D1550508

THE ROMANOVS

The Romanovs
Ruling Russia, 1613–1917

Lindsey Hughes

hambledon
continuum

Hambledon Continuum is an imprint of Continuum Books
Continuum UK, The Tower Building, 11 York Road, London SE1 7NX
Continuum US, 80 Maiden Lane, Suite 704, New York, NY 10038

www.continuumbooks.com

First published 2008
Reprinted 2008, 2009

British Library Cataloguing-in-Publication Data
A catalogue record for this book is available from the British Library.

ISBN 978 1 84725 213 5

Typeset by Pindar NZ (Egan Reid), Auckland, New Zealand
Printed and bound by MPG Books Ltd, Cornwall, Great Britain

Contents

Illustrations

Abbreviations, dates, spelling and transliteration

AAASS	American Association for the Advancement of Slavonic Studies
Bartlett and Hughes	R. Bartlett and L. Hughes (eds), *Russian Society and Culture in the Long Eighteenth Century: Essays in Honour of Anthony G. Cross* (Münster, 2004)
CASS	*Canadian-American Slavic Studies*
CWC	*The Complete Wartime Correspondence of Tsar Nicholas II and the Empress Alexandra, April 1914–March 1917*, J. T. Fuhrmann (ed.) (Westport, VA and London, 1999)
DR	*Dvortsovye razriady*
Evtuhov	C. Evtuhov, D. Goldfrank, L. Hughes, R. Stites, *A History of Russia: Peoples, Legends, Events, Forces* (New York, 2003)
FOG	*Forschungen zur osteuropäischen Geschichte*
JGO	*Jahrbücher für Geschichte Osteuropas*
Kritika	*Kritika: Explorations in Russian and Eurasian History*
M.	Moscow
MERSH	*Modern Encyclopedia of Russian and Soviet History* (Gulf Breeze, FL)
PiB	*Pis'ma i bumagi Imperatora Petra Velikogo*, 13 volumes to date, (St Petersburg, Petrograd, Moscow, 1887–2003)
PSZ	*Polnoe sobranie zakonov Rossiiskoi Imperii*, first series, 46 vols., St. P., 1830)
RH	*Russian History*
RR	*Russian Review*
RSH	*Russian Studies in History*
r.	Years of a tsar's rule
St. P.	St Petersburg
SEER	*Slavonic and East European Review*
SGECRN	*Study Group on 18th-century Russia Newsletter*
SIRIO	*Sbornik Imperatorskogo Istoricheskogo Obshchestva*
Soloviev	S. M. Soloviev, *History of Russia*, 48 vols to date., various translators/editors (Gulf Breeze, FL)

SR	*Slavic Review*
SSEES	School of Slavonic and East European Studies
Vernadsky	G.Vernadsky, *A Source Book for Russian History*, 2 vols (New Haven CT, 1972)
WOR	M. Di Salvo and L. Hughes (eds), *A Window on Russia. Papers from the Fifth International Conference of the Study Group on Eighteenth-Century Russia* (Rome, 1996)

Note on dates: For all Russian domestic matters up to February 1918, I use the Old Style (Julian) calendar, which in the 17th century was ten and in the 20th thirteen days behind the New Style (Gregorian) calendar in use in some Western countries. By the end of the 18th century most European countries were using New Style. For certain international events, e.g. treaties, I give both styles.

Spelling and transliteration: Russian is transcribed according to the Library of Congress system, with certain modifications, e.g. initial 'Ia' becomes 'Ya', hence Yakov, Yaroslavl, rather than Iakov, Iaroslavl; 'iia' at the end of feminine proper names becomes 'ia,' hence 'Maria', not 'Mariia', 'Anastasia, not 'Anastasiia, and so on; 'ii' and 'iy' endings on masculine proper names in the text become 'y', hence Vasily, Georgy, not Vasilii, Georgii, but all endings are rendered in full in italicised (e.g. bibliographical) references. A single quotation mark ['] denotes the Russian [silent] soft sign and double ["] – the hard sign. We use them only in full references, not in the text.

Names of ruling monarchs and some others, e.g. heirs to the throne, are anglicised according to convention; otherwise, the Russian is normally retained, e.g. Catherine II, but Ekaterina Dolgorukaia, Nicholas I but Nikolai Novikov. In some cases, e.g. Peter, the anglicised version is always used.

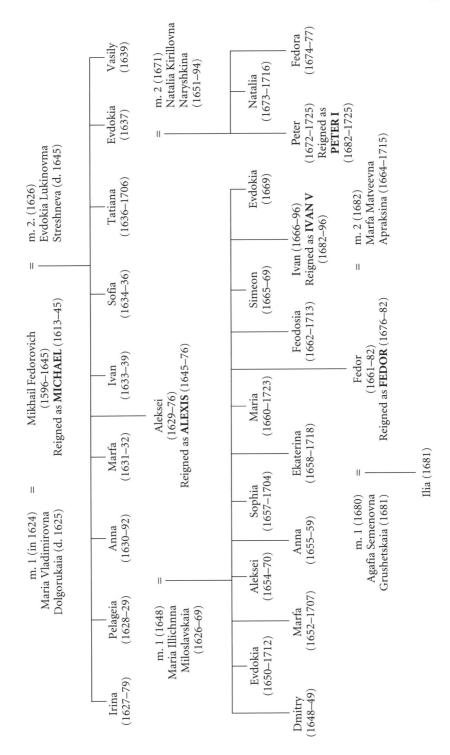

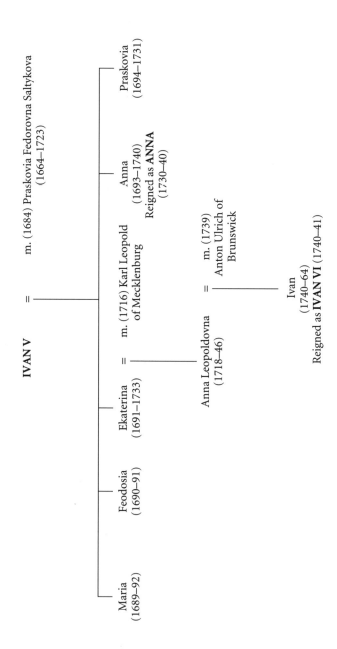

Maria
(1689–92)

Feodosia
(1690–91)

Ekaterina
(1691–1733)

=

Anna Leopoldovna
(1718–46)

=

IVAN V

=

m. (1716) Karl Leopold
of Mecklenburg

m. (1684) Praskovia Fedorovna Saltykova
(1664–1723)

Anna
(1693–1740)
Reigned as **ANNA**
(1730–40)

Praskovia
(1694–1731)

m. (1739)
Anton Ulrich of
Brunswick

Ivan
(1740–64)
Reigned as **IVAN VI** (1740–41)

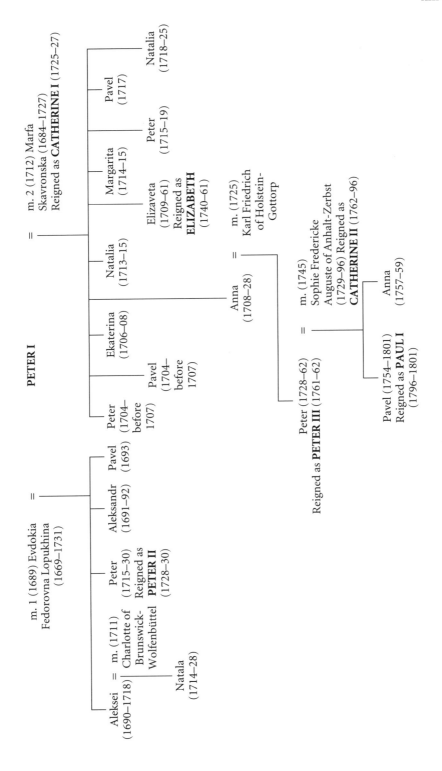

PETER I

m. 1 (1689) Evdokia
Fedorovna Lopukhina
(1669–1731)

=

m. 2 (1712) Marfa
Skavronska (1684–1727)
Reigned as **CATHERINE I** (1725–27)

Aleksei
(1690–1718)
= m. (1711)
Charlotte of
Brunswick-
Wolfenbüttel

Peter
(1715–30)
Reigned as
PETER II
(1728–30)

Aleksandr
(1691–92)

Pavel
(1693)

Peter
(1704–
before
1707)

Ekaterina
(1706–08)

Natalia
(1713–15)

Margarita
(1714–15)

Pavel
(1717)

Natalia
(1718–25)

Natala
(1714–28)

Pavel
(1704–
before
1707)

Anna
(1708–28)

Elizaveta
(1709–61)
Reigned as
ELIZABETH
(1740–61)

Peter
(1715–19)

=

m. (1725)
Karl Friedrich
of Holstein-
Gottorp

Peter (1728–62)
Reigned as **PETER III** (1761–62)

=

m. (1745)
Sophie Fredericke
Auguste of Anhalt-Zerbst
(1729–96) Reigned as
CATHERINE II (1762–96)

Pavel (1754–1801)
Reigned as **PAUL I**
(1796–1801)

Anna
(1757–59)

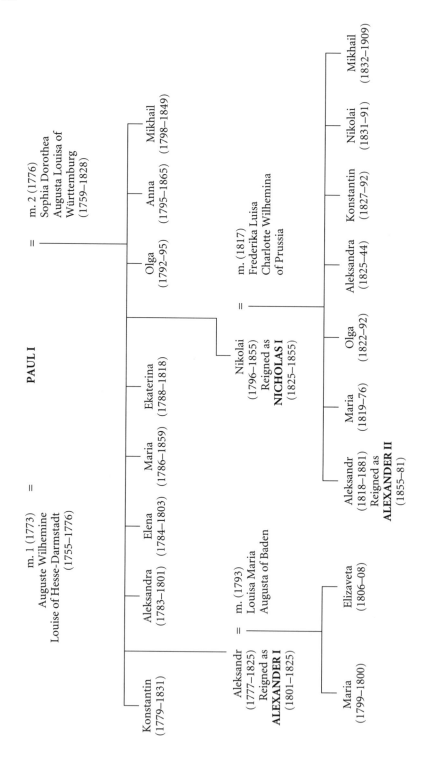

PAUL I

m. 1 (1773)
Auguste Wilhemine
Louise of Hesse-Darmstadt
(1755–1776)

=

m. 2 (1776)
Sophia Dorothea
Augusta Louisa of
Württemburg
(1759–1828)

Konstantin
(1779–1831)

Aleksandr
(1777–1825)
Reigned as
ALEXANDER I
(1801–1825)

=

m. (1793)
Louisa Maria
Augusta of Baden

Maria
(1799–1800)

Elizaveta
(1806–08)

Aleksandra
(1783–1801)

Elena
(1784–1803)

Maria
(1786–1859)

Ekaterina
(1788–1818)

Olga
(1792–95)

Anna
(1795–1865)

Mikhail
(1798–1849)

Nikolai
(1796–1855)
Reigned as
NICHOLAS I
(1825–1855)

=

m. (1817)
Frederika Luisa
Charlotte Wilhemina
of Prussia

Aleksandr
(1818–1881)
Reigned as
ALEXANDER II
(1855–81)

Maria
(1819–76)

Olga
(1822–92)

Aleksandra
(1825–44)

Konstantin
(1827–92)

Nikolai
(1831–91)

Mikhail
(1832–1909)

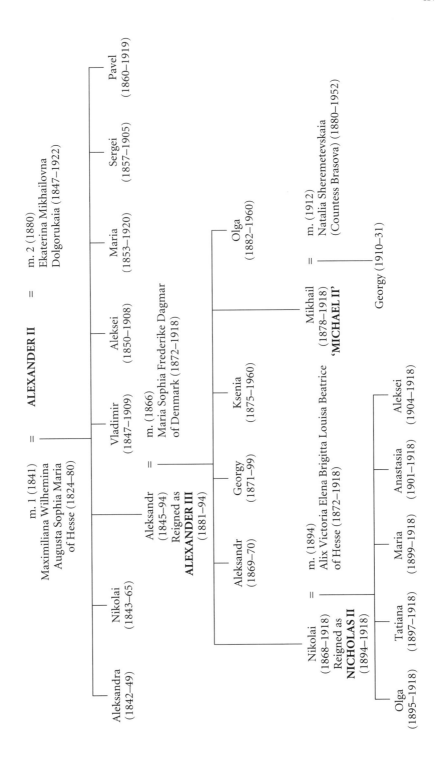

Aleksandra (1842–49)

Nikolai (1843–65)

ALEXANDER II = m. 1 (1841) Maximiliana Wilhemina Augusta Sophia Maria of Hesse (1824–80)

= m. 2 (1880) Ekaterina Mikhailovna Dolgorukaia (1847–1922)

Vladimir (1847–1909)

Aleksei (1850–1908)

Maria (1853–1920)

Sergei (1857–1905)

Pavel (1860–1919)

Aleksandr (1845–94) Reigned as **ALEXANDER III** (1881–94)

= m. (1866) Maria Sophia Frederike Dagmar of Denmark (1872–1918)

Aleksandr (1869–70)

Georgy (1871–99)

Ksenia (1875–1960)

Olga (1882–1960)

Mikhail (1878–1918) **'MICHAEL II'**

= m. (1912) Natalia Sheremetevskaia (Countess Brasova) (1880–1952)

Georgy (1910–31)

Nikolai (1868–1918) Reigned as **NICHOLAS II** (1894–1918)

= m. (1894) Alix Victoria Elena Brigitta Louisa Beatrice of Hesse (1872–1918)

Olga (1895–1918)

Tatiana (1897–1918)

Maria (1899–1918)

Anastasia (1901–1918)

Aleksei (1904–1918)

Preface

The inspiration for this book goes back many years, although the writing of it occupied far fewer. It was written with the benefit of my own extensive research on selected Romanovs, including my work on the regent Sophia and Peter the Great. It also drew heavily on the experience of researching chapters on the seventeenth and eighteenth centuries for *A History of Russia: Peoples, Legends, Events, Forces* (New York, 2003), co-authored with Catherine Evtuhov, David Goldfrank and Richard Stites. I thank my fellow authors for the inspiration of their own chapters on earlier and later periods. A major source of inspiration has been Richard Wortman's magisterial study *Scenarios of Power: Myth and Ceremony in Russian Monarchy* (2 vols, Princeton, 1995–2000). His interpretation of the Romanovs' self-presentation has undoubtedly influenced my own thinking and I have been grateful for the rich source material presented in his study. A visit to St. Petersburg in autumn 2005, with the financial support of the School of Slavonic and East European Studies UCL, allowed me to carry out essential work in the Russian National Library, as well as revisiting several Romanov sites. I am grateful to Elena Stolbova and Evgeny Anisimov for their help and advice during this and earlier visits to Russia, and also the late Elena Mozgovaia, whose friendship I so much miss. In the UK Roger Bartlett and Simon Dixon made constructive suggestions. At Hambledon, I am indebted to Tony Morris, for his enthusiasm about the project and for his forbearance when I missed the deadline. The latter stages of the work were carried out under trying circumstances owing to health problems and the book would not have been completed without the unfailing support of my husband Jim Cutshall, who helped in a thousand ways, from internet research to indexing and reproducing illustrations, but mainly just by being there for me. The book is dedicated to him. Any shortcomings are entirely my own responsibility.

Note

According to the date on the computer file, the words on page xvii were written on the morning of Friday 16 March 2007. The following day, Lindsey suffered what proved to be her final relapse, caused by the cancer with which she had been diagnosed fifteen months earlier. She died on 26 April and her funeral took place on 16 May, the 304th anniversary of the foundation of St Petersburg. Most of the text of this book was written when she already knew she was dying. It is a monument to her courage, as well as her scholarship.

To Lindsey's acknowledgements I must add my own grateful thanks to the following. To Ron Beaney and the staff of the London Bridge Hospital, whose care bought her the time to finish this book. To Ben Hayes, Ruth Stimson, John Sargant and Slav Todorov at Continuum Books. To Polly Blakesley at Pembroke College, Cambridge and to Jo Vickery and Luisa Langen at Sotheby's, for their generous help with the illustrations. To all those many friends and former colleagues of Lindsey's, especially from the School of Slavonic and East European Studies and the Study Group on Eighteenth-Century Russia, who have offered help in one form or another. To Peter Waldron at UEA. And above all to Simon Dixon at Leeds University, for his unstinting work to make the text ready for publication at a time when he was already more than busy enough.

In her prefaces, Lindsey never forgot to thank our cats for their part in the work. In the same spirit, I must thank Sophie, who lived just long enough to see the manuscript finished, and Henry, whose furry presence has helped see it through to publication.

Jim Cutshall
London,
December 2007

Introduction

TRUE SONS OF HOLY RUS! Today we celebrate a day of great solemnity, a day of great joy, the day, when three hundred years ago, after grave confusion, internecine strife and dissension, the Russian people invited the young boyar Mikhail Fedorovich Romanov to rule the Tsardom. His Royal Line, by God's blessing, has now ruled the Russian State for three hundred years. During those three hundred years under the wise rule of the Romanov Tsars Holy Rus has grown strong and expanded its borders. By their unfailing labours, undertaken with great love for the sake of the fatherland and the people, they created the strength and glory of the State and the welfare of its sons. So on this day of the tercentennial celebration may the fervent prayers of all the Russian people be borne aloft to the Throne of the Almighty. May the Lord remember in his Kingdom our deceased Crown-bearers and shield with his grace the now reigning Great Emperor Nikolai Aleksandrovich and give him strength and fortitude and strengthen his Rule and continue his Tsarist line for all time and forever may they grace the Throne of Russia. And may the holy image of the monk Ivan Susanin[1] live with them forever as a living example of that holy, great love for the Tsar and for his Fatherland with which every honest, loyal son of Russia ought to be filled and may their song of glory to the Tsar's line waft around its unbounded plains and blend into the single, mighty great song of the Russian people: GOD SAVE THE TSAR!

These words appear in one of many pamphlets issued to mark the tercentenary of the Romanovs in 1913.[2] Above the text to the left is a portrait of the dynasty's founder, sixteen-year old Michael (Mikhail Fedorovich), who on 21 February 1613 was chosen to ascend the throne following the failure of a series of contenders to establish their own lines after the expiry of the old dynasty in 1598. To the right is Nicholas II (Nikolai Aleksandrovich), now best remembered for being the last of the Romanovs, although technically speaking the dynasty ended on 2–3 March 1917, when Nicholas's short-lived successor, another Michael, abdicated.

In retrospect, the text, with its optimism about rule 'for all time', rings hollow. It is hard to escape our foreknowledge of the collapse of tsarism in February 1917, the Bolshevik Revolution in October and the gory postscript in July 1918

Front cover of a school certificate. St Petersburg Girls' Gymnasium, 1913.

in a cellar in the town of Ekaterinburg, when the ex-tsar, his family and their servants were slaughtered on Bolshevik orders. Popular imagination has been captured more by the Romanovs' end than their beginnings and, until recently, only in the West could both the popular imagination and scholarly speculation openly be indulged. Virtually everything printed about the Romanovs between the early 1930s and the late 1980s was produced by Western or émigré publishers. In the USSR in the late 1920s-early 1930s there were attempts to remove pre-revolutionary rulers from the historical record altogether in favour of material and collective forces as the levers of history. Even under Stalin, when the principle of the supreme leader or *vozhd'* was unabashedly celebrated, the only Russian rulers to be the subject of biographical studies were Ivan the Terrible and Peter the Great. Other monarchs were denounced with blanket charges of oppression and exploitation, with certain individuals identified as 'hypocritical', 'two-faced' or 'weak'. Mostly they were ignored.

Western and émigré authors displayed their own selectivity. There is to date no monograph in English on Michael Romanov and only a handful of works on his son Alexis. The eighteenth-century empresses Catherine I, Anna and Elizabeth have also been neglected. Alexander I and II have received adequate attention, but scholars have only recently begun to reassess the reign of Alexander III. At the tail end, however, studies of Nicholas II and his reign would fill several shelves, ranging from the solidly scholarly (the minority) to the sensational and sentimental, often with hagiographic or salacious elements.

Collectively the Romanovs have not fared much better in the historiography. It is striking how many accounts of the later Romanovs contain in their titles such words as 'sunset', 'twilight', 'doom' and 'curse'. They were Russia's 'tragic tyrants'. Not just studies of the last emperor but also longer narratives of Russian history, particularly those devoted to the Romanovs, take a teleological approach, preoccupied with the search for tragic flaws, looking ahead to the dynasty's fall in 1917, or, in the case of Soviet historians, to the triumph of Bolshevism.[3] Western historians have tended to focus on the 'otherness' of Russia and its rulers and in writing their history underline their deviation from what are perceived as Western norms, especially tsarist excesses of cruelty, despotism and conspicuous consumption. 'Autocracy' is a term applied consistently only to Russian monarchy. In the words of a popular study, the dynasty came to rule over 'a bizarre mixture of chanting priests and torture chambers' over a society that was 'both savage and perverse'. The same author quotes the view of Dr Samuel Collins, physician to Alexis, the second Romanov tsar, that the Russians were 'a people who differ from all other nations in most of their notions'.[4] 'Form for yourself the conception of a half-savage people who have been regimented without being civilized,' wrote the Marquis de Custine in 1839, 'and you will understand the moral and social condition of the Russian people.'[5] The exotic Russian flavour (epitomised by Rasputin) and the promise of an unhappy ending have undoubtedly boosted sales of works on the Romanovs, many of which, unfortunately, are not much more than potted biographies strung together with a second-hand historical narrative.

A more objective examination of the historical record, taking due account of the wider international context in which first the Muscovite state, then the Russian Empire operated,[6] reveals that for much of its existence the Romanov dynasty was strong, rather than weak – in its own estimation and that of others – and that its style of rulership represented a variation on Byzantine and European models, rather than a deviant 'Oriental' form. For all but eleven of their three hundred and four years the Romanovs ruled as unlimited autocratic monarchs and continued to regard themselves as such even after Nicholas II conceded legal limitations to his power in 1906. A Romanov ruler, however undistinguished or handicapped, was never a mere figurehead. Each had the power either in reality or potentially to decide Russia's fate. Moreover, there was little evidence of popular pressure to abolish or even limit autocracy for much of this period. Before 1905 there were only two serious collective attempts by representatives of the elite to obtain a share of power and thereby end autocracy, in 1730 and 1825, both carried out with the flimsiest of support from below. Two emperors, Peter III and Paul I, were murdered in palace coups, and one, Ivan VI, was deposed in the same way. Alexander II was the victim of revolutionaries. Peter III died in 1762 in a scuffle (murder is not ruled out), after being deposed in favour of his wife Catherine, and Paul I was murdered in 1801, the elite conspiracy to remove him endorsed by his son and heir Alexander I. Periodically, major popular rebellions erupted on the margins of the empire, deflecting resources from the centre, but never seriously threatening it. However, even the most devastating, led by the Don Cossack Emelian Pugachev in 1773–75, was carried out in the name of the tsar, Pugachev claiming to be Peter III miraculously returned to claim his throne. 'Naive monarchism' and pretenderism were staple features of Romanov Russia. Individual Romanovs may have displeased the people, but the belief that to thrive Russia must be ruled by the anointed representative of the legitimate dynasty was a potent one. For their part, Russia's 'crown-bearers' took their responsibilities seriously, although the degree of personal input and achievement varied. All believed that their endeavours were blessed by God.

In this study I propose to dwell as much on the Romanovs' successes as on their failures and to consider the strategies which allowed them to rule the biggest country in Europe for just over three hundred years, presiding over the expansion of a multiethnic empire, the acquisition and maintenance of great power status and, particularly in their final century, an astonishing flowering of culture. Lack of space dictates that my focus is on the rulers of the imperial house, as opposed to the wider Romanov clan, which proliferated rapidly from the early nineteenth century with the four sons of Nicholas I. Even so, I shall, where appropriate, explore the often tense relationships within the ruling family. This will include elucidating the political and cultural role of Romanov women, not just the eighteenth-century empresses, but also royal wives and daughters. Attention will also focus on the relationship between the ruling house and the ruling 'class', the nobility, which lacked corporate status or independent institutions for most of our period. I shall also consider rulers' fluctuating attitudes towards the mass of the Russian people (*narod*), some eighty to ninety percent of whom remained peasants well into the twentieth century. The conflict between, on the one hand, preserving peasant traditions (including serfdom to 1861) as the stable backbone of Russian economic and social life, and on the other, modernizing the economy and social relations, would be a major challenge. Another essential task for Russia's rulers was to define Russia's place in the world and especially its relationship with the major Western powers, while maintaining an empire that also looked east, and to strike a balance between asserting national identity and independence and imitating and assimilating new technologies and cultural trends from abroad.

This, then, is history from above, a study of rulers and rulership. It is not a comprehensive survey of Russian history. Limitations on space have forced me to dispense with any attempt to provide a 'prologue' outlining the history of

Sheet from a Romanov Tercentenary pamphlet. St Petersburg, 1913.

Russia before the seventeenth century, although I do characterize the Russia that Michael Romanov 'inherited'. There are many good histories available, the most up-to-date and reliable of which are indicated in the bibliography. Nor is this a series of 'potted biographies', although I have tried to maintain a clear narrative thread and to examine personalities and private lives in as much detail as possible. Russian politics remained a family business, in which clan and personal relations played a greater role than institutions. In particular, I focus on dynastic issues, on the Romanovs' awareness of their own history and role as a ruling clan. One aspect of dynastic identity, incidentally, was to retain the name 'Romanov' even after the male bloodline died out in the eighteenth century. Strictly speaking, with the accession of the foreign-born Peter III in 1761 the ruling house became Holstein-Gottorp. If one harbours doubts about the paternity of Paul, Peter III's alleged son, even this foreign dynasty was soon extinguished.[7] My own approach is to accept the dynasty's self-designation and assertions of continuity, which reached a climax during the tercentenary of 1913, while making clear its need to renew itself periodically. In this, as in many other ways, it resembled its European counterparts.

1

Romanov Roots: 1613–1645

MICHAEL

> 'Tsar Michael did not leave any profound mark
> on the political life of his country.'[1]

Just off Red Square in the centre of Moscow, on Varvarka Street (renamed Razin Street in Soviet times, after a seventeenth-century Cossack rebel), there stands a picturesque old building. Its foundations date back to the fifteenth century, but the visible structure is the result of centuries of alterations and reconstruction. The house was bought from an adjoining monastery by order of Emperor Alexander II in 1856, the year of his coronation. Today a plaque identifies it as the former residence of the boyars Romanov.[2] It may have been the birthplace of Michael, the first Romanov tsar, although we cannot be certain.

The boyars (nobles) who originally owned the house can be traced back to one Andrei Ivanovich Kobyla, who served the princes of Moscow in the mid-fourteenth century. Several clans claim him as their ancestor. The potential for confusion arises partly because the clan name Romanov (stressed, like the given name Roman, on the second, not the first syllable) emerged during a period in Russian history when, apart from some princely families, no one had fixed 'surnames'. Kobyla's son Fedor was known as Koshkin from his nickname 'Koshka': the cat. Before elite surnames stabilized in the late sixteenth century, a man might add to his given name his father's given name as a patronymic (ending in -ovich or -ich) and his father's patronymic (i.e. his grandfather's name), as a surname (ending in -ov or -ev). Occasionally, two or three names were strung together. Tracing the Romanovs' ancestry back to the mid-fifteenth century in this way, genealogists have shown that Zakhary Ivanovich Koshkin (d. *c.*1461) begat Yury Zakhar[ev]ich Koshkin-Zakharin (d. 1504), who in turn fathered Tsar Michael's great-grandfather, Roman Yurevich Zakharin-Yurev (d. 1543). And it was with the children of Roman Yurevich – the Romanovichi – that the rise to prominence of the future ruling dynasty began.[3]

In 1547, his daughter Anastasia became the first wife of Tsar Ivan IV Vasilevich (r. 1533–84). She was reputed to have a beneficial and calming influence on the man who later earned the epithet 'Terrible'.[4] Taking advantage of the perks available to royal in-laws, the 'Romanovichi' obtained lucrative positions at court and rose in the 'place system' (*mestnichestvo*) that largely determined

Дом боярь Романовых.—Maison des Boyards Romanoff.   Москва.

58

The Romanov House on Varvarka. Postcard, *c.*1910

appointments to military and civilian posts. When the eldest brother, Daniel, died in 1565, his place was taken by Nikita, who became one of four privy counsellors to Tsar Ivan and then to his son Tsar Fedor Ivanovich, who ascended the throne in 1584. Nikita's first wife died in 1544, apparently childless,[5] but his second, Evdokia Aleksandrovna Gorbataia-Shuiskaia, gave him six sons and six daughters. The latter married well, two of them into princely families, extending the network of marriage links that allowed their own clan to flourish.[6] The eldest son, Fedor Nikitich Romanov (1553? –1633) became a boyar in 1586.[7] He married Ksenia Ivanovna Shestova, allegedly at the behest of the future tsar Boris Godunov, Tsar Fedor's chief adviser and brother-in-law.[8] Of their six children, only one daughter, Tatiana (d. 1611), and a son Michael (Mikhail, born 12 July 1596) survived into adulthood. Two years after Michael's birth a chain of events began that would culminate in his election as tsar of Russia.

On 7 January 1598 Tsar Fedor Ivanovich died childless (a daughter had died in infancy) and the male line of the old Riurik[9] dynasty expired with him. 'Loss' of dynasty affected more than the immediate succession. Ivan IV and his publicists had worked hard to extend the ranks of his dynastic forebears after Ivan's coronation as tsar in 1547 made him dynastic leader of the extended clan. Their efforts included persuading the patriarchate of Constantinople to acknowledge a list of some 150 names from the tenth-century princes of Kiev onwards as evidence of continuity of power and to pray for them in Constantinople on the grounds that all 'belong to his [Ivan's] dynasty'.[10] Legends were propagated of the descent of the Riurikovichi from Prus, a legendary relative of Augustus Caesar, and the Byzantine origins of their regalia. Such underpinnings threatened to collapse once the clan lost its male leader, especially if one takes into account suspicions that it was extinguished by God's disfavour. They needed to re-establish a dynastic state – for Russia to be without a tsar was unthinkable – that rested not on an individual autocrat or despot but on the 'family firm' of an extended clan.

The weight of the extended family proved decisive and even outweighed the tradition of male-only succession. Among the proposed candidates for the throne were Fedor's widow, Tsaritsa Irina, who retired from the contest after initial acceptance, and Tsar Fedor's cousin, Fedor Romanov, nephew of the late Tsaritsa Anastasia. It was rumoured that the tsar tried to pass the sceptre to him on his deathbed, but in an act of self-sacrifice, to avoid bloodshed, Romanov ceded to Irina's brother, Boris Godunov, Ivan IV's favourite and the most powerful man at court.[11] After months of political struggle, involving endorsement by assemblies of the land (*zemskii sobor*) composed of representatives of various estates, Boris was duly elected and crowned in September 1598.

Despite the rhetoric that divine favour had determined the assemblies' decision, Boris never felt entirely secure on his throne and dealt harshly with potential rivals. Initially the Romanovs were his allies, but in 1600 relations cooled. He had the sons of Nikita Romanovich arrested on trumped up charges of treason, centring on a plot to do Boris harm by sorcery. Fedor was exiled to the Monastery of St Anthony at Siisk near Archangel, where he was forced to take monastic vows under the name Filaret. Equally reluctantly, his wife Ksenia took the veil and the new name Martha. Five-year-old Michael and his sister were separated from both their parents and sent with other relatives to live in Beloozero to the north of Moscow. The other Nikitichi were banished to various locations, where all apart from Ivan died.

In 1605 Boris Godunov died of natural causes, although later narratives suggested that his death was hastened by guilt about bloody deeds that cleared his path to the throne. His most notable victim was said to be Dmitry, son of Ivan IV, who died in suspicious circumstances in 1591. In fact, Boris's final years were plagued more by famine and social unrest beyond his control, with many parts of the country becoming ungovernable.[12] He was succeeded by his sixteen-year-old son Fedor Borisovich, but Fedor's reign was brutally curtailed. In May 1605 a man arrived outside Moscow with an army gathered from Poland and Russia's western borderlands, claiming to be the 'resurrected' Tsarevich Dmitry Ivanovich. The pretender's claim was dubious but many believed in him. A plausible narrative of his rescue and escape was devised and some witnesses claimed to recognize him from physical features such as the wart on his nose.[13] Many boyars welcomed the opportunity to prevent the establishment of a Godunov dynasty and False or Pseudo Dmitry I, as he was later known, also enjoyed the support of ordinary Russians, who believed that the restoration of a true tsar of the royal blood would gain God's blessing and end Russia's troubles. Some greeted Dmitry as the 'sun of righteousness' – 'Until now we have been sitting in darkness, but now the true light had dawned' – even believing that he had risen, Christ-like, from the dead.[14] The pretender's men murdered Tsar Fedor Borisovich and Dmitry was declared tsar. Among those exiles summoned back to Moscow to serve Russia's new ruler were the surviving Romanovs.

False Dmitry I's reign lasted only a year before some of his erstwhile supporters murdered him. Among their grievances were his neglect of Orthodoxy and his marriage to a Polish Catholic noblewoman, Marina Mniszek. For popular consumption what were earlier interpreted as signs of royal birth and God's grace were now presented as marks of the devil and proof of sorcery. Dmitry had, in the words of an official source, 'bewitched many people',[15] but the main reason for his downfall was probably that he was developing a programme of his own, with a decidedly Western orientation. Dmitry wore Western dress and was clean shaven with short hair (flouting Orthodox convention) and built a new palace in the Polish style. It has been suggested that he hoped to become king of Poland as well as Russia and that his 'Polish' behaviour was calculated towards this end.[16] The boyar Vasily Shuisky, the leading member of an extensive clan, became tsar, reigning from 1606–10, but he was soon challenged by a new and even less plausible 'Dmitry', known as the 'Brigand' or 'Thief' of Tushino. After Dmitry's death in 1610 his infant son the 'Baby Brigand' or 'Tiny Thief' by Marina, the widow of the first False Dmitry, was declared tsarevich. Other claimants to the throne included a False Peter, posing as a grandson of Ivan IV, and the king of Poland and his son. Russia sank deeper into the period of civil war known as the Time of Troubles, as social and economic conditions deteriorated and armed clashes for power occurred between rivals. Whole regions became detached from the centre, which lost control over taxation and recruitment. Bandits and Cossacks roamed the land. Villages were deserted.

The task of stabilizing Muscovy in the aftermath of the chaotic Time of Troubles was to be the main challenge facing the Romanov dynasty when Tsar Michael came to the throne in 1613. Meanwhile, the surviving Romanovs coped as best they could. Now was not the time for too many scruples. The able and ambitious Filaret, who had turned his talents to making a career in the church, was made metropolitan of Rostov and Yaroslavl by False Dimitry I. After the latter's murder, Filaret and his son Michael were reunited in Rostov. Michael was listed as a table attendant (*stol'nik*) in the register of boyars. After having verified for Tsar Vasily Shuisky what purported to be the miraculous relics of the real Tsarevich Dmitry, in October 1608 Filaret was captured and declared 'patriarch' by the Thief at his headquarters outside Moscow. (That a rival patriarch,

Hermogen, resided in Moscow at Shuisky's court added to the confusion.) In 1610 the exhausted Shuisky abdicated and with the sanction of a boyar interim government Filaret travelled with a delegation to Poland for negotiations about the candidature of the Polish Prince Władysław to the Russian throne. Filaret and fellow delegates would be imprisoned there until 1619. Polish and Swedish armies, originally in Russia at Shuisky's invitation, invaded the Smolensk and Novgorod regions respectively, culminating in the occupation of Moscow by a Polish garrison in 1610–12.

It is possible that during the Polish occupation Michael and his mother were reunited in the house on Varvarka, then moved to the nearby Kremlin. After the Poles were driven out in 1612 by an army of national resistance under Prince Dmitry Pozharsky, sponsored by the merchant Kuzma Minin, Michael and Martha moved south to Kostroma on the Volga, where there were family estates to support them, and took up residence in the Ipatiev monastery. Unknown to them, in December 1612 an Assembly of the Land gathered to choose a new tsar. As rhetoric dictated, 'without a sovereign the Muscovite realm cannot survive ... without a sovereign the Muscovite realm is being ruined utterly, without a sovereign the state is nothing and is being torn into many pieces by criminal intrigues as violence keeps increasing'.[17] Candidates included the Polish Prince Władysław, the Russian war heroes Prince Dmitry Pozharsky and Prince Dmitry Trubetskoy, selected boyars and even the Baby Brigant. The decisive voices were those of Cossacks, not members of the established Don or Zaporozhian Hosts, but a 'rabble' of renegades and dissidents who favoured the Romanovs because of favourable contacts in the camp of False Dmitry II and feared a strong ruler who might seek retribution. A recent revisionist study, which challenges the 'myth of the good Romanovs', refers to the 'February revolution' of 1613, arguing that the best candidate, the Riurikide prince and hero Pozharsky, was sacrificed for an 'untitled youth'.[18]

In the end the election of 21 February 1613 was framed in the words of Boris Godunov's election in 1598 rather than reflecting the 'true story' of dissent and dirty dealings. Chroniclers wrote of universal approval and rejoicing – a notion deemed essential if the rifts of the Troubles were to be healed. The election was underpinned by the claim that the new tsar was chosen and anointed by God. Preference for young Michael Romanov had little to do with his formal qualifications or character, which one historian has described as a 'blank'.[19] The Dutch envoy Isaac Massa, conceding that Michael had promise, doubted whether he was even literate.[20] A strong point in his favour was that Tsaritsa Anastasia was his great aunt. Under other circumstances a link through the female line might not have carried much weight, but after the Troubles even this tenuous legitimacy was a vital consideration for those who believed that dynastic extinction caused the Troubles in the first place. That Michael was too young to have been directly involved in feuding during the Troubles was also an advantage, although already in 1610 after the abdication of Shuisky he had appeared in a list of possible candidates for the throne.[21] To view the situation pragmatically, Michael was a useful figurehead for more powerful men, who could not themselves contend for the throne without precipitating further squabbles and were anxious to buy off troublesome Cossacks. Despite the Romanovs' earlier prominence, they had been radically reduced in numbers and the most powerful, Michael's father Filaret, was safely out of the way in Poland. The boyar council began issuing orders and edicts in Michael's name long before he returned to Moscow, including tax demands to various towns. In near-anarchy any acceptable tsar on the throne might restore order and fill the power vacuum. A strong, mature leader with a mind of his own was perhaps the last thing anyone wanted.

Michael and his mother, meanwhile, were oblivious of the turn of events in Moscow and of the possible dangers of their new celebrity. At about this time a band of Poles and hostile Cossacks, eager to capture Michael, are said to have arrested the peasant Ivan Susanin, elder of the village of Domnino near Kostroma, and tried to force him under torture to reveal the boy's whereabouts, but he refused and was killed. In the version in Glinka's opera *A Life for the Tsar* (1836, renamed *Ivan Susanin* in Soviet times) Susanin leads the Poles astray into impenetrable forests. Little evidence has survived, even of Poles in the locality, and the story may well have been invented by a relative of Susanin's seeking compensation and favour. Nonetheless, the tale of Ivan Susanin's heroic feat would become a staple of Romanov mythology, with its potent mix of the common folk's love for their future tsar, the work of divine providence in saving Russia's future ruling dynasty and xenophobia.[22] In the last decades of Romanov rule hardly a ceremony occurred unaccompanied by the strains of Glinka's opera, especially the final chorus in which a grateful people welcome Michael to Moscow.

In mid-March 1613 a delegation from Moscow headed by Fedor Ivanovich Sheremetev (?–1650), a leading member of the boyar council, arrived at the Ipatiev monastery to inform Michael that he was chosen tsar. The inclusion of leading clerics in the delegation, among them Metropolitan Feodorit of Riazan and representatives from the powerful Trinity-St Sergius monastery and leading Kremlin and Moscow monasteries and cathedrals, underlined the message that the mission was inspired by God. They carried with them some of the most revered icons from Moscow, which were joined by the wonder-working image of the Fedorov Mother of God from Kostroma. Many ordinary folk joined the procession to the monastery. Despite the pressure of earthly and heavenly forces, Michael and his mother agonized for hours, apparently from genuine reluctance rather than ceremonial show, as well as fear of acting without the approval of the absent head of the family, Filaret (who may well have coveted the throne himself).[23] In the end they agreed and Michael kissed the cross. His feelings can only be imagined, since no personal writings survive from any period of his life. His image and character come down to us through the rigid formulae of state papers and chronicles and the inevitably distanced observations of foreign travellers. This key moment in his life was no exception.

It took Michael and his retinue 42 days to reach Moscow from Kostroma, a journey that could be done in a few days in winter. The royal progress was slow not only because almost every step of the way was accompanied by religious ritual, but also because they had to wait in Yaroslavl for the roads to become passable in the wet spring season. Michael and his close circle also feared what awaited them in Moscow, as they travelled through deserted villages, some strewn with corpses. In letters they fretted about shortages of supplies and suitable accommodation, possible unrest and banditry in the vicinity of the capital, about the royal seal and the composition of the new royal household. There were fears of further Swedish penetration of Russia's north-western territory and of continuing attempts by the renegade Cossack Ivan Zarutsky to promote the Baby Brigand's claim to the throne. (Zarutsky and the four-year-old boy were eventually captured and executed in 1614, the latter by public hanging.)

In Moscow preparations to receive the new tsar focused on selecting representatives of the various estates for honours, from leading boyars to hold regalia to ordinary townsmen to present traditional welcoming gifts of bread and salt.[24] The procession culminated in prayers of thanksgiving and the swearing of an oath of allegiance in the Kremlin Cathedral of the Dormition (Assumption) of the Mother of God. This five-domed cathedral, built by an Italian architect in 1475–8 on the site of an earlier church, would remain a crucial landmark in the history of the Romanov dynasty, Russia's equivalent of London's Westminster Abbey or Reims Cathedral in France. The Virgin Mary, known in Orthodox tradition as the Mother of God, was the protector of Moscow, and the cathedral's holiest icon, the twelfth-century Vladimir Mother of God, was credited with saving the city on several occasions from Tatar attacks. In 1547 Ivan IV was the first tsar to be crowned there and the coronations of the Romanov tsars and emperors would continue to take place there, even after Peter the Great moved his capital to the new city of St Petersburg in the early eighteenth century. Rulers attended services of thanksgiving for military victories and prayed before the altar that contained some of Russia's holiest images and shrines. In this cathedral and other historical locations the 'upstart' dynasty affirmed its roots in earlier history and its continuity with generations of grand princes and tsars. The seventeenth-century Romanovs were married in the nearby Cathedral of the Annunciation (1484–9) and buried in the Cathedral of the Archangel Michael (1505–9), although Peter and his successor shifted these rituals to St Petersburg.

Dormition Cathedral. Postcard, *c*.1900.

On 11 July 1613 Michael was crowned Great Sovereign Tsar and Great Prince Mikhail Fedorovich. (Not until the reign of Peter I did Russian rulers adopt the Western practice of using a first name followed by a number.) The dynasty's first coronation was an event of immense significance. For the population of Moscow it marked a fresh start blessed by God. For Michael it entailed his anointing and symbolic investiture with regalia that were allegedly of Byzantine origins, reminding him that he was now God's representative. It allowed prominent men to assert their place – Ivan Romanov held the crown, Prince Dmitry Trubetskoy the sceptre, Prince Pozharsky the orb. There was no attempt to limit the tsar's powers, although it was understood that he had obligations and duties to his subjects and to God. The year of the coronation was inscribed in documents as 7121, that is, the 7,121st year since God's creation of the world as described in the book of Genesis, which some scholars calculated occurred in 5509 BC. Russia also followed the Byzantine practice of beginning the new year in September. Hence the first full year of Michael's reign, 7122, was due to start on 1 September 1613.[25] It would be a crucial period both for the Romanovs and for Russia.

Contemporary texts described Tsar Michael as 'most pious' and 'quietest', for the ideal of the devout tsar was the one most vigorously cultivated in official discourses. Contemporary rhetoric also referred to him as the all-powerful Orthodox tsar, yet he was arguably one of the least assertive of the Romanovs. It has even been suggested that his famed 'humility' was actually a euphemism for weak-mindedness.[26] He was, according to a biographer of his son, Alexis, 'autocrat in name but not in practice'.[27] For the first few years of his reign an Assembly of the Land was in permanent session, deciding a variety of issues, apparently with little active involvement on the part of the tsar.[28] Although not fixed in any written charter, it was understood that the Assembly had collective authority without limiting the tsar's power and that the joint deliberations of the tsar and 'all the land' strengthened central authority which not long before had been on the verge of collapse.

After Patriarch Filaret returned from exile in Poland in 1619 and until his death in 1633, historians talk of a 'dual power' or diarchy. 'Their royal majesty is indivisible', as a contemporary wrote. Filaret bore the title of Great Sovereign (*velikii gosudar*), which was usually reserved for the monarch, and presided at councils and receptions alongside his son. He was essentially a boyar in ecclesiastical robes, who secured his and his son's power through kinship and patron networks, elevating loyal men like his brother Ivan Romanov and kinsmen Ivan Cherkassky and Fedor Sheremetev, who remained senior members of the boyar council throughout the reign,[29] and limiting the power of others. As well as wielding secular power, Filaret built up a personal base in the Patriarch's Chancellery, which administered about 30,000 male peasants and kept several thousand armed retainers. Having been subjected to 'heretical' influences during his eight years of captivity in Poland, Filaret also felt compelled to refresh his Orthodox credentials. This was reflected in a programme of correcting and printing church books and in hostile pronouncements against 'Latins' and Lutherans, as Catholics and Protestants were dubbed.

As the sovereign of the biggest country in Europe, Michael was in need of strong support from kinsmen and the Russian elite. No maps were printed in seventeenth-century Muscovy and hand-drawn ones such as the Great Draft, made in the Kremlin in 1598–1600, have not survived. Existing maps were all made by foreigners, who needed them to trade and navigate the northern coasts and land routes to Moscow or to explore eastern tracks. The map made by the Dutch cartographer Hessel Gerritsz in 1613–14, for example, formed the basis for later atlases, such as those by Blaeu and Piscator.[30] This and other maps show a country of vast size, with enormously long and often ill-defined land borders. The land was intersected by river systems, on which the major trading towns were located. Beyond these the country was charted only locally.

The Russian heartland lay to the north of the Oka River, stretching to the ancient lands of Novgorod and the White Sea. Archangel on the Dvina River, Russia's only sea port during Michael's reign, was the point of entry for foreign ships. The forested heartland of mixed and coniferous forest was where the majority of the population was settled. To the south Muscovy was consolidating its position on the steppes, which offered the attraction of fertile agricultural land, while suffering the constant threat of raids by Tatars and other nomads, hence the area's designation as the 'wild field'. From the 1630s Moscow

Portrait of Tsar Mikhail Fedorovich, Russian School, 17th century.
Image courtesy of Sotheby's.

constructed the so-called Belgorod defence line, a series of garrisons to protect colonists.

In the south-east Moscow's foothold on the river Don ended below the Cossack settlements at Cherkassk. The port of Azov to the south was in Turkish hands. Russians had occupied the Volga to its mouth at Astrakhan on the Caspian Sea since the 1550s, but the shores of the Caspian were ruled by Persia. The Christian peoples of the Caucasus – present-day Georgians, Armenians and other nationalities – intermittently appealed for the tsars' protection, but Moscow's resources did not stretch much beyond occasionally entertaining visiting princes. Further west towards the delta of the Danube were the lands of Moldavia and Wallachia (present-day Romania), home to Orthodox Christian subjects of the sultan of Turkey. They also sought the tsar's protection, but remained beyond his practical reach or aspirations.

To the west, north-west and south-west lay the borders with Sweden and Poland. A foothold on the Baltic, dominated by Sweden, was still just beyond Moscow's grasp, as were the Polish-ruled territories of present-day Ukraine and Belarus, populated by Orthodox, Russian-speaking peoples, to which Muscovy laid claim as its 'patrimony'. The River Dnieper would provide a border of sorts after 1667, but in its southern reaches at the stronghold of the Zaporozhian Cossacks (Sich) it entered another wild frontier zone which belonged to no one. Cossacks and Tatars rode back and forth across it with impunity. The Russian-Polish border shifted dramatically westwards in the course of the seventeenth and eighteenth centuries.

To the east beyond the Ural mountains Siberia lay open without any sovereign powers to impede expansion until the Chinese borders (1619 saw the first Russian mission to Peking). In 1637 the Siberian Department was founded to administer the region. Russian colonists either wiped out local tribes or forced them into paying tribute in furs. Pioneer settlers established forts, which in turn attracted other settlers and grew into small towns. Yeniseisk was established in 1619, Yakutsk in 1632; Russians reached the Pacific in 1639. In the early modern period Siberia promised a tough but relatively free life. The government did not package out Siberian land with serfs to maintain military servitors for the reason that it was too far from the borders where mobilized armies were deployed. Thousands of peasants moved voluntarily to Siberia, in the wake of the independent or semi-independent Cossack units who conquered it. It is a striking fact that none of the lands on Michael's map would be permanently lost by his Romanov successors. On the contrary, the next three centuries saw a remarkable success story of expansion, which was already envisaged, if not achieved, in the early seventeenth century.

There may have been about seven million people in Muscovy in 1645, growing to about nine million by 1678, when a census of the male tax-paying population was carried out. Defining the tsar's subjects in terms of the duties they performed or the taxes they paid suited the authorities. These divisions provide a useful starting point for modern social historians, even if we accept that social status was not rigidly fixed.[31] People could confound expectations: for example, peasants lived in towns; provincial nobles worked their own land; free people in reduced circumstances took out contracts of bondage as slaves.[32]

At the top of the pile were the Russian elite, who will figure prominently in our narrative of the rise and fall of the Romanovs. Roughly the equivalent of the Western aristocracy, they were often referred to collectively as the boyars (*boiare*; sing. *boiarin*), a term which fell into disuse in the early eighteenth century. Historians also speak of the 'boyar elite' or 'upper service class' to stress their status at the pinnacle of the hierarchy of men who served the tsar.[33] In peacetime the boyars performed a variety of administrative and ceremonial duties. In wartime they commanded the Russian armies. Virtually all the boyars resided in or near Moscow and the upper crust were members of the tsar's court, which in Michael's reign numbered around 2,000 men. The elite within this elite, those closest to the sovereign, formed the so-called boyar council or duma, which in Michael's reign averaged about 30 members.[34] The numbers would grow in the course of the century, as we shall see, but the council never exceeded 3 per cent of the court.[35] This council had its own ranks – boyars proper, *okol'nichie* (sometimes translated as 'lords in waiting') and *dumnye dvoriane* (gentlemen of the duma). Most of the upper two ranks were occupied by senior members of some two dozen or so leading families, who became councillors by and large by hereditary right. Having another family member in the council increased a man's chances of promotion, but new blood was introduced by, for example, the entry of royal in-laws and by talented men of lower noble status who were raised by royal favour. Some powerful clans had men at the centre throughout the seventeenth and eighteenth centuries. Others enjoyed prominence only for a short time. Courtiers immediately below council rank bore the titles *stol'nik* (literally, 'table attendant'), *striapchii*, *dvorianin moskovskii* (Moscow noble) and *zhiltets*. Only a few of these would eventually attain membership of the council.

The absence of any reference to geographical location in the boyars' titles (equivalents of the English Duke of Bedford, Earl of Essex and so on) underlines the fact that their provincial estates, often scattered over dozens of different regions, were sources of income, not power bases.[36] Local loyalties were weak. Indeed, most boyars had no titles. The exception was *kniaz'* (prince), which indicated descent from the formerly independent rulers of principalities now incorporated into the tsar's domains or foreign, especially Tatar, princely origins. By Michael's time Russian boyars had no private armies. They had never enjoyed regional assemblies, still less a national parliament. Some historians point to boyar dominance of the Assembly of the Land during Michael's reign, but there was no promotion of corporate identity.

At court, etiquette prescribed ritual forms of abasement for even the grandest members of the elite. At first sight, the rhetoric employed even by boyars in their addresses to the sovereign suggested servile powerlessness: they referred to themselves as their lord's 'slaves' and prostrated themselves in the royal presence. Yet many of these men exerted themselves on behalf of their extended clans, for example to defend their positions in the code of precedence or 'place system', which determined the allocation of military commissions and other appointments on the basis of a man's service record, that of his clan and his seniority within it. The early Romanovs successfully played this system, which was abolished in 1682.

The Russian elite of this period has been condemned as 'abased' or 'supine'.[37] They lacked social cohesiveness, because of cut-throat competition for posts and land (which was always in short supply) and the need for state support to keep and exploit their serfs. Yet they apparently were motivated by a genuine belief in the divine origin of the tsar's power and that to challenge God's representative was a sin. The Romanovs' ability to command the loyalty and support of an overwhelming proportion of this elite would remain a crucial factor in their success story. In the eighteenth century the 'tsar's slaves' motivated by religion became 'true sons of the fatherland' inspired by civic duty. The rhetoric changed, but the relationship remained essentially the same: the elite enjoyed a near monopoly on top military and civilian posts; they owned landed property worked by serfs; they had an almost exclusive possession of high culture, but, with rare exceptions, they did not demand a share of power and continued to subscribe to the rhetoric of the all-powerful, divinely appointed autocratic ruler. Historians of the 1917 Russian revolution have generally focused on the breakdown of this relationship from the early nineteenth century onwards, what Nicholas Riasanovsky called the 'parting of the ways',[38] and its coincidence with the popular loss of faith in the Romanovs. That tsarism collapsed only in 1917, however, suggests that the relationship proved enduring.

Outside Moscow the ruler relied on his provincial gentry or 'middle' and 'junior' servicemen (*sluzhilye liudi, deti boiarskie*) to perform policing duties and serve in lower officer ranks of the army in wartime. These men were not close to the tsar, but they still enjoyed privileges, including exemption from taxes and the right to own serfs. Mostly they lived off their service lands or *pomest'ia*, which were granted and held conditionally, but increasingly were passed from generation to generation.

It has been argued that even boyars lacked the manorial tradition, civility and 'gentility' usually associated with noble status elsewhere in Europe. Russia also lacked the professional categories, such as physicians and teachers, found in most contemporary Western European towns of any size. The general picture of noble life in the provinces was one of 'almost unrelieved rudeness and coarseness, with a frequently repeated motif of drunkenness and violence'.[39] The Muscovite crown also deployed non-noble, non-serf-owning servicemen, among them the largely Moscow-based musketeers (*strel'tsy*), who formed army units in wartime and performed escort and guard duty in peacetime, carrying on small businesses and trades when off duty. Civilian personnel in the non-noble service category included secretaries and clerks (*d'iaki, pod'iachie*), the backbone of the government chancelleries.

A feature of this Moscow-centred configuration of power was the minimal development of towns outside the capital. Officially registered town dwellers accounted for less than 4 per cent of the population. During the process of 'gathering' the Russian lands by the princes, then tsars, of Moscow in the fourteenth to sixteenth centuries, the cream of local elites were transferred to Moscow, leaving the remaining 'sub-elite' to serve locally. The private fortunes and corporate privileges that allowed towns to flourish in the West did not develop. Moreover, the use of wood for virtually all buildings meant that whole towns could be reduced to ashes in a few hours. Most of the resident population of Russia's towns were bound to their communities by tax obligations. This applied also to merchants, who did not enjoy the right to own serfs. Including merchants, artisans and traders, the total male registered urban population in the 1670s has been estimated at just 185,000, although many more people, including peasants, resided in towns.[40] The married (white) clergy and, in some cases, monastic (black) clergy constituted another element of the urban population.

In seventeenth-century Muscovy peasants accounted for about 90 per cent of the population, a proportion which diminished only slightly over the next two centuries. Technically speaking, in Michael's reign it is too early to speak of serfdom, which was fixed in 1649 in legislation that closed loopholes in a system which had been in the making for a century and was accelerated by the economic ruin of the Troubles.[41] Some explanations for the appearance of serfdom in Russia emphasize action 'from above', with reference to the state's need to maintain and deploy military servitors, who were recompensed with land worked by peasants. The crown also demanded its share of peasants' resources in taxes and service. To ensure that the peasants paid up they had to be tied down. Another explanation emphasizes action from below, which included local indebtedness – peasants binding themselves in return for cash – that proliferated during the Troubles. Russia's harsh climate meant that many people lived on the margins of agricultural viability. Foreigners at the time pointed to Russians' 'natural servility', seeing master-slave relations as the model at all levels of society. Yet in Central and Eastern Europe, in countries such as Poland-Lithuania, the Baltic provinces and Austria, serfdom also was the norm. Russia was by no means unique.

Recent historical approaches to the phenomenon of serfdom have turned from Marxist analysis, with its emphasis on class struggle, oppression and exploitation, towards a more complex appreciation of divisions among the peasants themselves, treating serfdom as a 'viable and workable institution' which allowed the Russian empire to expand and maintain sufficiency, if not abundance.[42] By the mid-seventeenth century serfs proper, who were the property of noble landowners, could be bought and sold and passed their servile status to their children, accounted for about 50 per cent of the peasantry. Some nobles owned tens of thousands of serfs, others only a handful. The other 50 per cent belonged to the royal family, to the Church or were so-called state peasants, whose obligations and taxes were rendered direct to the authorities. In all sectors agricultural labour, based on a three-field system, was organized by various combinations of stewards and peasant self-regulation through the village commune, one of the most important functions of which was to repartition land to take account of changing household composition.[43]

The technicalities of the rural economy will occupy a modest space in this study of the Romanovs. However, the two-way relationship, idealized and mythologized, between the crown and the *narod* or common people, already embodied in the tale of Michael Romanov and Ivan Susanin, will be a constant thread. In reality, peasants in their everyday life had minimal contact with anyone directly representing the crown, including in many cases their own masters. (The exception were those serfs who worked as servants in the master's household.) This situation tended to reinforce the peasants' belief that the land was theirs by natural right because they worked it and landlords did not set foot on it. Their relationship with the ruler in Moscow was even more remote. Until well into modern times, Russian peasants were hardly aware of the personality or likeness of the currently ruling monarch, except on the coinage. They were, however, reminded of the tsar's existence, his God-given authority and the notion that he represented justice and retribution by admonitions to pray for the long life of the royal family in church and the arrival of the tsar's edicts about recruitment and taxation. A belief prevailed, referred to by historians as 'naive' or popular monarchism, that humble folk could obtain justice by bypassing the barrier or wall of 'wicked advisers' and approaching the tsar, the 'Little Father' (*batiushka*), directly. Given the theory that the Romanovs' eventual demise was closely linked to the peasants' loss of faith in their 'father', this is a topic to which we shall return regularly.

Faith in the 'true tsar' was inextricably linked with faith in his legitimacy and ability to continue his line, and a crucial issue in Romanov family politics from the start was the production of heirs. In Russia, as elsewhere in early seventeenth-century Europe, royal marriage had everything to do with politics

and little to do with love, but in Michael's Russia the politics were forced into a
domestic rather than a foreign framework. Marrying into foreign royal houses
was hampered by religious scruples (on both the Russian and the foreign sides)
and by the relatively low eligibility of Russian princes and princesses at the more
prestigious courts of Europe following the Troubles. The much-married Ivan IV's
proposal to Elizabeth I of England was regarded as particularly eccentric, but
even Boris Godunov's attempts to find foreign spouses for his children came to
nothing. At the start of Michael's reign efforts at consolidating the new dynasty
concentrated on finding Michael a suitable Russian bride, with due consideration
for minimizing clan rivalries. However, his first betrothal – to Maria Khlopova
in 1616 – was undermined by palace intrigues masterminded by his cousins
Boris and Mikhail Saltykov. Maria was declared sickly and unfit to bear children.
Thereafter Michael awaited the return of his father from exile. Filaret's efforts to
find a bride in Protestant Denmark, Sweden or one of the German principalities
(a Catholic was not considered) failed. In 1624 Michael was married off to the
Russian princess Maria Vladimirovna Dolgorukaia, but she became ill (reputedly
poisoned) and died just four months later. A traditional 'viewing' or bride show
was arranged of 60 or so eligible Russian girls, from among whom Michael
selected Evdokia Lukianovna Streshneva, the daughter of a provincial nobleman.
They married in February 1626.[44]

Thereafter Evdokia was almost constantly pregnant, giving Michael a total of
three sons and seven daughters in a little more than a decade.[45] Their first child,
Irina, was born in April 1627, their last, Vasily, in March 1639. Their first son,
Alexis, arrived in March 1629, but this energetic breeding produced a surfeit of
daughters and a fragile male legacy. Vasily died at birth two months after five-
year-old Ivan, leaving just one male heir, ten-year-old Alexis. The new dynasty
thus hung by a thread, threatening a repetition of the void left by Tsar Fedor's
death without issue in 1598. A faction of boyars, headed by Fedor Sheremetev,
proposed as a safety measure to invite the Protestant Danish Prince Waldemar,
a son of King Christian IV, to marry Tsarevna Irina and act as a 'spare' male
heir. However, his arrival in Moscow in 1644 sparked controversy. Russia had
no written law of succession and the sponsors of Tsarevich Alexis, with their
own political futures in mind, were anxious not to dilute the principle of male
primogeniture as long as Alexis was alive. Irina and Waldemar never married, in
fact never met. The Russian side even refused to supply a portrait of the tsarevna
on the grounds that such depictions represented a 'danger' to her health.[46] The
prospect of a Danish entourage at court raised hackles and Waldemar aroused
further hostility by refusing to convert to Orthodoxy. After an abortive attempt
to escape, he was released to return home only after Michael's death in 1645. As
we shall see, none of the daughters of the first two Romanov tsars married. Yet in
numbers, health and longevity they outdid their brothers and, when the occasion

arose, played an active role in defending family honour and fortunes. In 1672 Irina would be godmother to the future Peter the Great. After her death in 1679, her younger sister Tatiana (1636–1706) enjoyed considerable authority and lived to see the founding of St Petersburg. Alexis's daughter Sophia (1657–1704) acted as regent in the 1680s. In the eighteenth century, as a result of Peter I's quirky new succession law of 1722 and a dearth of eligible males, two Romanov daughters, Anna and Elizabeth, would rule as empresses.

Just as the right marriage created the proper framework for dynastic continuity, so suitably imposing buildings and symbolic sites formed a backdrop for the presentation of royal power. The Romanovs would prove particularly successful in matters of ostentatious architectural display and even cash-strapped Michael was no exception. The new regime set about repairing major sites damaged during the Time of Troubles. In the 1620s the Scot Christopher Galloway added ornate upper sections to the Saviour Tower, the main entrance to the Kremlin from Red Square, and installed a chiming clock that Muscovites regarded as a marvellous piece of foreign 'cunning'. In the 1630s Russian master builders added an annexe known as the Terem palace to the tsar's residence in the Kremlin, creating a set of richly decorated vaulted apartments linked by galleries and corridors to palace chapels and to a more public area of audience chambers and porches below. After Michael's mother Marfa died in January 1630, her husband and son founded the Znamensky convent on Varvarka in her memory and endowed it with the site of their adjoining residence. Michael made particularly lavish endowments to monasteries and churches in Kostroma, including the Fedorov Mother of God icon, a fragment of the Robe of Our Lord and numerous Gospels and other printed books.[47] In 1637 the Cathedral of the Icon of Our Lady of Kazan on Red Square was consecrated to commemorate the contribution of a wonder-working icon to the national resistance of 1612.[48] In 1642–3 a team of artists repainted the frescoes in the Dormition Cathedral, following the outlines of older paintings. In the seventeenth century the Romanovs could siphon off the best craftsmen from the provinces, attract a growing stream of foreign specialists, run the only printing press in the country (officially supervised by the church) and, in the 1670s, Russia's first and only theatre. There was no competition from boyars, nothing resembling even a semi-independent 'public' sphere, although the elite vigorously consecrated chapels on their estates and commissioned icons and other religious artefacts.

In Michael's reign both painting and architecture remained traditional and fairly impervious to foreign influences in their main features. This matched the conservationist mood of the post-Troubles period, as well as reflecting the essential conservatism of Orthodox art, which threatened icon painters who worked from the imagination with damnation. Western art, both religious and secular, insofar as it was known at all, was regarded with deep suspicion. There is written evidence that portraits of Michael, probably miniatures, were made in the early 1620s in connection with the search for a foreign bride, but none survives.[49] In 1647 his engraved portrait in traditional regalia appeared in the Holstein scholar and diplomat Adam Olearius's account of his travels. Olearius had an audience with the tsar in 1633, but the likeness is at best captured from memory.[50] The portraits reproduced in modern textbooks are invariably copies of invented images produced in the 1670s or later, which seem to extrapolate on contemporary images of Tsar Alexis, superimposing his father's supposed features on the conventional trappings of robes and regalia.[51] It was one of these which Nicholas II issued on coins and medals bearing their double portrait to mark the Romanov tercentenary in 1913. By way of comparison, Michael, we recall, was a contemporary of Charles I of England (r. 1625–49), whose appearance artists recorded year by year from his eighth birthday onwards.[52]

Orthodox conventions in the arts, for example the rejection of sculptures in the round as 'graven images' and the exclusion of realistically 'worldly' and 'fleshy' motifs from painting, restricted the possibilities for the direct borrowing and copying of Western art. Preserving the purity of religious art also reflected a wider agenda. Modern historians often speak of 'Moscow the Third Rome' or, more broadly, 'Holy Russia' (Rus). Neither term was common currency in Michael's reign; indeed they came into wide use only in the nineteenth century, but he and his circle endorsed the general principles even if they did not articulate them in a consistent manner. These included the belief that, since the fall of Constantinople to the Turks in 1453 and the ending of Mongol rule over Muscovy in 1480, Orthodox Russia was the only independent truly Christian country in the world. This belief was embellished with myths about the descent of Moscow's rulers from the Roman emperors and the symbolic transfer of authority by the emperors and patriarchs of Byzantium, for example, through gifts of regalia.

Of course, God could also punish his chosen people for their sins, as during the Time of Troubles: the normal way of explaining misfortune in the mediaeval religious world view. The violation of the sacred Kremlin by Polish 'heretics' in 1610–12, for example, was interpreted in this manner. At other times God bestowed his grace, and the restoration of a ruling dynasty in 1613 was viewed in this light, as a signal to Russia to resume its sacred mission. Past horrors fuelled a belief in the need for repentance and for ensuring divine protection. Thus in 1625 Muscovites welcomed a fragment of the Robe of Our Lord, a gift from the shah of Persia, which almost immediately was credited with miracles. 10 July was instituted as the new feast of the Deposition of the Robe, one of several added to the Muscovite calendar in the seventeenth century.[53] Major church festivals were celebrated with great pomp, alongside the royal family's name days. In general, Western visitors, hardly unaccustomed to religious ritual at their own courts, found Russian court life excessively overburdened with 'superstition' in the form of religious ceremonial, most of which they were barred from attending.

Michael presided as a figurehead over the restoration of printing and publishing at the Moscow Print House, the first new production of which was an annotated Psalter of 1615. This and other works published in the seventeenth century under Michael and his immediate successors contained prefaces and afterwords praising the tsars for spreading the light, sowing the good seed of education and eradicating heresies throughout the Russian land. Invariably they stressed that the pious monarchs were chosen and anointed by God and often, glossing over historical precision, that they were the 'grandsons' of Ivan IV and heirs to Augustus Caesar and Byzantium. Sometimes the motif 'chosen by all the land' features, with reference to both geography and social class, but the new dynasty preferred to play down the elective principle in favour of inherited legitimacy and divine providence.[54]

A sacred mission was, it might be argued, more a burden than a blessing, which overstretched the resources of Russia and its rulers. As a minimum, it required that defence of Russia against its enemies be embellished with heavy doses of rhetoric about saving the fatherland from infidels and heretics. On occasion it advocated the defence of fellow Orthodox Christians abroad while seizing opportunities for expansion into 'patrimonial' territory, as would happen later in the seventeenth century when Michael's son Alexis annexed half of Orthodox Ukraine from Poland, or in the early eighteenth century when Peter I tried unsuccessfully to 'liberate' Orthodox Moldavia and Wallachia from the Turks. Michael was forced to be a minimalist in this respect, with little room for manoeuvre beyond maintaining claims to occupied territory and Russia's independence. In February 1617 Russia and Sweden signed the Treaty of Stolbovo, under the terms of which Sweden returned the Novgorod region to Russia and recognized the new tsar and his titles, while Russia paid an indemnity and ceded part of Karelia (Kexholm) and Ingria (the site of the future city of St Petersburg). It proved more difficult to make terms with the Poles, who were disappointed by their failure to install Prince Władysław as tsar. In October 1618 Władysław marched unsuccessfully on Moscow. In December the peace of Deulino established a fourteen-and-a-half-year armistice, broken in 1632 when Russia declared war on Poland in the hope of regaining the town of Smolensk. In 1634 the Treaty of Polianovka ended the war in a stalemate. Smolensk remained in Polish hands. Some historians regard this campaign as Russia's contribution to the Thirty Years' War, indirectly as the ally of Sweden![55] In 1637 Don Cossacks occupied the Turkish fort at Azov and invited the tsar to accept it, but he felt unable to do so for fear of provoking war with the Turks: resources did not allow for a crusade against the infidel. The Cossacks abandoned Azov in 1642.

At the same time, the new Romanov regime tried to revive relations with Western Europe. In June 1613 an embassy went to England to inform King James I of the accession of a new tsar and to request financial and military assistance against Sweden and Poland. The tsar's letter to the king stressed the legality of Michael's position: the Assembly of the Land which elected him had acted by 'unanimous unchangeable advice' and was composed of all manner of people 'from small to great and even suckling babes'. It recorded the 'great injustices' committed by Poland, and complained that Poles had desecrated churches and spilled innocent blood. The king of Sweden had violated his agreement to aid Russia against the Poles, taking Novgorod 'by stealth' and doing much evil.[56] However, England's main interest in Russia was commercial. King James offered no assistance.

Michael and his advisers realized that Russia could not rely on foreign loans. His foreign policy would be underpinned by military reform, inspired by awareness of Western superiority in such matters as infantry warfare, training and weaponry. In 1630 the Scot Alexander Leslie of Auchintoul, then in the service of Gustavus Adolphus of Sweden, came to Russia and offered to organize two regiments along Swedish lines. (Leslie later converted to Orthodoxy and was rewarded with a landed estate and generous monthly allowances in cash and provisions.) These regiments formed the basis of Michael's 'new model army', a standing army based on infantry as opposed to the traditional levy of nobles as cavalrymen. The new units eventually numbered about 66,000 men, including 2,500 foreign officers, Scots, Poles, Germans and Italians. Modern weapons were imported and munitions produced in an ironworks founded by a Dutchman in 1632. The army and later the navy (founded by Peter I) were to provide the backbone of the Romanovs' 300-year rule, not only in war but also in peace, when court life was permeated by military parades and symbols. Michael never led his armies into battle in person, but spiritually and symbolically even this 'mild' tsar was regarded as a commander-in-chief. A posthumous image, from the 1670s, shows him on a trotting steed, wearing a gold breastplate and holding aloft a cross.[57]

In later life Michael spent more time making stately progress to church in robes of state than in armour on horseback. This is how he died on 13 June 1645, the day after his 49th birthday, having collapsed during a service in the Annunciation Cathedral. Doctors blamed an accumulation of 'evil humours'. A chronicler recorded formulaically: 'In the city of Moscow there was great lamentation and grieving among all the people, from men of all ranks.'[58] If most historians dismiss Michael Romanov as a mediocrity, it is because there is so little evidence of what he was like. He left virtually no personally revealing letters, diaries or memoirs and, perhaps more to the point, neither did his Russian contemporaries. Almost the only character-revealing assessments come from the pens of foreigners, who themselves had very restricted access to the tsar's person. In his youth he went bear hunting and on pilgrimages, but in his middle age he suffered from weakness in the legs, poor eyesight and kidney problems.[59] At his death official accounts stressed his meekness, mildness and piety; his main service to Russia was maintaining 'peace and quiet'. However, records of court cases of 'sovereign's word and deed' (involving charges of intending physical harm to or committing verbal abuse of the tsar and his family) contained less flattering assessments. Complainants interpreted Michael's pious meekness as failure to curb ambitious boyars and spineless capitulation to the 'schemes' of first his mother, then his father. Even the failure to produce vigorous male heirs was seen as a sign of weakness.

Official documents, of course, conserved the myth of the tsar's absolute power, which required no personal talent or dynamism to legitimate it. Chroniclers boosted his authority by developing myths of the new dynasty's unbroken links with the Riurik line. A 'weak' monarch like Michael was especially in need of myths stressing the sacredness of monarchy, whereas 'alpha male' kings could rely much more on personal authority.[60] Despite Michael's anonymity, however, there are good reasons for regarding his reign as a crucial period in Russian history. In 1613 Russia's very independence was at stake. The state coffers were empty. Whole villages had disappeared. Law and order had broken down. That by 1645 Russia was still a sovereign state and on the verge of expansion was in large part due to the re-establishment and acceptance, both at home and abroad, of the new ruling dynasty. Future Romanov rulers displayed varying degrees of individual energy and all who were capable accepted a leadership role in improving Russia and bringing 'civilization' in the widest sense. Even so, most contemporary foreign observers maintained the stereotype of the 'tyranny' and 'despotism' of Russian rulers, the foundations of which had been laid in the sixteenth century.[61] When, for example, Olearius wrote in 1656 that the Russian system of government was what political thinkers called 'a dominating and despotic monarchy', in which the tsar's subjects were 'his serfs and slaves, whom he treats as the master of the house does his servants', he was repeating ideas which had been current among European writers for at least a century.[62] This stock motif in the construction of Russian 'otherness' remained in foreign assessments up to 1917 and beyond. The reign of the first, 'pious' Romanov did nothing to dispel them.

2

The Pious Tsars: 1645–1696

ALEXIS, FEDOR AND IVAN V

Michael died on the night of 12–13 July 1645. His wife Tsaritsa Evdokia passed away less than a month later. They were survived by their three daughters Irina, Anna and Tatiana and by sixteen-year-old Alexis, now Tsar Aleksei Mikhailovich. Messengers rode all over Russia to assure people that Alexis was tsar according to his father's wishes and with the approval of the boyars and the patriarch. No one openly challenged the principle of hereditary succession. The new dynasty, it seemed, was established and accepted.

Alexis's reign would see a continuation of the policies that allowed Russia to recover from the Time of Troubles. Priorities remained the defence of borders; the maintenance of internal order (with a strong emphasis on enforcing service and tax obligations), and, not least, the consolidation of a stable monarchy. Like his father, Alexis cultivated an image that suggested tradition and continuity rather than change – he too would be known rhetorically as 'most pious' and 'quietest' or 'most serene' – but, as we shall see, he was also an innovator, even if official records did not emphasize this aspect. Staunch adherence to Orthodoxy was a Muscovite tsar's most essential quality; without it, neither he nor his realm could prosper. Therefore scribes listed almost obsessively the religious rituals and ceremonies in which the tsar participated, whereas activities which modern historians might consider more interesting, such as discussions with the boyar council, were not recorded at all. The few surviving contemporary portraits of Alexis reinforce the impression of pious passivity, showing a lone statuesque figure in heavy robes with symbols of office, apparently about to set forth in a religious parade.

Nineteenth-century Slavophile historians took these records rather literally, regarding Alexis as the ideal ruler. It was this static image that would appeal to the undynamic Nicholas II, too. In fact, Alexis's personality is much more clearly defined and his real reputation less 'mild' than that of Michael. Alexis's letters[1] reveal that he had the measure of the people around him, that he could be assertive and had an agenda of his own. Religious rituals emphasized his authority rather than detracting from it; he conducted government business during church services if necessary. The 'quietest tsar' once dragged his father-in-law round a room by the beard (as reported by the Austrian ambassador in 1661). His reign saw the disappearance or decline of institutions that might have diluted autocracy. He summoned the Assembly of the Land for the last time in 1553. The powers of the boyar council were diluted. The church lost out to the state.

Alexis's 'mild' reign witnessed the cruelty characteristic of his era all over Europe. Rebels in Astrakhan in the 1670s variously had their tongues ripped out, were quartered, burned and buried alive. In 1674 a pretender posing as Alexis's late son 'Tsarevich Simeon' had his limbs hacked off and his trunk impaled before being finished off in front of a crowd on Red Square. Female religious dissidents were starved to death in underground cells and male schismatics burnt at the stake. However, Alexis's ability to project a public image remote from such unpleasantness proved particularly important because of the many crises – wars, urban and Cossack revolts, religious power struggles and dissidence – that disturbed his reign. The reward for dealing with these outbreaks more or less successfully was a further consolidation of Romanov autocracy, including a decisive shift in the balance of power between the church and the state in favour of the latter.

In 1645 the young tsar was neither willing nor able to wield much personal power. He relied heavily upon his former tutor and 'substitute father' the boyar Boris Ivanovich Morozov (1590–1662/61).[2] When Alexis became tsar, Morozov, who had been a member of the boyar council since 1634 and had a personal substantial fortune, was able to extend his power base to key government departments. These included the Pharmacy (which guarded the tsar's health), the Department of Musketeers (the militia responsible for security in Moscow, including that of the royal family) and the Treasury. He consolidated his position further by marrying Anna Miloslavskaia, sister of Alexis's first wife Maria. Morozov's relatives and their clients in turn obtained key posts that allowed them access to the inner circle.

Some of the tsar's blood relatives also enjoyed prominence at court. In 1645 Alexis's first cousin, Nikita Ivanovich Romanov (? – 1654) was promoted to boyar and would head the government when his rival Morozov fell from power in 1648. He was joined in the ruling circle by Prince Yakov Kudenetevich Cherkassky (?–1666), another man with kinship ties to the throne, who became a boyar in 1645. Semyon Lukianovich and Vasily Ivanovich Streshnev, kinsmen of Alexis's late mother, were in charge of the Military Appointments Department. More informal positions were held by Afanasy Matiushkin, linked by marriage to the Sheremetevs, and Artamon Matveev, who had been one of Alexis's fellow pupils. In 1671 Matveev would become the tsar's father-in-law. Men gained prominence through a complex mix of royal favour and personal chemistry, marriage and kinship ties, talents and aspirations. There was no standard career path, although it was hard for complete outsiders to make inroads.

The first public occasion to showcase the new regime was the coronation on 28 September 1645. Fedor Sheremetev, the senior boyar of the council and probably the richest man in Russia,[3] held the crown during the anointing ceremony. Nikita Romanov scattered gold coins as Alexis left the cathedral. Surviving accounts reveal not the reality but the ideal or formulaic 'order', which was based on the Byzantine rite first used by Ivan IV in 1547 and repeated substantially at Michael's coronation in 1613.[4] The patriarch's sermon dwelt on the new tsar's duties to his people – to be merciful to his boyars and magnates and accessible and kind to all his Christ-loving troops and to 'care for and be merciful to all Orthodox peasants and have solicitude for them in your heart.'[5] A speech written for Alexis emphasized his hereditary right to the Muscovite throne. A prayer for the new reign stressed also the new tsar's universal role as Christian monarch. In 1649 the Patriarch of Jerusalem would urge him to 'liberate pious Orthodox Christians from the clutch of the infidels.'[6]

After the coronation Alexis set off on a pilgrimage to monasteries with Romanov connections – St Savva Storozhevsky at Zvenigorod (his mother's birthplace), St Nicholas at Mozhaisk and the Pafnuty monastery at Borovsk.[7] In 1650 he prayed at Uglich (where Tsarevich Dmitry was murdered in 1591), at the great Trinity-St Sergius monastery, the richest in Russia, and the shrine at Tver of Princess Anna, who saved the city from the Poles during the Time of Troubles. These and later pilgrimages involved the whole court. The aim was not merely publicity, allowing people outside Moscow to witness the royal progress, but also for the tsar and his circle to move in unison through selected sacred locations of the realm.[8]

Alexis's circle included clergy as well as laymen. He was particularly impressed by the ideas of a group of priests known as the Zealots of Piety, who wished to restore 'pure' practices to make the Russian church worthy of its leadership of the wider Orthodox world. Like the Puritans in England, the Zealots denounced drunkenness, sexual immorality and manifestations of 'pagan' folk culture. An edict of 1645 stated: 'Take great care that nowhere should there be shameful spectacles and games, and no wandering minstrels with tambourines and flutes'. Cartloads of banned instruments were burnt.[9] The Zealots also strove to stem the corrupting influence of 'Latins and Lutherans'. Following a series of measures in the 1640s against Protestant chapels and businesses operating in close proximity to Orthodox people, an edict of October 1652 finally removed 'unbaptized' foreigners to their own self-contained suburb on the eastern outskirts of Moscow, known as the 'New German Quarter', which in time would become a small corner of Western Europe.[10]

The strictures of the Zealots influenced Alexis's wedding on 16 January 1648 to nineteen-year-old Maria Ilinichna Miloslavskaia, daughter of the nobleman Ilia Danilovich Miloslavsky, who had marriage ties to a number of prominent courtiers, including the Morozovs.[11] No strong liquor was served and sacred choral music replaced the usual revels. There were no restrictions on eating, however. The guests feasted on swan, suckling pig, goose, pies, pancakes and various confections. Maria set about her main duties with initially spectacular success. In October 1649 a son, Dmitry was born, to 'universal rejoicing'. But within less than a year he was dead, the first of four sons who failed to fulfil their dynastic potential. The couple's second child was a girl, Evdokia, born in February 1650, as was the third, Martha, born in August 1652. In February 1654 another son was born, Aleksei, who would be declared his father's heir in 1667. He was followed by a quartet of girls – Anna (1655), Sophia (1657), Ekaterina (1658) and Maria (1660). This disappointing run was broken in May 1661 by the arrival of Fedor. Another daughter, Feodosia (1662) was followed by two more sons, Simeon (1665) and Ivan (1666). Sadly, Simeon died in 1669 and it quickly became apparent that Ivan suffered from debilitating physical and mental ailments.

Maria did not function solely as a breeding machine. As recent studies have argued, in Muscovite Russia royal women were empowered by religious symbolism and rhetoric as part of the extended family. They 'actively used the power of religious myth and ritual to create for themselves a meaningful role within a largely male-centered political system.'[12] For tsars' wives (*tsaritsy*) a substantial proportion of symbolism was devoted to the gender-specific myth of the 'blessed womb', but a tsaritsa's role also complemented that of her spouse, as protector, intercessor and champion of Orthodoxy. The tsar's daughters (*tsarevny*) were credited with similar powers of intercession. Royal women were compared with appropriate biblical, Byzantine and Russian prototypes such as Esther, Deborah, Pulcheria and Olga of Kiev, as well as their own patron saints. Although secular portraits of elite women remained taboo in Russia (we have no reliable likeness of Tsaritsa Maria, for example), they could be depicted in religious art in poses of reverence and supplication, as, for example, in the icon *The Tree of the Muscovite State* (Simon Ushakov, 1668), which has images of Tsar Alexis, Maria and their sons Aleksei and Fedor beneath a large icon of the Mother of God, the palladium of Moscow.

Foreign visitors rarely caught more than a glimpse of royal or boyar women, an odd experience for men accustomed to attending the courts of queens and socializing in female company. Curtained recesses in church and closed carriages for outings shielded elite women from prying eyes as they went about their round of devotions. In palaces and residences they occupied separate quarters known as the 'terem'. Foreigners drew understandable conclusions about the 'imprisonment' of women by men and/or their incarceration in convents, combining the evidence of their own eyes with preconceptions about the 'enslavement' of most of the Russian population under despotic rule.[13]

Following the ease of his accession to the throne, the strength and resolve of the new tsar were soon put to the test by the so-called Moscow revolt of 1648. The outbreak sprang from festering discontent over taxes, food prices and corrupt officials. Alexis had inherited a budget deficit which Boris Morozov took steps to reduce, increasing some indirect taxes, including the salt tax, which rose four times. In 1647 the tax was repealed, but by then the government was being bombarded with complaints from military servicemen about rich landowners luring away their peasants, and from townsmen denouncing non-taxpayers and corrupt 'blood-sucking' officials. In summer 1648 a mob made a direct appeal to the tsar and the tsaritsa on the road to Moscow, naming as the chief wrongdoer among officials a crony of Boris Morozov, Ivan Pleshcheev. The tsar's reassurances that Pleshcheev would be dealt with were quickly undermined by the intervention of representatives of those same officials, who attacked the crowd and made arrests. The authorities reacted to a second abortive attempt to engage the tsar in person by calling out the musketeers, but they too turned against elite 'wrongdoers'. The crowd's anger now focused on Morozov himself, whose retainers had killed a musketeer. They ransacked the boyar's house, but he escaped. The anger began to subside only after Pleshcheev and some 'accomplices' were executed and their corpses abused. Alexis made a last appeal to the crowd and banished Boris, who was replaced by some of his rivals on the boyar council, including Nikita Romanov and Yakov Cherkassky.

The striking feature of this and many other Russian revolts, in the seventeenth century and later, was that the troublemakers expressed themselves in the rhetoric of 'naive' or 'popular' monarchism. The musketeers, for example, made a distinction between the person of the tsar, whom they would protect, and 'traitors' and 'blood-suckers'. For the next two centuries the Romanovs to varying degrees exploited this phenomenon, secure in their paternalistic belief that the ordinary Russian people, the peasant *narod*, were loyal to their Little Father, to whom they appealed for justice against abuses of power by 'strong men', who themselves had no firm protection for either their person or property in law and could be exiled and expropriated on the tsar's whim.

Riotous destruction of property was a common feature of these revolts, as was the brutal murder and desecration of the corpses of selected victims. The authorities could not tolerate such anarchy, even if allegedly inspired by loyalty to tsarism. Alarmed, Alexis summoned an Assembly of the Land under the direction of his new associates. At the same time, he appointed a commission to collect and collate the laws, an enormous and daunting task motivated by constant complaints about the practical obstacles of obtaining justice. The Law Code (*Ulozhenie*) of the Assembly of the Land, published on 29 January 1649, comprising 967 articles arranged in 25 chapters, codified existing laws and edicts. This was the first Russian law code to be printed and it remained Russia's basic legal statute until the 1830s.[14] The first two chapters – on 'blasphemers and church troublemakers' and 'the sovereign's honour' – underlined its traditional priorities. Chapter 11 ratified serfdom by abolishing the time limit on owners recovering fugitive serfs. Serfs were bound to the land, with all their dependants and descendants, 'in perpetuity'. In general, it prescribed harsh punishments, including beatings with the knout, a notoriously vicious whip capable of inflicting death within a few blows, other whips or sticks, slitting of nostrils, amputation of hands and feet, burying alive, death by fire and drinking molten metal (for counterfeiters). The tsar's subjects were judged according to the particular law and in the particular court appropriate to their social status. In other words, the 1649 Code observed the old social hierarchies. With no independent judiciary (government officials doubled as judges) or professional lawyers, going to law remained a hazardous process, in which torture of both defendants and witnesses continued to be the approved method of taking evidence in an inquisitorial procedure. Serfs had no recourse to the laws as set out in the code. They continued to settle their disputes or be tried either through their communes or by their landlords

While Alexis grappled with his first domestic crisis, clouds were gathering beyond Russia's south-western borders. The focus of Alexis's foreign policy, like his father's, would be Poland. Indeed, for the Romanovs Poland, whether strong and independent as it was in the mid-seventeenth century, or a refractory part of their empire, as it became in the late eighteenth, would be a recurrent thorn in the flesh. The central issue for the seventeenth-century Romanovs was that the elected kings of the neighbouring Polish Commonwealth – since 1569 comprising the Kingdom of Poland and the Grand Duchy of Lithuania – ruled regions to which the tsar held territorial 'patrimonial' claim and whose Orthodox inhabitants he protected. Militarily Poland remained a strong enemy and its kings periodically laid claim to the Muscovite throne, as during the Time of Troubles.

In 1648 Bogdan Khmelnitsky, military commander or hetman of the Cossacks of Polish Ukraine, brought matters to a head by rebelling against the Polish crown, citing infringements by Polish magnates, persecution of Orthodoxy and encroachment on Cossack liberties and service opportunities. Khmelnitsky wanted an autonomous Orthodox state and he calculated that the Orthodox tsar in Moscow might help him to get it. At the same time, he endorsed the idea of a common Russian (*rossiiskii*) nation in which eastern Slavs could be united.[15] He appealed for Moscow's aid.

Alexis and his advisers viewed the Cossacks' request with mixed feelings. On the one hand, they felt ill-prepared for the war that would inevitably break out. On the other, expansion southwards was a tempting prospect. In 1653 Alexis consulted three Assemblies of the Land before deciding, in June, to accept the proposal. On 8 January 1654 Khmelnitsky swore allegiance to the tsar at the border town of Pereiaslav. The Cossacks understood this vow as an alliance between equals against Poland, but Alexis's envoy refused to take an oath on behalf of the tsar on the grounds that the tsar could undertake no such obligation to a subject, which was how Moscow now regarded Khmelnitsky and his successors. For their part, the Cossacks apparently saw their pledge of 'eternal loyalty' as mere words, since the terms of the treaty suggested self-rule, with Ukrainian nobles and cities retaining their rights and the Cossack army keeping its own laws and command structure. The new Russian-ruled hetmanate would survive for over a century.[16]

The Muscovites took 30 towns during the 1654 campaign, including Polotsk and Smolensk. Preparations for war were spiritual as well as material, deploying religious polemics against the Catholic Poles. In speeches to his troops, Alexis declared that he was ready to shed his blood for Orthodox Christians. The whole affair had the flavour of a crusade. In 1655 Alexis carried out a successful double-pronged campaign against Minsk, Vilna, Kovno, Grodno and Slutsk. At this point, alarmed by the tsar's progress towards their possessions on the Baltic, the Swedes intervened to occupy Warsaw in August and declared war on Russia. War with Sweden stretched Alexis's resources, even though the restoration of Russia's Baltic foothold had been on the agenda since the 1610s. In 1656 Alexis duly attempted to take Riga but his luck ran out. He could not blockade the city from the sea and had to abandon the siege at the end of the campaign season. Attempts to retain some Baltic territory faltered when Polish resistance revived in 1660. In 1661 Russia and Sweden signed the peace of Kardis, which brought no gains to either side and determined relations for the rest of the century.

For much of the mid-1650s to early 1660s Alexis was not only waging a battle on two fronts abroad, but also at home. In April 1652, Patriarch Joseph, in office since 1642, died. Joseph broadly supported the Zealots of Piety, eschewing some of their more extreme proposals but endorsing their programme for replacing the old church hierarchy with more reform-minded churchmen. One of these new men was Nikon (1605–81), who in 1649 was installed as Metropolitan of Novgorod. Nikon proved useful to the tsar in a number of ways, for example by identifying and bringing to Moscow the remains of selected saints having special links with Russia's past. In July 1652 Nikon became patriarch, with the tsar's approval.[17] As was the custom, Alexis promised to obey him as his spiritual father, but before long it became clear that Nikon regarded the tsar's obedience as more than mere rhetoric.

Nikon seems to have based his relationship with Alexis on the mode of the power-sharing between Michael and Filaret, in which the latter was the more powerful. When Alexis went to war in 1654, for example, Nikon revived the title Great Sovereign. He took charge of the tsar's wife and children, whose lives he probably saved by evacuating them from Moscow when plague broke out. Nikon also expressed his personal power with grandiose architectural projects. He built the new Cathedral of the Twelve Apostles and adjoining palace in the heart of the Kremlin and founded three new monasteries, of which the Resurrection at New Jerusalem (consecrated 1657), was the most impressive, with symbolic landscapes referring to Russia's status as a Holy Land in its own right. The Cathedral of the Resurrection was based on the church of the Holy Sepulchre in Jerusalem. Such symbolism had Alexis's approval, but he was less happy with the fiscal ramifications of Nikon's building programme. Nikon filched his neighbours' peasants and confiscated land from other monasteries. These and other acts, such as replacing heads of all major monasteries and demoting certain prelates, carried out in an 'atmosphere of arbitrariness and violence', alienated a substantial body of the clergy.[18]

Nikon continued reforms initiated by Joseph, who had invited learned monks from the Holy Land, Greece and Ukraine to correct service books and other texts. Conservatives duly accused the correctors of being covert Catholics, trained by Jesuits.[19] More controversially from the point of view of ordinary worshippers, in 1653–54, having revealed 'discrepancies' in Russian religious practice, Nikon issued a rule about making the sign of the cross not with two but with three fingers in the Greek manner; he also made changes to spellings in the Creed, the number of Alleluias sung and other liturgical details. In 1655–8, corrected service books and commentaries on the liturgy were published for use by all churches.

There was an immediate protest, initially from prominent members of the clergy, many of whom had their own axes to grind with Nikon. Foremost among them was Archpriest Avvakum (1620/21–1682), who argued that until Nikon's time the Russian Orthodox faith had been pure and undefiled.[20] By the 1660s, when the church and state actively persecuted individuals and congregations who adhered to the 'unreformed' religion, protest spread beyond Moscow. 'Old Believers' or 'Old Ritualists', as they came to be known, argued that to conduct a service or worship using the new books and symbols represented mortal danger to the soul. It was better to die than to submit. 'There was only one general conclusion possible; if Moscow, the Third Rome, had instituted religious changes which required the condemnation of itself and its own past, then Moscow had accepted heresy – and the end was at hand.'[21]

By the second half of the seventeenth century the split between the official church and the schismatics was a fact of life, and it continues to this day. Indeed, one should speak not of 'one great schism' but of 'numerous small schisms',[22] as religious dissidence was deeply ingrained. It was one of the factors that weakened the Orthodox church, making it less able to resist encroachment from the state, whose aid it needed to stem a further flow of believers from its ranks. Dissidence remained a complicating factor for Russia's Romanov rulers, who, as the empire expanded, had to contend also with the incorporation of non-Christian faiths into 'Holy Russia'. Alexis supported Nikon's reforms. He and his family and all their descendants would make the sign of the cross with three fingers and worship from the revised service books. But he lost patience with Nikon himself, sensing the general consensus that Nikon had gone too far in abandoning the Orthodox concept of communality (*sobornost*) in favour of 'papal' theocracy. Matters came to a head in 1658 when a boyar assaulted one of Nikon's officials in the Kremlin but Alexis refused to institute an inquiry, forbidding Nikon to use the title Great Sovereign. On 10 July 1658 Nikon conducted mass in the Dormition Cathedral in the Kremlin as usual, delivered a verbal attack on Alexis and walked out.

A council in 1660 failed to agree on whether Nikon was still patriarch, as did advisers on canon law. In April 1666 he stood trial before a church council, which resolved that '... out of his own caprice, of his own will, without the permission of His Majesty the tsar, without the approval of a council, and without anyone hounding him, he quitted the ecumenical and apostolic church and rejected the Patriarchate'.[23] At the same time the council admonished all present to accept his reforms, including the revised service books. Nikon was exiled as a monk to the Ferapont monastery in north Russia.

The triumph of the secular power over the ecclesiastical was crucial in the symbolic clash between tsar and patriarch and in defining the Romanovs' relationship with the Church until 1917. In the course of the seventeenth century the Orthodox Church lost power in others ways. Chapters in the 1649 Law Code limited the jurisdiction of the patriarch's court, created the secular Monastery Department whose officials could try any priest below the rank of patriarch in civil suits, and limited the expansion of church lands. Abandonment of the Byzantine 'symphony' of emperor and patriarch in favour of the secular power opened the way for the further strengthening of autocracy. These developments must not be confused with 'secularization' in the wider sense, however. The tsar's presence and power continued to be expressed in religious terms and his view of the world and understanding of how it worked remained rooted in religion rather than secular, rational explanation. Like all seventeenth-century Muscovites, for example, Alexis believed in miracles: that St Savva of Zvenigorod had saved him from a bear (he carried around one of the saint's teeth as a cure from toothache), that St Philip, whose remains were transferred to Moscow in 1652, performed dozens of miracle cures. Relics were particularly venerated. In 1655 Patriarch Macarius of Antioch brought as gifts for the tsar's children a finger of Alexis Man of God and various limbs of holy women.[24] Alexis conducted modern experiments in horticulture using foreign experts, but also had holy water sprinkled in the sign of the cross on fields. Russians were not alone in such beliefs – the comet which appeared over Europe in 1665 was generally interpreted as heralding disasters.

In the later 1650s Muscovite gains in the war against Poland began to be reversed. An interim agreement allowed Alexis to become king of Poland when the incumbent, John II Casimir (1648–68) died, but Polish bishops blocked this move with support from the Pope. Bogdan Khmelnitsky's successor Hetman Ivan Vyhovsky rejected Moscow and threw in his lot with the Crimean khan. In 1660–1 Russian armies suffered defeats in Ukraine and the Grand Duchy. Mogilev and Polotsk were lost. In 1663 King John Casimir invaded Left-Bank Ukraine with Tatar aid. Three years later, civil war broke out in Poland and the Polish-appointed hetman of Right-Bank Ukraine, Peter Doroshenko, defected to the Turks. At this point the Poles decided to sue for peace.

In 1667 the controversial truce of Andrusovo, set for a term of thirteen-and-a-half years, confirmed Moscow's possession of Smolensk, part of Belarus and Left-Bank Ukraine (territories east of the Dnieper river). Kiev, on the right bank, was leased to Russia for a further two-year period. In fact, Moscow retained Kiev until the Poles formally ceded it in 1686. Alexis continued to cherish the idea of a Russian on the Polish throne, grooming his sons Aleksei, and then Fedor, for the role. When John Casimir abdicated in 1668 and again in 1673 following the death of his successor King Michael, the Poles themselves asked for Fedor as a candidate to bring about 'the ruin of Islam', but on the condition that he become a Catholic. Alexis's offer of himself as king proved unacceptable. In 1674 John III Sobieski (died 1696) was elected, the last king of Poland not to be dependent on Russian support.

Muscovy's relationship with the Orthodox Cossacks of Ukraine was crucial to its influence in Poland-Lithuania, but that relationship was by no means clear-cut. Cossack leaders never fully accepted Moscow's authority. Some sought Tatar aid, others simply reneged on their agreements with Moscow. In 1663 Alexis appointed a 'reliable' hetman, Ivan Briukhovetsky, but in 1668 he too teamed up with the Tatars and attacked Muscovite garrisons, then in his turn was ousted by a rival who claimed leadership of all Ukraine. A weakened Poland brought new problems, too. In May 1672 the Turkish sultan attacked Poland and captured the fort at Kamieniec-Podolski, forcing the king to accept Turkish rule over Right-Bank Ukraine. As it turned out, this proved no more permanent than previous divisions of the Ukrainian cake. Alexis launched a campaign and installed a (temporarily) pro-Moscow hetman, Ivan Samoilovich, as hetman of all Ukraine. And so it went on. The fastening of the Romanovs' grip on their 'patrimony' was a troublesome process.

At home deliberations over such issues took place in the tsar's court, where the religious world view of the monarch and his circle, sacred ritual and symbolism were probably more powerful than in any other court in Europe. The absence of women at court, itself determined by religious scruples, was not the only oddity that struck Western visitors. Foreigners too, if non-Orthodox, were excluded from most of the court's activities, which revolved around the liturgical year, the anniversaries of living and dead members of the royal family, selected saints' days and special anniversaries of national events, many linked with the feasts of miracle-working icons. Muscovite court life was played out within a closely defined historical context which was reflected in ritual, rhetoric and art. The enclosed Kremlin residences and cathedrals provided a stage for regular dates in the court calendar, but processions sometimes spilled out into the territory adjoining the Kremlin, passing through the Saviour Gate on to Red Square and towards the Cathedral of the Protecting Veil of the Mother of God (1555–61), better known as St Basil's Cathedral. The most colourful of these events was the Palm Sunday procession, a ritual representation of Christ's entry into Jerusalem, dating from the sixteenth century. On these occasions, the patriarch, mounted on a horse representing a donkey, was led by the tsar, who walked ahead on foot in Christ-like humility to a service in the cathedral's chapel of the Entry into Jerusalem.[25] Other lavish re-enactment ceremonies were held on 6 January (Epiphany), when a procession went from the Kremlin to the River Moskva for the blessing of the water (at a spot designated 'Jordan'), when the patriarch sprinkled worshippers with holy water, and on 1 August for the feast of the Bringing Forth of the Cross, on the first day of the fast of the Dormition of the Mother of God. The blessing of the waters with Moscow's own fragments of the cross associated this festival with the baptism of Rus in 988.[26] The fullest programme occurred in Holy Week, when the tsar and courtiers attended several services each day, culminating in the feast of the Resurrection, the high point of the Orthodox year.

Courtly display was intended not so much to impress the tsar's subjects at large (few of whom caught even a glimpse of it), as to reinforce both the bonds and the distance between the autocrat and his elite servitors.[27] The boyars donned appropriate ceremonial robes and stood or walked in a sequence determined by their rankings in the code of precedence. Outside the court, however, the elite had little independent cultural life. There were no public theatres or music, no secular press, no schools or universities. Boyars' country estates were sources of income, not cultural oases. Travel abroad required the permission of the tsar and the patriarch, who issued warnings of the dangers of corruption. In other words, cultural and social life relied to an extraordinary degree on the sovereign himself. Although the cultural forms would change with Peter I's founding of St Petersburg and something resembling a 'public sphere' would eventually emerge in the latter part of the eighteenth century, compared with their Western European counterparts – even the kings of France – the Romanovs and their tastes would play a disproportionate role in determining the evolution of Russian elite culture over the next two-and-a-half centuries.

Alexis himself set a number of trends. For him a cultural turning point was his experience on campaign in Poland and the Baltic in the 1650s, where he saw Renaissance and Baroque churches and palaces that inspired him to convert some of his own residences to a Western style. In the words of his English physician Samuel Collins, 'Since His Majesty has seen the manner of the Princes' houses in other countries and ghess'd at the manner of their kings, his thoughts are more advanced and he begins to furnish his rooms with tapestry and contrive houses of pleasure abroad'.[28] He also had unique access to reports, materials and artefacts from Russian envoys abroad. An embassy to Italy in the 1650s sent back accounts of marvellous palaces, fountains, statues, gardens and theatres. He acquired prints, maps and illustrated books through the Foreign Office.[29] The Russian elite too obtained their knowledge of Western culture second-hand at the tsar's court, through collections of books and engravings and the oral accounts of the few among them who had the opportunity to travel abroad.

The hub of artistic production of icons, frescoes, banners, metal-work and enamel work, fabrics, decorative armour and saddles for the court were the workshops of the Kremlin Armoury, where in 1683 the first studio for non-religious art was created under the direction of the icon painter Simon Ushakov (1629–86).[30] Ushakov has sometimes been presented as a pioneer of 'realism' in Russian art, but this trend was limited. For example, the precisely delineated representation of the Kremlin walls in his icon *The Tree of the Muscovite State* (1668) shows that Ushakov sometimes worked from direct observation, but otherwise the iconography ignores real time and space, bringing together heaven and earth, architecture and holy men of different periods, all presided over by a huge image of the Mother of God, who blesses the 'founding' of Muscovy in the 1320s.[31] In his icons of the Saviour, Christ's face is more naturalistically moulded than in earlier images, but the composition remains conventional.

Secular Western styles and genres came to Moscow with a handful of hired Polish, German and Dutch artists and greater numbers of Belarusians and Ukrainians, who were familiar with Polish Renaissance and Baroque culture and able to paint portraits, historical subjects and 'perspective' studies. The first secular form of figurative art to emerge from these various sources were portraits, especially royal ones. Realistic likenesses of living persons, detached from any religious context and painted from life, a development of the Renaissance in the West, represented a bold novelty in seventeenth-century Russia, where 'portraiture' hitherto was confined to saintly images and lay persons could be shown only in attitudes of prayer and supplication. Tsar Alexis was painted from life several times, but even his portraits demonstrate the tenacity of iconic traditions.[32] The best-known surviving example is anonymous and undated, stiff and stylized, with much attention devoted to conveying details of costly

Engraving of Tsar Aleksei Mikhailovich by Cornelius Meyssens. Vienna, 1660s–70s.

fabrics, although there is a degree of three-dimensional realism in the construction of the background and the treatment of Alexis's face. It recalls similarly
static and decorative portraits painted on panels more than a century earlier in
England, where formal portraiture was also a relatively late development.

In architecture, too, the Romanov court set the trend. Alexis, for example,
owned a book of 'stone buildings of all German states' and works by theoreticians
of the Renaissance and Baroque eras.[33] Even traditionally constructed churches
capped with onion domes began to display decorative details drawn from the
Western Classical order system. (Belarusian and Ukrainian craftsmen seem to
have been major influences here.) A fusion of tradition and innovation may be
seen in the tsar's wooden palace at Kolomenskoe, begun in 1667 and redeveloped
more than once in the eighteenth century. With its turrets capped with double
eagles, the palace was fantastic and 'Oriental' looking to contemporary Western
eyes, but it also displayed broken pediments and twisting columns derived
from Western sources, a pair of automata in the shape of lions and signs of

the Zodiac painted on the ceilings. Both the tsar and his boyars purchased foreign imports such as mirrors, carved furniture, clocks, prints, maps and fabric hangings, although Muscovite houses remained unostentatiously equipped by Western standards. These developments hint at cautiously expanding cultural horizons.[34]

Non-traditional trends risked the censure of the Orthodox Church, which embraced novel decorative details in architecture only if they were not liturgically significant. In the 1650s, for example, Patriarch Nikon condemned as uncanonical the replacement of cupolas by 'tent' (tower) roofs on churches. Sculpture remained taboo because of its association with graven images and 'lasciviousness'. The most sensitive areas were printing and publishing, over which the church wielded a virtual monopoly. In the whole of the seventeenth century the single, Church-run press in Moscow published fewer than ten books which were not wholly religious in content.[35] Even liturgical and devotional works amounted to only a few hundred titles per year and were mostly intended for use in church. The private reader was hardly catered for in print, apart from books of sermons and homilies; the 'print revolution' in political discourse that burgeoned in Europe – for example in England during the Civil War – was quite alien to Russia. The Foreign Office produced handwritten translated news-sheets (*kuranty*) based on Western newspapers for use in the Kremlin, but there were no journals, almanacs or pamphlets, no plays, poetry or philosophy published. Muscovite 'best-sellers' were alphabet primers for teaching basic literacy, themselves composed mainly of religious texts. This bleak picture was mitigated by the availability of literature in manuscript and a flourishing oral tradition. Boyars and townspeople alike read chivalric romances, picaresque tales and parodic works like 'Liturgy to the Ale House', alongside the ever popular lives of saints and miracle tales of the Mother of God. Few Russians were capable of reading imported foreign language material, apart from a little Polish, which spread among the elite in the second half of the century.

The titles of the few secular works that appeared in print in Russian are instructive. They included the 1649 Law Code and a translated manual for training infantry regiments. In the early eighteenth century the number of state-sponsored instructional and practical publications, including government decrees, would rocket, but there was still no room for private, commercial publishing until the 1780s, and then on a small, vulnerable scale.

The weak development of print culture was inextricably linked with low levels of urbanization and education. There were no universities or even elementary schools, and study abroad was precluded on religious grounds. Yet under Alexis education was expanding modestly, with tuition for government officials, although here too the palace set the tone. As a boy Alexis learnt to read from primers and biblical texts, but later he had access to works on such topics as cosmography, astronomy, mechanics and ancient history. In the early 1660s the monk Simeon Polotsky (1629–80) was summoned from the Grand Duchy as tutor to Tsarevich Aleksei Alekseevich, who in 1667 delivered a speech in Latin and Polish to a Polish delegation. Polotsky pioneered the composition in Russian of verses on the Polish model, as well as writing plays and sermons, but most of his works were handwritten by scribes in bound copies for presentation to the tsar and his family, not aimed at a wider readership.[36] Even so he inspired a small school of Baroque poets in the Kremlin.

We should beware of exaggerating the cultural gap between Russia and 'the West'. For the mass of Europeans, the world was still explained by divine providence, not the laws of physics or astronomy. Book learning was for the few. However, succeeding generations of Romanovs were painfully aware of the peculiar limitations that their rural society and economy placed on spreading education and, more generally, 'civilization', beyond the elite. They were forced to be movers and shakers in educational reform, as in so many other spheres, even if, as individuals, their own intellectual achievements were distinctly patchy.

Tsar Alexis's theatre provides an interesting case study in cultural innovation from above. In October 1672 the tsar sat down alone to watch a company of German amateur actors directed by a Lutheran pastor perform *The Play of Ahasuerus and Esther*. The tsar had expressed an interest in theatre a few years earlier when he instructed the Englishman John Hebdon to hire actors, having discovered that European monarchs often attended plays.[37] After being vetted by Alexis himself, the tsar's playhouse opened its doors to the elite and was in operation until the tsar's death.[38] Its repertoire included such productions as *The Comedy of Bacchus*, which featured drunkards, maidens and performing bears, *The Lamentable Comedy of Adam and Eve*, which was performed on two stages, representing the heavenly and earthly spheres, and *The Comedy of Bayazet and Tamerlane*, whose main attractions were lively battle scenes and explosive special effects. The German Peter Engels, 'master of perspective', painted scenery for the productions.

In turn, the royal theatre encouraged the spread of Western-style instrumental music, which had been hampered by the restriction of music in church to the human voice. Outside church services the objection was not so much to the instruments themselves as to their misuse for 'pagan' entertainments; 'seemly' musical offerings at court functions and diplomatic receptions were tolerated. The tsar was at first hesitant about instrumental music for his new theatre 'as being new and in some ways pagan, but when the players pleaded with him that without music it was impossible to put together a chorus, just as it was impossible for dancers to dance without legs, then he, a little unwillingly, left everything to the discretion of the actors themselves'.[39] He duly hired musicians from abroad.[40] These were the modest beginnings of the Western strand of the great Russian musical tradition, which had its roots in choral music and folk song.

After the truce of Andrusovo in 1667 Alexis must have looked forward to some leisure for his cultural pursuits, but in 1669–70 he faced a major challenge to domestic security on the semi-lawless periphery of Cossackdom. The rebel leader, Don Cossack Stepan (Stenka) Razin, was a man of magnetic personality, who some of his followers believed had magical powers. The Cossacks, whose communities had been founded by fugitives from taxes, serfdom and conscription, jealously guarded their liberties and Orthodoxy. By the 1660s they faced fresh challenges. Some of the Don Cossack hierarchy accepted payment from Moscow in return for military service, but their communities attracted further renegades who made a precarious living, usually landless, stuck between the government-subsidized men of the regular Host and the Moscow authorities. Razin took up the cause of these so-called 'naked and hungry ones', leading some daring pirate raids on the Volga and Caspian. In 1669 he swore allegiance to the tsar, but in 1670 provoked a break with Moscow by murdering a royal envoy on the grounds that the envoy had been sent 'by the boyars and not the tsar'. Gathering supporters, Razin took Tsaritsyn on the Volga, then in June captured Astrakhan, amidst an orgy of murder and looting.

Turning in the direction of Moscow, Razin's motley army gathered various malcontents, especially from among the urban poor, who were attracted by the prospect of 'the Cossack way of life' and regarded Razin as a redeemer. In October 1670 superior government forces with artillery defeated Razin outside Simbirsk. Mass executions followed, but Razin himself escaped. An English witness recorded scenes of carnage reminiscent of 'the suburbs of hell'. Eventually Razin was captured by Cossack loyalists and executed in Moscow on 6 June 1671 for 'evil and loathsome acts against God'.[41]

Razin's programme was not anti-tsarist; on the contrary, his pronouncements were loaded with the rhetoric of 'popular monarchism'. He intended to march against the sovereign's 'enemies' and to eliminate 'the traitor boyars and the men of the duma and the governors and the officials in the towns' then grant freedom to the 'common people'. His entourage included a 'Tsarevich Aleksei' and a 'patriarch of Moscow'. Like all such rebellions in Russia, the main targets were boyars and bureaucrats, in the belief that changing the men at the top was the key to a better life. Razin was doomed by his marginal location, haphazard military organization and poor co-ordination, but his exploits lived on in folk memory. As for the Cossacks, their leaders would enjoy a changeable relationship with the Romanovs, which would culminate in the loss of all 'liberties' and the conversion of the remaining Cossacks into fiercely loyal guards and escorts of the last tsars.

Razin's production of a figurehead whom he claimed was the true Tsarevich Aleksei gave unwelcome publicity for the fragility of the Romanov succession. In March 1669 Tsaritsa Maria had died, six days after giving birth to another daughter, her thirteenth child Evdokia, who lived for less than a day. At this point Tsar Alexis still had the promising Aleksei as his heir apparent and the intelligent but frail eight-year old Fedor as a spare. Then in January 1670 young Aleksei fell ill and died, despite desperate attempts to find a cure, including resort to witchcraft and folk medicine. Suddenly the future looked more uncertain. Dynastic considerations were among the reasons that prompted Alexis to marry nineteen-year-old Natalia Kirillovna Naryshkina (1651–94), the daughter of Kirill Poluektovich Naryshkin, a fairly obscure provincial nobleman. There were suggestions that this was a freely made love match on the part of Alexis, who was still only 42 years old, with no parents or guardians alive to dictate his choice. In fact, as with all seventeenth-century Romanov marriages, the successful bride emerged among fierce clan rivalries connected with the rise to power of Natalia's sponsor, Artamon Sergeevich Matveev, and the realignment of court factions.[42] This second wedding took place on 22 January 1671 in a very different atmosphere from the tsar's first in 1648 (when he had been under the killjoy influence of the Zealots of Piety) with musical entertainments from organs, pipes and drums.

The marriage had a significant impact on relations at court. Members of the new tsaritsa's clan and their clientele moved into prominence. Her father entered the duma in 1671 and attained full boyar status the following year. Matveev rose from the fairly lowly grade of gentleman of the council to full boyar in 1674, and with him rose his allies.[43] The former in-laws, the Miloslavskys, and their clients moved out of the limelight, but at this stage there was no open conflict. Rather a balance was struck between old hands and newcomers. The new marriage also alarmed the Mikhailovny (daughters of Michael) and Alekseevny (daughters of Alexis). By the early 1660s there were nine unmarried tsarevny in the palace, the eldest, Irina, born in 1627, the youngest, Feodosia, in 1662. The abortive attempt to marry Irina to a foreign prince in 1644 was too fresh in the memory to be repeated; it apparently was acknowledged (although nowhere articulated) that foreign husbands brought religious complications and possible snubs. There were no eligible, independent Orthodox suitors available and marriage to Russian 'subordinates' might offend the honour of the tsarevny and, more crucially, disrupt and unbalance court kinship and patronage networks. In these circumstances the only alternative to marriage, as we have seen, was to emphasize the tsarevny's virtues of piety and chastity and their powers of intercession as part of the royal collective, but without forcing them to take religious vows. They had their own sphere of influence and allowances. Now they must concede prominence to a new tsaritsa, who was younger than several of them. Natalia's ascendancy was consolidated when on 30 May 1672 she gave birth to her first child, a boy, who was named Peter. Two daughters followed, Natalia (1673–1716) and Fedora (1674–7).

Tsaritsa Natalia remains a shadowy figure. Despite her contacts with the household of the 'Westernized' official Artamon Matveev (who organized amateur theatricals and owned a picture gallery) and reports that she occasionally broke the rules of seclusion,[44] Natalia conformed to the traditional 'pious tsaritsa' type. The only known portraits give little hint of her alleged beauty as a girl, showing her in nun-like widow's garb with her hair modestly covered. Records dwell on her good works and commissions for churches and icons. Even so, there is evidence that she liked to have fun and encouraged her husband's efforts in bringing new diversions to court, including the theatre and music. Summer outings to country estates around Moscow included hunting, falconry (Alexis's passion), bear-baiting and fights between wolves and hounds. Fools and dwarfs were a feature of the court, as they had been of Michael's. Alexis's children grew up with dwarfs, and he bought more than twenty for Natalia who was very partial to them, as was her son Peter.

The birth of a son to his second wife did not amend Alexis's plans for the throne. In September 1674 he presented Tsarevich Fedor to 'all ranks of people in the Muscovite state' as his successor. A carefully orchestrated procession of leading churchmen and boyars, bearing a precious icon of the Saviour, made its way from the Kremlin through a route lined with musketeers onto Red Square, where there was a specially devised ceremony and speeches. Fedor was to become tsar sooner than anyone expected or wanted. On 29 January 1676 Alexis died, aged 47, possibly from renal failure, although even modern biographies cannot pinpoint the exact cause in the absence of medical evidence.[45] He maintained enough composure to bless Fedor as his successor. The decline seems to have been gradual. In the early 1670s records show that he went hunting less frequently and usually rode in a carriage. Despite observing a healthy regime of fasting, he suffered from high blood pressure and obesity. He had always supplemented belief in divine protection with a cocktail of pills and potions and blood-letting, which were often administered by his foreign doctors without any examination of the patient and in a great deal of secrecy because of superstition surrounding the tsar's health.

Rumours of a plot by Artamon Matveev to declare three-year-old Peter tsar instead of Fedor were spread by Matveev's enemies, reflecting a complicated power struggle at court and the perception that Fedor might be 'unfit' to rule. (He had to be carried to his father's funeral on a stretcher.) On this occasion, at least, the principle of primogeniture prevailed even in the absence of a written law of succession. The boyars seated Fedor on a throne and swore allegiance to him. With Fedor's accession, Miloslavsky fortunes rose again and the Narsyhkins' declined: Fedor apparently entertained no personal animosity towards his step-mother and young half-brother, but the new tsar's favourites secured the banishment of leading members of Tsaritsa Natalia's party – including several of her brothers and Artamon Matveev – on trumped up charges of sorcery.[46]

Historians still disagree whether Fedor was a sickly nonentity, easily manipulated by unscrupulous favourites, or whether he showed promise of being a strong ruler. Oddly, no portrait on canvas survives of Fedor made during his lifetime, although there is documentary evidence that artists painted him. War with Turkey (1676–81) over disputed territories and forts on the Dnieper occupied most of his short reign, determining fiscal measures – a reassessment of the population's tax obligations was carried out in 1678 – and also generating a major reform, the abolition of the code of precedence in 1681–2. The registers of previous military appointments were burned, with the declaration that the code, 'hateful to God, creating enmity, hateful to brotherhood and destructive of love', should perish in the flames 'and nevermore be recalled for all time'.[47] The interests of military efficiency played a part, since the code's disappearance in theory gave more scope for making appointments on merit rather than precedent and seniority. Worthy 'newcomer' contenders for honours at court had proliferated over the past decades, but lacked a precedence record to help them climb the ladder. There was general agreement that honour disputes were disruptive, and the obligation to be ever alert for breaches of clan honour, lest some rival was promoted prematurely, was wearisome. What was not weakened in any way was the obligation to serve the tsar. The upper service class remained the 'slaves' even of sickly Fedor, liable to serve wherever he sent them and, short of fleeing abroad, with no alternative outlets for their talents.

Fedor is said to have studied Latin with Simeon Polotsky, but the record is silent on this point, indicating rather that the boy's education was fairly traditional.[48] Following his first marriage in July 1680 to Agafia Grushetskaia (?–1681), a noblewoman of Polish descent, Polish fashions became popular at court, from poetry to daring women's hats, but he had to take account of the current patriarch's suspicion of all Latin and German 'novelties'. Fedor duly closed his father's theatre and issued sumptuary laws banning certain items of expensive court dress, which at the same time outlawed specifically foreign styles. The evidence that he was a 'Westernizer' is patchy, although a number of the men around him, such as Prince Vasily Golitsyn (1643–1714), undoubtedly had advanced ideas.

In two respects at least Fedor presided over a continuation of his father's Westernizing trends. One of his last acts was to approve a charter for an academy in Moscow to teach grammar, poetics, rhetoric, dialectics, rational, natural and legal philosophy and the free sciences on the Jesuit model of the academy at

Kiev. It opened in 1687. In the 1670s the taste for dynastic portraiture also took off, as Fedor and then Tsarevna Sophia and her circle, paid tribute to their ancestors by commissioning their likenesses. In 1677 Fedor ordered portraits for the tombs of Michael and Alexis, and in 1682 two half-length portraits of his father. Rare equestrian portraits of Tsars Michael and Alexis also date from Fedor's reign. Other examples include the icon *Veneration of the Cross* (1677–8, Ivan Saltanov), in which Constantine the Great and St Helena honour the Life-Giving Cross together with Tsar Alexis, Tsaritsa Maria and Patriarch Nikon (whom Fedor admired).[49] The so-called Copenhagen portrait of Ivan IV also belongs to this cycle. Now usually dated *c.*1672–6, it was presented by Tsar Fedor to a Danish envoy.[50]

A striking example of these developments is the posthumous icon-like *parsuna* of Fedor Alekseevich himself on a wooden panel, probably commissioned by his sister Sophia for placing by his tomb in 1685/6. The prototype may have been a non-extant 1679 portrait of Fedor painted from life. The 'iconic' treatment of royal portraits, sometimes set within an actual icon, persisted well into Peter's reign.[51] Thus the portrait gallery of the Romanovs took shape along rather different lines from its Western contemporaries. Except in icons, the early tsars were never portrayed with their wives, for example, as long as the taboo on female secular images prevailed. This was true of aristocratic portraits, too. In the same period a few Russian boyars began to commission likenesses painted on canvas in oils in the Polish-Ukrainian manner, often incorporating coats of arms and heraldic verses. Some prominent individuals, such as Prince Vasily Golitsyn and Artamon Matveev, even organized galleries, but theirs were isolated examples. Not until the 1700s did a thoroughly Western idiom begin to prevail, created mainly by hired Western artists.

In July 1681 Tsaritsa Agafia and her new-born son Ilia died, an event which struck a severe blow to hopes of dynastic continuity given Fedor's poor health. In February 1682 the twenty-year-old tsar was hurriedly married off again, to the Russian noblewoman Martha Matveevna Apraksina (1664–1715). But on 27 April 1682 Fedor himself died, apparently from the cumulative effects of scurvy. Custom rather than written law dictated that his younger brother, sixteen-year-old Ivan, succeed him, but on the same day nine-year-old Peter (the future Peter the Great) was declared tsar on the grounds that Ivan was 'weak-minded' and Peter's mother was alive to guide him. The choice had the backing of Patriarch Joachim (incumbent 1674–90). Ivan's many afflictions, which included serious visual impairment and a speech defect, evidently would prevent him from playing an active part in either civil or military affairs. The German scientist and traveller Engelbert Kämpfer saw both boys at a diplomatic reception in July 1683. Ivan sat 'motionless with downcast eyes' and had to be helped by an attendant to acknowledge the ambassadors, whom he greeted with a sort of 'babbling noise'. Peter, in contrast, 'his face held upright and open, made a [positive] impression with his wonderful beauty and pleasant gestures'. Unlike the passive Ivan, Peter was so eager to ask questions that he had to be restrained.[52] Other foreigners recorded similar impressions.

Even without the wisdom of hindsight, Peter was clearly the 'better candidate for the job'. Yet from the Muscovite political-religious perspective Ivan, however impaired, was the heir by God's will, capable of fulfilling the symbolic functions of rulership as the pivot around which court ceremonial revolved. Piety, dignity and restraint in public, as we have seen, were important elements in the idealized image of a good tsar. From this perspective, lively Peter was by no means the 'better' candidate, but the absence of a written law of succession and practical palace politics still allowed the possibility of making his case on the grounds of utility. Crucially, the immaturity of both boys and the rewards for backing the winner made factional struggle inevitable.

In the days following Fedor's death it seemed that the Naryshkins had the upper hand, but they had not reckoned on a combination of unrest among the musketeers and the fury of the Miloslavskys, who found a spokeswoman in Tsarevich Ivan's 25-year-old sister Sophia (1657–1704), that 'ambitious and power-hungry princess', as a contemporary described her.[53] Sophia had been raised in the semi-seclusion described earlier, the fifth of Alexis's daughters, and she enjoyed the aura of pious authority accorded to all the Romanov women. But clearly she had more worldly ambitions and may have developed her own networks during Fedor's reign. In order to get her brother Ivan on the throne, which she believed to be his birthright, Sophia and her supporters, among them her kinsman Ivan Miloslavsky, had to go beyond boyar circles, where loyalties were fairly evenly balanced between the two boys. She turned to the musketeers, who at the time of Fedor's death were in dispute over pay and conditions and sensitive to rumours of abuses and injustice, their own particular variant of 'naive monarchism', according to which wicked officers poisoned the tsar against them and prevented their voices from being heard.

On 15 May someone spread a rumour that Tsarevich Ivan had been strangled by 'traitors', who were preparing to massacre the musketeers. Mutinous regiments grabbed their weapons and made for the Kremlin. Despite the evidence that Ivan was alive and well, the musketeers took the opportunity to butcher some of their own commanding officers and unpopular government officials. They especially singled out members of the Naryshkin clan and their associates as the chief culprits, accusing Tsaritsa Natalia's brother Ivan Naryshkin of the heinous crime of trying on the royal crown. Some 40 persons, including Artamon Matveev and several of Natalia's close kinsmen, fell victim, some of them hacked to pieces in front of Peter and his mother.

A compromise was found in joint rule or 'diarchy', with Ivan as senior tsar and Peter as junior, an arrangement justified by Byzantine precedents. There is no contemporary record of Sophia's formal appointment as regent, but she undoubtedly acted as such and from about 1686 began not only to add her name to those of her brothers in royal edicts but also to use the title *samoderzhitsa*, the feminine form of *samoderzhets* (autocrat). She commissioned portraits of herself – the first secular female images of their kind in Russia – wearing something similar to the tsar's regalia. However, titles and portraits could not disguise the dilemma that Sophia would have to step down when Peter came of age or when he and his supporters were in a position to assert themselves.

Neither Peter nor Ivan played any direct role in either the domestic or the foreign policy of the 1680s, even though their names appeared on all official documents and Ivan in particular actively participated in religious ceremonies, for Sophia was eager for him to enjoy prominence in almost the only activity of which he was capable. Another vital service was required of the handicapped Ivan. In January 1684 Sophia arranged his marriage to the Russian noblewoman Praskovia Fedorovna Saltykova (1664–1723), a member of a clan prominent since Michael's reign. A male heir would have been a considerable asset to the Miloslavsky party, but Praskovia did not become pregnant until 1688 and then produced five daughters in quick succession: Maria (1689–92), Feodosia (1690–1), Ekaterina (1692–1733), Anna (1693–1740, empress 1730–40) and Praskovia (1694–1731). Rumours circulated that this rich crop of girls was not Ivan's, although the identity of the 'real' father or fathers has never been established. Peter and his mother, in the meantime, spent more time at Preobrazhenskoe, a royal estate on the outskirts of Moscow, where Peter, as we shall see, organized and drilled his own troops and learned to sail.

In general, Sophia's government continued the policies of Alexis and Fedor in areas such as the founding in 1687 of the Slavonic-Greek-Latin Academy in Moscow and granting concessions to foreign merchants and industrialists. Efforts continued to stem the flood of runaway serfs and to persecute religious dissidents. The regime was particularly active in foreign affairs. In 1686 they signed a treaty of 'eternal peace' with Poland, which ratified the 1667 Truce of Andrusovo in return for Russia's agreement to break its 1681 truce with Turkey and Crimea in support of the Holy League against the Turks. In 1689 commercial treaties were signed with Prussia and in the same year, following hostilities with China, the Treaty of Nerchinsk established a border between the two countries in the Amur valley and regulated commercial relations. For all the instability of domestic politics, there was no deviation from Russia's goals of defence of its borders, territorial expansion and consolidation of its diplomatic and commercial position.

The brain behind most of these measures was Prince Vasily Vasilevich Golitsyn, probably the most able and experienced man of his generation in respect of foreign policy issues.[54] However, Sophia's over-reliance upon his lesser skills as a military commander was to hasten her own downfall as well as his. It is possible that she was blinded by love, too, although evidence of the couple's intimacy rests mainly on hearsay. Golitsyn was a cultured man who could converse in Latin, owned foreign books and decorated his house with portraits, mirrors and foreign furniture. Sophia too was a patron of architecture. Her major project was the Novodevichy convent in Moscow, where she honoured the cult of the miracle-working icon of Our Lady of Smolensk, commissioning several churches and numerous icons, vestments and items of church plate. Much of this ensemble was in the new fashionable style, later known as Moscow Baroque, which fused Western decorative features with more traditional Orthodox elements.

This cultured profile did nothing to keep Sophia and Golitsyn in power. Their Achilles' heel was court politics, which in the period 1682–9 were unusually complicated and tense, as contenders for honours proliferated and the extended 'Naryshkin' party regained strength as the 'second tsar' matured. On 27 January 1689 Peter's mother married him off, aged sixteen, to twenty-year-old Evdokia Fedorovna Lopukhina (1669–1731), the daughter of a middle-ranking nobleman. The wedding was commemorated by the production of an illustrated manuscript entitled *The Token of Love in Holy Matrimony*, containing verses and an allegorical drawing with a notional likeness of the tsar and his bride wearing traditional brocade robes and crowns. Floating above them on a cloud, Christ and the Mother of God and their patron saints Peter and Evdokia bless their union, while scrolls with appropriate biblical texts about marriage link the earthly and heavenly planes. This was a traditional marriage with traditional expectations, as emphasized by Evdokia's submissive pose.[55] The only known portrait of her painted in the Western manner shows her later in life, a flabby-faced woman in a voluminous fur-trimmed robe of dark fabric, her hair concealed under a dark head-dress. A contemporary wrote that in her youth she was 'fair of face, but of mediocre intellect and no match for her husband in character'.[56] Surviving letters which she wrote to Peter in her own hand in the early years of their marriage are formulaic texts dotted with conventional terms of endearment: 'Your wretched little wife Dunka [a diminutive expressing subservience] greets you … Be so good as to write to me, light of my life, about your health, so that your wretched wife may be cheered in her sadness'.[57] We do not know whether Peter was ever 'so good' as to write to her: no letters survive from him to Evdokia. But he did his duty: a few months after the wedding Evdokia was pregnant with what turned out to be a son. The tide was beginning to turn in the Naryshkins' favour.

To fulfil Russia's commitments to the Holy League, in 1687 Golitsyn led a large army south against the Crimea, but supply problems and epidemics forced him

Novodevichy convent, Moscow. (Lindsey Hughes.)

to turn back short of his goal. On a second campaign, in 1689, Golitsyn reached the Crimea and had several engagements with the Tatars, but again logistical problems forced the Russian army to retreat after suing for peace, with even greater casualties than before. Golitsyn's opponents seized the opportunity to undermine both him and Sophia, whose 'unseemly' appearances in public Tsar Peter had begun to criticize. The pretext for a confrontation came in August 1689 when rumours that Sophia was sending musketeers to kill him forced Peter to flee to the Trinity-St Sergius monastery. Following a stand-off, Sophia capitulated and was locked up in the Novodevichy convent, where she remained until her death in 1704. Golitsyn was exiled to the north of Russia, where he died unforgiven in 1714.

For the rest of his life Peter associated Sophia with the forces of opposition, especially when in 1698 she was again implicated in inciting the musketeers to rebel. He recognized his half-sister's intelligence, but in his view it was overshadowed by malice and cunning. In a letter to Tsar Ivan written in mid-September 1689, Peter declared: 'And now, brother sovereign, the time has come for us to rule the realm entrusted to us by God.'[58]

Although some historians insist on making 1689 the start date of Peter's reign, the removal of Sophia and Golitsyn did not mark the beginning of Peter's independent rule, still less of his reforms. Peter's letter to Ivan was probably penned on his behalf by one of his circle. It was the Naryshkins and their clients, with Tsaritsa Natalia as figurehead and backed by Patriarch Joachim, who for a few years continued to set the agenda within a vastly inflated boyar council which in 1690 numbered more than 153 members, including 60 boyars proper. There were 33 new entrants during those years. (This may be compared with a council totalling 28 at the end of Michael's reign.)[59] The most prominent of Peter's maternal relatives was his uncle Lev Kirillovich (1664–1705), dismissed by a contemporary as 'a man of very mediocre brain and an inveterate drunkard'.[60] The new ruling faction was easily persuaded by the patriarch to take a conservative line on 'Latins and Lutherans'. They cancelled several concessions made to foreigners during Sophia's regency and adopted closer supervision of aliens in general to stem the ingress of heresy. In October 1689 the Jesuit fathers Georgius David and Tobias Tichavsky were expelled from Moscow and the Protestant mystic Quirinus Kuhlman was burned on Red Square together with his works. The governor of Novgorod was warned to take care that 'no more such criminals enter the country' and to question all foreigners at the border.[61]

Patriarch Joachim's Testament to the tsars graphically illustrated this xenophobic policy. 'May our sovereigns never allow any Orthodox Christians in their realm to entertain any close friendly relations with heretics and dissenters', he wrote, 'with the Latins, Lutherans, Calvinists and godless Tatars (whom our Lord abominates and the church of God damns for their God-abhorred guile); but let them be avoided as enemies of God and defamers of the church.'[62] Joachim's successor Adrian, consecrated in August 1690, held similar views. Religious life at court, with the pious Tsar Ivan Alekseevich at its centre, proceeded as before, the court scribes meticulously recording every detail. For a time, even Peter found himself forced to put in regular appearances. On Easter Sunday in April 1690 we find the two tsars processing into the Dormition Cathedral for matins past ranks of servitors clad in robes of gold thread, walking round the church behind icons and crosses, then processing to pray first at the tombs of their ancestors in the Cathedral of the Archangel Michael, then in the Cathedral of the Annunciation, after which they attended mass in a private chapel. In the next couple of years, however, Peter would begin to set his own ceremonial agenda, ushering in a new style of Romanov rule.

3

Transformation: 1682–1725

PETER THE GREAT

Peter the Great is known as the Tsar Reformer. So radical were many of his reforms that some contemporaries believed that the Romanov male line ended with Tsar Ivan Alekseevich and that Peter was either a changeling, substituted at birth for a daughter, or the son of a German, exchanged while the real Peter was abroad, or, worse still, a work of the Devil. The very adoption of the title Peter *the First* suggested discontinuity, an impious claim of primacy, since previous Russian rulers were known by their name and patronymic, not number. Others regard Peter as the greatest of the Romanovs, who eclipsed the memories of his predecessors and was a role model for all his successors, male and female. Among his greatest admirers were Catherine II and Nicholas I, but all later Romanovs honoured the 'Petrine legacy'.[1]

Peter had no doubts about his identity. Anyone caught spreading rumours about his illegitimate or 'Satanic' origins was swiftly dispatched to the torture chambers of the Preobrazhensky Department, which investigated *lèse majesté*. He did not regard his reforms as unprecedented, freely acknowledging his debt to his father. In the preface to the *Military Statute* (1716) he wrote: 'Everyone is well aware of the manner in which our father of blessed memory and eternally worthy of remembrance … began to use regular troops and how a Military Statute was issued; and thus the army was established in good order'.[2] (Either Peter was unaware of or chose not to mention his grandfather's achievements in this area.) The preface to the *Naval Statute* (1720) tells the story of Alexis's ship *Eagle*, built by Dutchmen on the Caspian Sea in 1667–8 and burned by Stenka Razin. When Peter built ships in the 1690s, 'then did the seed of Tsar Alexei Mikhailovich begin to sprout' into the new Russian navy.[3]

Peter took seriously his obligation to defend the lands gathered by his ancestors, by which he meant all earlier Russian rulers. When he had to justify going to war with Sweden in 1700 he referred to the 'injustice' of the Swedish occupation of Ingria and Karelia, which had been 'forced' on Russia when it was vulnerable during the Time of Troubles. The lost lands, he wrote, 'belonged to our ancestors, the great sovereigns of Russia, for many centuries, but the

Swedish crown in truth treacherously snatched them by dishonest military means during a time of major internal upheavals.'[4] Peter and his publicists blended the discourses of continuity and innovation from the start.

There was little in Peter's early upbringing to suggest his future radicalism. His first tutors were Russian chancellery clerks who instructed him in basic literacy and churchmen who inculcated the fundamentals of Orthodoxy. But he was avidly curious, as foreign visitors attest, and the arrangements of the 1680s for his joint rule with Ivan allowed him to shirk many ceremonial duties and to indulge his curiosity to the full with the help of the foreign companions to whom he was strongly drawn. At Preobrazhenskoe, where he and his mother mostly resided, he began to train the 'play' regiments that eventually formed the Preobrazhensky and Semenovsky guards and to learn to sail, all under the instruction of foreigners. These included the Dutchman Franz Timmermann, the Scot Patrick Gordon (1635–99), who was one of the German Quarter's leading Catholics, and the Swiss mercenary Franz Lefort (1655/6–1699), to whom Peter became particularly close.

The fusion of Orthodox piety and foreign novelty was evident in the celebrations for the birth of Peter's first son in February 1690, when he offered 'thankful praise to the Lord God, our blessed protectress the Mother of God and the Moscow miracle workers and all saints, asking them to grant … many years of health … to the new-born, pious Sovereign Tsarevich and Great Prince Aleksei Petrovich of all Great and Little and White Russia'.[5] He also celebrated with cannon fire and drum beats, as foreign-led infantry regiments marched through the Kremlin. The Naryshkins and Tsaritsa Evdokia's relatives, the Lopukhins, had good reason to celebrate, for nothing was more important to a dynasty than male heirs. Ironically, the son whose birth they celebrated so enthusiastically was to prove a great disappointment.[6]

Peter increasingly turned his back on traditional court ritual, indeed on the Kremlin itself. Boris Kurakin records: 'First the ceremonial processions to the cathedral were abandoned and Tsar Ivan Alekseevich started to go alone; the royal robes were abandoned and Peter wore simple dress.'[7] In fact, the apparent simplification of court ritual involved both the elaboration of a new court calendar, from which old feasts were dropped and new ones added, and the addition of 'mock' ceremonies. Peter's lifestyle became more Westernized. Among foreign goods shipped for him to Archangel in 1692 were mathematical instruments, two globes, a large organ, four clocks, five kegs of Rhine wine and a barrel of olive oil.[8] Arguably, in making such purchases Peter was merely continuing trends encouraged by his father and brother, but the accumulated effect of the things he bought and the company he kept created a more Westernized environment than they had known. In October 1691 Peter attended a party at the home of the German innkeeper Johann Georg Mons, which is probably when he first met his mistress Anna, Johann's daughter. Peter acquired other skills from his foreign friends, taking lessons in Dutch, dancing, fencing and riding. In July 1693 foreign friends accompanied him to Archangel to pursue his passion for seafaring.[9] (Just before departing he visited his father's favourite place of pilgrimage, the St Savva Monastery at Zvenigorod.) There is little evidence of formal education or serious reading, however.

On 25 January 1694 Tsaritsa Natalia died. Scribes noted, 'the great sovereign tsar and great prince Peter Alekseevich ... did not process behind the body of the pious tsaritsa and did not attend the burial'.[10] Peter visited her tomb the day after, but mainly it was left to Ivan alone to attend the requiem masses for Natalia's soul. As letters reveal, Peter's grief was genuine, but with Natalia's death more links with the past were broken and lip-service to the old ways could be abandoned further. In September 1694 Muscovites witnessed a display of Peter's 'play' troops, in what were known as the 'Kozhukhovo manoeuvres'.[11] Armies commanded by 'King' Fedor Romodanovsky of Pressburg (now Bratislava, in Slovakia) and 'King' Ivan Buturlin of Poland paraded through the city. The subsequent mock battle left 24 dead and 15 injured. Peter himself posed as 'King' Fedor's loyal subject, participating as an ordinary bombardier. This was one of countless demonstrations of tsarist authority operating under the guise of assumed humility. The most famous of Peter's mock institutions was the All-Drunken, All-Jesting Assembly which engaged in parodic religious ceremonies, presided over by a 'Prince-Pope' (kniaz'-papa) and other pseudo-churchmen, including Peter himself as Archdeacon Gedeon. The best-known Prince-Pope was Peter's former tutor Nikita Zotov, referred to in some sources as 'Patriarch Bacchus', holder of the post until his death in 1717. The Drunken Assembly had no consistent programme or parodic source. Peter elaborated elements as it pleased him, for example 'papist' terminology of 'conclaves' and 'cardinals'. It contained features of Russian Yuletide revelries as well as foreign carnival. The British in Russia, for example, specialized in bawdy humour; the 'British Monastery' or Bung-College in St Petersburg, had its own Father Superior and included among its members 'the staff surgeon and pickle smith or prick farrier'.[12] Once glossed over as an aberration, even though it was in operation until Peter's death, more recently the Drunken Assembly has commanded serious scholarly attention.[13]

Peter also constructed a parallel mock court, presided over by His Majesty Prince-Caesar (kniaz'-kezar'), who appeared dressed in traditional Russian robes alongside the Prince-Pope in a parody of the Byzantine symphony of tsardom and priesthood. For more than twenty years the mock crown was worn by Prince Fedor Romodanovsky (1640–1717), who was succeeded by his son 'Tsarevich' Ivan. As Prince-Caesar, Romodanovsky had his own residence at Preobrazhenskoe and was also director of the feared Preobrazhensky Department, the tribunal for investigating treason. In January 1695 the mock court and Drunken Assembly combined to celebrate the wedding of Yakov Turgenev, a secretary in the Department, in which the bride and groom rode in the tsar's 'best carriage' with a retinue of boyars and courtiers in fancy dress pulled by bullocks, goats, pigs and dogs.[14] A new cultural topography was being constructed which paralleled the traditional 'sacred landscape' in which Tsar Ivan and Patriarch Adrian continued to function. Peter's role in this constructed world was variously as the humble subject (trainee bombardier or trainee shipbuilder) of Prince-Caesar or deacon in attendance on Prince-Pope. He set the rules and allocated the roles.

An enthusiastic devotee of such play-acting was Peter's friend Alexander Danilovich Menshikov (1673–1729), a man 'of low birth, lower than the gentry', initially without close links with any of the families of the Muscovite elite.[15] His father may have come to Russia as a prisoner of war from Lithuania and served as a non-commissioned officer in the Semenovsky guards regiment. His was a 'rags to riches' tale, a poor boy raised above boyars and princes of ancient lineage to become the most titled man in the realm after the tsar himself, although later he constructed a narrative about a more elite ancestry. Peter's relationship with Menshikov was a complex one, possibly with a homosexual dimension, which changed over the years, through their subsequent marriages. Menshikov may have become rich and powerful, building up his own clientele networks, but he was ultimately Peter's creation. They could never be equals.[16]

In 1695 Peter faced the first real challenge of his reign. In the wake of the disastrous Crimean campaigns of 1687 and 1689, Russia began to lose confidence in the Holy League, fearing to be sidelined in future peace negotiations with the Turks. In an attempt to gain a stronger bargaining position with the allies and ward off Turkish attacks on Ukraine, Russia launched a campaign against the Turkish fort of Azov at the mouth of the river Don.[17] In this, as on many subsequent occasions, Peter ceded nominal command to others, himself serving as a bombardier in the Preobrazhensky guards. The campaign was a failure, which Peter blamed on an unclear command structure, tactical errors and technical deficiencies. (In particular, the Turks were able to replenish supplies by sea.)

On 29 January 1696 Tsar Ivan died and was buried on the following day next to his brother Tsar Fedor in the Archangel cathedral.[18] This ceremony was the last of the old-style royal funerals. Peter's departure from this world almost exactly 29 years later was to be marked in a different place and a different manner. From now on Peter was freer than ever to elaborate his own ceremonies, while the traditionalist camp, headed by Patriarch Adrian, found themselves without a tsar. Both the defeat at Azov and the death of Ivan forced Peter to take stock. Early in 1696 he prepared for a second campaign, which involved the building of galleys and other craft at Voronezh on the Don, a huge effort in which thousands of the tsar's subjects were expected to do their bit, from the churchmen and merchants who supplied cash to the hapless labourers drafted in to hack vessels out of unseasoned wood. Late in May 1696 Peter's land and water-borne forces laid siege to Azov. A Russian flotilla took to the sea and cut off the Turks' access to reinforcements. On 18 July the fortress surrendered.

Peter's first military victory prompted some striking celebrations. Services of thanksgiving and prayers for the souls of the dead were supplemented by secular parades bristling with 'pagan' symbols, imperial Roman references and imagery. Triumphal gates of Classical design were erected, bearing Julius Caesar's words: 'I came. I saw. I conquered'. There were references to the Christian Roman Empire, too, and stock comparisons of Peter with the Emperor Constantine the Great. Imperial Roman parallels would become standard features in celebrations of Romanov successes. Peter's first major public display of the new manners also featured Prince-Pope Nikita Zotov blessing his 'flock' from a carriage. These and other examples of Western and parodic ceremony drew criticism from tradition-alists, one of whom described Peter's entourage as 'a swarm of demons'.[19] Shortly afterwards, Peter had to crush a conspiracy masterminded by representatives of leading families who were alarmed by Peter's imminent plans to travel abroad and to send a group of young nobles to the wicked West to study.

In March 1697 Peter set off on a Grand Embassy, one of the aims of which was to publicize Russia's recent success at Azov in the hope of obtaining further aid for the Holy League.[20] For Peter it was to be a personal voyage of discovery. He would see with his own eyes the extent to which Russia differed from the countries that he visited in its social, economic, technological and cultural development and to find confirmation of what he already must have sensed in Moscow's German Quarter, with its tantalizing glimpses of Western urban life. Not the least of the problems he had to confront was Europe's negative image of Russia, and indeed of himself, as the exotic ruler of a 'rude and barbarous kingdom' who attracted more curiosity than respect.

The 250-strong contingent which left Moscow with 1,000 sledges was headed not by the tsar but by Franz Lefort. It was accompanied by 35 Russian 'volunteers' bound for the Dutch Republic to study shipbuilding and navigation, among them one Peter Mikhailov and his friend, Alexander. Peter's decision to travel incognito has usually been attributed to his desire to retain the freedom to work and observe without getting bogged down in official duties, but as a sustained attempt to conceal the identity of a man who was now 6ft 7in tall it was doomed to failure. In some ways the Embassy 'charade' was a natural extension of the play regiments and the mock court, a variation on the theme of role-playing.

Peter's semi-incognito was to provoke some awkward incidents. In Riga in Swedish Livonia in March 1697 the governor forbade Peter to inspect ships in the harbour and to sketch fortifications, having made no special arrangement to honour Mr Mikhailov. Fulminating against the 'insult' and the high price of accommodation and transport, Peter left Riga early. Turning the West-East rhetoric of 'them and us' on its head, he later referred to his reception as 'barbaric and Tatar-like'.[21] For the time being relations with Sweden remained officially cordial. In December 1697 Peter congratulated sixteen-year-old King Charles (Karl) XII on his accession.

Peter's travels next took him to Brandenburg to meet Frederick III, since 1688 King Frederick I of Prussia, with whom Lefort signed treaties on friendship, trade and training opportunities. Frederick's wife Sophia-Charlotte and her mother, Sophia electress of Hanover, later remarked on the tsar's 'rustic' table manners, his shyness and lack of gallantry. He seemed more at ease with the dwarfs in his party than with the German ladies, whose whalebone corsets puzzled the 'Muscovites' who had little experience of socializing in mixed company. Even so, the women believed that Peter had 'much merit and much native wit'.[22] Such unnerving social encounters were an essential part of Peter's (and Russia's) Western education and contributed to his vision of civilizing Russia, which included ending the traditional segregation of the sexes.

In August he rented a room at the back of a blacksmith's tiny house in the Amsterdam suburb of Zaandam and prepared for his shipbuilding training. He was however forced to quit after a week by curious crowds. Peter's guide in Amsterdam was the burgermeister Nicolaes Witsen, who had visited Russia and shared the tsar's interest in ships and collecting curiosities. The Dutch East India company agreed to admit 'the distinguished personage living incognito' together with ten of his companions to work in their yards. On 1 September in Utrecht Peter had his first, secret, meeting with the Dutch stadtholder William III of Orange-Nassau, since 1689 also King William III of England. Peter expressed his admiration for William ('the most brave and most generous Hero of the Age'), his distrust of France and his desire to promote trade.[23] This proved an inopportune moment, however, to request money from the Dutch, who pleaded poverty as a result of the recent Nine Years' War with France.

Peter's four-and-a-half months in the Dutch Republic were highly instructive. He was particularly fascinated by curiosities and rarities, assembled from all corners of the globe, some of which later ended up in his own museum. He attended some of Professor Ruysch's gruesomely illustrated public lectures at the Amsterdam Anatomical Theatre, one of the places where he acquired a taste for performing dissections and autopsies. The Dutch urban order which Peter admired – clean streets and solid houses, thriving commerce and crafts, the intersection of cities by canals, and embankments, the formal layout of gardens and the use of brick and tile – he later introduced in his new city of St Petersburg, which came to be known, among other things, as 'New Amsterdam'.

On 9 January 1698 Peter I sailed across the Channel to England (not on his original itinerary) to acquire theoretical knowledge 'in the Mathematical way' and tempted by the gift of the frigate *Royal Transport*, the most modern vessel of its kind afloat.[24] In fact, most of Peter's time in England, too, was devoted to practical activity and visiting the sights rather than to theoretical studies, for which he had little aptitude. Near the Royal Naval Dockyards at Deptford the Russian trainees lodged in the diarist John Evelyn's house at Sayes Court, where their destructive antics resulted in a bill for £350 9s and 6d. Evelyn's servant referred to the Russian guests as 'right nasty'.[25]

British motives for welcoming their odd guest were chiefly commercial. As far as political alliances were concerned, they still regarded Russia's role in the world as marginal. They acknowledged success at Azov, but the port's location further encouraged the view that Russian foreign policy was distinctly Eastern-oriented.[26] Over the next two decades Britain would watch the growth of Russian sea power in the Baltic with growing anxiety, but for the time being relations were cordial.

The highlights of Peter's visit included sailing on the Thames and attending a naval review at Portsmouth. In London he visited the Royal Observatory, the Mint (in the Tower), the Arsenal and the Royal Society. He went to Windsor Castle and spent a night in Christ Church, Oxford. He enjoyed 'the choicest Secrets and Experiments' conducted for him by the physician Moses Stringer, which included dissolving and separating metals,[27] and some trips to the theatre, which he liked less. Peter visited Sir Christopher Wren's Kensington Palace, the new wing at Hampton Court and the Royal Naval Hospital at Greenwich. The imposing scale of the still incomplete St Paul's Cathedral may have reminded Peter that even in a country like Britain, where the Church was firmly subordinated to the Crown, grand ecclesiastical architecture remained a prominent feature in the capital city and glorified the monarch as well as God. He met the archbishop of Canterbury at Lambeth Palace, where he saw an ordination and a service. He was particularly interested in the supremacy of the English kings.[28]

Peter also attended a joint session of the Lords and Commons. The Lords may have struck him as not much different from his own boyar council, even though they did not prostrate themselves before the king or refer to themselves as his 'slaves', practices which Peter was trying to eliminate at home. He probably regarded the king as an absolute monarch much like himself. He was less impressed by the principles behind the Commons, allegedly declaring that 'English freedom is not appropriate here [in Russia]... You have to know your people to know how to govern them. I am happy to hear anything useful from the lowest of my subjects; their hands, legs and tongues aren't fettered'.[29] This anecdote represents the relationship between tsar and subjects in traditional, patrimonial terms. People could appeal or speak to the tsar (although direct petitions were discouraged), but not channel their appeals through institutional bodies. The independent judiciary, parliament and corporate assemblies, which in Britain regulated relations between ruler and ruled, were absent.

Engraving of Peter I, the Great, by John Smith
(after Kneller). London, 1698.

In 1698 the 25-year-old tsar comes to life in the full-length portrait painted in
London at William III's behest by the eminent court painter Sir Godfrey Kneller
(1646–1723). Kneller probably painted only Peter's face, which apparently is
a good likeness, immediately recognized by contemporaries, while assistants
did the rest. The master set the same formulae – column and crown to our left,

warship in the background to the right, the tsar in royal ermine and armour – as he used in his portrait of James II (1683–4, National Portrait Gallery, London). The emblematic armour (of a kind which was no longer worn in battle) and a marshal's baton conventionally honoured Peter as a military leader. This was an unambiguously Western royal image in the grand register. For perhaps the first time a Russian ruler was depicted as 'one of us' as opposed to 'one of them'.[30] Peter's aim, it seemed, was 'to see countries more civilised than his own, and especially nations who have developed a Navy, which is his master passion' and 'to take patterns for civilising his own rude people'.[31] If imitation is the best form of flattery, the British had every reason to approve Peter's good sense and forgive his rude behaviour.

In April 1698 Peter returned briefly to the Dutch Republic before heading for Vienna, where he had talks with Emperor Leopold. In early May news came from Prince-Caesar in Moscow about a mutiny of the musketeers, which apparently had been successfully quelled. In Vienna a highlight of Peter's stay were two costumed balls, one given for his nameday on 29 June/9 July and another on 11/21 July, which Peter attended dressed as a Friesian peasant, whom Emperor Leopold, getting into the spirit of things, toasted with the words: 'I know that you are acquainted with the great Russian monarch, so let us drink to his health.'[32] There was little substance to the formal negotiations, for the Austrians were on the point of making a separate peace with the Turks, signed at Carlowitz late in 1698.

Peter was about to leave for Venice when news arrived that the musketeers had mutinied again. Subsequent reports that the revolt had been suppressed did not persuade him to resume his planned itinerary. On his homeward journey Peter met Augustus II, Frederick Augustus I, elector of Saxony (1670–1733), the new king of Poland, one of the most colourful characters of his era, whose election had been supported by Russia and Denmark over a French-backed candidate. Peter expressed his wish to avenge the 'insult' suffered at Riga in 1697 and learned that Augustus had designs on Swedish Livonia. He also knew that Denmark was eager to reduce Sweden's possessions in north Germany. The outline of alliances against Sweden took shape.

In terms of its stated diplomatic aims, the Grand Embassy failed, although it produced many tangible results such as the hiring of foreign experts and the purchase of technology. In terms of Peter's view of the world, its influence was incalculable. He came back more convinced than ever that Russia must change. The Embassy crystallized further Peter's image of Europeans, in the immediate, concrete sense of what they looked like and how they behaved in their surroundings. And what in the first instance divided Russians and Western Europeans (of both sexes) into 'us' and 'them' were clothes and hairstyles. Peter made his initial onslaught on his subjects' appearance on 26 August 1698, the day after he returned to Moscow, when he wielded a razor to cut off the beards of the boyar council. Apart from the patriarch and a few elderly men, 'all the rest had to conform to the guise of foreign nations, and the razor eliminated the ancient fashion'.[33] Peter committed another offence to tradition, when he failed to observe the 1 September New Year ceremonies. In December 1699 Peter decreed that, following the example of many European Christian nations, henceforth Russia would adopt the practice of numbering years from the birth of Christ, not the beginning of the world, and would begin the New Year in January, not September.[34] Traditionalists protested in vain.

The attack on beards was thus part of a wider package of cultural reform imposed from above. In 1705 Peter introduced a beard tax on a graduated scale for those who insisted on retaining their beards. Members of Peter's immediate entourage mostly had already adopted a Westernized appearance, but further afield the measures aroused bitter protests on religious grounds. The British engineer John Perry recounts the tale of an old Russian carpenter at Voronezh who hid his shaved-off beard under his shirt with the intention of taking it with him to the grave.[35] Peter's own clean-shaven visage and 'German' attire and his imposition of the same on others were frequently cited as evidence of his ungodliness.[36]

Dress reform followed. In February 1699, Peter cut off the long sleeves of some of his officers and ordered returning envoys to wear 'German dress'. Formal decrees imposing Western dress on urban men and women were issued in 1700 and 1701.[37] It was no accident that Peter's assault on beards and traditional clothing occurred as he did battle with the musketeers, whom he had come to regard as symbols of Old Russia. The rebels' petitions to the authorities confirmed Peter's worst fears: they vowed to kill the 'Germans' who were 'destroying Orthodoxy' and to wipe out the new guards regiments, their perceived rivals. They harboured vague notions of driving out 'traitors' and foreigners, establishing leaders sympathetic to them and restoring the 'old order' under which they, the musketeers, had enjoyed a privileged position.

The musketeer trials aimed at eliciting information on 'accomplices' and motives, including the involvement of Tsarevna Sophia. Sophia denied everything and Peter resorted to inflicting a symbolic death on his troublesome half-sister by forcing her to take the veil.[38] One thousand, one hundred and eighty-two musketeers were executed and 601 flogged and banished. Men were broken on the wheel, heads were displayed on poles, corpses strung up, some in front of Sophia's windows. The execution of the musketeers became one of the symbols of Peter's ruthless determination to root out opposition. The message was not lost on the elite, who, as we shall see, remained by and large culturally obedient and subservient. For the next two centuries they maintained clean-shaven faces and

Western dress, distinguishing themselves from the mass of the traditionally clad and bearded population, always taking a sartorial lead from the Romanovs.

Peter had another symbol of the past to deal with. In 1697 he had written from abroad to close associates proposing that his unloved wife Evdokia take the veil. The 'pious tsaritsa' turned out to have a mind of her own, and had to be unceremoniously dispatched to the Intercession convent in Suzdal, where she lived under armed guard. In May 1699 Peter sent an agent to Suzdal to force her to take the veil under the name Elena, although apparently she quickly discarded her nun's habit. Evdokia would outlive both her husband and her son and was regarded by traditionalists as Peter's rightful spouse.

On 18 August 1700 Russia celebrated a 30-year truce with the Ottoman Empire and the following day declared war on Sweden on the grounds of its failure to give satisfaction for the 'insult' at Riga and its illegal occupation of the Baltic provinces of Ingria and Karelia. Anti-Swedish coalitions with Denmark and Augustus II boded well for Peter's plans to re-establish and extend Russia's foothold on the Baltic, but optimism seemed ill-founded. Denmark was soon forced to withdraw from the coalition. In the first campaign, at the Baltic port of Narva in November 1700, Charles XII's men killed or captured thousands of ill-prepared Russian troops after a month-long siege. The ease of the victory convinced Charles that Russia was finished and he turned his attention to Augustus II's Saxon army. This and the outbreak of the War of the Spanish Succession in May 1702, which lessened the likelihood of intervention by Western powers, left Russian troops free to advance into pockets of the Baltic and in autumn 1702 Peter captured the Swedish fortress of Nöteborg on Lake Ladoga, which he renamed Schlüsselburg, the 'key' to the River Neva. In May 1703 the Russians captured the fort of Nyen downstream on the Neva. Nearby Peter built his own modest earthwork fort, dedicated to his patron saints Peter and Paul, the beginnings of his future capital city, St Petersburg.

In the 1710s St Petersburg would become the residence and seat of government, although no official declaration was ever issued to this effect. One cannot over-exaggerate its significance for Peter and his successors. It became inextricably linked to the Romanovs not only as their capital (only Peter II abandoned it for Moscow for a short time) and as a modern commercial port and centre of imperial-sponsored arts and culture, but also as the dynasty's sacred landscape, with symbolic and mythological associations, which linked or paralleled the Romanovs' history and mission with such distant events as the founding of Byzantium and the legendary travels of St Andrew in the region.[39] If Moscow was the creation of the Riurik dynasty, St Petersburg was unequivocally the creation of the Romanovs. The idea that it was built on 'empty' land also contributed to the myth that Peter created his new Russia 'from nothing', although there were actually a number of Swedish settlements in the area.

Sankt-Piter-burkh (spelt initially in a Russified Dutch manner) had a special personal significance for Peter, who referred to it as his 'Paradise' despite its disadvantages, such as mosquito-infested summers and long, cold, sunless winters, floods, half-finished buildings and expensive food, since nearly everything had to be imported long distances. Only after 1709 did the city really take shape.[40] The Summer and first Winter Palace (the existing building dates from the 1750s–60s) were begun in 1710, as were the mansions of Menshikov and other magnates, and the Alexander Nevsky monastery. In 1711 a central avenue, later named Nevsky Prospect, was laid. The Cathedral of SS Peter and Paul was begun in 1712. The city was intersected by canals and straight streets according to a plan and the main streets had a uniform roof line, in contrast to Moscow's haphazard maze of lanes. Outside the city on the south shore of the Finnish gulf Peter built grand palaces at Peterhof and Strelna, both sometimes referred to as his 'Versailles'. The chief architect of many of these projects was the Swiss-Italian Domenico Trezzini, who came to Russia in 1703 and died there in 1734. All the major architects of early St Petersburg were foreigners, working in the latest European styles and passing on their skills to Russian apprentices.

Peter's court artists also came from the West, mainly to paint portraits – men such as Louis Caravaque and Johann Tannhauer. Peter also collected Old Masters for his new galleries. Russian painters fully trained in Western techniques remained, like architects, in short supply during Peter's lifetime, and information about them is sparse. The best known is Ivan Nikitin (*c.* 1680–after 1742), whom Peter sent to study in Italy, but the catalogue of his works, mainly portraits, is fragmentary. Engraving caught on more quickly, with Russian artists producing prints and maps of St Petersburg, battle and naval scenes and processions for wide distribution. Sculpture in stone and metal, still stigmatized by the church as the art of graven images, was slower to develop. An equestrian statue of the tsar by Carlo Bartolomeo Rastrelli (1675? –1744) had to wait until Paul's reign to be erected.[41]

In 1718 Peter established a 'police' administration for St Petersburg, in the eighteenth-century sense of provision for civic order, cleanliness and welfare. Public hygiene and safety measures involved setting up a regular refuse collection and a fire service, reducing the pollution of waterways and clearing beggars from the streets. Better-off districts were provided with street lighting (which Peter had seen in Amsterdam), drainage pipes and paving. Other decrees, such as compulsory tree-planting, aimed to beautify the city. Exhortation was supplemented by penalties. For example, owners of horses were ordered to bring a cartload of manure for each horse they possessed to a designated place or pay a one rouble fine. St Petersburg was constructed by teams of state peasants drafted in for the summer building season, fifteen or twenty thousand at a time. Casualties were high and conditions harsh. Nobles too were subjected to

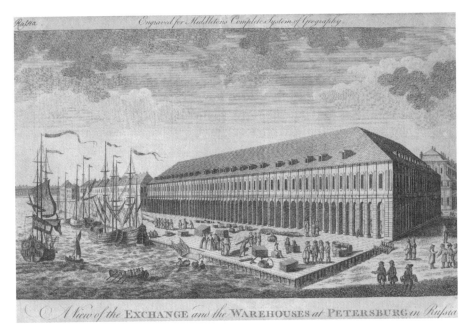

Stock Exchange (Bourse) and warehouses, from Middelton's *Geography* of 1778.

compulsion: in 1714 a thousand noble families were ordered to move permanently to St Petersburg. In the same year Peter passed an unpopular law of Single Inheritance that curtailed a nobleman's right to divide his estate among all his children, in the hope that disinherited sons would put their efforts into service. There was no escape from Paradise, except temporarily with the tsar's written permission.

In Peter's battle for international recognition, St Petersburg was more than a naval base or port, more even than 'a great window recently opened in the north through which Russia looks on Europe'.[42] It was a sort of clean sheet, an anti-Moscow on which Peter could create a model for his new Russia. The city's layout was, at least on paper, planned,[43] and its spirit was rational. The foreign design and decoration of the new buildings, the foreign-sounding names of institutions (*Senat, Kollegii, Kunstkamera*), the European fashions that inhabitants were forced to wear – all were calculated to make foreigners feel that they were in Europe rather than Asia. Peter felt at home there, too. Critics, on the other hand, have regarded St Petersburg as the prime illustration of the high cost of imperial indulgence 'from above', especially under Peter's successors, as well as a symbol of the fundamental error of discarding tradition. 'How many people perished, how much money and labor was expended to carry out this intent? Truly, Petersburg is founded on tears and corpses,' wrote the historian Nikolai

Karamzin in 1810.[44] Dislike of the new 'artificial' capital was an important element in later critiques of Peter's reforms.

Creating St Petersburg presupposed a programme for the 'transformation of savage manners', the creation of a Westernized elite. The peasant masses of necessity were excluded from this process, from rules on dress, shaving, habitations and education. Peter worked hard to inculcate Western manners in those around him, although the often boorish tsar was not the best of role models. Trips abroad aided the transformation of a select few, while at home they could read behaviour books such as *The Honourable Mirror of Youth* (1717), which included advice after Erasmus on how to behave at table and make polite conversation. In 1718 Peter issued a decree on Assemblies in an attempt to extend polite society beyond the court. Access to social gatherings in private houses was open to any decently-dressed persons. Peter used a characteristic degree of compulsion both in the manner of their introduction and their subsequent supervision. For example, hosts' homes were visited by the police to check that everything was in order and the authorities sometimes demanded guest lists.

Ladies were required to abandon seclusion, discard their traditional shapeless garments for Paris fashions and show off their hair dressed in the latest style. New consumer items such as wigs, fans and coffee services appeared. Paintings and sculptures featuring female nudes were unthinkable in the prudish Muscovite period. But they found a place in Russia's Baroque palaces. The leading lights and role models in this cultural experiment were the ladies-in-waiting to Peter's second wife Catherine (see below). These already privileged women took every opportunity to make a brilliant marriage and receive lavish gifts.[45] At the same time, chapters on 'Maidenly Honor and Virtue' in the *Honourable Mirror* made clear that women were expected to blend the new social graces of the French drawing room with Muscovite bashfulness and decorum. It would be premature to speak of female 'emancipation' or even of an enhanced political role for Russian elite women. This continued to be the case even under the strong female monarch Catherine II.

Early on Peter understood that education was a key to unlocking Russian potential. His first experiments were practical and concrete, such as the Moscow School of Mathematics and Navigation (1701), modelled on the Royal Mathematical School at Christ's Hospital in London and staffed by British teachers. In 1715 it formed the prestigious St Petersburg Naval Academy, the graduates of which were allocated to teach in the so-called cipher or arithmetic schools, first mentioned in decrees of 1714. Without a diploma from such a school, nobles were not allowed to marry. However, richer nobles preferred to educate their sons at home. Others were sent abroad. The Academy of Sciences (opened 1725) is generally regarded as the major achievement of Peter's programme, although all the first academicians were foreigners.

Peter's reign has been associated with a printing 'revolution', one hundred times more publications being produced during it than in the whole of the seventeenth century.[46] In 1701 the Moscow Printing House was placed under state control. One of its new products (from 1702) was Russia's first newspaper, *Vedomosti*, which had a target audience of government officials and army and naval officers. In 1707–10 Peter commissioned new Russian typefaces for non-religious works, the so-called civil script. The schedule of new books, virtually all translations, included titles on the etiquette of letter-writing, geometry, locks, siege warfare, fortification, artillery, engineering, geography, history, calendars, descriptions of triumphal gates and manifestos of the kings of Poland and Denmark. Even larger numbers of liturgical and devotional works continued to appear in the older church script, accounting for over 40 per cent of books published. There was no private publishing and no outlet for individual authors outside the state publishing establishment. By Western European standards, publishing output remained modest; few individuals bought books and probably even fewer read them, the biggest demand being for calendars and primers. For most readers tales and stories popular in the seventeenth century continued to circulate in manuscripts, as did chronicles, saints' lives and other religious works with interesting narratives. In elite literature celebratory verse, written mainly by churchmen, was the dominant poetic genre, almost always harnessed to the praise of the monarch and the state.

In 1719 the new *Kunstkamera* opened in St Petersburg.[47] The museum was just one example of Peter's efforts to introduce his subjects to a wider world of curious, sometimes gruesome objects gathered from all over the globe. He encouraged map-making and surveying, and sponsored the expeditions of the German Daniel Messerschmidt to Siberia and the Dane Vitus Bering to Kamchatka. Petrine science and learning, like Petrine art and architecture, were a public, propagandistic exercise directed from above, which sowed the seeds of a future native 'intelligentsia', but failed to bear much fruit in Peter's lifetime. Petrine education was a compromise, with native and foreign, religious and secular elements. It was closely supervised, usually selectively elitist, imposed by the state for the interests of the state, not the enlightenment of the individual, and it was under-funded. This was not so very different from the situation in many other countries, but in Russia apathy and hostility among all classes of a population with no tradition of education outside the home and which thought itself overburdened by other obligations, often frustrated the government's best efforts. Russians returning from abroad found themselves subject to ridicule by their fellows and, once in retirement, some reverted to comfortable old Muscovite lifestyles. After Peter's death, however, under the influence of foreign travel and books, a select few began to think about the deeper implications of becoming more 'civilized' and to demand that Russian nobles be treated more like their peers abroad. Peter's cultural reforms thus produced both the loyal imperial service elite, devoted in its duty to the house of Romanov, and, in the nineteenth century the Russian intelligentsia, alienated from the crown which had transformed their ancestors.

St Petersburg and its culture could not have flourished without further military and diplomatic successes. Soon Peter found himself dragged into the conflict between Augustus II and Charles XII in Poland-Lithuania. In 1706 Charles forced Augustus to abdicate and break his alliance with Russia, while the Swedes installed their own Polish king, Stanisłas Leszczynski, and Peter faced the prospect of a Swedish invasion to which his initial response was a scorched earth policy along Russia's western borders. At the end of 1707 he learned that a Swedish army 45,000 strong was marching towards Russia. Charles, it was anticipated, would make for Moscow or even St Petersburg, but in mid-September 1708 the main Swedish army turned south towards Ukraine in search of supplies. The winter of 1708–9 turned out to be one of the most severe in living memory, further undermining the Swedes, who were already exhausted after two years on the move in alien terrain. Charles made a secret agreement with the Cossack hetman Ivan Mazepa, but in November Menshikov stormed and burned Mazepa's headquarters and stores.[48] The 'new Judas' was excommunicated and in his absence an effigy was hanged. Mazepa, however, did not see himself as Peter's subject, believing that Peter had reneged on his duties towards Ukraine. Subsequent Romanovs regarded Ukraine as 'Little Russia', an integral part of their patrimony.

Swedish attempts to enlist the support of the Crimean khan and Zaporozhian Cossacks also failed. In spring 1709 Charles's army holed up near the small Ukrainian town of Poltava, where Peter struck on 27 June 1709 with numerically superior forces. This was Peter's first encounter in command of troops in a pitched battle with the enemy's main army, once regarded as the most formidable in Europe. Charles, immobilized by a leg wound, anticipated a quick breakthrough with cavalry, only to witness guns from the Russian camp laying his men low, 'as grass before a scythe'.[49] The tattered remnants of the Swedish army surrendered to Menshikov the next day. Charles escaped into Turkish territory, where he made a nuisance of himself for the next five years. It has been said that Russia itself, with its vast distances, harsh climate, sparse population, poor villages and a social structure based on serfdom destroyed Charles's army.[50]

In the summer and autumn of 1710 Russia made further gains on the Baltic, including the ports of Riga, Reval (present-day Tallinn) and Vyborg. Peter renewed alliances with Denmark, Prussia and Poland. Outside observers watched such developments with some foreboding. Gottfried Leibniz wrote to the Russian envoy in Vienna: 'You can imagine how the great revolution in the north has astounded people. It is being said that the tsar will be formidable to the whole of Europe, that he will be a sort of Turk of the North.'[51]

The Turks themselves were perturbed by Russian successes, particularly by Russia's rapidly growing influence and presence in Poland. In late 1710 they declared war. Russia made routine peace proposals to the Swedes in the hope of avoiding war on two fronts, but Charles refused to relinquish even one province to buy what he regarded as a shameful peace. On the eve of departure for the campaign in February 1711 Peter listed the names of ten men 'to govern in our absence' in a Senate. The senators' main duties were to act as judges, supervise state expenses and eliminate unnecessary ones; increase revenues ('since money is the artery of war'); recruit officers; increase and regulate trade and commerce.[52] Everyone, churchmen and laymen, must obey the Senate as they did the tsar himself, under threat of cruel punishment or death. With most of his close circle already in major posts, Peter's first group of senators was a largely unprepossessing bunch, who behaved 'in the old stupid manner'.[53] Later the institution comprised many of Peter's top associates, and the Senate continued as the highest court of the realm until 1917.

Peter's subsequent campaign against Turkey was a near disaster. Attempts to turn it into a crusade foundered when the Orthodox rulers of Moldavia and Wallachia failed to deliver promised support and the Russian army ran short of supplies. In July 1711 38,000 Russian troops faced a Turkish and Tatar force of 130,000 men on the River Pruth in Moldavia. The battle was inconclusive, but the Russians lacked the resources to fight on. Disaster was averted by the moderateness of Turkish demands. Russia had to sacrifice Azov, to destroy its southern fleet and raze forts on the Dnieper. Slowness in evacuating Azov provoked further declarations of war by the Turk; a final settlement was reached in June 1713 in the Treaty of Adrianople. In April 1714 the sultan recognized the restored King Augustus II's possession of Polish Ukraine, which in effect ratified Russian influence. The peace allowed Peter once more to concentrate his efforts in the north, but in the 1710s international politics and diplomacy rather than warfare became the central issue and stumbling block to reaching peace. In April 1713 the War of the Spanish Succession ended, allowing Britain and France more leisure to intervene in northern affairs. Prussian and Danish claims to Sweden's remaining German territories restricted Peter's actions. From now on Russia aimed for pockets of influence rather than further territorial conquests.

This inspired an energetic programme of dynastic marriages. In 1710 Peter married his niece Anna to the duke of Courland, who died, probably from alcoholic poisoning, shortly after the wedding. Still, Peter insisted that the seventeen-year-old widow proceed to Courland and reside there with her retinue to maintain a Russian presence. In 1711 Peter's son Alexis wed Princess

Charlotte-Christina-Sophia of Wolfenbüttel (1694–1715) and in 1716 his niece Ekaterina married the duke of Mecklenburg. He betrothed his daughter Anna (born 1708) to Duke Karl Frederick of Holstein-Gottorp, whom she married in May 1725. These marriages laid the foundations for Russia's close dynastic links with European, predominantly German, Protestant courts for the next two centuries. They increased the range of foreign candidates to the Russian crown, as we shall see, but limited the access of the Russian nobility to status and privilege by marrying into the Romanov clan.

Of all these marriages that of Alexis and Charlotte, which took place at Thorn in Poland on 13 October 1711, was the most significant for the dynastic future of the Romanovs. The Brunswick-Blankenburg-Wolfenbüttels were related by marriage to many of the royal and princely families of Europe. Charlotte's father was Duke Ludwig-Rudolf, her mother Princess Christina-Louisa, the aunt of Duke Anton Ulrich of Holstein-Gottorp. Charlotte's sister was married to the Habsburg Emperor Charles VI. Under the terms of the marriage contract, Charlotte was allowed to retain her Protestant faith, but children were to be raised in the Orthodox religion.[54] It was an ill-fated union. Alexis found his bride unattractive and was influenced by his religious friends' disapproval of a foreign Protestant bride, who was said to be cold and standoffish and always surrounded by her German entourage. In 1714 Alexis formed a liaison with Efrosinia Fedorovna, the serf of one of his tutors. For seventeen-year-old Charlotte being hauled off to St Petersburg to live with a reluctant husband was hardly an attractive prospect, either, although only perhaps an extreme version of the duty required of many girls in her position. A portrait of Alexis painted by Johann Tannhauer in about 1714 shows a thin-faced young man with a long nose and large brown eyes, high forehead beneath a receding hairline. The portrait hints at ill health: by this time Alexis was diagnosed with tuberculosis, exacerbated by 'corrupt Habits' and excessive drinking.[55] Tannhauer painted a companion portrait of Charlotte, of which a copy survives. It shows a pleasant, narrow-faced young woman fashionably dressed, indistinguishable from hundreds of other female portraits of the period. The marriage produced a daughter, Natalia, in 1714 and a son, Peter, in 1715.

In February 1712 Peter himself married for the second time, to Marfa Skavronska (1684–1727), a woman of Livonian peasant stock, who in Orthodoxy took the names Ekaterina (Catherine) Alekseevna, the latter from her godfather Peter's son Alexis, Ekaterina from her patron St Catherine of Alexandria. When the Russian army entered Livonia in the summer of 1702 Martha was working as a servant in Dorpat in the home of a Lutheran pastor. Peter met her in 1703 after, according to rumour, she was passed on by Menshikov. Laconic references to her in Peter's letters show that by 1706 she was an established fixture in the royal entourage, having borne him three children. The couple had ten children, but only two survived into adulthood, Anna (1708–1729) and the future empress Elizabeth (1709–1761).[56] Peter and Catherine may have married secretly in November 1707, but on the eve of the Turkish campaign of 1711 Peter swore to provide for his wife and children's future security and to have a formal marriage ceremony, should he return. Catherine accompanied him to the Pruth and later won official acclaim for her 'manly' courage during the ordeal. Their public wedding took place on 19 February 1712 in St Petersburg, with a strong naval flavour in the choice of trappings and naval personnel as witnesses and attendants.[57]

The marriage was controversial, not least because Tsaritsa Evdokia was still alive (and possibly not divorced), Catherine was a foreign convert of humble origins, and, according to strict reckoning of degrees of kinship, Alexis being her godfather made the union incestuous. Peter, however, revelled in the choice of an 'unsuitable' wife, just as he constantly undermined other traditional hierarchies. This was a love match of mutual choice. Catherine was physically strong and shared her husband's fondness for crude practical jokes and alcohol. She rarely seems to have been intimidated by him, even when he was in a rage. Whilst loving her down-to-earth ways, Peter also deemed it politic to elevate her in the eyes of the elite. In 1714, for example, he introduced the Order of St Catherine for distinguished women and made her its first recipient, in recognition of her courage at the Battle of Pruth, where she behaved 'in a manner more male than female.'[58] In May 1724 in a lavish ceremony in the Kremlin he would crown Catherine as his consort, which would pave the way for her emergence in 1725 as his heir. Hers was a remarkable success story.

In 1713 the Russians launched a sea-borne campaign in Swedish Finland, in the first year taking Helsingfors (Helsinki) and Åbo (Turku) and in 1714 winning a battle against the Swedes off Cape Hangö, hailed as the 'naval Poltava'. The conquests turned out to be symbolic rather than practical as Peter did not have the resources at this stage to occupy and rule Finland. In 1712–14 the war seemed to reach a stalemate as Russia found itself bogged down in north German affairs, embroiled in rivalries over Swedish possessions in Pomerania, and frustrated by Denmark's failure to honour agreements to launch a landing on the Swedish mainland and Poland's reluctance to supply Russian troops stationed there.

The difficulties of war were exacerbated by personal tragedy. In 1715 relations broke down between Peter and Alexis. Nothing Alexis did was quite good enough for Peter. He was often sick and unenthusiastic about Peter's pet projects, especially the fleet and St Petersburg, preferring devotional literature to books on shipbuilding. Peter wrote Alexis several letters in which he expressed his fears for Russia's future were Alexis to survive him. October 1715 saw a series of events of crucial significance for the dynasty. On 11 October Peter delivered an ultimatum: 'I have not spared and do not spare my own life for my country and my people, so why should I spare you who are so unworthy? Better a worthy stranger [on the throne] than my own unworthy son.'[59] On 12 October, the tsarevich's wife Charlotte gave birth to a healthy son, named Peter, but on 21 October she died of postnatal complications. On 29 October Catherine gave birth to another Peter. This sudden abundance of male heirs and his wife's death prompted Alexis's reply to his father's ultimatum. He expressed his willingness to relinquish his claim to the throne, in view of the fact that he was 'unqualified and unfit for the task', his memory was gone and his health undermined 'by many illnesses'. He would enter a monastery.[60] This was not the reply Peter had hoped for. Peter generally regarded the monastic life as 'shirking', an option only for the aged and disabled and a few high-flyers destined for posts in the Church hierarchy. The matter remained unresolved.

In February 1716 Peter set off on another major tour of Western Europe, which took him back to the Netherlands and to Denmark for the first time. The highlight of the tour was his first visit to France in summer 1717, the only diplomatic outcome of which was a friendship treaty. Hopes of detaching France from its traditional Swedish connection and forming an anti-Austrian alliance were unfulfilled. Culture provided the main rewards. In Paris Peter visited the Botanical gardens, Tuileries, the Arsenal, Observatory, Academy of Sciences, Sorbonne University and other sights. He made several visits to Versailles, which made a deep impression, especially its fountains, which he replicated in St Petersburg. The best-known image from France is the portrait by Jean-Marc Nattier, which shows Peter clad in shining armour, his right hand holding a baton and resting on a mediaeval helmet complete with extravagant red plume. Nattier went to the Hague to do a companion piece of Catherine, every inch the empress. However, Peter did not take her to Paris, for fear, apparently, that her lowly origins would not command respect.[61]

From Copenhagen in 1716 Peter had summoned Alexis to join him. Alexis set off, but headed south and sought asylum with his brother-in-law, the Habsburg Emperor Charles VI. Peter wrote to inform Alexis that although he had acted 'like a traitor', he was ready to forgive him if he returned to Russia. Peter's agents Peter Tolstoy and Alexander Rumiantsev went to Alexis's refuge in Naples and persuaded him to do just that, together with his pregnant mistress Efrosinia. In fact, upon his return Alexis found himself under pressure to name the 'accomplices' who had helped him to flee Russia and allegedly plotted against Peter's life. On 3 February 1717 Peter announced a manifesto setting out the reasons for removing Alexis from the succession and naming Peter Petrovich, the tsar's two-year-old son by his second wife, Catherine, as the new heir, since he could not keep an heir 'who would lose that which with God's help his father had obtained and who would overturn the glory and honour of the Russian people, for which I spent my health, in some cases not even sparing my life.'[62] Many dignitaries wept, as at a funeral.[63]

Medal showing Peter I crowning Catherine I, 1724.

An investigation followed, which included interrogation of Alexis's mother
Evdokia and his aunt Tsarevna Maria Alekseevna. Particularly alarming for
Peter were testimonies which revealed that Alexis enjoyed the sympathy of
many members of the old nobility, as well as the higher clergy. This was hardly
surprising while he was still heir to the throne, but there was evidence that such
men were weary of the unrelieved burdens of the war and associated impositions,
although none expressed a strong desire to restore Muscovite traditions. The
tribunal accused Alexis of moral and physical failings and indifference to the
common good. The crucial charge, for which there was fragmentary evidence,
was that he had sought armed assistance to overthrow and assassinate Peter,
to which Alexis confessed under torture. On 24 June 1718 the tribunal, which
included many men Alexis had identified as his supporters, delivered a sentence
of death, but the torture continued, for Peter was desperate for more information.
On 26 June Alexis was dead, allegedly of an 'apoplectic fit'. Rumours circulated
that Peter had strangled him or had him suffocated. Ultimately Peter was first
and foremost a monarch, a father only second. He could not separate Alexis's
fate from the fate of Russia. Even so, the tsar's plans for the succession were
frustrated. Peter Petrovich died on 25 April 1719, leaving Alexis's son Peter as
the only male heir.

In December 1718 Charles XII was killed in Norway, and in 1719 Russia prepared
to resume the Swedish campaign, scoring several naval victories and bombarding
the Swedish coast. With Britain planning an anti-Russian coalition and sending
a squadron to the Baltic, the situation looked bleak for Russia, but international
tensions came to the rescue. France and Austria, for example, hesitated to side
with Britain and in 1720, after further Russian victories off Sweden, the British
squadron withdrew. 'Eternal peace' between Russia and Sweden was finally signed

at Nystad in Finland on 30 August/10 September 1721. In 24 clauses Sweden ceded Livonia, Estonia, Ingria and part of Karelia, and Russia agreed to evacuate Finland and to pay Sweden cash compensation. Peter's territorial acquisitions on the Baltic were modest in size, but of enormous significance. Not least, his military successes allowed Peter to be declared Emperor (*imperator*) in October 1721 and Russia to be officially designated an empire (*imperiia*), even though many countries were slow to recognize its new status. At the same time Peter accepted the title 'the Great', in imitation of both Alexander and Constantine, and the imperial Roman appellation 'Father of the Fatherland'.[64] Russia's new international role was summed up by one of King George I's officials in Hanover: 'Germany and the entire North have never been in such grave peril as now, because the Russians should be feared more than the Turks ... and are gradually advancing closer and closer to our lives.'[65] In 1722–3 Peter waged a successful campaign along the western shore of the Caspian, capturing Derbent and Baku. It proved impossible to maintain these conquests and in the 1730s Russia let them go.

In the last four years of his life Peter consolidated and rationalized a number of piecemeal measures into regulations and statutes that made a lasting impact on the way the Romanovs ruled and their subjects served.

In February 1720 he issued the General Regulation for the administration of the Colleges or collegiate boards (Foreign Affairs, Military, Admiralty, Commerce, Justice, State Revenues, State Expenses, State Accounting and Mines and Manufacture) that he had set up in 1717–18 on the Swedish model.[66] Boards of officials overseen by a president and vice-president (initially the former was a Russian, the latter a foreigner), operated 'collegiately' on reaching majority decisions. As the preface to the Regulation decree explained, Peter founded the Colleges for the sake of 'the orderly running of ... state affairs and the correct allocation and calculation of his revenues and the improvement of useful justice (*iustitsiia*) and police (*politsiia*)'.[67]

In 1724 Peter specified that the General Regulation must be read aloud to officials in the same way as the Military Statute of 1716 was read to soldiers.[68] The 1720 law was a 'regulation of regulations', the proliferation of which accorded with Peter's belief that the common good was best served by a large body of well-drafted legislation, initiated from above.[69]

Another major piece of legislation regulated the Orthodox Church and its relationship with the state. In the seventeenth century the Church already had conceded ground, but the notion of the parallelism or 'symphony' of Church and State was not officially revoked. The patriarch still enjoyed a place of honour at ceremonies and a residence in the Kremlin. The Church remained a substantial landed proprietor which, by and large, served the State rather than opposing it. It catered to spiritual life through worship and rites of passage. Priests did such duties as reporting persistent absentees from church, ensuring that people coming to be married were eligible to do so, announcing decrees and declarations of war and peace. It was these latter aspects that Peter chose to build on, while limiting the powers of the Church institutionally. He refused to accept its claims to wield power outside the sphere of worship and (to some degree) morality, for in so claiming the Church challenged the state's need for a free hand in deploying resources.

When in October 1700 Patriarch Adrian died, Peter appointed a 'stand-in', Metropolitan Stefan Yavorsky, a Ukrainian, but made no provision for an election. In 1700–1 he re-established a secular Monastery Department to supervise Church courts and run Church lands. Part of monastery income went for the upkeep of almshouses and other good works. The minimum age for women to take the veil was set at 40, later 50, to discourage evasion of child-bearing duties. During the Northern war sons of priests and deacons, a largely hereditary caste, were drafted into the army or civil service. Education for priests was improved, including tuition in delivering sermons. Priests were also expected to act as disseminators of public information such as treaties and edicts on taxes, and to keep registers of births, deaths and marriages. Church-run schools were strongly encouraged.

In 1721 Peter published the Spiritual Regulation, which established the Holy Synod, modelled on the government Colleges, comprising eleven churchmen, plus a twelfth 'honest, right-thinking person of secular rank'.[70] The Regulation made clear that the Synod was interlocked with the state apparatus and, like it, subjugated to the tsar. There was no room for a 'second sovereign' (the patriarch). In 1722 Peter created the post of Over-Procurator of the Synod, who, like the Procurator-General of government departments (see below), was to act as the 'sovereign's eye'. Restrictions on taking monastic vows were strengthened, with the result that between 1724 and 1738 the numbers of monks and nuns in Russia almost halved. In 1722 Peter added a new task to the clergy's policing duties: they must report revelations of 'evil intentions' against the sovereign, his family or the state made during confession, although there is little evidence that priests complied with this ruling.

Peter did not secularize Russia. Although he no longer saw his main function as facilitating the salvation of his subjects' souls, he freely acknowledged the agency of the Almighty in human affairs. As he said after Poltava: 'To God alone belong the glory and honour (for this is a divine deed: he raises up the humble and subdues the mighty).'[71] For Peter, like his fellow European monarchs, life without religion was inconceivable. He himself attended church assiduously. Orthodoxy proved remarkably resilient not only in ordinary people's everyday lives but also in the life of the imperial court. It also remained on the agenda of Romanov foreign policy, be it protesting against the persecution of Orthodox Christians abroad or giving moral support to fellow Orthodox rulers. For Peter, the ideal of Russian leadership of the Orthodox world remained more a religious abstraction than an active policy. Some of his successors would promote it more vigorously.

In the secular sphere, perhaps none of Peter's decrees was so influential as the Table of Ranks (24 January 1722). Peter imposed a rational framework on a mainly pre-existing jumble of foreign terms that emerged as old Muscovite ranks fell into disuse. The Table was based on Prussian, Swedish and Danish models, dividing the service elite into four main columns – army, navy, civil and court – its very layout reflecting Peter's passion for orderly, regulated legislation. The vertical columns were then divided horizontally into fourteen numbered grades, each containing a variable number of offices or posts, thus correlating seniority across the different branches of the services. The most crowded column was the civil service, with sometimes a dozen or more offices packed into one grade in order to accommodate Peter's newly-created central and provincial officials.

One of the most widespread misconceptions about this most enduring of Peter's reforms – it lasted until 1917, making a deep impact on elite mentality – is that it demonstrated a consistent commitment to meritocracy to the detriment of lineage. Peter's own example is often quoted. 'By taking upon himself both a Post in his Navy, and in his Army, wherein he acted and took the gradual Steps of Preferment, like another Man', wrote John Perry, '[Peter wished] to make his Lords see that he expects they shall not think themselves nor their Sons too good to serve their Countrey, and take their Steps gradually to Preferment.'[72] Certainly the Table was strict about promotion procedures for actual offices or jobs. No candidate who was unqualified for the duties involved must be appointed, which in practice meant serving for periods deemed sufficient to gain experience. Neither grade nor office could be inherited or bought and there were strict penalties for demanding deference or position higher than one's rank at social gatherings.

However, birth and marriage continued to confer privilege, as they did elsewhere. The first explanatory clause confirmed the precedence of princes of the blood and royal sons-in-law. Another clause blended two principles: it conceded 'free access' to the court to sons of princes, counts, barons and the aristocracy 'before others of lowly office', but stressed that the emperor expected such people 'to distinguish themselves from others in all cases according to their merit'; they would not be awarded any rank until they had served the fatherland in a post. Newcomers from non-noble families who reached grade 8 in the civil service or grade 14 in the military officer lists became *hereditary* noblemen.

The Table of Ranks, then, did not promote such modern concepts as equality of opportunity or a leg up for the disadvantaged. It was intended to encourage the service elite to perform more efficiently than hitherto. Nobles remained natural leaders of society: hence high-flying commoners who reached the required grades were granted noble status, including its heritable aspects. In the words of the Holstein secretary Bassewitz: 'What [Peter] had in mind was not the abasement of the noble estate. On the contrary, it all tended towards instilling in the nobility a desire to distinguish themselves from common folk by merit as well as by birth.'[73] After Peter's death the existing nobility would close ranks, making it harder for commoners to become nobles through the mechanism of the Table, although not by imperial preferment, which always remained an option.

On 5 February 1722 Peter extended the concept of merit in a Manifesto on the Succession to the Throne, which concluded: 'we deem it good to issue this edict in order that it will always be subject to the will of the ruling monarch to appoint whom he wishes to the succession or to remove the one he has appointed in the case of unseemly behaviour, so that his children and descendants should not fall into such wicked ways as those described above, having this constraint upon them'.[74] The rationale behind the decree was explained in the book *The Justice of the Monarch's Right to Appoint the Heir to the Throne* (1722), co-authored by Peter's chief publicist Feofan Prokopovich (1681–1736), who identified the divine basis of monarchical power, but also used a Western frame of reference to stress affinities with European natural law theory. The author argued that succession by the first born son (primogeniture) was a mere custom which could be set aside for a higher purpose, giving numerous examples. The underlying principle was that the monarch's power was absolute.

For all its recourse to utility, Peter's new law of succession was rooted in personal conflict and tragedy. The 'wickedness' of Tsarevich Alexis is referred to in its opening lines. The law had radical implications, replacing the notion of God's will by the will of the emperor. It also potentially weakened the continuity of a hereditary dynasty by allowing the possibility of choosing any 'worthy' successor from outside the family. As it turned out, none of the dynastic crises that dogged the eighteenth-century Romanovs, starting with Peter I's failure to nominate a successor, was solved in this radical fashion. Peter's policy of marrying his offspring and nieces to foreigners gave scope for keeping the crown within the extended family.

Another important edict (April 1722) set out the duties of the Procurator-General, who was to ensure that the Senate 'does its duty and acts in all matters which are subject to [its] scrutiny and resolution truthfully, diligently and correctly, without wasting time and in accordance with the regulations and edicts' and that 'business is completed not only on paper but also put into effect according to instructions.' As the 'tsar's eye', if he discovered negligence or dishonesty, he must immediately bring the matter to the Senate's attention.[75] Peter's appointee to the post was Pavel Ivanovich Yaguzhinsky (1683–1736), son of an organist in the Lutheran church in Moscow. In 1724 his duties were extended to the Colleges, where he was expected to keep an eye on the office personnel, for, as Peter admitted, 'I am sure that much wrong-doing goes on behind our back'.[76] In general, Peter lacked confidence in his subjects from the highest to the lowest, as is vividly summed up in a manifesto of November 1723: 'Our people are like children who, out of ignorance, will never get down to learning their alphabet unless the master forces them to do so.'[77] His subjects failed to respect the laws, playing with them 'like cards, one suit being picked up after another', undermining the 'fortress' of the law.[78]

Peter was not immortal. In the winter of 1723 the disease that finally killed him – inflammation of the urinary tract and bladder, possibly linked with venereal disease – confined him to his sick bed. In the autumn he was on the move again, inspecting works on the Ladoga canal. On 17 January 1725, the keeper of the court journal recorded: 'His Imperial Majesty was ill and did not deign to go anywhere.'[79] After days of agony caused by a recurrence of the old bladder problem, Peter died on the morning of 28 January 1725. In accounts of Peter's final days, an incident stands out. Shortly before losing consciousness, he is said to have summoned his eldest daughter Anna and scrawled an unfinished note: 'Leave everything to …'. In fact, the story appears in only one contemporary source, the memoir of a retainer of the duke of Holstein, whose aim may have been to persuade readers that Anna, the duke's fiancée, was Peter's intended heir. Peter may even have been grooming the duke for the throne in the hope that sons from the marriage would create a new male line, in order to pass over his nine-year-old grandson Peter Alekseevich, whom traditionalists backed as the rightful heir. In terms of seniority and legitimacy, Peter's niece, Anna Ivanovna, duchess of Courland, had a claim, although she had no conspicuous support. Peter's younger daughters Elizabeth and Natalia (1718–25) were also contenders.

In the end it suited a group of powerful men at court led by Menshikov, with whom she has always maintained close ties, to have Catherine as empress. The belief that Peter had signalled his wish for his wife to succeed him by crowning her as his consort in 1724 helped to secure the backing which Menshikov's party needed, notably from the guards. Peter's funeral was orchestrated to smooth the succession.[80] His corpse lay in state in the Winter Palace until mid-March 'after the manner of other European countries', surrounded by emblematic statues and devices, then his coffin was taken to the Peter-Paul Cathedral in a lavish procession, which stressed universal mourning and military might. Because the cathedral interior was still unfinished the coffin was not placed in its vault in front of the right-hand wing of the iconostasis until 1731.

Officially, the reputation of the man who had transformed Russia from 'non-existence into being', as an associate declared at the Nystad celebrations, had never been higher, but in reality Peter left a number of unresolved issues after decades of relentless mobilization. These were particularly evident in the countryside, in parts of which poor harvests triggered famine. Peasant flight remained endemic, exacerbated by recruitment and forced labour. There were no concessions on serfdom; in fact more categories of the population found themselves enserfed. Provincial reforms in 1708 and 1718–19 had done little more than rationalize the collection of revenues, which was further addressed in the 1710s–20s by new censuses of the tax-paying population based on a male head count rather than household, which produced the poll tax, collected for the first time in 1724. Peter established many factories to aid the war effort and in 1721 allowed merchants to purchase serfs, but most industry remained under state control. In 1726 a group of Peter's close associates would give a frank assessment of Russia's condition in a memorandum to the new empress, 'nearly all affairs – both spiritual and temporal – are in disarray and require speedy correction … Not only the peasantry, on whom the maintenance of the army is laid, are in dire need and are being reduced to complete and utter ruin by heavy taxation and continual punitive expeditions and other irregularities, but other areas such as commerce, justice and the mints are also in a state of decay'.[81] There was no word of criticism against Peter himself, however. The Petrine principles of devotion to duty, concern for the common good, pride in Russia and its armed forces, determination to maintain and expand the empire and win respect abroad were to remain the models for his successors, even if some paid only lip service. Western cultural norms were never reversed among the elite, even if later in the eighteenth century some questioned the wisdom of excessive borrowing of alien cultures and in the nineteenth some embraced Neo-Russian culture and ideas. Ironically, Peter's very successes added to his successors' burden, for the maintenance of an empire required a standing army, based on peasant conscripts and reliable revenues. Diplomacy demanded a splendid court, which in turn put pressure on the nobles to maintain their own expensive households, based on serf labour. Meanwhile, outside St Petersburg, Moscow and a few other towns, life continued much as it had always done. Extending 'civilization' was to be tackled by Peter's successors, with mixed results.

4

The Age of Empresses and
Palace Revolutions: 1725–1762

CATHERINE I, PETER II, ANNA, IVAN VI, ELIZABETH, PETER III

The period 1725 to 1762 saw seven rulers ascend the Russian throne, four female and three male, as the house of Romanov suffered a series of dynastic crises and its very name was threatened with extinction. Historians once treated this as the 'Doldrums' of Russian history. Of Russia's first three women monarchs, Catherine I (r. 1725–7) is remembered as an illiterate foreign peasant who died of drink, Anna (r. 1730–40) was fat, had a reputation for cruelty and a liking for dwarfs, and lazy Elizabeth (r. 1741–61) is renowned for the 15,000 outfits discovered in her wardrobes after her death. The three emperors barely got started: Peter II (r. 1727–30) was fourteen when he died from smallpox; Ivan VI (r. 1740–1) was deposed at the age of eighteen months; and Peter III (r. 1761–2) reigned for a mere six months before he was overthrown.[1] Catherine II, the Great (r. 1762–96) more or less wrote off the 37 years between Peter I's death and her own accession by forging a direct line to Peter and referring to herself as his 'spiritual daughter', signalling a return to true Romanov values.

To underline the absence of a strong personality at the helm of the ship of state, a leading Russian historian dubbed the period up to Catherine II's accession as 'Russia without Peter'.[2] There has been a tendency to attribute the intermittent crises to 'weak' female rule, which Peter I inadvertently initiated. His 1722 Law on Succession, for example, did not specify the gender of the successor. His programme of foreign marriage alliances produced eligible female candidates beyond the home-grown tsarevny, as well as males of the female line. Peter also made women visible in elite society, providing his wife Catherine with her own court. Yet it would be wrong to regard 'female rule' as the chief issue of the period.[3] A woman on the throne was hardly a shocking idea, even in Russia. In Byzantium, Rus and Muscovy a woman representing her absent, dead, under-aged or incapacitated male relative was well accepted. (Tsaritsa Irina, we recall, was regarded as a possible successor to her husband in 1598.) The problem was not so much how a woman stayed in power – all four Russian empresses died in office of natural causes – as how she behaved in order to rule effectively, or to allow men to do so.

In early eighteenth-century Russia the discourse of female rule was invented by the promoters, not the detractors, of women monarchs. Most of the Russian nobility supported the current feminine 'scenario of power' and vied to get a part in it.[4] There was little recorded dissension over the suitability of women to rule (not surprising, perhaps, given the lack of a free Russian press or public sphere of debate) and if an empress was criticized it was generally not with reference to her gender. This is probably because a woman on the throne, even Catherine II, did little to reduce male dominance of power structures. The empresses needed escorts, preferably men who would not antagonize members of the established elite, who accepted an empress's need for male company as long as the chosen companion did not threaten their own power bases. Other women at best wielded influence through 'informal channels', and a few token women made careers, but they were exceptions. Under female and male sovereigns alike, favouritism, patronage and intrigue, too, 'remained overwhelmingly the purview of men'. Women stayed in the 'private' sphere.[5] A highly visible empress posed no threat.

Even for female rulers Peter I became the approved model. Catherine II's three female predecessors, too, were bound to emphasize their relationship with and dependency on Peter to gain currency. Immediately after Peter's death, Catherine I was presented to the public as both the great man's grieving widow and his worthy successor. Her selection as empress may have been illegal according to the 1722 law (Peter did not explicitly nominate her), but her short reign, which lasted from 28 January 1725 to 6 May 1727, provides a good illustration of how autocracy continued to operate successfully under an unassertive ruler who had little talent for or interest in governing. The men who ruled Russia, foremost among them Alexander Menshikov, presented Catherine's feminine 'weakness' as an asset rather than a handicap (as, indeed, it was for their purposes), promoting her with the rhetoric that not only would she rule in Peter's spirit, but had actually been 'created' by him.[6] She had proven masculine qualities, having accompanied Peter on his military campaigns, but they were softened by attractive feminine ones such as kindness and motherliness, for the last thing the men close to the throne actually wanted was another bullying Peter. A woman monarch promised respite from burdens and more space for men to organize affairs to their own satisfaction, as long as stability was assured by consensus about her credentials to rule. Peter's publicists had already cultivated the cult of St Catherine for his convert wife to emphasize her true Orthodox devotion, a campaign that continued while Catherine was on the throne. If one adds the rhetoric that Catherine was an all-loving Mother, caring for orphaned Russia as she cared for her orphaned daughters, and throw in some stock comparisons with Classical rulers and goddesses, the illiterate peasant woman was transformed into Empress of All Russia and a true

Romanov. Similar devices could be applied to transform the most unpromising candidate.[7]

The issue of the succession arose before Catherine was even crowned, as no one wished for a repetition of the confusion at Peter's deathbed. Catherine left a testament in which Menshikov persuaded her to bypass her own daughters Anna and Elizabeth, who had been born out of wedlock, in favour of Peter's grandson, Peter Alekseevich, the last surviving Romanov of the male line. If he died or remained without issue, the daughters of Peter and Catherine became heirs, with a preference for their male offspring. The arguably senior line of Ivan V Alekseevich was ignored. Menshikov then pulled off what looked like a brilliant move, outsmarting Tsesarevich Peter's own supporters, including members of the powerful Dolgoruky and Golitsyn clans, by taking the boy under his wing and betrothing him to his daughter Maria. Heading a nine-man regency council, Menshikov probably hoped to rob the 'old' nobility of its base while gaining popularity by restoring the male line.

Catherine died on 6 May 1727, probably of drink-related problems. That day three yachts moored in front of the Winter Palace were festooned with flags to celebrate the anniversary of her coronation as Peter's consort in 1724, 'but this sad event prevented it ... Then to mark the decease of Her Majesty, from the Peter and Paul fortress all guns were fired at one minute intervals.'[8] According to another source, the funeral, which took place on 16 May, was conducted 'without any particular pomp'.[9] The comparatively short lying-in-state was necessitated by warm weather. (In Orthodoxy, it will be recalled, the coffin remained open until the funeral service.) For four years the caskets of Catherine I and Peter I stood together in the centre of the still unfinished Peter-Paul Cathedral, where in November 1728 they were joined briefly by their daughter Anna Petrovna, whose body was brought from Holstein for burial after she died a few months after giving birth to a son, the future Peter III.[10] On 29 May 1731 the two coffins were finally lowered into a vault under white alabaster sarcophagi 'as a memorial for future generations'.[11] They occupied prime positions near the cathedral's south wall close to the iconostasis, to be joined over the years along the altar to the north wall by the remaining eighteenth-century Romanovs, then by later rulers spread throughout the nave of the cathedral.

Peter II Alekseevich was duly proclaimed emperor. At first Menshikov managed to keep him under his control as his prospective son-in-law, planning also to marry Peter's sister Natalia (1714–28) to his son Alexander. On 25 May 1727 the betrothal of Peter and Maria was publicly celebrated, then Menshikov fell ill and was absent from court, where his many enemies intensified a campaign against him. His situation was not improved by the return from banishment of his implacable enemy, the new emperor's grandmother, ex-Tsaritsa Evdokia. In September 1727 the German foreign policy expert Andrei Osterman and several members of the aristocratic Dolgoruky-Golitsyn faction had Menshikov arrested on charges of embezzlement and 'tyranny' and banished to Siberia, where he died in wretched circumstances in November 1729. Several members of his family, including Maria, also perished.[12]

Peter was taken to Moscow to be crowned in the Dormition cathedral on 24 February 1728. His chief adviser was now Prince Aleksei Dolgoruky, father of his personal favourite Ivan, but the power behind the throne was Osterman. Both were members of the Supreme Privy Council (founded 1726), which included other powerful men from Peter I's regime: Fedor Apraksin, Gavrila Golovkin, Dmitry Golitsyn and Vasily Dolgoruky. After his coronation Peter stayed in Moscow, where he devoted himself to favourite pursuits such as hunting. A close companion was his aunt Elizabeth, whom rumours suggested he might even marry. There is no evidence, however, that the move to Moscow indicated Peter's wish to return to the 'old Muscovite ways', although some magnates welcomed the opportunity to spend more time on their estates in and around the old capital and enjoyed the relaxation of Peter I's insistence upon St Petersburg being the centre of everything. A lull in foreign affairs and domestic crises allowed departments of state to operate at a low level and officers and officials to enjoy a sort of extended vacation. In November 1729, taking a leaf from Menshikov's book, Aleksei Dolgoruky betrothed Peter to his daughter Ekaterina, but the wedding, scheduled for January 1730, never took place. On 6 January 1730 Peter caught a chill during the outdoor Epiphany ceremonies. On 19 January he died, apparently from smallpox, and was buried in the Archangel cathedral, the only member of the post-Petrine house of Romanov apart from Ivan VI not to rest in St Petersburg.[13]

Peter II passed away without naming a successor. At the sickbed Dolgoruky tried to persuade him to nominate his fiancée Ekaterina, but Peter was too sick to sign a testament. There was some support for ex-Tsaritsa Evdokia or Elizabeth (who according to Catherine I's testament was the rightful heir), but Dolgoruky and his allies, chief among them Prince Dmitry Golitsyn, decided to install a ruler from the neglected line of Tsar Ivan Alekseevich, Anna Ioannovna[14] (1693–1740), widowed Duchess of Courland, and to impose limitations on her power.

Dmitry Golitsyn, one of the most educated men of his generation, drew up a list of Conditions for Anna's rule.[15] She must not marry or designate a successor; she must maintain the Supreme Privy Council, without the consent of which she must not start a war or make peace, raise new taxes, make promotions in any branch of the services or court, deploy the guards, deprive members of the nobility of life, possessions or honour without trial, grant landed estates or spend state revenues.[16] Leading men outside the Golitsyn-Dolgoruky circle were alarmed by this 'conspiracy of privy councillors' and submitted counter-proposals, which included appeals for the extension and clarification of nobles' privileges.[17] Counter-petitions begged Anna to rule with the same powers as her predecessors, pleading, as Feofan Prokopovich expressed it, that one autocrat was preferable to multiple tyranny by Dolgorukys and Golitsyns. A delegation advised Anna to forge a personal link with the guards by becoming their colonel-in-chief, a move which was in breach of the Conditions. Two weeks later, with the guards' acclaim, she tore up the document.

If implemented, the Conditions, although incomplete – the sovereign continued to appoint the Supreme Privy Council, for example – would have made Russia a constitutional monarchy. Instead, there followed yet another reshuffling of the ruling elite under an autocratic female sovereign, in which power passed to Andrei Osterman in the Foreign Office, Count Burchard Christopher Münnich (1683–1767), head of the War College, Anna's Courland chancellor Ernst Johann Biron (Bühren) (1690–1772) and R. G. Löwenwolde, grand marshal of the court. Anna, her powers restored but with little enthusiasm for exercising them, settled down for a ten-year reign.

It is difficult to form a fair impression of Empress Anna Ioannovna, but mostly negative judgements prevail.[18] She is generally dismissed, for example, for being virtually a German and cut off from things Russian since her marriage in 1710, although, in fact, during the 1710s–1720s she spent long, well-documented periods in Russia with her mother, dowager Tsaritsa Praskovia (1664–1723) and sisters Ekaterina (1691–1733) and Praskovia (1694–1731).[19] In 1716 Ekaterina Ioannovna was unhappily married off to Duke Charles Leopold of Mecklenburg-Schwerin, 'the coarse, uneducated, wilful and highly eccentric owner of a scrap of German soil',[20] but after 1722 returned with her daughter Anna (born 1718) to live in Moscow. Praskovia secretly wed a Russian nobleman, Ivan Ilich Dmitriev-Mamonov, by whom she had a son in 1724.[21]

Anna's reputation is not enhanced by the best-known image of her – the bulky mass of Carlo Rastrelli's bronze statue (1739), made even less acceptable to modern eyes by the addition of a black servant holding a globe. To her contemporaries its very weightiness, the opulence of the jewel-studded robes and the symbols of imperial might in the regalia must have conveyed an image of powerful rule, while the servant denoted the loyalty appropriate to all Anna's subjects. Poets praised the empress's 'masculine', warlike virtues,[22] although Anna never set foot on a battlefield and seems to have been governed by common sense and instinct rather than bravery or intellect. She liked active pastimes such as tobogganing and hunting and also picked up some habits from her uncle Peter, enjoying his weddings for dwarfs and masquerades and his collections of 'monsters', exotic beasts and jesters. Anna's reign has been condemned as a 'Dark Era' dominated by the 'Bironovshchina' or 'bad rule' of her favourite Biron, who from 1730 served as her senior chamberlain. His was a personal

Anna Ioannovna. Eighteenth century.

power grounded in strong emotional ties with Anna, although the precise nature of their relationship remains a matter of conjecture. Biron was demonized by those critics, both contemporary and Soviet, who associated Anna's reign with foreign or 'German' domination, which, it is argued, Biron promoted for his own ends. In fact, contemporaries were largely relaxed about 'Germans' serving in government and the armed forces, especially Russia's 'own' Germans such as Count von Löwenwolde, one of many well-educated immigrants from the Baltic to forge careers at court. At least two of Anna's entourage – Münnich and Osterman – were first promoted under Peter I. Analyses of the origins of men in the Table of Ranks during Anna's reign fail to demonstrate a preponderance of non-Russians, still less an imminent threat of Germans taking over power.[23] There was room for talented foreigners to advance, but the old Russian nobility maintained a firm presence.

Anna herself has been condemned as 'cruel'. Notorious trials conducted by her Secret Chancellery included those of the Dolgorukys and Prince Dmitry Golitsyn and of cabinet minister Artemy Volynsky, who had his tongue ripped out for making unflattering remarks about the empress in a letter in 1740.

Some fellow 'conspirators' were beheaded, knouted and/or banished. There was nothing new, however, in the procedures of the Secret Chancellery, which was established under Peter I for the trial of Tsarevich Alexis, supplementing the Preobrazhensky Department. The interrogation of both accused and accuser under torture, a whole culture of denunciation, were deeply rooted in Russia's past.[24] Elizabeth long enjoyed a better reputation than Anna and was praised for abolishing capital punishment, but her Secret Chancellery continued to operate much as before. A group of courtiers alleged to have made derogatory remarks about the empress, for example, were flogged, had their tongues shortened and were banished to Siberia. In 1743 the noblewomen Natalia Lopukhina and Anna Bestuzheva were banished to Siberia after being flogged and having their tongues cut out for an alleged plot inspired by their husbands against the empress.[25] No amount of revisionism will turn 'German' Anna into an appealing personality, but there is probably less to choose between her and 'Russian' Elizabeth than traditional narratives have admitted.

The childless Anna was keen to keep the succession on her father's 'senior' side of the Romanov family by nominating as her heir a future child of her niece Anna Leopoldovna (1716–46). The empress signed a testament to this effect in 1731, long before Anna was even married. In 1739 she was duly wed to the 'mediocre' Protestant Duke Anton Ulrich of Brunswick and in August 1740 gave birth to a son, Ivan Antonovich, whose line on the basis of male precedence should have been Brunswick, not Romanov. On 17 October the empress died from kidney disease, having nominated Biron as regent to Ivan; but Biron, who had fallen out with Anna Leopoldovna and her husband, was arrested and imprisoned on the orders of Münnich, who installed the baby's mother as regent. The beginning of Ivan VI's short reign was overshadowed by the postscript to Anna's, whose funeral was delayed until 23 December to wait for the ice on the river to harden to form a path to the fortress, allowing crowds to flock to the palace to see a sumptuously clad Anna lying in state. There were so many visitors that the black draperies at the entrance were damaged by the crush and had to be changed several times.[26] The funeral parade closely followed that of Peter I, with some amendments for gender. Eight sculptures on the theme of universal grief were placed in the cathedral, representing the reciprocal love of the empress's subjects and their ruler. Anna's coffin was lowered into a vault next to the iconostasis on 15 January 1741, a procedure that necessitated moving the adjacent coffins of Peter and Catherine to accommodate it.[27]

The acts of the Brunswick government's one-year rule suggest continuity with Anna's, with no evidence of blatant mismanagement or abuse. Indeed, after the banishment of Biron foreigners predicted a period of calm and prosperity. With the prospect of more than a decade under a regent, however, the infant Ivan VI's regime fell more as a result of its vulnerability than its obvious inadequacy. Anna Leopoldovna and her circle were keen to establish the Brunswick line on the Russian throne. Given high infant mortality, it was hinted, to hang on to power it made sense for Anna to be declared empress herself and the succession to be restricted to Ivan's future siblings if he died young.[28] This alarmed rival groupings at court and the 22-year-old regent, described as 'not without self esteem, but of limited intelligence and firm will',[29] became the target of gossip and scandal, fuelled by allegations, for example, of a lesbian affair with a lady-in-waiting. In turn, rumours spread of a conspiracy in support of Elizabeth, who seized her chance on 24–25 November 1741, on the eve of the departure of guards regiments for an unpopular war against Sweden. She personally accompanied Preobrazhensky guardsmen to arrest Anna and her husband and deposed the infant Ivan VI. (The guardsmen were instructed to wait for him to wake up before carrying him away.) The ex-imperial family ended up in the Far North, where Anna gave birth to two daughters and two sons before her death in 1746. The ex-emperor Ivan was to die in Schlüsselburg fortress in 1764, the victim of an ill-conceived plan to release him and restore him to the throne.[30] Elizabeth sentenced Osterman and Münnich to death for their support of Anna, but reprieved and banished them to Siberia at the last minute. Her coup had the support of the French and Swedish ambassadors, who hoped that the grateful empress would restore territory to Sweden, but this was not to be. 'Indolent' Elizabeth had a mind of her own in this as in other matters and would not easily relinquish land conquered by her father.

Elizabeth was Peter and Catherine's fifth illegitimate child, born in December 1709, the year of Poltava.[31] Officially she never married or had children, although in November 1742 she secretly and morganatically married the Ukrainian, later Count, Aleksei Grigorevich Razumovsky (1709–71), a singer in the court choir.[32] Her trump card was undoubtedly that she was Peter I's last surviving child and her publicists compensated for her lack of personal talents by frequent and long references to Peter's heritage, a ready-made model of reform that assumed similar actions on her part without the need actually to do anything very much. She had 'saved' Peter's legacy, she was 'victorious over the "wicked wreckers of the fatherland"', a heroine who had 'wrested Peter's heritage from the hands of foreigners'.[33] Elizabeth's accession was publicized as an act of salvation, carried out by a woman who had the right to rule not only by descent but also by acclaim, for the guards begged her to rule in the name of her subjects. The 'oppression' she had suffered since her father's death was exaggerated for rhetorical effect so as to appear like an insult to Peter himself.

In fact, proving herself worthy to be Peter's daughter was a tall order for a woman who regarded reading as injurious to health and banned conversations on scientific topics in her presence. She shared some of Peter's worst characteristics, including impatience, unpredictability and inability to stay for long in one place, but lacked his vision and dedication to hard work. She was an instinctive ruler with a sense of self-preservation, made cautious, even fearful by her years on the fringes of power. However, her actual abilities were less important than the way she was presented and packaged. Elizabeth laid claim to honorary male virtues, assuming symbols of military leadership. These included, for example, sometimes wearing the uniform of Peter's Preobrazhensky guards and attending sailing regattas. Her coronation in Moscow in April 1742 was preceded by a triumphal entry parade, mimicking those organized by Peter after military victories. The whole occasion, from the ceremony in the cathedral to the firework displays, masquerades and balls that followed, was lavish in the extreme, infused with a 'scenario of demonstrative rejoicing'.[34] Elizabeth's devotion to Orthodoxy was also a selling point in her popularity.[35] Her schedule included visits to monasteries and convents, especially those with strong associations with her father, such as the Trinity-St Sergius monastery to the north of Moscow. For Russia's non-Orthodox people this attachment had its negative side: Elizabeth persecuted Old Believers, expelled Jews from Russia and had mosques demolished.

In recent years Elizabeth has emerged as something more than a figurehead attractively packaged by her publicists. Revisionist Russian historians such as Viktor Naumov and Konstantin Pisarenko,[36] for example, offer us a more dynamic, proactive Elizabeth, especially if one extends investigation to palace politics and to court culture, which historians once tended to overlook or denounce as manifestations of Elizabeth's 'wastefulness'. That Elizabeth devoted little time to regular government business may be explained in part by the fact that she rarely got up before noon and stayed up all night. She was uninterested in anything to do with state finances and trade or domestic legislation. However, records show that she took a keen interest in foreign affairs, for diplomacy and dynastic matters were natural extensions of court life.

Elizabeth was unwilling to entrust policy-making to any one person. She operated through a number of advisers, including Mikhail Vorontsov, her vice-chancellor, whom she regarded as a trusted friend, until he alienated her with his pro-Prussian sympathies in 1745. More personal ties were forged with the brothers Razumovsky, Aleksei (her husband/lover) and Kirill, president of the Academy of Sciences and hetman of Ukraine. A high-flier of Elizabeth's circle was Peter Shuvalov (1710–62), who married Elizabeth's maid of honour in 1742, rose to dominate financial affairs and made (and lost) a vast personal fortune. He in turn promoted the career of his cousin Ivan Shuvalov (1727–97), who made his mark in cultural affairs as co-founder and curator of Moscow University and first president of the Academy of Arts. Elizabeth preferred to operate through conferences (*konferentsii*) of advisers – at first informal gatherings, from 1756 more regular – although never defined in statute. These bodies initiated a number of projects, for example a commission in 1755 to recodify the laws.

For both Anna and Elizabeth the natural and everyday setting of 'political' life was the court, where business and pleasure merged. It was their courts, rather than those of the early Romanovs or Peter I, that produced the much criticized model of conspicuous, rather vulgar consumption associated with the dynasty up to its overthrow. The conservative Prince Mikhail Shcherbatov (1733–90) complained in his exposé of the 'corruption of morals' in Russia that ladies would spend 10,000 roubles or more on their costumes for court spectacles, thus contributing to the impoverishment of the nobility.[37] The sheer expense of court life could ruin even influential men like Peter Shuvalov, who died leaving enormous debts. Soviet historians denounced big spending as incongruous and insensitive when the mass of the population lived in poverty and serfdom. More recently the view has partly prevailed that the cultural achievements of Anna's and Elizabeth's reigns in particular allowed Russia to be an equal, indeed a source of envy, to courts all over Europe as historians turn the spotlight on court ceremonies and settings.

In 1732 Anna formally confirmed the return of the court to St Petersburg. Using the model of her court in Courland, she established its formal structures, extending the list of salaried post holders introduced and sporadically awarded within Peter I's Table of Ranks under such German-sounding titles as *ober-kamerger* and *ober-gofmeister* and junior level *kamer-iunkery* and *freiliny*. As one foreign observer remarked, Anna loved magnificence in her household and encouraged luxury and outward display until they 'rivalled that of the court of France'.[38] But if some writers regarded Anna's as the first Russian court with any claim to refinement, others were more struck by lingering elements of 'Asiatic' taste. For example, Anna relegated several nobles to the role of jester, most memorably Prince Mikhail Golitsyn, who had to pretend to be a chicken and sit on eggs in a large basket. In 1740 she married him off to a Kalmyk woman. The newly-weds were transported on an elephant, with attendants in carriages drawn by camels, goats and pigs, to a palace on the ice of the Neva river, where they had to lie naked on an ice bed wearing ice night-caps and slippers.[39] Playing the fool may have been regarded as just another form of Russian state service, a throwback to Peter's day, but such occurrences tended to confirm in Western eyes that the Russian aristocracy did not enjoy much respect or dignity.

Elizabeth was famed for even more lavish, but less bizarre, entertainments in which her own attractive person took centre stage, for example in the transvestite balls which showed off her fine legs to advantage.[40] The future playwright Denis Fonvizin observed: 'I confess sincerely that I was amazed by the splendour of the court of our empress ... The palace seemed to me the habitation of a being higher than mortal.'[41] The fact that Elizabeth was regarded as a beauty, albeit an overblown one in her latter years, and had a graceful bearing was vital to her success, as was her love of dancing and dressing up. She literally filled the

Engraving of Empress Elizabeth by G.F. Schmidt (after Tocque)
St Petersburg 1760.

space around her. A painting by the French artist Tocque, much reproduced in etchings, shows her in the voluminous skirts of the period, the billowing folds dotted with double eagle emblems wrapping themselves around the curvaceous legs of furniture in rococo style. She really did own thousands of costly outfits, mostly worn only once. Both she and Anna issued rules on court dress and accessories that included restrictions to ensure that the empresses' own costumes and hairstyle were not duplicated or surpassed.

Music and ballet were important at both Anna's and Elizabeth's courts, although Elizabeth was the more actively involved, enjoying singing Italian and Russian folk songs.[42] Foreign masters wrote new works for the court orchestra, composed mainly of Italian and French musicians, and directed operatic and ballet spectacles involving lavish and intricate scenery, lighting effects and costumes. Court life both influenced and was influenced by new architectural designs and spaces, as it was all over Europe. Linked *enfilades* of rooms were required for promenading, grand halls with high ceilings for balls. The court maintained heated winter and unheated summer palaces, the latter with opportunities for outdoor entertainments, and smaller stop-over palaces for rest and snacks. By Elizabeth's time there were 25 of the latter on the Moscow–St Petersburg road alone.

Little of Anna's architectural setting, mostly built of wood, survives today, although she completed several buildings begun by Peter I, including the Kunstkamera and the Peter-Paul Cathedral. She did, however, launch the career of mid-eighteenth-century Russia's most influential society architect Bartolomeo Francesco Rastrelli (1700–71), the son of the sculptor Carlo. The younger Rastrelli won fame as the master of 'Elizabethan Baroque', a prime example of which is the grand Catherine Palace (1740s–50s) at Tsarskoe Selo outside St Petersburg. This shallow, two-storey building incorporates a splendid series of rooms stretched out along an extended facade, with turquoise exterior walls set off by white stone orders, gilded ornamentation and ornate plaster work. Inside the rooms were decorated in gilt, with painted ceilings and full of rare furniture, paintings and porcelain, mirrors and chandeliers. One of the highlights was the so-called Amber Room, decorated with amber panels and carvings presented to Peter I in 1717 by the king of Prussia. The even bigger Winter Palace on the Neva River in St Petersburg, the fourth on the site, completed in 1762, had a more central, public presence. It was, in Rastrelli's words, created 'for the glory of Russia', and became synonymous with the seat of power, although not all Romanovs resided there permanently. It eventually combined living quarters and public ceremonial areas, including throne rooms and chapels, with all the cultural paraphernalia of art galleries, library, theatre and hanging gardens. Rastrelli also built the blue and white Smolny convent with its ornate five-domed cathedral for devout Elizabeth as a possible retreat in her old age, although she never used it as such. It would later become a school for the daughters of gentlefolk and in 1917, in adjacent buildings, Lenin's headquarters.[43]

The royal palaces provided steady work for foreign artists, as well as for their Russian pupils such as Ivan Vishniakov (1699–1761) and Aleksei Antropov

The Winter Palace and the Alexander Column (Lindsey Hughes).

(1716–95). Particularly in demand were copies of Russian royal portraits, including the seventeenth-century Romanovs: no palace could do without them. Contemporary portraits and decorative panels were especially popular, but many more art works were purchased abroad. It took time for the full repertoire of Western genres to be assimilated and produced on the spot. Not until the latter half of the eighteenth century, for example, did history painting, commonplace in Europe, make an impact. In particular, Peter I's efforts to create a school of Russian sculpture failed and most statues continued to be imported from abroad. In 1752 Elizabeth founded the St Petersburg Academy of Fine Arts on the initiative of Ivan Shuvalov to provide not only training but also a career path for Russian artists. It was initially reliant on foreign teachers, but Russians of any social class, occasionally even serfs, could gain access. The Academy retained a virtual monopoly on training and studio space in the capital until the mid-nineteenth century, again illustrating the concentration of patronage within the imperial court and the lack of opportunity for private initiatives. The main exception, ironically, were the serf artists and artisans trained up to produce all manner of art and artefacts for the grander noble estates, for example the Argunov serf dynasty who belonged to the Sheremetevs. A substantial middle-class and professional clientele was lacking, although Russian merchants commissioned family portraits from local artists who usually doubled as icon painters.

Peter I's immediate successors, none of whom was personally well educated or attached to scholarly pursuits, inherited distinctly patchy educational provision. As we have seen, Peter I's educational experiments were undermined by poverty and popular indifference. The Russian nobility accepted institutional education only when it was directly linked to service and privilege – the Cadet Corps school (founded 1731), for example, which allowed quick promotion to first officer grade and was closed to outsiders. For the rest, the best schools were still run by the Church. After Peter I's death some seventeen ecclesiastical academies were created, which, along with older religious establishments, in turn prepared most of the staff and students for secular higher schools. Peter's most substantial secular bequest, which his successors developed, was the Academy of Sciences opened in St Petersburg in August 1725, with an all-foreign research faculty.[44] Only a quarter of eighteenth-century academicians were Russian-born, of whom the first and most renowned was Mikhail Lomonosov (1711–65), son of a White Sea peasant, who after training in the Moscow Academy was sent abroad to study in Germany. Lomonosov went on to distinguish himself as a chemist, linguistician, poet, historian and maker of mosaics and glass.[45] Lomonosov hero-worshipped Peter the Great and was a firm supporter and enthusiastic eulogizer of the unique role of the house of Romanov in promoting Enlightenment in Russia. Russian science would have foundered without imperial sponsorship. Elizabeth's crowning achievement in education was Moscow University, founded in 1755 by Ivan Shuvalov and Lomonosov. It took many decades for the university to become Russia's leading institution of higher education. In the nineteenth century it would break away from its imperial roots, embedded in state service, to become a focus of dissent and tension between the small but growing educated class and the government.

The lack of time for nobles still harnessed to state service to cultivate the arts or to develop a taste for books meant that Russian literature, indeed print culture in general, was slow to develop in the early eighteenth century.[46] The late 1720s saw only about twenty books published annually. Literary life picked up in the reigns of Anna and Elizabeth, but even then original output by Russian writers represented an insignificant proportion of what was published and some important Russian work remained in manuscript until later in the century: the satires of Antiokh Kantemir (1708–44) – whose verses heaped scorn upon detractors of Enlightenment – did not appear in print until 1762. Most authors of the immediate post-Petrine generation, such as Vasily Trediakovsky (1703–69) and Lomonosov, specialized in panegyric verses to the crown. Both men were also interested in theories of literature and to establish European norms and registers in such areas as genre and versification. A few Russians began to write seriously for the theatre, as classical drama came into vogue. In 1756 Elizabeth appointed A. P. Sumarokov (1717–77) as the first director of her Russian theatre. His play *Khorev* (1747) was the first Russian classical tragedy, with allusions to the relationship between the monarch and the nobles and warnings against tyranny, excessive favouritism and arbitrary disgrace. It played alongside Sumarokov's version of *Hamlet* (1748).[47] None of the rulers until Catherine II, however, had a literary bent. Although Elizabeth, for example, had an impressive library it is difficult to ascertain what, if anything, she read. At least she had little inclination to interfere in literary matters. Censorship remained light, perhaps not surprisingly given the absence of independent publishing.

The phenomenon of a European state acquiring classical architecture, sculpture, painting, poetry, fashion, foreign languages, schools and academies for its elite more or less from scratch was unprecedented, driven by the idea that learning was essential in a civilized country and that European cultural values, based on Classical models, were universal. In Russia knowledge was pursued for the welfare of the state, not the personal development or satisfaction of the individual; as ever, the ruling dynasty, advised by members of their circle, set the trends. Only in the second half of the eighteenth century did art and culture spread more widely from the court to noble households, when a few individuals began to explore the roots of national culture and react against 'Gallomania' and other varieties of blind imitation of foreign models.

Apart from the imperial family and its immediate circle, the chief consumers and beneficiaries of the new court culture, arts and educational opportunities were nobles. In the decades after Peter I's death the Russian nobility continued to be a service elite, for state service remained compulsory, and promotion was achieved formally through the Table of Ranks. Performing some form of state service for the house of Romanov was the one factor that still united the nobles as a class, for outside service there were virtually no acceptable outlets for a nobleman's talents.[48] Agriculture held no attraction for most, although towards the end of the century some enlightened nobles did begin to take at interest in running their estates. Unlike their British counterparts, Russian nobles did not, with rare exceptions, enter the Church and there was no legal profession or parliament. With no institutional bodies through which to defend corporate interests, nobles tended to be rivals rather than allies.

Nevertheless, a noble consciousness did begin to emerge, as expressed, for example, in draft projects produced during the 'constitutional crisis' of 1730. Nobles engaged with the government on such issues as the period and terms of service, access to promotion and inheritance law. Peter's unpopular Law of Single Inheritance was repealed in 1731. In 1736 Anna reduced the service requirement to 25 years and allowed one son to stay home to look after the estate. In 1762 the requirement would be abolished altogether. However, nobles still complained about their lack of personal property rights, the threat of arbitrary exile or confiscation and the absence of representative institutions. Again and again, what they thought to be secure was violated, especially in the reign of Paul I, as we shall see. At the same time, existing nobles resented infiltration by outsiders. In practice the Table of Ranks became more of a closed shop and achieving noble status through service became harder. Peter's social Assemblies, which any decently dressed non-peasant person could attend, met a similar fate. For purposes of socializing and entertaining, the nobles closed ranks.

The economic status of nobles varied enormously. A mere 1 per cent owned more than a thousand male serfs, while over 50 per cent owned fewer than twenty, some none at all.[49] Many wealthier nobles owned not one single, extended estate, but many packages of land acquired separately over generations. Those who owned the most often took the least personal interest in agriculture because the general rule was that the greater the wealth and number of serfs, the greater the imperative to seek status in high office, which meant residing in St Petersburg. Nobles tried, with some success, to regain some of the control over their peasants lost to the state during Peter I's reign and to increase their share of peasant labour at the state's expense. In 1742, for example, serfs were forbidden from enlisting voluntarily in military service.

For the majority of noblemen military service continued to occupy a couple of decades of their lives, and there was no lack of opportunity to see active duty in the period 1725–62. Deprived of Peter I's driving force and with an apparent shift to domestic politics, with interruptions by palace 'coups' and succession crises, the Romanovs might have reverted to the status of the minor electoral houses of their various marriage alliances, or worse. In March 1730 a writer in the *British Journal* wrote, perhaps subject to wishful thinking, that 'unless the Empire of Russia rouses itself from under the lethargic slumber, which it is now fallen into, their furred Gowns and long Petticoats will return upon them; and all the sordid affectation of a singularity from all the world, which made them so truly contemptible before, will do the like again'.[50] The predictions proved false. There was no return to 'Asiatic' isolation. Territorial expansion was insignificant, but Russia maintained embassies and missions all over Europe and had a voice in all the major disputes on the continent of Europe and some beyond. There was a cost, however. Throughout the eighteenth century Russia needed to maintain not just European-style infantry and cavalry together with siege and field artillery, but also the means to fight steppe nomads. The fleet, too, was kept up as a useful bargaining chip and a symbol of national pride, even though it rarely saw action.

It has been argued – by Geoffrey Hosking, for example[51] – that in the process of building a multi-ethnic state between Europe and Asia, the Romanovs failed to create a Russian nation, severely restricting the development of either a civic or an ethnic consciousness vital to nationhood. An empire ruled from St Petersburg required the preservation of autocracy and serfdom and the categorization of the population in terms of service or tax liabilities rather than rights and privileges. The majority of subjects remained 'slaves'. Another cost of empire was the rift between the 'two Russias' – the peasant masses and the elite – which widened as the elite became increasingly Westernized as a way of demonstrating Russia's right to a place among the European great powers. By 1762 a generation of nobles had grown up who felt at ease in Western clothes, could converse in French and felt closer to German or English counterparts than they did to Russian peasants. At best, nobles took a paternalistic attitude to the 'souls' under their protection. Territorial expansion should, in theory, bring blessings, and empire-building did stimulate the economy in various ways.[52] Metalworking flourished in Anna's reign, with Russia becoming the world's top producer of iron ore by 1740. Russia's industrial workforce grew, but the dilemma of staffing factories in a serf economy remained. Despite some concessions, such as tax amnesties, the government continued to squeeze the peasants for taxes.

As the previous examination of Romanov priorities suggests, in the 1720s–50s Russia's ruling circle did not agonize about social dilemmas as their successors would do; there was little public theorizing about the peasant question or national identity, including the fraught issue of national minorities. By and large, the official mood of the period was upbeat. The distance of Russia's major cities from the main theatres of war in Europe gave Russia an advantage similar to that conferred on Britain by the English Channel. The eighteenth-century wars in which Russia engaged barely touched ethnic Russian territory proper. The population, it is true, suffered from the severe demands of conscription and taxation and from war casualties on a grand scale – 100,000 dead in the Russo-Turkish war of 1735–9 alone, for example – but not from occupation of home territory by alien troops. None of Peter's immediate successors was involved personally in armed combat. For the rest of the century Russia's rulers, like their foreign counterparts, had substitutes fight their battles while they themselves could either be wreathed in the imagery of victory without the need to face the dangers of actual combat or, in the case of defeat, distanced from the mess that the generals had created. Military success and limiting the impact on the home front were major factors in maintaining autocracy intact.

The international challenges facing Russia in this period sprang from Peter I's successes in the Baltic, his failure against Turkey and the advantage that he established over Poland and Ukraine. Yet one should not forget that for all their Western ways, the Romanovs remained rulers of eastern tsardoms, as incorporated in their titles, with aspirations to further expansion. In this respect their Eurasian empire was unique. In 1727 the Treaty of Kiakhta settled the border with China and regularized trade. In 1737–52 the Russians constructed about 2,000 miles of new fortified lines from the mouth of the Yaik River at the Caspian Sea to the upper reaches of the Irtysh in Siberia. In 1743 Orenburg was founded on the line, as the focal point of Russian trade with the Kazakhs. But the territories won by Peter I on the Caspian in 1722–3 proved too costly to maintain and a new balance of power between Persia and Turkey allowed Russia to withdraw from the southern shores of the Caspian in 1730s. In 1728 the Dane Vitus Bering (1681–1741) sailed north-eastward along the Pacific coast and discovered the strait that bears his name. Thirteen years later he and the Russian A.I. Chirikov discovered the southern coasts of Alaska, and on their return voyage the Aleutian Islands. Russia's mapped and charted territories continued to grow as the Romanovs sponsored the exploration of exotic lands in the relative comfort of their own borders.

European powers were reluctant to recognize the imperial titles claimed by Peter after the 1721 Treaty of Nystad: Austria and Britain did so only in 1742, France and Spain in 1745. However, they were all anxious to maintain a presence in St Petersburg. Russia also benefited passively from the shifting balance of power in Europe, where France, protector of Russia's enemies Sweden, Poland and Turkey, declined and the mutual enmity of Austria and Prussia grew. A Russo-Austrian treaty of 1726, renewed in 1746, underpinned Russian alliances for much of the century. Austria reckoned to limit Russian interference in Habsburg Orthodox territories, while allowing Russia a freer hand in Orthodox lands ruled by Poland and Turkey. The pact determined the outcome of the War of the Polish Succession (1733–4), in which Russia and Austria headed off the election of a French candidate for the Polish throne, the former Swedish 'puppet' Stanisłas Leszczynski. Anna dispatched a Russian corps to dispute the latter's 'illegal' election, allowing a Polish confederation to elect the Austrian candidate Augustus III (1733–63), son of Augustus II.

In 1735 Russia, with Austrian support, went to war with Turkey and successfully invaded Crimea and Moldavia. The costly victories secured the restoration to Russia of Azov and some adjoining lands after France intervened to determine the terms of the Peace of Belgrade (1739). Russia still lacked access to the Black Sea, but Turkey was in trouble and was soon to lose its French backing. In the Russo-Swedish War (1741–3) Sweden failed to recover any of its lost territories in return for helping Elizabeth to depose Ivan VI. By the Treaty of Åbo (1743) Russia extended its occupation of the Vyborg area. In 1744 Vyborg province was formed, which in the early nineteenth century became known as 'Old Finland' to distinguish it from the Finnish provinces added to the empire in 1808. Thus the Romanovs saw a modest expansion of their empire, which publicists extolled.

The succession in 1740 of Frederick II to the Prussian throne and Maria Theresa to the hereditary Habsburg lands set off a chain of events which would profoundly influence Russian foreign policy. Frederick's seizure of most of Silesia and part of Maria Theresa's Bohemian crown lands sparked off the War of the Austrian Succession (1740–8), which lined up France, Prussia and Bavaria against Austria, Britain and Holland. In 1743 a pro-Prussian party at Elizabeth's court headed by Mikhail Vorontsov secured a mutual aid alliance with France, Prussia's friend. However, Elizabeth was hostile to Frederick II and in 1745 the anti-Prussian Aleksei Bestuzhev-Riumin seized the initiative, envisaging alliances with Britain, Holland, Saxony and Austria. A Russian expeditionary force on the Rhine hastened the conclusion of the peace of Aix-la-Chapelle (1748), which left Silesia to Prussia.

For the next six years Russian policy aimed to contain Prussia, one of the results of which was the 'Diplomatic Revolution' of 1756, with Britain and Prussia forming one alliance and France, Austria and Russia another. In the Seven Years' War Russia's armies enjoyed some tactical successes against Prussia, for example at Grossjägersdorf in 1757, Zorndorf in 1758 and Kunersdorf in 1759, and in 1760 even temporarily occupied Berlin. However, there were major deficiencies in leadership and logistics and huge loss of life, notwithstanding patriotic Russians' pride in their success in battle against the highly regarded Prussians. One of the chief reasons why Russia did not exploit the military possibilities of the war was internal misgivings over war aims. Mounting financial problems and desertion rates in 1761, then Elizabeth's death at the end of that year, led to Russia's withdrawal, at the initiative of the new emperor Peter III, who regarded Frederick II as one of 'the greatest heroes in the world'.

The future Emperor Peter III was born Karl Peter Ulrich in Kiel in Holstein on 10/21 February 1728.[53] Through his father, it would be claimed, he had direct descent from Riurik.[54] His mother, Peter I's daughter Anna Petrovna, died the following May, possibly of consumption. From 1721 until their marriage in May 1725 Peter's father Duke Karl Frederick (1700–39) had spent several uncomfortable years at Peter I's invitation courting Anna in and around St Petersburg, at times under the impression that Elizabeth, her younger sister, was his intended bride. The marriage contract specified that the couple renounce their own claim to the Russian throne, but this did not apply to any issue of the marriage. Despite Peter III's female Romanov genes, through his father's line he was a Schleswig-Holstein-Gottorp, which title some historians insist on applying to the dynasty thereafter.[55] However, there do not seem to have been any serious proposals for a name change, because of Elizabeth's fierce loyalty to her father's legacy. On his father's side Peter was related to the Swedish royal family – Karl's mother Hedwig was a sister of the childless Charles XII – and hence had a claim to the Swedish throne. Karl was raised as a Lutheran and educated in the Prussian military style. The project of wresting Schleswig from Denmark was impressed upon him from an early age.

After Elizabeth brought Peter to Russia in 1742 to be groomed as her heir, he received instruction in the Russian language and the Orthodox religion, to which he converted. In 1745 he was married off to the German Princess Sophie Fredericke Auguste of Anhalt-Zerbst (1729–96), who took the name Ekaterina Alekseevna when she converted to Orthodoxy, but is better known to posterity as Catherine the Great. Elizabeth's choice was determined by personal factors

– Catherine was the niece of her own late fiancé – and by the desirability of an alliance with a Protestant clan in Prussian service to strengthen ties with northern Germany. She wanted and expected a pliable, dutiful spouse who would be grateful for being plucked from obscurity.

Catherine's *Memoirs* paint a bleak picture of this teenage marriage. Initially the two may have been attracted to each other and found mutual support – they were, after all, both Germans, both outsiders in an alien environment – but Catherine admitted that any physical attraction disappeared after Peter, no oil painting to begin with, was disfigured by chicken pox. Unsavoury incidents stick in the mind: Peter spying through a hole in the wall on Empress Elizabeth and her lover, court-martialling rats and bringing hunting dogs into the bedroom and tormenting them.[56] Catherine suggested that Peter was retarded and childish. Moreover, in her final version of her memoir she hinted strongly that their marriage was never consummated and that her son Paul (born 1754) was fathered by a lover.[57] Peter was not a husband at all, it seemed, and his acquisition of a long-term mistress, 'ugly' Ekaterina Vorontsova, as well as intermittent dalliances with ladies-in-waiting, was something of a relief to his wife, who reciprocated by taking lovers of her own. Catherine also found solace in books, graduating from novels to more serious fare, including the works of Voltaire.

Catherine had good reason to blacken the reputation of the husband whose throne she later snatched – even in the 1790s when she last revised her memoir. Her self-justifying strategy undoubtedly influenced not only contemporaries but also the longer-term reputation of her 'inadequate' spouse. Revisionist historians paint a more positive picture, pointing to Peter's wide cultural interests (music, painting, collecting books and coins), his interest in the Cadet Corps school and in trade and industry. During his short rule he was an energetic and 'serious' monarch.[58] Even so, many witnesses corroborate the essence of Catherine's portrait of her husband, who seems to have been immature to the point of childishness (in his obsession with dolls, for example), thoughtless, impulsive and unpredictable. A Prussian envoy wrote in 1747: 'It's incomprehensible how a prince of his age can behave so childishly'.[59] Many of his pursuits were perfectly routine – for example his love of military affairs and drawing fortifications – but could be taken to extremes, in this case a near obsession with correct uniform and drill. His interest in real and toy soldiers often merged. At his estate at Oranienbaum he set the 2,500 serfs to work building a small fortified town called Peterstadt, in homage to Peter I. His main cultural pursuit was 'sawing away' at the violin, which again was hardly a crime, but annoyed his wife. His appearance was against him: surviving portraits, even those that strive to flatter, suggest a weedy, unprepossessing gangliness.

Being 'childlike' was not sufficient reason for a Russian ruler to forfeit his rightful throne, however. Indeed, some of Peter's vices were uncomfortably close to those of his grandfather Peter I, such as enjoyment of practical jokes and heavy drinking. It is significant that in his accession manifesto he pledged 'in everything to follow in the footsteps of our most wise sovereign, our grandfather, Emperor Peter the Great'.[60] Unlike Peter I, however, Peter III never established his undisputed authority to do pretty well whatever he wanted, nor did he command loyalty. Powerful courtiers might have accommodated him had he acted according to consensus, but he alienated the guards, who over four decades had gained the confidence that they could remove or enthrone anyone, legitimate or not. In this respect, Peter III's greatest mistake was not the peace that he made with Prussia in 1762, which had some sympathy at the Russian court, but launching a new personally motivated campaign, unpopular with the Russian military, to obtain Schleswig. There were rumours that he intended to bring men from Holstein to replace existing guards, who were required to wear Prussian uniforms in place of those devised by Peter I himself. It was no secret that he believed that the guards had degenerated into a 'dissolute' lifestyle under Elizabeth.

A few months before his overthrow it seemed that Peter might after all win noble support. The impending peace with Prussia probably triggered the most famous piece of legislation of his short reign, a manifesto releasing the Russian nobility from compulsory state service (18 February 1762). The reasons for ending compulsion were, in the words of the edict, that 'coarseness in those who neglect the general good has been eradicated ... useful knowledge and assiduity in service have increased the number of skilful and brave generals in military affairs, and have put informed and suitable people in civil and political affairs'. The decree was not an invitation to wholesale retirement, however. The emperor commanded 'all our obedient and true sons to despise and scorn all those people who have never served anywhere, but spend all their time in sloth and idleness, and do not subject their children to any useful education for the benefit of the fatherland, for they are negligent of the common good, and they will not be allowed to appear at Our Court, or at public meetings or celebrations'.[61]

The emancipation of the nobility has been attributed to pressure both from above – the state ridding itself of superfluous staff – and from below – nobles demanding more rights, the culmination of trends since the death of Peter I towards reducing the period of state service. As the memoirist A. T. Bolotov wrote, this 'magnanimous act filled the whole nobility with indescribable joy ... and our satisfaction was universal and most sincere'.[62] The timing of the end of the Seven Years' War was crucial. Officers returning from active service could be redeployed into the management of estates and local affairs. Nevertheless, most nobles continued to serve for the sake of salaries, perks, honours and prestige, for which the Romanovs were grateful for they could hardy have survived, not to mention retained a high profile in international affairs, without a strong backbone of professional and loyal 'sons of the fatherland'.

The emancipation act and several other measures helped to build Peter III's reputation as a ruler with promise, although the nature and degree of the contribution made by his advisers remains to be calculated. The most powerful men of his regime were the procurator-general Alexander Glebov and privy secretary and president of the College of Foreign Affairs Dmitry Volkov. During his six-month reign he issued almost two hundred edicts,[63] including the abolition of the notorious Secret Chancellery, acts on trade and sailcloth manufacture in Siberia, reduction of the salt tax, a temporary ban on the purchase of serfs for factories and exile of landlords who murdered their serfs, and the lifting of some sanctions on Old Believers. He also transferred about two million peasants on church estates to the jurisdiction of the state College of Economy, which the peasants themselves regarded as an improvement in their status. In conjunction with the emancipation of the nobility, the last measure increased speculation that Peter might be planning to emancipate the serfs. His positive credentials were enhanced by the fact that he matched the criteria of both the new and old conventions of succession. Under the law of 1722 he was nominated almost twenty years before he came to the throne and groomed to succeed. He was male and a grandson of Peter I.[64]

None of this saved Peter III, whose fate, it seemed, was further sealed by his neglect of Orthodoxy. It was even falsely rumoured that he intended to convert Russia to Lutheranism, probably based on his desire to introduce certain rational Protestant practices. Accusations of importing alien faiths were stock ones against Russian rulers, such as False Dmitry I, who came from outside. True or not, they served the purposes of Peter's many opponents, most notably the guards on whom he imposed unwelcome discipline and reforms. On 28 June 1762 his wife Catherine seized power with the support of guards regiments and her lover Grigory Orlov. 'It was evident to all true sons of the fatherland', a manifesto declared, 'what danger there was to the entire Russian state, and above all what a threat to our Greek Orthodox faith.'[65] After vain efforts to rally support, Peter abdicated (29 June) and was placed under house arrest on his estate at Ropsha. Between 3–6 July he died, officially of 'haemorrhoidal colic', but rumours hinted at assassination by poison, strangulation, suffocation, beating or shooting. The officer in charge of the ex-emperor's escort reported an unfortunate scuffle. No one was charged, but even if Peter was not killed on Catherine's explicit orders, his death did not arouse her regret, although at times it came back to haunt her.

5

Philosopher on the Throne: 1762–1796

CATHERINE II

With the accession of Catherine II as empress in June 1762, Romanov blood at best flowed thinly in the veins of the ruling house. Only Catherine's son Paul could now be traced back to Michael Romanov, his great-great-great grandfather, and he through the female line.[1] As we have seen, however, Catherine hinted that Paul was in fact the son of her lover, the Russian nobleman Sergei Saltykov, who courted her assiduously from the summer of 1752, having been virtually thrust upon her 'to secure the succession' when she failed to produce an heir after almost ten years of marriage. The governess of the Young Court, Maria Choglokova, stated that 'there was no question of [Catherine and Peter] having children, that this could not happen without a cause and although Their Imperial Highnesses had been married since 1745, the cause of children did not exist'.[2] Catherine suffered a miscarriage in summer 1753, but in February 1754 was pregnant again. Paul was born on 20 September and rumours immediately circulated that Saltykov was his father. Peter III's reaction is not recorded. However, in 1758, when Catherine was pregnant with her daughter Anna, presumed to be the child of her lover the Pole Stanisław Poniatowski, Peter apparently commented: 'God knows where my wife gets her pregnancies. I really do not know if this child is mine and if I ought to recognize it'.[3] Later, however, she writes that he seemed 'very happy about the birth of this child', who was named after his mother.[4]

Catherine had nothing to gain by denying Peter's paternity, for producing a male heir of the imperial blood made her position more secure. Indeed, in an earlier version of her *Memoir*, written in 1771–3, she suggests that the marriage to Peter may indeed have been consummated (and Paul conceived) in 1754, perhaps after both had gained sexual experience with their respective lovers.[5] In the 1790s, when she had occupied the throne for 30 years and she and Paul were barely on speaking terms, she had less to lose by acknowledging Saltykov except for upsetting her beloved grandsons Alexander and Constantine with doubts about their ancestry. But even in the 1790s her *Memoir* was still a very private matter. So she keeps us guessing, perhaps because she herself did not know for sure. Paul, who closely resembled Peter III in appearance, never doubted his parentage.[6]

Whatever the biological facts, that many regarded Paul as Russia's legitimate ruler was a source of anxiety throughout Catherine's reign, especially as mother and son became ever more distant. Among the reasons suggested for their poor relationship is that Catherine was prevented from bonding with the infant Paul, whom Elizabeth whisked away into her own apartments immediately after his birth, where he was 'literally smothered by her care'. Catherine did not see him for 40 days and meetings thereafter were infrequent.[7] After Elizabeth lost interest, Paul was cared for by a succession of nannies, then male tutors. In June 1762, when Catherine named him in a manifesto as her heir, she knew that she would be under pressure to act as regent for a few years rather than assume the headship of the house of Romanov until her own death in 1796. At the same time the 1722 Law of Succession did not require a blood link, only nomination of the 'worthiest' successor. Catherine considered herself nominated by popular acclaim; thereafter her rule would be justified by her achievements and Paul would have to wait.

As it turned out, the 34-year reign of Catherine II was one of the most successful in Russian history, judged by the standards of its time, and had to rely little upon 'scientific' claims to legitimacy. She and her capable helpers expanded the empire, gave charters to nobles and townspeople, reformed provincial government, developed public education, sponsored literature and the arts and much more, following the Petrine model of reform from above. Unlike any of her predecessors, except to some extent Peter I, Catherine also provided ideological underpinnings for her policies, developing ideas from her readings of the leading writers of the French and German Enlightenment, causing her to be dubbed a 'philosopher on the throne'.

In this respect, historians once portrayed Catherine as a vain 'hypocrite' who sought applause by providing the veneer of reform without the substance. Some observers dismissed her cultural activities as the trappings of vanity or blatant wastefulness, while her renowned contacts with thinkers were denounced as a subterfuge to persuade the sages that Russia was a happy country. She was chastised for 'pretending' to pity the peasants while actually enslaving them even more. In foreign policy, Catherine's contribution to the dismemberment of Poland in the 1770s and 1790s aroused moral indignation. That she lived with a series of lovers evoked the unedifying spectacle of empress and escorts cavorting while the masses suffered. Since the 1970s Western scholars have revised these views, followed in the late 1980s by Russian colleagues, developing a picture of 'monarchy without despotism' within the context of its time.[8] As a pioneering Russian historian wrote, 'Catherine's image has been monstrously distorted, and this in turn has distorted our understanding of the whole epoch'. It turns out that she was perhaps 'the most successful Russian reformer because she succeeded in creating without any serious social, political and economic upheavals a planned programme of significant transformation'.[9] With the ongoing scholarly publication of official and private correspondence, memoirs and other papers of the period, historians are in a better position than ever to assess the contribution of Russia's foremost woman ruler.[10]

Catherine was born Sophie Fredericke Auguste on 21 April/2 May 1729 in the town of Stettin (now Szczeczin in Poland) to the minor German Prince Christian August of Anhalt-Zerbst and his wife Johanna Elisabeth of Holstein-Gottorp, the sister of Duke Karl Frederick. As we have seen, in 1745 Catherine married her cousin, Karl's son, the future Peter III, after converting to Orthodoxy. A contemporary portrait by Georg Christoph Grooth shows a slender, dark-haired young girl, wearing the order of St Catherine and lightly brandishing a closed fan. Later in life Catherine would add weight to her image in all senses of the word. Life at Elizabeth's court, which Catherine recorded in frank and sometimes squalid detail in her *Memoirs*, was at times unbearable. Neglected by her husband, who soon installed a mistress, Elizabeth Vorontsova, Catherine spent much time reading and dabbling in or avoiding the consequences of court intrigues, which towards the end of Elizabeth's reign began to focus on making Catherine regent to her son Paul or empress instead of her husband. To this end she received encouragement from foreigners, notably the British, eager to steer Russian foreign policy in new directions. The British ambassador Sir Charles Hanbury-Williams was a trusted confidant and was probably the intended recipient of the first version of the *Memoirs*.

Catherine felt increasingly insecure as friends at court were removed and secret correspondence with foreign diplomats threatened to come to light. Any plans to pre-empt Peter's succession were discouraged by the fact that she was secretly pregnant in December 1761, but as we have seen, six months into his reign Peter had undermined his own position. His public ill-treatment of his wife at court brought Peter further unpopularity and the emperor's opponents focused on his imminent departure for an unpopular campaign against Denmark in mid-June as a signal to act. The declaration of Catherine's accession took place on 28 June while Peter was at his estate at Oranienbaum on the Finnish gulf. The following day she donned the uniform of the Preobrazhensky guards and went there to arrest her husband, although the two did not meet. The confused Peter was powerless to act.[11]

The manifesto that Catherine now presented, co-authored by Nikita Panin (1718–83), her foreign minister in all but name from 1763 to 1781, and her secretary Grigory Teplov, condemned Peter for being contemptuous of Russia and Orthodoxy. It distracted attention from Catherine's own 'outsider' credentials and lack of formal entitlement to his throne. The manifesto contrasted her concern for Russia with Peter's lack of it, her 'love' with his 'hatred' for both the fatherland and, crucially, the guards regiments. 'All the respected traditions of our fatherland are being trampled underfoot. So we, being conscious that it is the honest desire of all our loyal subjects, and having God and justice on our side, have ascended the throne as Catherine II, autocrat of all Russia.'[12]

Catherine did intend to rule in the best interests of her adopted people. For the time being, however, she was inexperienced and vulnerable, dependent upon the loyalty of a close group of friends and officials. These men (and a few women, such as Princess Ekaterina Dashkova) provided crucial support for a young widowed female ruler who did not intend to be a mere figurehead. Her leading adviser in both domestic and foreign affairs was Panin, but it was characteristic that Catherine failed to implement his proposal of December 1762 for the creation of an imperial council that would have limited her powers.[13] The driving force behind the June coup was her lover of the moment, the war hero Grigory Orlov (1734–83), one of five prominent brothers who all supported Catherine's bid, a big man who, according to Horace Walpole 'dances gigantic dances and makes gigantic love'.[14]

The historian can hardly avoid the issue of Catherine's lovers, for the 'institutionalization' of favouritism was an essential element in her style of rulership and had an impact on relations at court and beyond.[15] Catherine had twelve official lover-consorts, all men, consecutively over a period of 44 years, nine of them after 1762 when she was a widow. Grigory Orlov enjoyed a decade as favourite. When in 1772 Alexander Vasilchikov replaced him, Orlov departed with generous gifts. This set the tone for future redundancy packages. Catherine preferred to be on good terms with retiring lovers. Her best-known consort was the guards officer Grigory Potemkin (1739–91), latterly His Most Serene Highness Prince of the Holy Roman Empire, Prince of Taurida, Field Marshal, Commander-in-Chief of the Russian Army, Grand Hetman of the Black Sea and Ekaterinoslav Cossacks, Grand Admiral of the Black Sea and Caspian Fleets and President of the College of War, whose tenure as lover lasted just over two years in 1774–6. Potemkin remained Catherine's best friend and virtual co-ruler, a major actor in foreign and military affairs, and probably her husband (from 1774), until his death on war service in 1791.[16] Their passionate affair settled into friendship in an extended household, which included the prince's own mistresses and Catherine's current favourite. Potemkin's reputation once suffered as much neglect and distortion as Catherine's. Among the many myths about him, for example, is that he created fake villages to impress the empress when she toured her new southern territories in 1787, a slander spread by his enemies. In fact, Potemkin actually helped create many real towns in the conquered areas.

In 1776 the Ukrainian Peter Zavadovsky briefly became favourite, to be replaced by Simon Zorich (aged 32), who made way in 1778 for Ivan Rimsky-Korsakov (aged 24). Catherine was devoted to his successor, Alexander Lanskoy (aged 22), whose death in 1784 drove her almost mad. Both he and his successor, thirty-year old Alexander Ermolov, were aides-de-camp to Potemkin, which prompted rumours that Potemkin 'procured' the empress's younger lovers. Alexander Dmitriev-Mamonov (aged 26) took over in 1786, and, having betrayed Catherine with a younger mistress, was replaced in 1789 by the even younger Platon Zubov, who remained in post until the empress's death. Catherine's lovers from Orlov onwards shared certain common features. All but one (Zavadovsky) were guardsmen, mostly from minor noble clans; they were all younger than her, the age gap increasing as she grew older. Charm and good looks provided the initial attraction. Mostly the lovers shared Catherine's cultural interests, while she saw herself as 'educating' them, a metaphor, perhaps, for enlightening Russia. Banished from the bedroom when Catherine grew tired of them or they erred, they were generally gently dismissed and compensated to minimize the danger of continuing rivalries and tensions.

In the 1770s and especially in the 1790s the foreign press (there was no Russian independent media) began to equate the empress's appetite for territorial expansion with her greed for sexual conquests.[17] In fact, the tone of Catherine's private circle was of dullish domesticity rather than orgies and she rarely allowed her love life to disrupt her orderly timetable of work. The everyday routine of the palace was low-key – private parties, cards, conversation, with the occasional masked ball or visit to the theatre to liven things up – and became more so as Catherine grew older. People enjoyed Catherine's company. She had an ability to put them at their ease and a sense of humour, coupled with a skill at manipulation. She successfully juggled the demands and ardour of her latest lover with those of older courtiers.

The first few years of Catherine's reign were devoted mainly to clearing up her predecessors' unfinished business, including ratifying Russia's new relationship with Prussia, the transfer of church peasants and the freedom of the nobility, with some restructuring of central and provincial government. In July 1764 there was an attempt to free the ex-emperor Ivan VI from Schlüsselburg fortress. The guards followed the procedures for dealing with an escape bid and killed Ivan, thus ridding Catherine of a potential embarrassment. In the eyes of some observers, her reputation never recovered from suspicions of double regicide, although she had, of course, played no part in the fate of the Brunswicks in 1741.

In the late 1760s Catherine unfolded a wider vision for Russia. In 1767 she published her Great Instruction or *Nakaz*, 526 articles for the guidance of a Legislative Commission, which she summoned that year to discuss the recodification of the laws, initiated under Peter I. Defining the nature and purpose of the *Nakaz* has been central to historians' assessment of Catherine and her regime. Some critics have treated it as a sort of a check-list of promises to be matched against concrete measures. It has been mistakenly described as a draft law code or, equally unjustly, as a piece of propaganda to get easy publicity abroad, but not widely distributed in Russia. Recent scholarship sees it in a more positive light.[18]

The *Nakaz*'s main theme was the improvement of law-based monarchy, rooted in the premise that laws must conform to the historical nature of the people for whom they are intended, and sovereigns must rule in harmony with them and regard them as binding. Chapter 1, article 6 stated confidently that 'Russia is a European state', for which the right form of government was monarchy, not the despotism that some writers thought appropriate to vast non-European empires. At the same time, the monarch must be absolute, 'for there is no other authority except that which centres on his single person that can act with a vigour proportionate to the extent of such a vast dominion' (chapter 1, article 10). Thus Catherine set her mission squarely in the European context, but with due consideration for the special nature of her dominions.

Catherine approached the composition of the *Nakaz* not as an original work but as an exercise that drew unapologetically on other sources. Some 294 articles were borrowed from *On the Spirit of the Laws* by Montesquieu (1689–1755).[19] Catherine accepted the French writer's advocacy of the separation of legislative, executive and judicial powers and the need for fundamental laws, but would not concede independent powers for the nobility. Freedom from oppression and encroachment as guaranteed by law did not mean licence to do anything you liked: as article 38 stated, 'Liberty is the right to do everything which the laws permit'. By the same token, equality implied subjugation to the same laws which were appropriate to other members of one's estate, not having the same laws for princes and peasants alike.

Another 108 articles came from the Milanese jurist Cesare Beccaria's *On Crimes and Punishments*, which advocated that punishments must be humane. Capital punishment, torture during investigation and cruel punishments were condemned. Other sections of the *Nakaz* were based on modern European writings on social welfare, trade and prosperity. The work contained many concepts that were novel for Russia: for example, that a person was innocent until proven guilty. Sanctions on torture, capital and corporal punishment were radical in the European context, not just in Russia.

The initial audience for the *Nakaz*, the Legislative Commission, was convened in Moscow on 30 July 1767, when the document was read out. The Commission met 204 times, in Moscow and St Petersburg, with between 518 and 580 delegates drawn from most sections of Russian society, excluding serfs and clergy (there was a single deputy from the Holy Synod). At a specially-convened session at Moscow's Golovin palace, the commissioners begged Catherine to accept the titles 'Great' and 'All-Wise Mother of the Fatherland', which she declined, although they were widely used anyway. The Commission last met in December

1768, after which many deputies left to serve in the war against Turkey which had just broken out.

The Legislative Commission was not a political forum in the modern sense, still less a proto-parliament, but rather an attempt at preparation for recodifying the laws. It formed the basis of a package of measures implemented in the 1770s–80s. Catherine hoped to get her more educated subjects thinking along the right lines. When it came to national issues, however, even the noble delegates were ill prepared. If they grasped the principles in the *Nakaz* at all, many found them too radical. Catherine, like Romanovs before and after, may have concluded that the overwhelming majority of her subjects were deeply conservative and that radical reform was impossible. Action from above was the only alternative.

Catherine's thinking owed a great deal to her relationship with leading figures of the French and German Enlightenment. Her correspondence with Voltaire was launched after he published his *History of Peter the Great* (1760–2) and continued to his death in 1778. They shared a number of pet hates – the Turks, the Catholic Church, fanaticism and superstition. Voltaire was a monarchist, opposed to the idea of immediate freedom for serfs and thought it natural that rulers and their courts should be the driving force for improvement. In 1765 Catherine bought the library of Denis Diderot, which he was forced to sell to meet debts, allowing him the use of it in his lifetime. Diderot visited Russia in 1773–4, and several times each week conducted informal conversations with Catherine. He expressed the view that Russia was a 'blank sheet' which would be easier to reform than Western countries with their set ways. Catherine, however, found his schemes for reform unrealistic. 'You only work on paper, which will put up with anything', she complained, 'whereas I, poor empress, work on human skin, which is notoriously irritable and ticklish.'[20] Catherine's closest confidant was the German thinker Friedrich Melchior Grimm, and she was also much influenced by the writings of German political theoreticians such as Jakob Bielfeld and Johann Justi and the British jurist William Blackstone.

Accusations that Catherine 'fooled' the *philosophes* into thinking that she was reforming Russia according to their principles fail to take into account the limitations of the *philosophes* themselves, whose writings were not blueprints for reform but, to a great extent, philosophy for philosophy's sake.[21] Catherine herself adopted their terms of reference. Thus, in speaking of her 'republican soul',[22] she was not advocating the overthrow of monarchies, for 'the sovereign is the source of all political and civil power' (*Nakaz*, article 19). Republican regimes (in the strict political sense) were suitable for small countries, but larger countries could still apply some of the good features of republican government by fostering commerce and manufacture and tolerating different beliefs, for example. Catherine's wider reading of European writers, her appreciation of Russian precedents and her perception of the Russian people as in need of firm direction pushed her to favour the model of a *Polizeistaat* – a 'policed' state in the eighteenth-century sense of strong central concern for the common good on the basis of regulations implemented by officials to foster good order. In this she built on Peter I's model.

An essential pivot of the Enlightenment was educational reform. In the words of the *Nakaz*: 'The rules of education are the first principles which prepare us to be citizens.'[23] All the ruling heads of the house of Romanov would be concerned with education at all levels and, as we shall see, as the imperial family proliferated, individual grand dukes and grand duchesses acted as patrons of individual institutions. For the time being, however, Catherine took on the task more or less single-handed. Initially, her plans were ambitious: schools would create a new type of person, who would augment Russia's 'civilized' population. She summed up her ideas in the *General Plan for the Education of Persons of Both Sexes* (1764), which stressed a rational, well-ordered regime, personal hygiene, suitable clothing and exercise. (In the spirit of overcoming superstition and encouraging science in 1768 Catherine and her son Paul were inoculated against smallpox. More than 150 nobles followed her example within a month, and inoculation clinics were subsequently established in several Russian towns).[24]

Children were best isolated from parental influences. In 1764–5 two separate schools for boys and girls from non-noble backgrounds were established. The Moscow orphanage and foundling homes (1763–4) were supposed to turn orphans and outcasts into anything the state wanted, but sadly high mortality rates prevailed in these and other establishments. More successful was the Smolny Institute for Noble Girls (1764), which provided a finishing school for generations of young ladies. There were further provisions for schools under the terms of the 1775 Statute on Provincial Administration.[25] In August 1786 the Statute on National Schools initiated Catherine's most ambitious educational project, which adopted the methods of the Prussian educationalist Johann Felbiger, whose system was in operation in the Habsburg empire. The idea of a uniform curriculum and uniform methods throughout an empire seemed appropriate in the Russian context. The Statute provided for a two-tier system of co-educational high schools and primary schools in provincial and district towns. Tuition was to be free of charge; corporal punishment was outlawed; the curriculum was secular. Subjects included geography, natural history, physics and architecture; at the same time, set texts such as *On the Duties of Man and Citizen* (1783) stressed obedience to the authorities, fulfilment of social obligations and contentment with one's lot.[26] A pedagogical institute was founded in 1783 to recruit and train teachers.

By the end of Catherine's reign only about 62,000 children were being educated in 549 state institutions, supplemented by private and church schools. The new schools suffered from inadequate funding, teacher shortages and local indifference or hostility. Most people could not see the point in educating their children. Even so, in the Russian context, where there was still no state provision for rural education, the schools may be regarded as an achievement.

For all Catherine's enthusiasm for reform, the outside world continued to assess Russia and its ruling house on their record in war and diplomacy. As Sir George Macartney, the British minister to St Petersburg, remarked in 1768 Russia was 'a great planet that has obtruded itself into our system, whose place is yet undetermined, but whose motions most powerfully affect those of every other orb'.[27] Russia was moving into the first rank, but had not yet arrived. From the start of her reign, Catherine neither felt tied to one particular orbit nor had any doubts about the powerful role which Russia must continue to play in the world. She appreciated the difficulty of guaranteeing both her northern and southern borders by alliances, but was helped by the fact that all Russia's neighbour-enemies in the eighteenth century – Sweden, Turkey, Poland – were satellites of France, which was in decline. In April 1764 Russia signed a treaty with Prussia, which sanctioned joint intervention to place Catherine's ex-lover Stanisłas Poniatowski on the Polish throne, to counteract French and Habsburg moves to elect a Saxon candidate. This represented a first step in Nikita Panin's 'Northern System', which envisaged a protectorate over Poland. An ex-lover on the throne did not guarantee a compliant Poland, however, and generally Poland would be a thorn in Romanov flesh until the fall of the empire. Catherine's attempts to champion the rights of disenfranchised Orthodox and Protestant Polish 'dissidents' and to promote representation for all religions in the Polish government were strongly opposed as King Stanisłas instituted his own con-stitutional reforms and played down the dissident issue. Russia responded with armed intervention. As hostilities encroached on its dependent territory, Turkey declared war.

Initial Russian successes in the First Turkish War (1768–74) were impressive. In 1769–70 Russia captured all Turkey's strongholds in Moldavia and Wallachia, including Bender, the key fortress on the Dniester River. With Britain's co-operation and some British officers on her ships, Catherine dispatched her Baltic fleet to the Mediterranean. In 1770 the Russian squadron won a naval victory over the Turks at Chesme in the Aegean. Crucially, in 1771 a Russian army occupied Crimea, which in late 1772 accepted the Russian offer of nominal independence in return for Russia's occupation of most of its ports. Crimea proved the biggest stumbling block to Russian and Turkish negotiations, but the Pugachev rebellion (see below) hastened a resolution in the form of the Treaty of Kuchuk Kainardji (Küçük Kaynarca, 10/21 July 1774), which gave Russia part of the Black Sea coastline, the port of Kerch, the freedom for Russian merchant vessels to navigate the Straits and an 'independent' Crimea.

Europe's major powers viewed Russia's military and naval successes with alarm. The Austrians – determined to keep the Orthodox principalities of Moldavia and Wallachia under the Ottomans – in 1772 offered them diplomatic help in return for the cession of Bukovina. Prussia and Austria offered Russia a share of Poland in compensation. There followed the First Partition of Poland (1772) between Austria, which annexed territories comprising about 2,700,000 people, Prussia, which gained most of northern Poland to the west of East Prussia, and Russia, which acquired 'ancestral' lands in the Grand Duchy of Lithuania (eastern Belarus) and south-eastern Latvia, bringing some 1,800,000 new subjects into the empire.[28]

In the midst of war and diplomacy Catherine did not neglect pressing dynastic questions. In the 1760s she had successfully resisted suggestions that she serve as regent to Paul, who was painfully aware that his mother could legally disinherit him by choosing an alternative successor. For her part, Catherine feared the formation of factions around Paul, but at this stage had no viable successor to consider. Paul was groomed as heir, well educated by the standards of the time. His first tutor was Nikita Panin, whose knowledge of foreign affairs was unsurpassed, supplemented by a number of specialist teachers who taught languages (he had an excellent knowledge of French), science, mathematics, drawing and horsemanship. Generally, the grand duke was schooled in the precepts of the Enlightenment, which were underpinned by conversations with men of learning.[29]

In the early 1770s Catherine sensed a wave of enthusiasm for Paul, now eighteen, that put her on her guard against some sort of move to place him on the throne. She sought a bride for Paul to mark his coming of age on her own terms and to switch his attention from Panin, whose reign as tutor was ended with rich rewards. In September 1773 a marriage was arranged with the German princess Augusta Wilhelmina Louisa of Hesse-Darmstadt (1755–76), who was known after conversion to Orthodoxy as Natalia Alekseevna.[30] She died painfully after giving birth to a stillborn son in April 1776. Paul was inconsolable – at least until he learned (almost certainly from his mother) that his 'vivacious' wife had been unfaithful to him.[31] In September he married another bride of the empress's choosing, Sophia Dorothea Augusta Louisa of Württemberg (1759–1828), known as Maria Fedorovna after her conversion to Orthodoxy. 'I found my intended to be such as I could only have dreamed of', Paul wrote to Catherine. 'She is tall, shapely, intelligent, quick-witted and not at all shy.'[32] She returned his love and at the beginning at least their marriage was happy and productive: she gave him four sons and six daughters.

Catherine's grandchildren proved to be one of the joys of her older age, although they did not mitigate her unsatisfactory relationship with her son. She adored Alexander (1777–1825) and Constantine (1779–1831), removing them from their parents' care into her own apartments, as Empress Elizabeth had done with Paul. The future Nicholas I (1796–1855) she knew only as an infant and the couple's last son Mikhail (1798–1849) not at all. Her six granddaughters Alexandra (1783–1801), Elena (1784–1803), Maria (1786–1859), Ekaterina (1788–95), Olga (1792–5) and Anna (1795–1865) became part of the empress's extended family, although she declared that she 'loved boys far more than girls'.[33] Catherine attempted to extend the family further when in 1793 she married Alexander, just fifteen, to thirteen-year-old Louisa Maria Augusta of Baden (1779–1826).[34]

Despite Paul's status as father of a growing family, Catherine kept him away from government and actual military service, even when he begged to be allowed to serve against the Turks in 1788. Official visits abroad occupied some of the couple's time, notably an eighteen-month grand tour in 1781–2, which they undertook as the Count and Countess of the North, which included Vienna, Naples and Paris. It was crucial in shaping their cultural tastes. Maria Fedorovna enthusiastically sponsored interior and garden design and collected fine art. At home Paul's major occupation was drilling two thousand troops on his barracks-like estate at Gatchina, a gift on the birth of his first daughter in 1783. Even though Catherine hated the military atmosphere at Gatchina, she apparently never saw the troops as a threat, rather believing that this 'mad military establishment' kept her son harmlessly occupied and undermined his reputation among high-ranking Russians.[35]

Successes abroad helped to maintain Catherine's grip on central government, but governing the Russian provinces effectively remained as problematical as it had been for her seventeenth-century predecessors. Rather than enjoying 'autocratic', still less 'despotic', powers that penetrated all parts of their dominions, the Romanovs suffered from a shortage of power in the countryside, being unable to count on a sympathetic response from the noble elite – who acted as proxy servants of the state – to their reforming edicts. In one respect at least, the self-governing of the mass of the population through the peasant communes and other local bodies allowed the government to conserve its resources as long as taxes were paid and recruits were conscripted. The equilibrium was constantly disturbed in the countryside, where acts of violence were a fact of life, as they were in other countries in eighteenth-century Europe. However, few outbreaks involved outright attacks on the status quo. Serfs killed each other more often than they killed their masters or mistresses. Conflict occurred between state peasants and government agents, between rich nobles and poorer ones. Recorded peasant revolts usually involved refusal to fulfil obligations, and flight remained the preferred method of defying the system.[36]

Sporadically a wider crisis occurred, as it did under the impact of the first war with Turkey, associated with conscription, taxation and bubonic plague, which killed an estimated 100,000 people in the Moscow region alone in 1770–2. Like revolts in the seventeenth and early eighteenth centuries, the rebellion led by the Don Cossack Emelian Pugachev began on the periphery of the empire.[37] The catalyst was action by Cossacks of the Yaik River over loss of privileges and increased service requirements. Protests against the recent crushing of a mutiny in Yaik by government troops resurfaced in 1773, bringing further reprisals. As if in answer to their appeals, a man declared himself as the true Tsar Peter III come to claim his rightful inheritance, of which he had been robbed by 'wicked advisers'. Peter III was an ideal candidate for pretendership. He had been the legitimate male ruler and his reign had shown promise, but his God-ordained rule was cut short under circumstances which remain suspicious to this day. Many believed that the 1762 emancipation of nobles was the first stage of a general emancipation package which representatives of the landowners had attempted to abort by trying to assassinate the would-be liberator. Peter III/ Pugachev told a story about how he, Peter, had wandered abroad, which would have seemed perfectly plausible to anyone who wanted to believe it.

Pugachev's first edict in the name of Peter III (September 1773) was addressed to the 'army of the Yaik' and set a pattern for later manifestos with its assurances of imperial favour, confirmation of Cossack status in perpetuity and promises of material rewards in return for slave-like loyalty. Customized decrees were issued to Old Believers, nomadic tribes-people, factory workers and peasants. The texts contained dire threats of retribution for anyone who refused to serve 'Peter'. Worries about 'German' female rule played a fairly minor role in raising rebellion in areas where most people probably had the haziest of notions of what the court in St Petersburg actually comprised. The main point is that the male pretender promised to replace fake, usurper Romanovs and their courtiers and institutions with his own genuine ones, including his own 'College of War'. The Romanov dynasty would be purified.

In late 1773 the Pugachev revolt came to resemble the 'peasant war' described in Soviet history books, as the rebels entered territory with a mainly Russian peasant population. To them Pugachev addressed a number of manifestos, most famously to Penza province. Former serfs would be his 'loyal slaves' in return for 'the ancient cross and prayers, heads and beards, liberty and freedom and to live forever as Cossacks, with no demands for recruit levies, poll tax and other money taxes, with possession of lands, forests, hay fields and fisheries and salt lakes without compensation and without quitrent; and we liberate all from the taxes and burdens hitherto imposed on the peasants and on all the people by the wicked landlords and bribe-taking judges in the towns.'[38]

The manifesto commanded peasants to capture and execute the 'wicked landlords'. Rebels duly butchered 1,572 nobles (including 474 women and 302 children), 1,037 officials and 237 priests, and plundered estates. In September 1774 disillusioned former supporters handed Pugachev over to the authorities. He was brought to Moscow in a cage, where he was sentenced to the prescribed punishment for his crime, which was severing the limbs by quartering, followed by hanging. Catherine, however, followed Enlightened principles by ordering the executioner to hang him first.

The major outcome of the Pugachev rebellion was the Statute on Provincial Administration (November 1775), Catherine's longest and most complex piece of legislation. 'There is', the act admitted, 'both an insufficiency of administration and a shortage of people capable of administering.'[39] The Provincial reform divided Russia into 38 (later 50) provinces or *gubernii*, further subdivided into districts (*uezdy*). Each province had a capital with a resident governor (grade 4 on the Table of Ranks), directly appointed from St Petersburg. The Statute established a complex system of courts, on the basis of separate lower courts for nobles, townspeople and state peasants, and higher courts of appeal.[40] Serfs remained outside the system. One of the aims was to galvanize the nobles into taking established elected posts, for example as assessors and judges in courts, on the grounds that the nobles should fulfil a public role above and beyond policing their own serfs. In the view of Jacob Sievers, the governor of Novgorod, the nobles had been 'loafing around since 1762' and had 'lost interest in the common good'.[41] Boards of Public Welfare, with elected representation from the free estates, were set up in each province to found and run schools, hospitals, foundling homes, almshouses, mental asylums, homes for incurables, workhouses and houses of correction. The Provincial reform was backed up by the 1782 Police Statute, which contained more detailed legislation for running towns. The Statute regulated not only law and order, but also the maintenance of streets and buildings, waste disposal, lighting, fire fighting, beggars and religious dissidents, public decorum and good behaviour in church.[42]

Both the Police and the Provincial statutes reflected a trend towards decentralization in Russian government, with more powers vested in local courts and boards, but always under the supervision of governors, who were responsible directly to the Empress. Both the number and quality of officials improved and in some places, especially St Petersburg and Moscow, local boards did good work in establishing hospitals and welfare organizations. The basic structures remained until Alexander II's local government reform of 1864.

Despite the shock of the Pugachev revolt and new pressures on reluctant nobles, most historians consider that the semi-mythical 'golden age' of the Russian nobility reached its apogee in Catherine II's reign. All Soviet and many Western historians constantly emphasized that the nobles lived at the expense of the peasants, while conceding that the foundations of Russia's great nineteenth-century literary and artistic culture were laid precisely in this landowning milieu.

When Catherine came to the throne she was faced with the reality of a nobility no longer liable for state service but whose services she required. She was forced to devise a revised relationship between monarch and nobles, not just for the purposes of safeguarding her own position and the security of the house of Romanov, but also from a sincerely felt desire to improve the nobles' legal status and thereby to encourage public-spiritedness and enterprise. In 1785 she issued her Charter to the Nobility, which confirmed that the Russian nobility 'shall enjoy freedom and liberty in future generations for all time in perpetuity'.[43] If the old historiography regarded the Charter as yet more perks for the already privileged at the expense of the 'have-nots', revisionist historians see it as a first step towards civil rights, a modernizing rather than a conservative measure. The Charter codified existing laws and manifestos, as part of an overall vision of a well-regulated society in which each social category knew its place. It confirmed the nobles' freedom from compulsory service, taxes and corporal punishment. Nobles must not suffer deprivation of their titles or property without trial by their fellow nobles. They had the right to enter the service of friendly foreign powers; to purchase villages and to exploit their lands through the sale of products, mining and industry, but the document said nothing explicit about their powers over their serfs. Importantly, it recognized the nobles' inalienable right to their property. Even if a man was convicted of a serious crime, his estate passed to his heirs.

However, the Charter still defined the nobility in subservient terms with reference to 'service, fidelity, zeal and industry', enjoining them to respond to the government's summons, 'sparing neither effort nor life itself in service of the State'. Nobles who had not served were barred from holding office and voting in local elections. All other nobles had a duty to participate in provincial and district Noble Assemblies and to elect representatives to local courts and boards. There was no hint of an institutional presence in central government or any share of political power. Autocracy remained unadulterated.

Most nobles continued to do a stint in the military, retiring to their estates after they had done their duty for a decade or so. The manor house became the scene of literary and cultural pursuits. Enterprising nobles also developed the commercial potential of their estates and a few even tried to improve the lot of their serfs. The developments of the 1760s–80s were important for the Russian nobles' self-image and self-confidence. If the first half of the eighteenth century was about painfully reinventing themselves as Europeans following orders from on high, the second half saw them asserting some sort of personal and national identity rather than just aping Western ways and being cogs in the wheels of state. An elite section was poised to break away from its dependency on the court and its loyal relationship with the House of Romanov, with important consequences for Catherine's successors.

These were developments for the future. Russia did not yet have a civil society grounded in the urban middle classes and in this sense lacked 'civilization', notwithstanding its aristocratic cultural oases. The urban population as a proportion of the whole remained no more than 4 per cent even by the 1790s, which continued to mark Russia out sharply from more urbanized countries further west. Most Russian towns were big villages, and Catherine's challenge was to expand them with the 'right sort of people' to create corporate pride and a prosperous entrepreneur class from the available human resources. In 1785 she issued her Charter to the Towns, published on the same day as the nobles' Charter and modelled on it.[44] The Charter set up town councils (dumy) comprising representatives of each of six hierarchical categories, which in turn elected a six-man executive and a mayor. However, the alien character of some of the provisions limited their effectiveness. Restrictions on movement between towns meant that townspeople continued to be 'attached' to their towns rather as the peasants were attached to their land and communes.

Catherine's biggest challenge was posed by the 90 per cent of the population comprising the peasantry (half of them serfs in bondage to a private lord, the remainder owned by the imperial family or administered by the state), whose very existence seemed to undermine the Romanovs' efforts to 'civilize' and educate their subjects, not least in the eyes of foreigners. 'The peasants in Russia [...] are in a state of abject slavery; and are reckoned the property of the nobles to whom they belong, as much as their dogs and horses', wrote the Scot, William Richardson.[45] In 1766 the Free Economic Society for the Encouragement of Agriculture and Good Husbandry, founded by Catherine herself, launched a prize essay competition on the topic: 'Which is more beneficial to society, that the peasant should own land as property or only moveable property, and how far should his rights to this or that property be widened?'[46] The winner argued for peasants with land. Other entries were more radical. 'We sell our fellow-men like pieces of wood and pity our cattle more than our people', wrote an entrant. Most conceded, however, that only abuses of the system, not the system itself, should be tackled, a principle that early on Catherine acknowledged. As in other areas, she was ahead of Russian educated opinion, a fact which was brought home when she was preparing her *Nakaz*, and counsellors advised her to tone down pronouncements on limiting serfdom. The published *Nakaz* said almost nothing about the peasantry, apart from the observation that governments should refrain from reducing people to slavery except in the case of utmost necessity and that mass enserfment was to be avoided (articles 253 and 260). Catherine believed that serfdom must and would disappear. However, this did not mean that the people were ready for freedom or that their owners were economically or psychologically prepared for emancipation. The politically expedient decision to safeguard the landowning rights of the nobles made it impossible to free peasants with land unless the masters voluntarily gave some up. Catherine sought to mitigate the 'peasant problem' with bans on the enserfment of orphans and illegitimate children in state homes, prisoners of war and state peasants assigned to factories. A law of 1775 forbade the re-enserfment of freed serfs. However, a proposal to emancipate children born to serfs after 1785 proved far too radical. Catherine has been accused of turning as many as 800,000 free peasants into serfs. In fact, most of her grants came from crown lands or from lands already farmed by serfs in partitioned Poland, the proportion of state peasants to serfs remaining more or less constant.

Ironically, it was the successes of Catherine's reign – when Russia experienced rapid territorial expansion, more authority in world affairs, relative political stability and economic prosperity – that prevented her from doing more for the peasants. Agriculture was the source of Russia's wealth. Peasant life was hard, but the population managed to feed and renew itself. There was no demographic crisis and the Pugachev revolt was to be the last great popular outbreak until 1917. In short, the serf economy was producing the goods, marginal though they often were. Serfdom was ended in 1861 only when it began to hamper Russia's status in world affairs, at which point, as we shall see, the Romanovs faced additional internal pressures.

Unable to do much with the social structure, Catherine and her circle devoted much time and effort to the built environment. 'The passion for building is a devilish thing', she wrote. 'It eats up money and the more one builds the more one wants to build. It is intoxicating.'[47] Her town squares and civic buildings still form the heart of many Russian towns. St Petersburg provided a blueprint for the empire, bringing Catherine's preferred Classicism, the style favoured by fellow rulers further west, to the provinces. From London to Berlin, architects based their designs on the conscious imitation of Greek and Roman originals, which were believed to reflect the essence of true art. Space and proportion, not ornament, were the watchwords. Buildings that reflected Romanov taste for the Classical include Potemkin's Tauride Palace in St Petersburg (1783–9, architect Ivan Starov). Inside there was a magnificent ballroom and winter gardens, but the facade was modestly plain, demonstrating 'antique elegance'. One of Catherine's favourite architects and designers was the Scot Charles Cameron (1746–1812), whose works included a gallery addition in the form of a Greek temple to the Catherine Palace at Tsarskoe Selo for the display of a collection of antique busts, and Pavlovsk, a Palladian summer residence built in 1782–6 for Grand Duke Paul, set in a picturesquely landscaped 'English' park dotted with Greek temples.

Catherine's old and new palaces contained impressive art collections, acquired not for personal vainglory but for national prestige, in an age when the visibility of the monarch was crucial. The tally of acquisitions includes approximately

Andrei Efimovich Martynov (1768–1826). 'View over the Great Lake and the Cameron Gallery, Tsarskoe Selo'. Image courtesy of Sotheby's.

4,000 Old Masters, 10,000 engraved gems, 10,000 drawings, 16,000 coins and medals and countless snuff boxes, watches, instruments, pieces of furniture and objects of porcelain. She bought 225 paintings from the Berlin collector Johann Gotzkowski after Frederick the Great could not afford to buy them. This was the collection of Sir Robert Walpole, which his heirs were forced to sell, the Pierre Crozat collection, which included eight Rembrandts, six Van Dycks, three Rubens and one Raphael, and the 944-piece Green Frog Service ordered from Josiah Wedgwood in 1773–4, which featured scenes of British stately homes, castles and parks.[48] The ability to buy lavishly was itself a sign of Russia's international power to the extent that the loss of the Walpole collection to Russia was associated with British decline. Such events showed that Russia had entered the 'fast lane' of culture:[49] foreigners should be overwhelmed, Russian nobles should be moved to emulate on a more modest scale.

Inside and outside the capitals, nobles adopted the new tastes emanating from the court. Gracious dwellings sprang up, often built of wood, but of a regular Classical design, typically a square house with two wings fronted by a columned portico. On the first floor a procession of rooms created spaces for entertaining. Landscaped gardens in the 'natural' English style were popular, with artificial lakes and waterfalls, pavilions and temples to Friendship, the Muses, the Graces and other ornaments to suggest historical, allegorical and philosophical themes. Many British landscape gardeners found work in Russia. The larger noble estates could, of course, function only thanks to armies of serfs, whose masters in some cases organized them into choirs, theatrical troops or horn bands. Examples of such estates survive at Kuskovo and Ostankino outside Moscow, both built by members of the Sheremetev clan, the wealthiest in Russia.

The arbiter of artistic output in Russia remained Elizabeth's Imperial Academy of the Three Fine Arts (architecture, sculpture and painting), which Catherine issued with an imperial charter in 1764, placing it directly under the sovereign's patronage. The curriculum was based on the French and German academic systems, which required the study of history and mythology and drawing from engravings, classical sculpture, Old Masters and life models. Successful graduates were sent abroad for further study. Few nobles contemplated a career in painting or sculpture, which continued to be regarded as high-grade trades; most academy students came from the 'middling' class. The most successful court artist was the Ukrainian Dmitry Levitsky (1735–1822), who painted the leading figures of his time, including several portraits of the empress herself. Among his best-known works are seven canvases (1770s) depicting students of the Smolny Institute for Noble Girls, commissioned by Catherine to celebrate her ideal of talented young womanhood. Other Russian artists, such as Fedor Rokotov (1735–1808) and Vladimir Borovikovsky (1735–1825),[50] worked alongside foreigners such as Vigilius Eriksen (famous for the painting of Catherine in guards uniform on her steed Brilliant), Giovanni Battista Lampi the Elder and Alexander Roslin, who tended to produce imperial portraits in the grand manner.

Wealthy nobles trained their own serf painters and architects, sometimes whole dynasties such as the Argunovs, serfs of the Sheremetevs. Ivan Argunov's painting *Unknown Woman in Russian Dress* (1784) suggests ambiguities of identity: it is unclear whether his subject is a peasant in her Sunday outfit or a young noblewoman wearing fancy dress. (Catherine herself promoted the wearing of loose-fitting 'Russian' dress at court.) Generally, however, contemporary life was sparsely reflected in art: buyers did not favour everyday Russian genre subjects and landscapes, preferring studies of Italian urchins and classical landscapes. The wealthier bought and commissioned foreign originals. Portraits and icons continued to provide the bread and butter for most home-grown artists.

Another area in which Catherine and the court sought to influence the elite was in literary tastes.[51] Russian readers still represented a tiny fraction of the population. One estimate puts male literacy in the empire in the 1790s at 3–7 per cent (compared with 47 per cent in France, 68 per cent in Britain and

After Vigilius Eriksen(1722–1782). 'Portrait of Catherine II'.
Image courtesy of Sotheby's.

80 per cent in Prussia). Published native authors represented an even tinier
proportion. At the beginning of Catherine's reign practically all the literature
published in Russian was imported from abroad, translations from the French
still accounting for one in four of all books published in the second half of the

eighteenth century. Translations (from the French) of novels by British writers also became popular, providing models for the first Russian novelists. Britain also provided inspiration for literary journals, of which 500 or so existed in the 1780s, most of them short-lived with subscriptions restricted overwhelmingly to nobles. In 1769 the first issue of *About This and That* appeared, containing anonymous articles by Catherine herself, sparking a debate about the nature of satire, whether it should be aimed at human vices in general, as Catherine believed, or against named individuals. Catherine would be the last Romanov to take a conspicuous lead in guiding her subjects' literary tastes. By the late eighteenth century a more independent literary public was forming. From 1783 private individuals were allowed to run printing presses. Talented Russian writers such as Gavrila Derzhavin (1743–1816) and Nikolai Karamzin (1766–1826) formed literary circles. Freemasonry, of which Catherine soundly disapproved and from which, as a woman, she was excluded, provided networks for men of letters and officials alike, independent of the court.[52]

There was plenty of music at court – Italian and French comic operas being especially popular – despite the fact that Catherine claimed to be tone deaf. As before, foreign composers and musicians predominated, but native talents such as D. S. Bortniansky (1751–1825) laid the foundations of the great Russian classical music of the nineteenth and twentieth centuries. Catherine's enthusiasm focused on the Imperial Theatre Department, whose repertoire of foreign and Russian plays included her own works such as *O Time!* (1772), a satire about meanness, gossip and superstition.[53] In 1783–6 the Hermitage theatre was built as an extension to the Winter Palace. Although foreign works dominated the repertoire, Russians could watch plays by Denis Fonvizin (1744–92), whose comedies of manners *The Brigadier* (1769) and *The Adolescent* (1783) poked fun at such trends as 'Gallomania', and comic operas on Russian themes by the likes of Yakov Kniazhnin and Alexander Ablesimov. The scores of these and other Russian operas were based on well-known Russian folk songs orchestrated in a classical idiom. Westernization did not eliminate popular culture from the lives of the Russian elite, for as long as Russian nobles were raised by peasant nannies and visited their country estates, they could hardly avoid the culture of the 'other Russia'.[54] Catherine herself had no Russian roots, but even she wrote a folk story, 'The Tale of Prince Khlor' (1781), for her grandson, Alexander. In the nineteenth century finding ways of getting even closer to the ordinary Russian folk (*narod*) would pose a major challenge to the last Romanovs, as the *narod* itself became subject to urbanization and a degree of Westernization that threatened to dislocate the traditional relationship between crown and people.

At the same time Catherine's empire had to accommodate more and more non-Russian, non-Orthodox peoples, particularly after the Second Turkish War

(1787–92) and the Second and Third Partitions of Poland (1793, 1795). In the early 1780s Russia leaned towards the anti-Turkish Greek Project, the brainchild of Grigory Potemkin, the goal of which was the creation of a new Russian Greek empire at Constantinople, with Catherine's second grandson Constantine on the throne.[55] In 1780 Catherine and Emperor Joseph II of Austria, who aspired to expand southward into the Balkans, made a secret alliance which allowed Russia to impose the outright annexation (1783) of Crimea. Prussia responded to the Austro-Russian alliance in 1785 by forming a league of German princes. Catherine still went ahead on a tour of her new territories in Joseph's company, visiting Crimea and Russia's new naval base at Sebastopol early in 1787, an act regarded as particularly provocative by the Turks. An allegorical painting by Ferdinand de Meys, much reproduced in prints, shows the empress holding a lighted torch progressing through her territories in a chariot as hovering goddesses place a victory wreath on her brow and hold attributes of enlightenment. Grateful new subjects strew her path with flowers and produce. Peter the Great looks down from heaven holding a globe, accompanied by Zeus. By August that year, Britain and Prussia were allies (in 1788 Britain declared war on Russia, then backed down) and in September the Turks, irritated at Russian attempts to interfere in Moldavia, Wallachia and Georgia, declared war on Russia, who also waged a short war against Sweden (1788–90).

In 1788–9 Russia captured territory in the Dnieper and Dniester regions down to the Black Sea. The Austrians took Belgrade in September 1789. Then in 1790 Joseph II died and his successor Leopold II pulled out of the war. The young sultan Selim III had no intention of conceding, however, and declared a Holy War. The Russian Black Sea fleet and armies pressed on, taking Izmail and other Ottoman fortresses on the lower Danube, under the legendary field commander Alexander Suvorov (1729/30–1800). Eventually Prussia persuaded Catherine to reduce Russia's demands to territory between the lower Dnieper and lower Dniester. The Treaty of Jassy (January 1792) confirmed the 1774 Treaty of Kuchuk Kainardji and Russia's possession of Crimea, Ochakov and an extension of its Black Sea coast.

In the meantime patriotic Poles were pressing for more independence. Catherine's policy had been to maintain King Stanisłas and the status quo and keep Russian troops in Poland, but in 1788 the Warsaw *sejm*, encouraged by a defensive treaty with Prussia, initiated a reform of the monarchy. The Constitution of May 1791 planned, with the king's backing, to replace Poland's elective monarchy with a hereditary one. It proposed, among other things, the disenfranchisement of landless nobles and the reduction of the privileges of the Catholic Church. A stronger monarchy did not look particularly revolutionary, but the reduction of noble privileges did, as did the abolition of the disruptive *liberum veto*, by which a single noble could block any measure in the *sejm*.

Catherine was alarmed by the spectre of a revived Poland with a real army, allied to Prussia, with reduced opportunities for Russia to interfere in Polish affairs. In 1792 she sponsored a confederation of dissident Polish magnates and dispatched almost 100,000 troops. The Russians and Prussians then cheated on their Polish allies and announced a new partition, whereby Russia obtained central Belarus and the eastern three-fifths of what had been Polish Ukraine, while Prussia got the western sections of ethnic Poland. Events in revolutionary France prompted further uprisings in Poland in 1794 under the leadership of Tadeusz Kosciuszko. A force under Suvorov quickly beat Kosciuszko's troops and ended the Warsaw resistance in October 1794 by massacring about 15,000 civilians. A third partition followed, with Austria and Russia limiting Prussian gains. Prussia and Austria shared the remainder of ethnic Poland and Russia obtained Lithuania, Courland and the remains of western Belarus and Ukraine. Poland vanished from the map. The powers vowed not to use the name again.

Catherine regarded the elimination of Poland as a blow against the 'disease' and 'madness' of the French Revolution. She and her allies had foiled a plot to spread a pernicious new doctrine throughout Poland and thereby destroy both its own peace and the peace of its neighbours forever. Others took a different view. In Britain, for example, caricatures appeared in the press featuring gruesome images of slaughtered Polish women and children, with Catherine herself as a bloody-handed butcher.

Imperial expansion was, it seems, the resounding success story of Catherine's reign and of the eighteenth-century Romanovs in general.

In 1719 the population was estimated at 15.5 million, in 1762, 23.2 million, in 1782, 28.4 million and by 1795, 37.2 million (41 million including the Polish provinces). Between 1750 and 1791 Russia acquired 8.6 million square miles of land. Imperial successes brought fresh permutations of the old challenge of how to cope with newly annexed populations of different races and faiths, in some cases hostile to their new masters, when the new masters also cherished deep-seated prejudices, especially against Muslims, Catholics and Jews. In Catherine's reign Russia did penetrate further west – to underline the claim that Russia was a European state – but at least half the empire lay outside Europe and the European sections were not all Russian. By the mid-1780s the proportion of ethnic Russians in the empire was less than 50 per cent, a figure which did not change much until the fall of the Soviet Union in the 1990s. Figures for the 1780s estimate about 18 million Russians, 7 million Ukrainians, 5 million Belarusians, 2 million Poles, half a million or more of Finns, Tatars, Latvians, Jews, Lithuanians and Estonians, smaller numbers of Chuvash, Moldavians, Germans, Swedes, Mordvinians, Bashkirs, Urdmuts, Karelians, Komi, Mari and others. Faiths apart from Orthodoxy included other Christians (Old Believers, Uniates, Catholics, Protestants of various denominations, dissidents such as flagellants and self-castrators), Muslims, Jews, Buddhists and pagans. The Russian empire now ruled all the Estonians, Latvians, Belarusians and most Lithuanians, up to a half of the world's Jews and about four-fifths of Ukrainians.

Catherine got to know her empire as best she could. She visited the Moscow region several times, went to the Baltic in 1764, the middle Volga in 1767, the post-Partition western provinces in 1780, Ukraine and Crimea in 1787. In 1767 she wrote to Voltaire from Kazan: 'Here I am in Asia. I wanted to see it for myself. There are in this city twenty different peoples, who bear absolutely no resemblance to each other. However, I have to make them a suit which will fit them all. It is not hard to find general principles, but what about the details?'[56] Catherine favoured as far as possible governing the multinational empire uniformly. Minorities, she believed, should 'by the gentlest means be brought to the point where they Russify'.[57] However, Russification on a major scale did not occur until the end of the nineteenth century. Local languages were used in schools and some local law codes remained in force. In the many Jewish communities acquired by Russia during the partitions, the councils known as *kahals* continued to perform a number of functions, and Jews could also elect members to new local bodies. However, opposition from local non-Jews ensured that a number of restrictions remained.[58]

The expansion of empire brought gains to the Russian economy. In particular, the fertile black-earth lands of New Russia, which gave much better yields than those in Russia proper, offered great potential for grain export, in combination with new ports such as Odessa, founded in 1795. But the cost of expansion was high. Overall, Russia's industrial capacity expanded in terms of quantity if not quality – in textiles for example – with the nation missing out on the technological developments of the early Industrial Revolution, spearheaded by Britain in the latter eighteenth century. The Russian economy continued to develop in the second half of the eighteenth century by expanding the potential of a serf-based economy under the direction of the central authorities. Growth rates were similar to those in England but from a different starting point, with profits remaining in agriculture rather than being reinvested in industry. Levels of prosperity across the regions varied greatly.

Russian expansion continued to arouse fears in Europe of a 'monstrous empire', centring on possible Russian influence in the Mediterranean via Constantinople. Prince Mikhail Shcherbatov's comment that 'the whole reign of this monarch has been marked by events relating to her love of glory'[59] is ambiguous in the eighteenth-century context, if not in the twenty-first, for adding to his or her country's prestige was regarded as a sovereign's true calling. The high costs of Catherine's foreign policy provoked some anti-expansionist sentiments at court, but opposition was not sustained. Paul, who disapproved of his mother's costly foreign policy, abandoned a campaign on the Caspian launched just before her death, but his successors revived the policy in the nineteenth century when imperial rivals played the 'Great Game' to win or maintain power and influence in Transcaucasia and Central Asia, a natural extension of Catherine's exploits.

In the 1790s events in revolutionary France were followed with varying degrees of dismay all over monarchist Europe. Catherine initially regarded the Revolution of 1789 as a sort of palace coup. French culture had become so well assimilated among the Russian elite that it was inconvenient to admit that there was a real problem. In 1792, when the republic was declared, Catherine was still speaking in fairly mild terms of 'the frivolous and flighty spirit and the inborn recklessness of the French nation'.[60] However, when Louis XVI was executed in January 1793, Catherine at once broke off relations with France in outrage at 'the killing of the sovereign anointed by God'. She forbade French ships entry to Russia or Russian nationals to take goods to French ports, and banned French newspapers and periodicals. French nationals who remained in Russia had to renounce 'seditious principles' on oath.

The French Revolution went against the whole ethos of Catherine's approach to government and she attached some of the blame to the *philosophes*. She wrote to Grimm in February 1794: 'And so you were right for never expressing the wish to be included among the luminaries, the illuminés, and the philosophes, since experience proves that all this leads to destruction; but whatever they have said and done, the world will never cease to need an authority.'[61] In fact, she had little reason to fear the spread of revolutionary ideas into Russia beyond the narrowest of circles. Their influence was to lie dormant until more than a quarter of a century after her death. Pockets of radical opposition were rare.

Soviet historians, faced with the task of charting the rise of the Russian intel-ligentsia, which would culminate in Lenin and the Bolsheviks, seized upon the beginnings of a split in the eighteenth century, when former servants of the state, 'emancipated' in 1762, turned into its critics. According to this scenario, greater distance from the establishment, more leisure to read and to travel abroad, and events in France and Poland, raised doubts and bred discontent. The nobleman and civil servant Alexander Radishchev (1749–1802), whose fictional travelogue *Journey from St Petersburg to Moscow* was published privately in 1790, was declared the most radical of Russia's aristocratic rebels. Barely known in 1790 – only thirty copies reached readers before the print run of 600 was confiscated – in Soviet Russia the *Journey* became the most famous single work of eighteenth-century Russian literature. It was most radical in its approach to the peasant question – on which Radishchev advocated emancipation – and condemnation of tyranny. For Catherine the purpose of the book was quite blatant. Its author was infected with 'French poison', in trying to break down respect for authority; he was 'maliciously inclined'.[62] As she famously wrote in the margin of her copy: 'He is a worse rebel than Pugachev'. Radishchev was sentenced to death, commuted to exile in Siberia. Broken by the experience, he committed suicide in 1802. A less radical nobleman whose ventures enraged the empress was Nikolai Novikov (1744–1818). Initially he won Catherine's approval by printing extracts from early Russian legislation, chronicles and memoirs, then survived an investigation in 1785 of a Masonic circle around Grand Duke Paul. When in 1790 a search of the publisher's premises revealed forbidden works, Novikov – a 'fanatic', in Catherine's view – was imprisoned in Schlüsselberg fortress.[63]

Radishchev and Novikov had no followers. By and large, Russia's small literate public shared a belief in a combination of autocracy and serfdom 'without cruelty'. Opposition, when it occurred, came mainly from conservatives who believed that Westernization had gone too far. Such men regarded themselves as true 'sons of the fatherland' with a duty to tell monarchs the truth. Catherine had no experience of the sort of public political life that existed in Britain and France. Russia had no political cartoons with rude captions portraying monarchs in undignified or obscene poses, no 'pamphlet wars', no electoral hustings. There was no Russian Hogarth or Gillray. It suffered not so much from censorship, of which there was little before 1793, as from low levels of urbanization and literacy, the absence of liberal professions and over-reliance on Romanov initiative and sponsorship from on high in everything from the first satirical journals to translations. In principle, Catherine encouraged public participation; in practice, she found it hard to handle. The paradox of her 'enlightened absolutism' was that cultivation of enlightenment and self-knowledge came from above, with the message to literate subjects not of 'know yourself' but 'know your place'. Maternalism on her part presupposed obedience rather than independent criticism on theirs, always with the danger that nagged children might turn against their parents.[64]

The last years of Catherine's life were a mixture of family happiness, provided by her numerous grandchildren, and grief caused by feuds with Paul and the death of Potemkin in 1791. 'Nothing will ever be the same', she wrote to Grimm. 'It is impossible to replace him since another person like him would first have to be born, but the end of this century somehow hardly presages any heroes.'[65] Many trusted advisers predeceased her, while the new blood at court was incarnated in Catherine's last lover, Platon Zubov, ambitious and unscrupulous. Catherine's mind was a sharp as ever, but her health was deteriorating and she may have felt that she was losing control over court politics. It must have been a great disappointment, for example, that her adored grandsons Alexander and Constantine seemed to enjoy the crude parade-ground atmosphere at their father's residence at Gatchina more than the cultured ambience of her own court. They even wore Paul's special Prussian uniforms which Catherine had outlawed in her presence.

On 2 November 1796 a maid found the empress collapsed in her water closet in the Winter Palace following a massive stroke. She was too heavy to lift into bed and died 36 hours later on 6 November, still on a mattress on the floor surrounded by weeping attendants, while in an adjoining room Grand Duke Paul was preparing his accession manifesto. Paul would do his utmost to undo his mother's work and to cast aspersions on her political legacy, but he was too aware of family honour and sensibilities to rake up scandals, much as he had disliked most of Catherine's lovers. Russians could not publish openly on such matters. Commentators abroad, however, unleashed a torrent of unfounded revelations of prodigious and perverse sexual activity. Subsequent writers were much influenced by Jean-Henri Castéra's *Life of Catherine II* (Paris, 1797), which alleged that Catherine 'contrived to blend the most daring ambition, that ever distinguished the male character, with the grossest sensuality that ever dishonoured the vilest of her sex'.[66] At home, those who knew her better cherished fonder and less sensational memories of what came to be a mythologized 'Catherinian age'. For many the 'gentler' era of Catherine would contrast favourably with the harsher regimes of her son and grandsons.[67] Her legacy would be a particular challenge for her military-minded, male Romanov successors who, with the exception of Alexander I who in his early years found it expedient to govern for a time in Catherine's 'spirit', had trouble identifying personally with a female ruler. It is hard to imagine Nicholas I wearing Catherine II's dressing gown for inspiration as he did Peter I's, for example.[68] For his 'Russophile' descendants, Alexander III and Nicholas II, the German Catherine was even harder to accommodate in the myths of the ruling house with its roots in the seventeenth-century 'Holy' tsars.

In both foreign and domestic policy, Peter the Great was Catherine's official inspiration – she often donned the uniform of the Preobrazhensky guards – even though she was never shy about exerting her independence in changed times or lauding her own achievements.[69] In the Peter-Paul Cathedral in August 1770, for example, Catherine laid naval trophies from Chesme at Peter's tomb. Archbishop Platon exhorted the Great Monarch to arise and look upon his handiwork; 'it has not decayed with time and its glory has not dimmed'.[70] In a poem recalling this event, Vasily Ruban wrote:

> Come Peter from the heavens, Look down on your city now
> And behold Catherine reigning there.
> She shares with you the fruit of her victories,
> Holding sacred your labours for the good of all.[71]

Falconet's 'Bronze Horseman' statue on St Petersburg's Senate Square, unveiled in 1782, bore the inscriptions in Russian and Latin 'To Peter I from Catherine II'.[72] She cultivated a number of Petrine virtues, such as getting up early, working hard and not wasting time. Unlike Peter, however, she never resorted to physical violence or practical jokes. Privately she deplored the crudity of his era. Her preference was to get people to do things by thinking it was their own idea. As she wrote to Jacob Sievers in 1776: 'You know better than anyone my repugnance for violence of all kinds. On every occasion I have preferred the paths of gentleness and moderation to extremes.'[73]

Catherine's style of rulership contained a strong element of showmanship. On the one hand, she cultivated 'simplicity', as reflected, for example, in her tastes in architecture or in the upbringing of her grandsons in an atmosphere of healthy pursuits and a plain diet. On the other, she appreciated that a monarch must dress for the occasion and be framed by impressive settings, for both subjects and foreigners had certain expectations of the imperial personage. Her favourite portraits of herself, by Roslin and Levitsky, showed her in sumptuous robes framed by Classical orders and symbols of imperial power; she was less fond of Borovikovsky's homely depiction of her with her dog in the garden at Tsarskoe Selo (1794), looking like a stout *Hausfrau*. Catherine was confident that Russians could prosper under an autocratic regime with all the trappings because she had confidence in her own ability to blend 'republican' virtues with firm rule from above, implemented with 'a good heart and good intentions', hard work and astute publicity. The short reign of her successor Paul was to show how few guarantees actually existed to prevent autocracy reverting to despotism under the wrong sort of ruler.

6

The Napoleonic Era: 1796–1825

PAUL I AND ALEXANDER I

> The Emperor Paul, leaving his palace one day, ordered a sergeant on guard duty to board his sled, saying 'Climb in, lieutenant.' The man protested, 'Sire, I am but a sergeant.' Paul replied, 'Climb in, captain.' Three days later the newly commissioned officer, by now a lieutenant colonel, caused the emperor some offense and found himself reduced to the ranks as suddenly as he had risen from them.[1]

One of Paul's first acts as his mother drew her last breaths was to search her private papers for a document disinheriting him. Either none was found, or, if a paper nominating Alexander did exist, he destroyed it. There was no challenge to the succession. In his accession manifesto Paul I proclaimed that he had ascended 'the throne of our forefathers, which we inherited',[2] with the emphasis firmly on fathers, not on nomination by his predecessor. Paul could hardly deny the biological fact of his maternal line, but he was determined to remind people of his paternity by according Peter III rites that he had been denied after his murder in 1762. On 9 November, three days after his mother's death, the new emperor issued an edict: 'On the occasion of the death of our beloved mother, … we have appointed a Commission of Mourning to organize the transfer of the corpse of our beloved father, Sovereign Emperor Peter Fedorovich of blessed memory, from the Holy Trinity Monastery of St Alexander Nevsky to the cathedral of SS Peter and Paul, and the burial of the body of Her Imperial Majesty in that same church.'[3] Peter III's remains were exhumed from their vault in the monastery, where assembled relatives were obliged to kiss them. On 25 November Paul enacted a posthumous coronation for the uncrowned monarch by placing a crown from his own head onto Peter's casket, which, to quote Wortman, 'symbolically and posthumously dethroned Empress Catherine', creating 'a symbolic fiction of continuity and hereditary right'.[4] On 2 December Peter's casket was brought to the Winter Palace to the sound of cannon fire in a solemn parade of army units, among whom walked Aleksei Orlov, the sole survivor of the conspirators of 1762, holding a crown over the coffin in an act of penance. The coffin was placed beside Catherine's catafalque for a joint lying in state, to which crowds were admitted 'without any regard to station, apart from badly dressed peasants'.[5]

A double funeral service was held on 6 December in the Peter-Paul cathedral.[6] There followed almost two weeks of vigils and requiem masses, after which on 18 December the coffins were lowered side by side into a double vault in front of the iconostasis, although at floor level separate sarcophagi mark the graves. Paul had done his duty by his father, oblivious to what might have been the reaction of his mother to reunion with her despised spouse in death.

Paul had comparatively little time for domestic reform in what turned out to be a brutally curtailed reign, apart from undoing as much of his mother's work as possible. As his son Alexander's wife Elizabeth wrote to her own mother early in 1797, she had been shocked by the emperor's lack of grief, 'as if it were his father who had just died and not his mother, for he speaks only of the former, providing every room with his portrait and saying not a word of his mother, except to condemn and roundly abuse everything that was done in her day'.[7] In symbolic gestures Paul released thousands of Polish prisoners, personally receiving the rebel Tadeusz Kosciuszko, as well as freeing Radishchev and Novikov. His major assault, however, was on what he perceived as Catherine's concessions to the 'pampered' nobility, as ratified in her 1785 Charter. Compulsory state service was restored (ironic in view of the fact that it was Peter III, not Catherine, who freed the nobles in 1762), local noble representation was reduced, corporal punishment and confiscation of property were sanctioned.

Paul seems to have had a passion for regulation for its own sake, producing five times more legislation per month than even Peter I, and issuing an astonishing 48,000 separate orders in 1797 alone.[8] Among the more memorable was a decree of April 1797 specifying that peasants should not work more than three days per week on their lords' land and that Sunday be a day of rest, a gesture interpreted more as a warning to the nobles than a kindness to the serfs. Paul offset these measures somewhat by restricting outsiders from becoming nobles, making lavish rewards to individual favourites and firmly maintaining serf-owning privileges, all underpinned by the general ethos that he was 'improving' the nobility, making it less 'soft' than in Catherine's day. Few perceived any benefits, however. Individuals felt vulnerable, liable to be exiled or arrested at any moment for some minor infringement of new rules. Those nobles who could took refuge on their estates, where they were able to cultivate a more independent salon society away from Paul's uncongenial court without abandoning the voluntary service ethic encouraged by the 1762 Manifesto and 1785 Charter.

Paul was also addicted to pomp and ritual, which required the compliance of his noble retinue. In spring 1797 he travelled to Moscow for his coronation in the Dormition Cathedral, the tremendous significance of which was enhanced by its coincidence with Holy Week. The royal party entered the city of Moscow, often associated with Jerusalem in early Russian texts, on Palm Sunday. On the eve the whole family took communion in the Kremlin Miracles Monastery and on Sunday 5 April 1797, Easter Day, Paul was crowned. This was very much a family affair; never before had the Romanovs lined up so visibly in such strength. A painting by the Moravian artist Martin Ferdinand Quadel (1736–1808) shows Paul crowning Maria Fedorovna while the rest of the family gather around, Alexander and Constantine twin-like in their glittering uniforms and orders, accompanied by emblematic knights in armour and plumes.[9] Paul energetically commissioned images of his impressive extended family, with its rich promise for the dynasty's future, its network of diplomatic marriages and implied collective responsibility for Russia's well-being. A painting by Vasily Istomin (1801), for example, shows the transfer of the Mother of God of Tikhvin icon from the Church of the Nativity to the Dormition Cathedral in Tikhvin on 9 June 1798, with the whole family escorting the miracle-working image. That the saint had been a patron of the royal family since the time of Ivan the Terrible underlined the clan's historical Russian roots.

Paul was hardly consistent in his promotion of the Romanovs' Russian identity, however. Some of the trappings of the coronation were distinctly Prussian, for example the Gatchina troops in their German uniforms brought to Moscow for the occasion. Paul rode to the cathedral on horseback and even wore a sword at the altar, 'like a general taking command of his armies'.[10] But Orthodoxy remained at the centre of the proceedings. For example, Paul dismounted and prayed at the chapel of the Iberian Mother of God at the entrance to Red Square.[11] As Wortman and others have underlined, Paul believed that he had a special religious mission, which extended to being head of the Church and even officiating at services in priestly garments, a claim that alarmed the higher clergy. He particularly enjoyed Orthodox ceremonies that incorporated a military element, assiduously attending the annual blessing of the 'Jordan' outside the Winter Palace at Epiphany.[12] A 'fusion of commander and cleric' is how Wortman puts it.[13] Paul loved wearing a crown, sometimes even for informal occasions and military parades, although just as often he adopted a mix of plain 'Petrine' and 'Frederick the Great' style. Portraits of short, pug-nosed Paul often give him a slightly comical caricatured look, as though the crown is too big or about to tip over. The commander who never led his troops into battle assumes an over-confident and bombastic pose, which artists were happy to accommodate.[14]

On the day of his coronation Paul issued several new fundamental laws concerning the imperial family. The longest, comprising 208 clauses, dealt with the hitherto neglected topic of the family's establishment and upkeep. Both the detail and the opening statement stressed Paul's almost obsessive commitment to this piece of legislation: 'Among the essentials for the thriving condition of any State, that contributes to all the other advantages and benefits comprising its basis, is the increase of the sovereign's family, for which the firm establishment of uninterrupted, continuous rules for the succession to the Throne must be a prime

Stepan Semionovich Shchukin (1762–1828)'Portrait of Paul I
(1796–1801)'. Dated 1797. Image courtesy of Sotheby's.

consideration.'[15] Russia had already enjoyed the blessing of seeing the throne pass to Paul, but he deemed it vital to secure proper provisions for the upkeep of his large and growing family by setting up a Department of Appanages (*udely*, estates), to provide independently of the state establishment, with incomes set out according to the order of succession and blood relationships. There were also clauses on inherited and purchased estates; salaries and maintenance; administration, agricultural economy and the monitoring of imperial estates; titles, arms and liveries. The heir to the throne (*naslednik*) bore the unique title Tsesarevich and was addressed as Imperial Highness (*Imperatorskoe Vysochestvo*) and Grand Duke (*velikii kniaz'*).[16] The last two titles applied also to younger sons and daughters (*velikaia kniazhnia*, Grand Duchess), grandsons and great-grandsons, granddaughters and great-granddaughters of the emperor, who also had the right to use the imperial coat of arms. Thereafter male descendants reverted to Highness and prince of the imperial blood, while women went by their father's or husband's titles.[17]

A manifesto on Orders of State was issued on the same day, giving a brief history of the Russian imperial orders, to which imperial offspring now had a right by descent. When they came of age (at twenty or upon marriage) all grand dukes were entitled to wear the orders of St Andrew, Alexander Nevsky and Anna (founded by Peter III in honour of his mother), and all grand duchesses the order of St Catherine. The ceremonial days when full medals were worn were 30 November (Andrew), 24 November (Catherine), 30 August (Alexander) and 3 February (Anna), with a general order day dedicated to the Archangel Michael (a favourite saint of Paul's) on 8 November.[18] Peter I's notion of the receipt of orders being linked to tangible service and/or imperial favour was weakened, even though assiduous service was still regarded as the duty of grand dukes in recognition of their new security of status.

The third edict was the Manifesto on the Succession, which Paul read out after taking communion, then placed at the altar in a silver receptacle. It set out the presumed order of descent from Alexander and his male successors according to male primogeniture, based on German statutes. In the event of the disappearance of the male line, the succession would revert to a male of the female line, since to 'avoid complications of the transfer from one dynasty to another (*iz roda v rod*), a male person is to be preferred to a female'. However, in the last resort, a female ruler of the blood was to be preferred to an outsider; her husband was not eligible to become sovereign. This act would ensure 'that the State is never without an Heir. That the Heir is appointed always according to the law. That there is not the slightest doubt who should succeed. To preserve the right of the dynasty to the succession without flouting natural law and to avoid complications in transfer from one dynasty to another [...] We desire that this Act should bear witness to all the World of our most profound love for our Fatherland, the love

and harmony of our marriage and the love for our Children and Descendants.'
It was signed Paul and Maria.[19]

The Romanov family became the basis and guarantor of Russia's security
and prosperity as it had never been in the eighteenth century, when in theory
any outsider could rule. The new laws set it apart from the rest of society. Russia
was the hereditary property of the dynasty. Its pecking order, finances and titles
were all carefully defined in law, to the extent that it was 'little more than another
instance in the military-governmental hierarchy'.[20] At the same time, right of
succession demanded high moral standards. Illegitimacy, morganatic ('unequal')
marriage and deviation from the Orthodox faith precluded candidates and their
line from the throne.

The right marriage – nearly always to a royal foreign Protestant, who if female
converted to Orthodoxy – remained vital. Russian nobles, still less 'commoners',
could not make their fortunes by marrying into the imperial line, although such
marriages, including marriages within the clan, became more common later in
the nineteenth century as junior branches of the Romanov family proliferated.
After Paul's death the family extended its roots and branches into European royal
houses to such an extent that only real enthusiasts try to unravel beyond one
or two generations the complicated permutations of dynastic alliances, which
for the purposes of our Russia-focused narrative will generally have to remain
unexplored, especially in relation to the marriages of Russian grand duchesses.

The marital history of the Pavlovichi and Pavlovny is, however, worth a brief
examination as it has a bearing beyond private concerns. Alexander, as we saw,
was married in 1793 to Louisa Maria Augusta of Baden (Elizabeth), Constantine
in 1796 to Juliana of Saxe-Coburg, an aunt of Queen Victoria.[21] The latter were
separated and divorced, childless, in 1820, after which Constantine contracted a
morganatic marriage that would make a significant impact on dynastic history.
An act of 1820 precluded the dynastic rights of any children from the union.[22]

In October 1799 at Gatchina Paul and Maria celebrated the weddings of
their daughters Grand Duchesses Elena to Frederick Ludwig of Mecklenburg-
Schwerin, and Alexandra to Archduke Joseph, son of the emperor of Austria, with
an impressive royal guest list from all over Europe.[23] Maria Fedorovna, if not
Paul, lived to see the rest of her children married. Maria Pavlovna married Karl
Frederick of Saxony-Weimar-Eisnacht in 1804. Ekaterina, the close confidante
of Alexander I, described as 'one of the brightest stars of the early nineteenth-
century Russian court' was married twice, in 1809 to Prince George of the Danish
house of Oldenburg, who was a nephew of Empress Maria Fedorovna (this was
after rejecting a proposal from Napoleon), and in 1816 to King Wilhelm I of
Württemberg, who was also related to Maria.[24] In 1816 the youngest daughter,
Anna, married William II of Orange-Nassau, king of the Netherlands from 1840,
having, like her elder sister, been the object of Napoleon's attentions. (Empress

Maria refused to give her charming girl to a 'Corsican cannibal' and sent the polite excuse that Anna was still too young to wed.[25]) The future Emperor Nicholas I married Fredericke Louisa (in Orthodoxy Alexandra Fedorovna), the daughter of the king of Prussia, in 1817. Finally, in 1824 the baby of the family, Michael, married the highly educated and accomplished Fredericke Charlotte, daughter of Prince Paul-Karl of Württemberg, another relative of Maria Fedorovna. Elena Pavlovna, as she was known after conversion, was a model grand duchess, more popular than her somewhat pedantic and parade-loving husband. The couple's residence in the Michael Palace (the present building of the State Russian Museum) became a haven for poets, artists, musicians and scientists. Elena's largesse extended to founding and sponsoring schools and institutes for girls, hospitals and refuges. During the Crimean War she formed the first Russian organization of military nurses, the Society of Sisters for the Care of the Sick and Wounded dedicated to the Exaltation of the Cross. The Elena Clinical Institute in St Petersburg opened after her death. As a staunch opponent of serfdom, she was also one of several Romanovs who ventured into the realm of politics.[26]

Scratching beneath the surface of many of the unions listed above one would find marital infidelity, sometimes tolerated or even welcomed as integral to the smooth running of arranged marriages, sometimes deeply resented. Paul's by and large happy relationship with Maria Fedorovna was no exception.[27] The most enduring of his affairs (according to some, a platonic relationship) was with Ekaterina Nelidova (1758–1839), a lady-in-waiting to the empress, whose elegant image was captured on canvas by Dmitry Levitsky when she was studying at the Smolny Institute in the 1770s. Nelidova's successor, Anna Lopukhina (1777–1805), arrived on the scene after doctors advised Paul and Maria to curtail marital relations following the difficult birth of Michael in 1798. Anna, sixteen at the outset of the affair, was set up in her own mansion next door to the residence that her sister shared with her husband, Paul's valet Ivan Kutaisov, which was next door to the house of Kutaisov's mistress.[28] Later she moved into the palace. Lopukhina's influence over the emperor was significant – she was the only woman on whom he conferred the Maltese order – and brought about a cooling of family relations.[29]

For her part, Empress Maria Fedorovna was not only the matriarch of the nineteenth-century Romanovs, whose fecundity assured the dynasty's survival. She was also the first of the patroness empress-consorts, a role model for those who came after. She presided over the building and furnishing of palaces and the laying out of gardens, which was a particular passion of hers.[30] She was a talented artist in her own right, working portraits in intaglio. In particular, the palace at Pavlovsk demonstrates her taste, with its elegant classical interiors and gardens with allegorical pavilions and furnishings and rich collections of applied art acquired abroad. After Paul's death, as dowager empress Maria continued to enjoy precedence at court, much to the chagrin of Alexander I's wife Elizabeth. The 'soft' nature of her youth matured into something rather more unyielding.

Despite Maria's love of family life in elegant domestic interiors, the main setting for Paul's reign was the masculine milieu of the parade ground, which set the tone of each day with the *Wachtparade* or morning reveille. Military discipline became 'a principle of governmental organisation to be applied ruthlessly and literally throughout the state apparatus'.[31] These principles reached their height in the 'Gatchina' system. On the estate troops were drilled under the tuition of the martinet Prussian Baron von Steinwehr, a stickler for strict discipline and brutal punishments. Like a drill sergeant in front of his troops Paul tried to be all-seeing, and at the same time the focus of all attention whether on parade or off duty, which made for an uncomfortable atmosphere at court and increasing alienation even from the few men and women who professed to be his friends. The laid-back attitudes of Catherine's day in which little attention was paid to strict details of uniform and drill were quickly banished by the issue of endless rules and regulations about everything from the shape of hats to the thickness of moustaches, much of it governed by Paul's distaste for 'French' degeneracy.[32] Attacks with shears on people's clothing in the streets recalled Peter I's assaults on traditional caftans and beards, but now anything reminiscent of French as opposed to Russian dress, including associated vocabulary (*gilet, pantalon*), was suspect. Paul banned certain books, music and foreign travel, much as Catherine had done after 1793 in her understandable response to the French Terror, but the need for such sanctions now seemed unconvincing, as did the introduction of a host of niceties of etiquette that victimized nobles who under Catherine were beginning to enjoy some degree of security. Demands such as the one that ladies curtsy to the emperor in the street and thus drag their clothes in the mud seemed demeaning. For men, the wrong belt buckle or a step out of place would result in a humiliating beating or banishment.

A number of anecdotes illustrating Paul's arbitrariness and his disrespect for social hierarchies survive in the literature: 'In Russia only the man with whom I am speaking is important and only while I am speaking with him' (attributed to the Swedish ambassador); 'This clothing is pleasing to God and good enough for you' (in response to protests against Prussian-style uniforms); the command 'Quick march to Siberia!' allegedly issued to a regiment that made errors during a drill parade.[33] For those foreign observers who expected Russia to revert to its 'barbaric' and isolationist roots, such incidents simply confirmed their prejudices about the master-slave relationship between ruler and people that they took to be the Russian norm. Paul was just a 'typical' Russian despot.

The Russian nobility found certain of Paul's idiosyncrasies hard to fathom. Especially baffling was his sponsorship of the Catholic Order of the Knights of St John of Malta, already an 'anachronism' by the time Paul took up their cause.[34] Paul had been inspired by the knights' history as a youth and by the existence of a priory in post-partition Poland awaiting his protection. In November 1797 he oversaw a convention of the Order in St Petersburg in which Alexander and Constantine were knighted and the empress received the Order's grand cross.[35] In June 1798 Napoleon occupied Malta, which prompted Paul to accuse the current grand master of cowardice and treachery for surrendering and to accept the invitation to become grand master himself, expressing his determination to carry on opposition to Napoleon and also to strengthen the Order with the inclusion of Russian knights. He duly opened a priory for almost 100 Russians.

The Russian artist Vasily Borovikovsky's painting of Paul in his grand master's attire (1800) captured the emperor's pride in his new, bright red and gilt trappings. Some observers regarded the complex regalia and high-blown sentiments about mediaeval knights as merely comical, rooted in a vision of chivalrous orders that had never existed in Russia; others as threatening diplomacy with 'delusions of grandeur'. The relationship between an Orthodox monarch and a Catholic order sponsored by the Pope naturally raised eyebrows, but for Paul this did not constitute a barrier – he saw himself as the Order's saviour, who would restore its former glory, just as he aspired to return Russia to some sort of mythical golden age.

Napoleon's rise to power had a decisive influence on Paul's regime. Despite his antipathy towards the French and Napoleon's republicanism, Paul initially abandoned the anti-French coalition that his mother had entered, but in December 1798, after Napoleon moved into Egypt and seized Malta, he joined the Second Coalition against France with Austria, Britain, Naples and Turkey. The veteran General Alexander Suvorov was recalled to lead an Austro-Russian army to operate in Italy. After brilliant successes in Lombardy, when Russian troops entered Milan and Turin, Suvorov was forced to evacuate his army across the Alps to save it from destruction. The perception that Paul treated Suvorov with disrespect when he returned to Russia, dying a few months later, alienated many veterans of the Italian campaign. Admiral Fedor Ushakov's occupation of the Ionian Islands off Greece was another success in a campaign which brought Russian troops to parts of Europe where they had never ventured before, successes which Paul was unable to exploit.

In 1800 Paul suddenly broke off with Austria and Britain, withdrawing from the Second Coalition and declaring friendship with Napoleon, who felt inclined to offer Malta to his new friend. But the capture of the island by the British in September precipitated a final, disastrous turn in Paul's foreign policy, at least as regards his own security. The Russian elite's dislike of Paul was now exacerbated by the perceived danger that his erratic policies and behaviour posed to the

Fatherland. The perception that the emperor was 'literally not in his senses' was shared by foreign observers, too,[36] in particular as evidenced by a rash scheme to send Russian troops to challenge the British in India, which aroused fears of a British attack on St Petersburg in retaliation. General Orlov's army of 22,500 Cossacks had reached Orenburg en route for India when Paul's death was announced in March 1801.

Paul brought a growing sense of isolation and vulnerability right into the city centre with his project for the new Michael Fortress (Mikhailovsky Zamok), where he and his family moved on 1 February 1801 after the new building was completed at breakneck speed. This castle-like structure, designed by Vasily Bazhenov (died 1799) and Vincenzo Brenna (the nature of their respective contributions continues to excite controversy), was furnished with a moat, five drawbridges, inner courtyard/parade ground, and cannons, with the added protection of a chapel dedicated to the fiery Archangel Michael, one of the patrons of the house of Romanov. It was Michael, according to legend, who advised Paul to build his new residence on the site of his aunt Elizabeth's wooden summer palace, where Paul himself had been born.[37] Outside, the walls were painted red, the colour of the robes of the Maltese order. Inside, the formal rooms were decorated in the latest Neo-Classical style favoured by the empress: light airy plasterwork, fine sculpture (including a copy of a famous statue of Laocoön and his sons), pictures and murals by the likes of Jacob Mettenleiter, Giovanni Battieste Scotti and Guiseppe Valeriani. Some halls had emblematic programmes, for example on the subject of virtue and power in Ancient Rome and scenes from Russian history, including Grigory Ugriumov's *Election of Tsar Michael*, a rare reminder of early Romanov history. The Marble Gallery and adjoining circular throne room were designated by Paul for assemblies of the Maltese order. Paul's private apartments also reflected his enthusiasms: in the bedroom hung a portrait of Frederick II and prints of guards uniforms. The empress, his sons Alexander and Constantine and their wives also has their own suites of rooms; everyone could be safely locked in.

Private demons motivated Paul to set up in front of the palace an equestrian statue of Peter I as a counterpoint to Falconet's 1782 monument, which was a target of Paul's apparently undiminished acrimony against his mother. Falconet's statue disturbed Paul not by its design or imagery, on which he made no comment, but by the inscription 'To Peter I from Catherine II', with which Catherine laid claim to her 'spiritual' descent from Peter. Paul could hardly remove Falconet's monument, which would have appeared like a gesture against Peter, but he did make his point by retrieving Carlo Rastrelli's statue (made in the 1720s, eventually cast in 1747) from the shed where it had languished since Empress Elizabeth's time. A new inscription echoed his mother's to Peter: 'To the great grandfather from the grandson'.

The year 1800 on the monument's plaque was significant. Peter I had 'begun' the eighteenth century and now his descendant was making a triumphal entry into the nineteenth. A biblical inscription in Slavonic on the façade read: 'Holiness becometh thine house, O Lord, for ever' (Psalm 93.5).[38] In fact, Paul only lived in his house for a mere 38 days into the new century before his reign was cut short by assassination. The initiators of a plot to remove Paul as early as 1799 were Count Nikita Petrovich Panin and Admiral Ribas. In 1800, however, Panin had been banished to one of his estates and Ribas was gravely ill. Others took their place, but they were reluctant to act without Grand Duke Alexander's backing. This was obtained in March 1801, when Alexander finally agreed to a plan that Paul be 'restrained' and a Regency established. (The example of George III in England came to mind.) The ringleader on the day was Count Peter Ludwig von Pahlen, who had won Paul's confidence to become governor-general of St Petersburg, as well as director of the postal service and the Foreign Office. His wife was head of the empress's household. In other words, conspiracy penetrated to the very heart of Paul's government and household. Pahlen depended on the support of the powerful Zubov brothers, Platon, Nikolai and Valerian, who recruited their associates. They were joined by the German-born General Leo Bennigsen. An analysis of 68 members of the conspiracy shows them to be 'a homogenous group drawn from the highest layer of Russian society' – the guards, Senate and government offices, with links with each other and Alexander, but not reflecting anything like 'public' opinion of Paul. In other words, they were men who had suffered directly at Paul's hands or feared that they might do so in future.[39] In view of the turn in foreign policy, the British, too, had an interest in Paul's removal (ambassador Lord Whitworth had discussions with some of the conspirators before he was recalled to London), although it is difficult to pinpoint the British contribution. Significantly, both the commanders of the Preobrazhensky and Semenovsky guards were in the plot, as was Paul's trusted aide-de-camp Peter Argamakov, who helped to gain access to the castle on the fateful night. Paul picked up rumours of a conspiracy but was partly reassured by Pahlen's assurances that all was secure.

On 11 March 1801 conspirators broke into Paul's bedchamber to place him under arrest.[40] The emperor, who earlier had enjoyed a good dinner with family and friends, hid behind a fire screen and at first only his feet were visible. 'What have I done to you?' Paul asked. The answer came: 'You have tortured us for four years!' (This according to Bennigsen's memoir.)[41] Moments later 47-year-old Paul was dead, officially of 'an apoplectic stroke' inflicted by Divine Providence. Paul, it seems, began to argue (the details remain unclear), there was a scuffle, one of the panicking conspirators (probably Nikolai Zubov) struck him over the head with a heavy snuffbox, he fell and conspirators piled on top of him. The guilt was collective: no one admitted to the fatal blow, which may have been caused by strangulation. They woke Alexander and told him he was emperor. The distressed Alexander expressed his abhorrence of ruling under such circumstances, but Pahlen chided him, 'Stop being a child. Go and reign. Show your face to the Guards. The welfare of millions of people depends upon your resolve'.[42] Alexander accepted the oath of allegiance from those present. Empress Elizabeth later wrote: 'His sensitive soul will remain tortured by it forever.'[43]

The assassins were dismissed from service but did not stand trial because, officially, no crime had been committed. Murder was not mentioned in official sources for years to come. Many offerings for the 1913 jubilee, for example, when numerous Romanov biographies were produced, referred laconically to Paul's 'sudden' (*skoropostizhnaia*) death, while hinting broadly at the grievances that caused his reign to be cut short.[44] None of Paul's descendants much wanted to live in the Michael Fortress, which became linked with urban tales of haunting and poltergeists. It was stripped of imperial valuables and later turned over to the School of Engineering (hence its later name the Engineers' Fortress), where, among others, the writer Dostoevsky studied. In the late 1990s it was opened to the public as a branch of the State Russian Museum with exhibitions in the state rooms and separate art displays.[45] At the time of writing Paul's bedchamber was not open for viewing.

Historians long maintained that the obsessive and inconsistent Paul was mentally unstable, a 'Tsar madman'. More recently, revisionists have searched for method in his apparent madness, arguing, for example, that Paul was motivated by deeply-held moral principles and a strong sense of duty and order. Even Gatchina showed better sides of his character, displaying his fine taste in paintings and sculpture and a magnificent library. He built churches, schools and a hospital there and presided over a benevolent regime for his 6,000 serfs. He had good reason, also, to cut back on his mother's expensive foreign policy and lavish court. The problem is that he did neither, embarking on his own costly campaigns and changing the style of the court rather than reducing expenditure. By alienating the elite he fell victim to the fact that under an autocratic regime that lacked representative higher institutions assassination was sometimes the public's only means of making its voice heard.

Alexander I was not in the bedchamber as Paul expired, but he had followed and at least tacitly sanctioned plans for his father's overthrow.[46] As early as September 1797 he had written to his former tutor La Harpe: 'When my father came to the throne, he wished to reform everything. The beginning of his reign was indeed bright enough, but its continuation has not fulfilled expectations. Everything has been turned upside down ... I think that if ever the time comes for me to reign, rather than go into voluntary exile myself, I had far better devote myself to the task of giving freedom to my country and thereby preventing her from becoming in the future a toy in a madman's hands.'[47] He went on to speak of translating useful books with his friends and when his turn came to find a way of 'representing the nation' by a 'free constitution', after which he could 'retire'. The message was mixed. On the one hand, Alexander offered the prospect of radical reform. On the other, he spoke of withdrawal from public life, a motif that would recur several times before and during his reign. No wonder that his personality, close relationships and episodes in his life, culminating in the rumours about the faking of his death in 1825, continue to excite speculation.

Alexander was dissatisfied with everything when he came to the throne, and just as his father had reacted to Catherine's regime so he, with greater justification, reacted against his father's. He had even suffered the anxiety in 1799 of seeing his father name his younger brother Constantine as second 'Tsesarevich', a title that the fundamental laws of 1797 had restricted to the eldest son and heir. Alexander had no reason to believe himself exempt from Paul's arbitrary ways.

It is highly significant that from his birth on 12 December 1777 Alexander was raised by his grandmother, who separated him from his parents on the understanding that she would do a better job of caring for him than they would. He was, in her eyes, the promise for the future of the house of Romanov and too precious to entrust to her unreliable son. (Ironically, when in 1801 Alexander pledged to rule 'according to the laws and heart of our late grandmother',[48] he also condemned himself to sharing her reputation among Soviet historians for 'hypocrisy' and adopting a 'mask' of liberalism and republicanism.) Alexander was a precocious pupil if we believe half the praise that Catherine heaped on him in her letters to Grimm and others. She provided modern tuition following the precepts of Rousseau, with due attention to diet and clothing (a one-piece suit for the toddler of Catherine's design survives) and a hands-on regime of play, which included writing fairy tales for Alexander and his brother Constantine, born April 1779, who was also separated from his parents at birth. The two boys were close in years and in the burden of expectations placed on them. Richard Brompton's double portrait of 1781 shows them in uniform with sword and spear against a backdrop of military standards and helmet, in imitation of their patrons Alexander Nevsky and Constantine the Great, to whom Catherine often alluded.[49] Military service and conquest would be their destiny, with a strong element of enthusiasm for the trappings of militaria. Politically speaking, Alexander inherited from Catherine a firm commitment to autocracy 'without cruelty'. His 'republicanism', like hers, acknowledged the sharp differences between countries of different sizes, histories and social structures.

In 1784 Alexander's tuition was entrusted to the Swiss Frédéric César de la Harpe, who initially worked with three Russian tutors and the French writer Frédéric Masson under the supervision of General N. I. Saltykov, to ensure that Alexander's education covered everything from the catechism and Russian grammar to how to use a plough and the culture of the Renaissance. From La Harpe he learned the latest ideas in philosophy, including those from revolutionary France. 'I am beholden to him for everything', Alexander said in 1811.[50] Under La Harpe Alexander extended his knowledge of arts and humanities and shone at conversations on history, politics, philosophy and literature in salons all over Europe. No previous Romanov was as well educated and informed as Alexander, but his education encouraged breadth of knowledge rather than depth. He learned to toy with ideas and use them for effect, a dangerous habit for a man who wielded real power.

There was no escaping dynastic duties, either. Alexander was just fifteen when in September 1793 Catherine married him off to Louisa Maria Augusta of Baden (1779–1826), who in Orthodoxy was known as Elizaveta Alekseevna (Elizabeth).[51] His parents were not consulted, but both were charmed by the prospective bride, one of five eligible sisters and a mere thirteen years old when she arrived in Russia; luckily, there was mutual attraction, as surviving notes between the pair attest.[52] 'Everyone said they were two angels pledging themselves to each other', Catherine enthused after the betrothal; it was, as she expressed it in another letter, the marriage of Cupid and Psyche.[53] Reports indicated that Elizabeth was 'one of the most beautiful women of her time'.[54] Allowing for marriage market hyperbole, numerous portraits by leading artists of the 1790s–1820s attest to her elegant profile, fine features and slender upright figure. One of the most evocative, painted by Marie Vigée-Lebrun in 1795 by order of Catherine II, shows Elizabeth wearing the order of St Catherine and jewels donated by the empress, her hair entwined in roses, plucking a bloom from a bowl of the same. A dour portrait bust of Alexander presides in the top left hand corner, reminding the spectator of the girl's status and loyalties.[55]

There were two children, both girls, Maria (1799–1800) and Elizabeth (1806–8).[56] Neither survived, much to their parents' grief. The marriage endured only on a formal basis after Alexander allegedly grew cold towards his wife and for a decade after the start of his reign the two lived separate lives, Alexander with his mistress Maria Antonovna Naryshkina (1779–1854), by whom he had three daughters. The first, born in 1804, lived only a few months, the second, Zinaida, died in 1810. The death of Sophia (1807–1824) from consumption was a particularly grievous blow, which Alexander, by then generally sunk in gloom, ascribed to his own sins. Unlike his father, Alexander never moved his mistress into the palace, but Naryshkina and their children were central factors in his life, even after he formally split with her in 1818, having been convinced of the sinfulness of the union at a time when his quest for spiritual perfection was at its most intense. Elizabeth's confidants were the Polish nobleman Adam Czartoryski and the cavalier guards officer Aleksei Yakovlevich Okhotnikov, who was stabbed to death under suspicious circumstances in 1807. He may have been the father of her second daughter.[57] Elizabeth continued to appear as empress consort at formal occasions and to support her husband, in the belief that only she truly understood him, and towards the end of their lives they drew closer together. Elizabeth's presentation as the grieving widow in numerous paintings and engravings of 1825–6 was genuine. 'Our angel is in heaven', she wrote to dowager Empress Maria Fedorovna on the day of Alexander's death. She outlived him by six months, dying on her return journey to St Petersburg in May 1826.

Probably the major influence in Alexander's life was his father, both in life and in death. Although Catherine dominated Alexander's boyhood, as a teenager he gravitated from the 'soft' atmosphere of her apartments towards Gatchina, where he relished the strict discipline and Spartan conditions. He loved parades, drill and uniforms, willingly donning the Prussian style that Catherine despised, although his own tastes were more refined. Father and son respected each other. However, Alexander had to tread cautiously between the warring mother and son, putting on an appropriate face at their respective courts. Rumours that came to light in 1794 of Catherine's intention to disinherit Paul in favour of Alexander, for example when Elizabeth produced a son, increased tensions, while Paul's fears about being disinherited were fanned by the growth of the brilliant 'young court' in St Petersburg and the popularity of the young couple. Alexander sought reconciliation with his father and was punctilious about attending manoeuvres at Gatchina. They found common ground in their disapproval of Catherine's policies towards Poland, which was deepened by Alexander's friendship with Prince Adam Czartoryski, whom Catherine invited to Russia in 1795. Alexander admired him as a man of the world and convinced liberal with whom he could share his own convictions. Other strong influences were the Gatchina commander Aleksei Arakcheev and the nobleman Viktor Kochubei.

It was to Kochubei that in May 1796 Alexander expressed his fears about the future: 'There is incredible confusion in our affairs. In such circumstances, is it possible for one man to rule the state, still less correct abuses within it? This is beyond the strength not only of someone endowed with ordinary abilities like myself, but even of a genius; and I have always held to the rule that it is better not to attempt something than to do it badly. My plan is to settle with my wife on the banks of the Rhine, where I shall live peacefully as a private person finding happiness in the company of friends and in the study of nature'.[58] Whether this indiscreet outburst was prompted by the awareness that his grandmother's days were numbered and that she had in mind to pass the throne to him or was simply a romantic fancy is hard to say. In September 1796 Catherine may indeed have raised with Alexander her wish that he succeed her, although both the content of papers that she passed to him and Alexander's response remain unclear. A few months later Catherine was dead.

After Catherine's death, as we have seen, Alexander had to endure his father's attempts to obliterate Catherine's memory and legacy, then his alienation from practically everyone in court circles. Despite all this, Alexander found his father's assassination – as opposed to his removal from power – hard to bear and awareness of the sin that he had committed continued to haunt him, especially when life became difficult. On his accession to the throne Alexander chose to focus not on his father's personal mistakes but on the state of Russia and the need for reform. His first measures included the restoration of civil rights, the release of nobles from exile, the abolition of the Secret Chancellery, the relaxation of censorship and bans on foreign travel, and reconfirmation of Catherine's Charter to the Nobility.[59] He allowed others to make explicit comparisons between his reign and Paul's, for example by obliterating the role of Paul (and his immediate predecessors) in promoting Russia's greatness by drawing a direct line of descent from Peter I through Catherine: '…soon the Almighty God gave Catherine's sceptre to Alexander', wrote I. M. Dolgoruky in 1802, while Alexander Radishchev imagined Peter and Catherine watching over Russia and the new century.[60] In the area of image, Alexander did not have to do much at all to benefit from the contrast between him and his father: Paul was small and ugly-looking, Alexander 'godlike' in his tall, blond, handsome appearance. If Paul was a demon, Alexander was an 'angel', a motif that was heavily exploited throughout his reign and beyond. (The angel on the Alexander Column, erected by Nicholas I in 1833, looking down from on high on Palace Square, has Alexander's features.) It was also an image that suggested remoteness, ambiguity and androgyny.[61]

At the same time, Paul's assassination provided informal guidelines about what not to do, especially with regard to the nobility whose Charter Paul had revoked. This was crucial, for Alexander sensed the dangerous drift among the elite away from court life to salon and estate settings and was aware of the need to retain or regain their loyalty. Alexander associated with the nobility: he was one of them. He appreciated and practised the refined tastes and behaviour of 'salon culture', he spoke French, read the same books. Whether this sympathy would go as far as allowing them a hitherto forbidden voice in government was a crucial question which Alexander was to some extent able to postpone as the demands of war pushed to the fore.

Thus began the so-called 'good half' of Alexander's reign, a concept to which historians have resorted to balance what came later during the 'bad' half, after 1814, when the 'promising young liberal' abandoned the ideals of his youth in favour of military discipline and religious obscurantism. During this good period, the story goes, Alexander benefited from the advice of the so-called Unofficial Committee or 'young friends' composed of Adam Czartoryski (1770–1861), Count V. P. Kochubei (1768–1834), N. N. Novosiltsev (1761–1836) and Count P. A. Stroganov (1772–1817). Their methods of operation were based on a cult of friendship and constrained by secrecy. As Stroganov wrote in his 'General Plan for the Work of the Emperor on Reform' (1802), 'reform must be entirely due to His Majesty and ... every measure must be taken so that nobody suspects that this work is in progress'. At the same time, the emperor had to be aware of 'public opinion', in other words of the views of educated, free citizens. Stroganov broached the subject of a constitution, which he believed had roots in the Charters, the main aim of which would be to end arbitrariness, especially in regard to property rights. The final paragraph referred cautiously without naming it to the emancipation of the peasantry, which must be done 'without shocks'.[62] Alexander was well known to favour at the very least a curb on the further spread of serfdom.

In the 'good half' of his reign, it has been argued, Alexander had every intention of granting Russia a constitution. However, what he understood by the term has been much debated, and one still feels inclined to agree with Marc Raeff that, despite consulting foreign examples, Alexander did not have in mind American or British precedents, still less representative institutions or limitations on autocracy. He saw no room for corporate or 'party' interests, no role for formally consulted public opinion. Alexander was tsar because he inherited the throne. He was 'very jealous of his autocratic power and prerogatives' and sought rather an 'orderly system of government and "mechanical harmony" based on the rule of law'.[63] It is no coincidence that the celebratory medals issued at his coronation in September 1801 has the inscriptions 'LAW. Such is the guarantee of universal happiness'.[64] In August 1801 Alexander set up a Commission on Laws. A preamble to an associated project for a Charter to the Russian people reiterated the tenet that he had imbibed from La Harpe, that 'it is Monarchs who have been established by Divine Providence for the benefit and welfare of the peoples living under their rule'.[65] The project included guarantees on property, freedom of thought, creed and speech. It safeguarded not only nobles but also merchants and townspeople (their 1785 Charter was confirmed) and to some extent the free peasants.

The concrete outcome of Alexander's first reforming effort was an administrative restructuring that put an end to Peter I's College system and restored the Senate to its former powerful position. In 1802 eight ministries – Commerce, Education, Finance (supplemented in 1810 by the ministry of State Economy), Foreign Affairs, Internal Affairs, Justice, Navy and War (amalgamated in 1810) – were created on the French model, with ministers directly appointed and answerable to the emperor. A Committee of Ministers co-ordinated their work. Provincial governors were also appointed by the emperor and subordinate to ministers. In 1810 Alexander created the State Council as an advisory panel with authority over the Committee of Ministers and the Senate but subject to the tsar's decisions. There was no public accountability, still less any electoral principle. According to one historian of the period, 'central government had been made neither more efficient nor more independent'.[66]

A significant early reform was the Law on Free Agriculturists (February 1803), which allowed landowners to liberate serfs with a parcel of land. Few nobles took advantage of this law, but the principle of increasing peasant land ownership was in keeping with the thinking of the time, as was the idea that the responsible behaviour of citizens (and the right, for example, to vote) were inextricably linked to having a stake in the existing order in the form of property. A law of 1801 allowed merchants, townsmen and state peasants to purchase land. Laws allowing nobles to engage in foreign trade (1802) and peasants in trade (1812) made for more social mobility.

In 1804 two new universities – Kazan and Kharkov – were created, and existing ones – Dorpat in Livonia, Moscow (founded 1755) and Vilna in Lithuania – were expanded and issued with new charters, with the explicit purpose of producing public servants. St Petersburg University opened in 1819. Graduates of the new system proceeded directly to grade 12 of the Table of Ranks. In 1803 a school diploma was made a requirement for appointment to civil service posts. From 1809 entry to grade 8 in the civil service required a university degree. Such measures did not have the universal approval of the nobility and were widely ignored, but they underlined the government's determination to improve the quality of public servants.

There were hopes that Alexander would go beyond institutional tinkering. The most ambitious scheme for constitutional reform was produced by the state official Mikhail Speransky (1772–1839), son of a parish priest, who rose to become the emperor's closest associate thanks to his rescue of the country from financial disaster by limiting the irresponsible printing of paper money. However, this did not guarantee the success of his 1809 Introduction to the Codification of State Laws, based on the Napoleonic Civil Code, the key element of which was that 'administration cannot be based on law if the sovereign power alone makes the law and executes it ... Therefore one must of necessity admit popular participation in the making of law.'[67] Speransky hedged these radical ideas with extreme caution. Legislative initiative must be left entirely to the government, i.e. to the sovereign power (the autocrat). Judges would be elected 'by the persons for whose sake the court is established', but judiciary procedures would be safe-guarded from above. At the same time the 'legislative body' was elected and no law could have legal force unless it was drafted by the same.[68] There would be common rights enjoyed by all, such as no punishment without trial, and rights pertaining to the few, such as ownership of landed property. Only those with property had political rights. The legislative order would be based on township or village duma, district duma, provincial duma, and a state duma, equal to the

Senate and ministry. In the end, the only elements of Speransky's scheme to survive were the State Council and a reconfiguration of ministries. Speransky himself was ousted in 1812.

If Alexander's focus on civil reform reflected his grandmother's legacy, his devotion to military affairs inherited from his father remained undiminished. The emphasis was as much on style as substance, focusing on the cut of tunics, the positioning of a feather or the angle of a step, with French style as the model. The members of Alexander's military suite, with their splendid uniforms, refined manners and good looks, were as influential as his Unofficial Committee and bear witness to the continuing role of Guards officers in Russian political life. Alexander found it difficult to get on with rough and ready old soldiers, and they in their turn resented his excessive devotion to aesthetic minutiae.

Love of the military was reflected in architecture in the Alexandrian Neo-Classical or Empire style, which produced some large-scale buildings on key sites, modelled on Greek temples and Roman arches and decorated with martial and naval motifs. Key buildings were the new Admiralty (Andreian Zakharov, 1806–23), which linked Palace Square with Senate Square on the Neva embankment with its long façade and pavilions. The new cathedral of the Icon of Our Lady of Kazan on Nevsky Prospekt (Andrei Voronikhin, 1801–1811) was one of the key shrines of the Romanov dynasty, its design based on St Peter's in Rome. (It would house the Tercentenary services in 1913.) Dominating the tip of Vasilevsky Island were Thomas de Thomon's Stock Exchange (1805–10) and Voronikhin's Mining Institute (1806–11). Most striking was the curved arch of Carlo Rossi's General Staff Headquarters (1819–29), which completed the ensemble of Palace Square at the heart of the imperial capital. Alexander I's prominently sited public buildings were redolent of the grandeur of an empire and a dynasty with their mythical roots in ancient times. It was the architecture of the parade ground.

The visual arts were dominated by male portraits, especially of veterans of the wars (*Denis Davydov* by Orest Kiprensky (1782–1836) is a dashing example). Alexander himself appeared in numerous paintings, nowhere more impressive than in François Gérard's full-length study of the conquering hero (in copies by, for example, K. A. Shevelkin), in tight fitting jacket and breeches with lavish epaulettes set against a romantically turbulent sky or in the Englishman George Dawe's much copied full-length study in black uniform.[69] In sculpture powerful male figures ousted the allegorical female previously favoured, as part of the celebration of the masculine physique. The style of the period, from furniture to porcelain, was refined and elegant, reminiscent of the Regency period in Britain. The Alexandrine era was remembered as a golden age of creativity, which saw the culmination of Russian Sentimentalism and Romanticism, as well as a growth in national themes.[70] The early work of Alexander Pushkin (1799–1837), Russia's greatest poet, encompassed lyric and narrative poetry, stories and plays, produced and discussed within a circle of friends dedicated to literature concentrated first at the Lycée at Tsarskoe Selo (founded by Alexander), then in the so-called Arzamas society. An admirer of Lord Byron and his imitator in his passion for female company, Pushkin suffered banishment during the latter part of Alexander's reign for 'revolutionary' motifs in his writing. Works written in this period included *The Prisoner of the Caucasus* (1821) and *The Fountain of Bakhchisarai* (1822), as well as numerous lyric poems. Pushkin, as we shall see, went on to write his major works under the apparently less civilized and cultured regime of Nicholas I.

The subject matter of much art and literature was inspired by events abroad, as Alexander presided over wars in all corners of his vast empire. From 1801 the annexation of mountainous Georgia and subjugation of its wild tribesmen inspired exotic Caucasian themes in literature, as did war with Turkey (1806–12), from which Russia acquired Bessarabia. Conflict with Sweden resulted in the annexation of Finland (1808–9). The empire seemed destined to expand to its 'natural' limits and beyond. These acquisitions in themselves might have been enough to assure Alexander's place among the pantheon of Romanov empire builders, but they were put in the shade by the war against Napoleon in Europe.

Things did not at first go well for Russia, which entered the third anti-French Coalition with Britain and Austria in 1805. The main Austrian army was forced to surrender at Ulm in mid-October, and on 2 December 1805 Russian and Austrian troops were all but destroyed after attacking the French at Austerlitz under the command of the tsar himself. Austria left the coalition and witnessed the dissolution of the Holy Roman Empire. Russia fought on, now with Prussia, but their combined forces were defeated at Friedland in June 1807. On 27 July 1807 Alexander was obliged to accept Napoleon's terms for the Peace of Tilsit, signed on a raft in the river Nieman. Here the tsar surrendered the Ionian Isles and Cattaro to the French and saw his Prussian ally 'reduced to a thin, indefensible wishbone of territory east of the Elbe'.[71] Russia and France now found themselves allies. The anti-British nature of the deal – in which Alexander agreed not only to break with Britain but even to go to war if Britain would not make peace on his terms – is reflected graphically in a famous British cartoon showing Napoleon embracing Alexander on the raft. A crown topples from the latter's head as he exclaims, 'Zounds, Brother, you'll squeeze me to death. … besides, I find my side of the raft is sinking very fast!', as waves lap over his feet. Alexander may have hoped to strengthen his partnership with France by showing that Russian help was indispensable for humbling the British. However, he had little option.[72] Tilsit was confirmed by the Erfurt convention on 30 September 1808 as a *traité de paix et d'amitié*, with exchanges of gifts, honours and compliments. But it remained a hopelessly one-sided agreement.

Peace with France did not last. The failure was hastened by French occupation of the land of the duke of Oldenburg, the husband of Alexander's sister Ekaterina, and by Russia's resumption of trade with Britain and imposition of a tariff on French goods. In 1811 the threatening appearance of French troops in the Grand Duchy of Warsaw was followed by invasion in 1812. Alexander received the news in Vilna on 24 June. After inconclusive encounters at Vitebsk, Mogilev and Smolensk, two Russian armies retreated eastwards under the cautious command of Prince Barclay de Tolly and Prince Peter Bagration, reluctant to offer Napoleon the opportunity for the sort of decisive engagement on which he thrived. In August the two sides finally clashed at Borodino, west of Moscow, in a battle of attrition which exhausted both sides: some 100,000 men perished on one day from Russia's total of 110,000 and France's of 130,000. The Russian General Mikhail Kutuzov (1745–1813) withdrew, having decided not to defend Moscow, which was evacuated, allowing Napoleon to enter, with Kutuzov's army stationed to the south. Cut off from supplies, Napoleon decided to withdraw before winter set in, but his already weakened forces were picked at and killed off by cold, starvation and partisans. Only 15,000 or so of the original 600,000-strong army survived, including Napoleon himself. A Russian army pursued the French for a 'final' confrontation at Leipzig in October 1813.

Tales of Moscow's suffering at the hands of foreigners who 'offended faith, ravaged provinces, profaned altars and the ashes of our fathers, outraged their graves' were potent,[73] as was Moscow's rapid re-emergence from the ashes 'like a Phoenix'. Events re-established its status as the mother of Russian cities (St Petersburg was physically untouched) and contributed to its rise at the core of Russian national identity, an identity later promoted by Russia's last two tsars. The devastation of Moscow revived its significance in the popular imagination as the original seat of the ruling dynasty and a continuing site for national tradition, in, for example, 'the sacred shrine where our sovereign was crowned'. (The French had the Dormition cathedral mined ready for demolition, but on the night that Napoleon left there was a downpour and the fuses were doused, as if by divine intervention.)[74] Napoleon's invasion recalled the 'barbaric' incursions of Tatars in earlier times, which the founders of Moscow had heroically contested, as well as later raids by Poles and Swedes.

Such sentiments inspired Alexander publicly to proclaim a plan to build a commemorative church in Moscow in a manifesto of 25 December 1812, the same day as he praised the heroism of the Russian people in expelling the enemy: 'To preserve the eternal memory of that matchless effort, loyalty and love for the Faith and the Fatherland which the Russian people displayed in those hard times, we shall establish a church. And may this church stand for many centuries and may the incense of the gratitude of future generations rise up before the holy altar of God, together with the love and emulation of the deeds of their ancestors.'[75]

Some historians have read the project as an exculpation of guilt for Alexander's connivance in the assassination of his father, a crime which he believed had caused God to unleash the enemy upon Russia.[76]

The first foundation of the Cathedral of Christ the Redeemer was laid on Sparrow Hills above Moscow in October 1817 on the fifth anniversary of Napoleon's retreat from the city. The architect, Alexander Vitberg, devised a grandiose scheme for a vast edifice of Classical design based on symbolic elements representing the Body, Soul and Spirit, which had to be scaled down over time as technical problems pushed the project more and more behind schedule. In 1827 Vitberg and other members of the building commission were convicted (unjustly) on corruption charges.[77] Even the site had to be abandoned when it was found to be unstable. Alexander's successors would rescue the project.

The Romanov bicentenary in 1813 attracted little attention, probably because Alexander was fully occupied with the continuation of the war. One exception came in the form of a tribute by Georg von Pott, who strove to link the 'double miracle' of 1812 with the anniversary in a eulogy to Alexander. He asked Catherine II to look down and behold 'the new, unprecedented happiness of the Russian people who are so dear to you; testify to heaven of the splendid epoch being created by your great Grandson and bear witness that on the almost thousand year-old Russian throne for two centuries the most august House of Romanov has ruled with glory, blessed by millions'.[78] In 1817 a new 'great bell' was cast for the Kremlin, inscribed with the names of Alexander and living members of the dynasty.[79] In general, however, Alexander made few symbolic gestures to underline the collective nature of Romanov authority, perhaps influenced by his growing perception of his own unique role in Europe's destiny and his lack of male successors. As Russian troops entered French territory for the first time in December 1813 he delivered a message that encompassed his image of himself as peacemaker: 'let us carry to [our enemies] not anger and vengeance, but friendliness and a hand stretched out for reconciliation. It is the glory of the Russian to overthrow the armed enemy and, after wresting the arms from his hand, to be charitable to him and to his peaceful brothers'.[80] In 1814 Alexander entered Paris in his 'hour of apotheosis'.[81]

In the international settlement at the Congress of Vienna in 1814–15 Russia, Prussia, Austria and Britain redrew the map to reflect pre-Revolutionary Europe and acknowledged new realities, such as a German confederation, a United Netherlands of Holland and Belgium and an independent Switzerland, and the restoration of constitutional monarchies in France (the Bourbons under Louis XVIII) and Spain (Ferdinand VII). The Russian empire expanded as Congress Poland came under Russian control and the annexation of Finland was confirmed. Much less concrete was Alexander's scheme for a Holy Alliance to bring 'Christian precepts of justice, charity and peace' to international life, which was signed by the rulers of Austria, Prussia and Russia on 14/26 September 1815 as representatives of 'one and the same Christian nation'. Lord Castlereagh regarded the Holy Alliance as 'a piece of sublime mysticism and nonsense', Metternich as 'a loud-sounding nothing'.[82] The ideas behind it had the approval of the religious mystic Baroness Julie de Krüdener, with whom Alexander had several meetings in Paris, but also reflected the direction of Alexander's own thought since 1812, which was dominated by all-encompassing schemes. For Alexander the meetings of 1814–15 represented a mystical experience linked with divine providence and his own special mission, which was bolstered by general adulation from enthusiastic crowds that was likely to turn anyone's head. In 1814 he came to London, where the press hailed him as 'Christian, Patriot, and Hero', 'magnanimous Liberator of Europe'[83] and 'the Christian Conqueror'[84] of the evil and godless Napoleon. At home the Senate, Synod and State Council offered him the title *blagoslovennyi* (blessed), which he modestly refused to accept but which stuck anyway.

For Russia the growth of national pride in the wake of 1812–14 was double-edged, especially for troops returning home. The last decade of Alexander's reign represented a sort of watershed, characterized by the growing contrast between Russia's external glory and its internal stagnation. Russia's rulers could endorse the use of the Russian language instead of French, support the restoration of desecrated national monuments and even pay lip service to elite appreciation of the peasants who had fought so heroically against Napoleon. However, when inevitably the issue of serfdom was raised, caution set in. It was to be several decades before Alexander's nephew Alexander II was forced to grasp that nettle. The same caution determined the issue of extending political power to the elite who had commanded the victorious armies. The new Kingdom of Poland was self-governing, with its own constitution which safeguarded the elected national assembly (the *sejm*), courts, administration and army, as well as civil liberties. Finland, too, enjoyed a constitution and independent government. In the Baltic regions of Estonia, Courland and Livonia between 1816–19 the serfs were liberated. Yet nothing of the kind was extended to Russia, despite recommendations from Speransky and later from Novosiltsev on constitutions for Russia and from Arakcheev on emancipation. Once the opportunity was lost, attempts by the elite to take power for themselves or on behalf of the Russian people – the Decembrists in 1825, various Populist groups in the 1860s–80s – pushed the tsarist regime further into reaction and the conviction that Russia would be saved only by firm government from above backed by popular (peasant) support from below.

Alexander came to rely more and more on Aleksei Arakcheev, that 'hated symbol of frustrated hopes and repression'.[85] Significantly, Arakcheev's career had begun under Paul I at Gatchina where he rose to be camp commander. Military colonies were his brainchild, and they appealed to Alexander's sense of order: state peasants, soldiers and their families were all supposed to live side by side in mutual assistance. The reality was deep resentment on the part of peasants whose traditional way of life was disrupted by such demands as shaving, forced marriages and drill. Alexander's obsession with spiritual improvement also lost him sympathy. Even good projects suffered from bad advice. Thus the efforts of the Russian Bible Society, initiated in 1813 by Prince A. N. Golitsyn, the procurator of the Holy Synod, to disseminate a translation of the Bible into Russian were undermined by the monk Photius, who succeeded in having all copies burned.[86] In 1822 Photius lobbied successfully for the closure of Masonic lodges. From 1817 Golitsyn presided over the Ministry of Spiritual Affairs and Education, which declared 'Christian morality' to be the basis of all true education. This had its enlightened side: for example Old Believers, Muslims and Jews enjoyed protection, but it also meant religious instruction in schools (which under Catherine were secular) and the emergence of advisers more reactionary than Golitsyn. In 1819 the educational inspector Mikhail Magnitsky closed departments of philosophy in Kazan University, expelled some professors and burned dubious books. There were increased restrictions on the press, with particular emphasis on stamping out foreign influences.

Alexander himself never formally converted to Protestantism – as Russian emperor and virtual head of the Orthodox Church this was unthinkable – but saw himself as a leader of world Christendom who must extract fundamental principles from the Bible in the Protestant manner. This was a new version of what modern historians dub 'Moscow, the Third Rome', stripped of its specifically Orthodox mission and reliant upon the personal convictions of the emperor himself. Praying in Paris at Place de la Concorde with troops on Easter Day 1814 and reviewing his troops and praying near the town of Vertus for the feast of St Alexander Nevsky in August, Alexander sensed a special mission to 'forgive' and 'purify' the French and to inaugurate a new era reflecting Russia's military and religious might.[87] The danger was that the perfection of outward show became even more central, an aspect that Alexander would concentrate on when he returned to Russia, at odds with an elite who wanted substantial reform. At the same time, Alexander was more inclined to support 'legitimate regimes', even when their overthrow might appear to be more in tune with Russian aspirations. This was the case with the Greek revolt of 1821, spearheaded by the army officer Alexander Ypsilantis, where Christian Greeks challenged their Ottoman overlords. Despite a great deal of popular support for fellow Orthodox, Alexander backed the Ottoman regime. This was to be one of several popular revolts in Europe that touched the imagination of Russian noble dissidents, who became increasingly frustrated with Alexander's policies. Ironically, Alexander chose to ignore evidence of the growth of 'secret' societies of young nobles in Russia itself, including those whose activities would culminate in the Decembrist revolt of 1825, preferring to see such activities as forgivable 'errors' about politics and society that he himself had once shared.

In 1817 Alexander turned 40, a landmark that may well have made the childless emperor think further about the succession to the throne.[88] According to the fundamental laws of 1797 his heir was his brother Grand Duke Constantine, but in 1819 Alexander and Constantine seem to have reached a private arrangement that the throne would pass to their younger brother Nicholas. Whether this constitutes 'a violation of the dynastic order', as Wortman suggests, is debatable since Nicholas was the next in line after Constantine according to the letter of the law, but it did reveal a loophole in the law in the event of renunciation by the legal heir.[89] The likelihood of Constantine, now Commander-in-Chief of Poland, being crowned emperor became even more remote when in 1820, having divorced his first wife, he made a morganatic marriage to the Polish Catholic Countess Johanna Grudzinska. In 1822 Constantine again expressed his intention to renounce the succession, a decision that was formally accepted by Alexander in 1823 when a manifesto declared Nicholas the heir. But all this was kept secret, even from Nicholas himself,[90] a bizarre oversight which would cause difficulties when Alexander unexpectedly died on 29 November 1825 in Taganrog on the Sea of Azov, a port developed by Peter the Great in the 1690s.

The location and unexpectedness of the emperor's death – all previous rulers had the good grace to die at home – presented considerable logistical problems for the Commission of Mourning in St Petersburg, which had to direct the preparation of appropriate furnishings for a lying-in-state in Taganrog Cathedral, arrange road transport home with selected stopping places and follow the model laid down by Peter I for the funeral in St Petersburg. The circumstances of the death and Alexander's state of mind gave rise to rumours: Alexander had committed suicide, been murdered or not died at all. The coffin was said to be empty, or filled with a dummy or a substitute corpse. When Empress Maria Fedorovna asked for the casket to be opened in St Petersburg, she was discouraged from viewing the corpse on the grounds that 'the body is decayed and giving off a strong stench'.[91] Many years later a hermit in Siberia called Fedor Kuzmich (?–1864) claimed that he was Alexander, having staged his own death. The legend's adherents included Leo Tolstoy; some still believe it today.

No such doubts were allowed to cloud official proceedings. The funeral procession on 13 March 1826 was a grand affair, recorded in paintings, prints and written descriptions, to underline, as had such occasions since the time of Peter I, the glory of the deceased and his dynasty in death as in life, when heroic deeds were recalled and the legacy underlined and a grateful public paid its respects. Alexander was laid to rest to the left of the iconostasis of the Peter-Paul Cathedral.

Elizaveta (Elizabeth) would be buried in 1826 next to him, to the right, Maria Fedorovna in 1828 to the left and to the right of Paul, who lies beside the north wall of the cathedral.

Alexander I has been described as a 'chameleon', a 'sphinx' on the throne as Prince P. B. Viazemsky dubbed him 50 years after his death,[92] an actor given to theatrical gestures in the spirit of the Sentimental era, a tendency which was intensified by the real-life dramas of the Napoleonic wars. Rarely did a monarch get such an opportunity to bestride the world stage. At the same time, he was the prisoner of his upbringing and inheritance with regard to basic institutions such as autocracy and serfdom. He shelved projects proposed by aristocrats that would have limited his power in order to safeguard against the sorts of abuses committed by Paul. There was little contradiction in the 'liberator' of Europe exercising extreme caution in granting freedoms at home.

For foreigners Alexander's legacy was inevitably linked with the events of 1812–14. His achievements confirmed foreign opinion that in Russia everything had to be achieved 'from above' and that the ruling dynasty continued to be the movers and shakers and the hope for the future. 'It cannot be forgotten', wrote the British traveller Robert Lyall in 1823, 'that it was this family which gave the first and mightiest impulse to civilization, and prepared the development of those powers of mind which have since continued exerting themselves in a thousand forms of restless activity, elevating the country which they honour, in the scale of intellectual reputation.'[93] This included schemes for emancipating the serfs, 'notwithstanding the interested and vehement opposition to His Imperial Majesty's benevolent views from the nobles'.[94] Later historians saw the cracks in this progressive scenario, as the imperial government, pressing reform on its obstinate subjects with the backing of a loyal elite, began to experience the reluctance and in some cases outright opposition of that elite, and found itself cast in a reactionary light as in the 'good half'/'bad half' story of Alexander's reign. In Paul's reign opposition was closely tied to the immediate interests of the elite, rather than broader political or ideological motives – the wish to escape sudden banishment or expropriation, for example. By the end of Alexander's reign, the experiences of active service in the wars, the lessons of seeing European civilization, education, reading of politics and philosophy, had grown more ideological/political roots, which culminated in what came to be known as the Decembrist uprising. Whether Alexander really planned his own 'death' or not, it is easy to see why he might have wished to do so, as easy assumptions about the progressive role of the autocracy were undermined and it became harder for the ruling house to maintain its role in relation to the elite and the people while keeping up appearances as a top nation in foreign affairs. Alexander left Russia much bigger and, arguably, much greater than he had found it, but at the cost of his own peace of mind and the viability of autocracy itself.

7

Consistent Autocracy: 1825–1855

NICHOLAS I

The emperor of Russia is an autocratic and unlimited monarch.
Obedience to his supreme authority is commanded by God
himself, not only from fear but also from conscience.[1]

'God! What sort of start is it to a reign when the first step taken is to order grape-shot to be fired at one's subjects?' asked the recently widowed Empress Elizabeth in December 1825.[2] She was speaking of the 'Decembrist' uprising of young army officers drawn from some of Russia's most distinguished families. Organized hastily and chaotically on the pretext of preventing Nicholas I acceding to the throne, the revolt was the culmination of several years of clandestine activities in response to disappointment with Alexander I's reactionary final years, liberation movements abroad and Western ideas imbibed through reading, travel and association. All participants were united on the need to abolish serfdom and end autocracy. A minority demanded the execution of the imperial family.[3] It is indeed hard to imagine a much worse start to a reign, or, indeed, 30 years later, a much worse ending. Nicholas I died after a series of defeats in the Crimean War, Russia's first humiliation after a seemingly endless golden age of military triumphs and authority in world affairs. There were rumours that he had committed suicide.

In the interim and after his death, Nicholas's reputation suffered both at home and abroad. He was 'the perfect despot'[4] and 'the most consistent of autocrats'.[5] Few admitted to liking him. He was, to rephrase Schiemann, the 'most consistent of Romanovs', always painfully aware of the burden of the dynastic legacy that he bore, handed down via his hero Peter the Great to his grandmother, father and elder brother, and of his role as Russia's promoter in world affairs. For his sheer dedication to duty Nicholas has won his admirers and apologists, both during his lifetime and more recently.[6] However, he received few of the accolades enjoyed by 'angelic' Alexander I and almost none of the legendary adulation heaped upon that equally 'consistent' autocrat Peter I.

When Alexander I died in Taganrog on 19 November 1825 almost no one knew that Nicholas was his heir. According to the 1797 law, the throne passed to Alexander's younger brother Constantine; no public declaration had been made to the contrary. Specimen coins with Constantine's head were hastily designed. Apparently only a handful of people, including Metropolitan Filaret and Empress Maria Fedorovna, knew of the letters dating from 1823 which ratified his renunciation of the throne.[7] Under these circumstances, Nicholas, apparently in some confusion and reluctant to appear to be 'usurping' the throne, initially took the oath of allegiance to Constantine, in anticipation that the latter would formally abdicate. To his consternation, no message arrived from Warsaw, where Constantine resided, and Guards regiments in the capital began taking the oath to Constantine I. At this point, on 13 December, Nicholas issued his own accession manifesto to the State Council. It was this apparent sidelining of the 'rightful' heir that spawned rumours of mischief in high places and gave a pretext for the conspirators to bring rebel troops onto the street to defend Constantine's rights, reminiscent of the mukseteer rebellion of 1682 when confusion over the claims of sibling candidates to the throne and rumours that one was being cheated and 'harmed' sparked a revolt. In 1825, too, 'naive monarchism', including the belief in the vital necessity of having a true tsar on the throne and fears of corruption by power-hungry advisers, was still a factor in shaping popular views, while for the elite conspirators, who had no particular affection for the conservative Constantine, an 'interregnum' promised to provide a breathing space in which their own preference for constitutional government or a republic could be imposed.

Nicholas was thus faced with the prospect of spilling blood on the first day of his reign. As he confessed in a memoir, 'I felt the necessity, but I confess, when the time came, I could not venture on such a measure and horror overcame me.'[8] He pulled himself together after one of the rebels shot and killed the Governor General of St Petersburg, Mikhail Miloradovich, a hero of 1812. Some 3,000 rebellious troops, gathered around the statue of Peter I on Senate Square, were scattered by 9,000 loyalists. Five ringleaders – Nikolai Bestuzhev-Riumin, Peter Kakhovskoy, Sergei Muraviev-Apostol, Pavel Pestel and Kondraty Ryleev – were executed on 13 July 1826 and many more rebels exiled to Siberia.

The Decembrist uprising set the agenda for the rest of Nicholas's reign, the twin objectives of which became to maintain order at home while continuing Russia's special mission in world affairs. Nicholas was conscience-stricken – 'Dear, dear Constantine', he wrote to his brother. 'Your will has been done: I am emperor, but, my God, at what a price! At the price of my subjects' blood!'[9] – but was inclined more to firmness in government instead of relaxation or concession. The emperor personally interrogated all the insurgents prior to their trial and kept a copy of the trial testimonials permanently on his desk. In his view, they were inspired by alien, Western ideas that could be counteracted only by adherence to Russian traditions and loyalty to the dynasty. Their defeat was inspired by God. The heart of Russia was and would be 'impervious' to their ideas, even though revolution stood on its threshold.[10] After 1825 the Romanovs could never really relax, for the split between the radical elite – the offspring of formerly loyal classes – and the crown proved impossible to seal.

Nicholas was reluctant to trust in the nobility as a class. He also distrusted not only the spectacle-wearing 'intelligentsia' but also elements of the regular, institutionalized bureaucracy, in the firm conviction that Russia must be ruled by a God-fearing autocrat with the help of good, personally chosen advisers. Among Nicholas's circle, army officers and Baltic nobles featured prominently, none more that the adjutants of his suite, some 540 of whom were appointed; they filled military commands during wartime as well as being promoted to some civilian posts. It was, after all, generals and loyal troops who had rallied round on 14 December. Nicholas required 'not wise but service-orientated' advisers.[11]

Nicholas's upbringing determined that his approach was centred in military discipline, without the ambiguous legacy that Catherine II's tuition programme gave to his brother Alexander. His earliest education was received during his father's reign. A formative influence from 1800 was his tutor, the ill-tempered disciplinarian Count M. I. Lamsdorf, whose methods included corporal punishment. Later Nicholas apparently showed little interest in formal study of political economy or law; the military remained his passion and he was deeply frustrated when Alexander I barred him and his younger brother Michael from active service in the war against Napoleon, although he did participate in the military parades at Vertus in France in 1815, which left a deep impression.[12] 'Here [in the army] there is order', he wrote. 'All things flow logically one from the other. No one here commands without first learning how to obey. No one rises above anyone else except through a clearly-defined system. Everything is subordinated to a single, defined goal, and everything has its precise designation. That is why I shall always hold the title of solder in high esteem. I regard all human life as being nothing more than service because everyone must serve.'[13] 'The Czar of Russia is a military chief, and each of his days is a day of battle', wrote the Marquis de Custine, who seems to have admired and resented Nicholas in equal measure.[14] Duty was a guiding principle: 'Duty! yes, that is not a meaningless word for one who from childhood was taught to understand it as I was. This word has a sacred meaning before which every personal impulse must give way.'[15]

As a young man, Nicholas was strikingly good looking: tall and slim, with classic 'Greek' chiselled features, 'the handsomest man in Russia'.[16] Patriotic observers went into raptures about his 'inspiring and majestic beauty' and 'Olympian profile'.[17] As he grew older, however, his features settled into sternness, giving him a rather severe and gloomy look which could turn menacing. Custine saw 'a worried severity'.[18] His was not a kind face. Queen Victoria, who met him in 1844, noted that he rarely smiled.[19] He maintained an upright military bearing, with the help of a corset, to look all the better in the guards uniforms

Engraving of Nicholas I by H.T. Ryall (after Kriegekal). London, 1841.

that he favoured, and hardly ever wore civilian dress. This personal preference was extended to other civilians, such as university students, who when in uniform were expected to salute when encountering military personnel. Even when visiting Windsor Castle in 1844 he brought his own camp bed and asked for clean straw to stuff the mattress. He died on a narrow iron bed, covered with a soldier's greatcoat, 'as if death had overtaken him amidst the austerities of a military camp and not amidst the luxury of a splendid palace'.[20] All this contributed to the 'parade ground' atmosphere that so many foreign visitors commented on, none more emphatically than Custine: 'The Russian government is the discipline of the camp substituted for the civil order: it is a state of siege become the normal state of society.'[21]

Nicholas was devoted to his family. In 1817 he married Fredericke Louise Charlotte Wilhelmina (1798–1860), daughter of King Frederick William III of Prussia and his wife Louise of Mecklenburg-Strelitz, and a great-granddaughter of Frederick the Great. The couple met in Berlin in 1814 and apparently fell in love. This dynastic link with the Prussian Hohenzollerns was to be a key factor in Russian foreign policy until the end of the nineteenth century. The alliance was, as Alexander I described it at the time, an expression of 'sacred friendship',[22] strengthened by the shared values of the two royal houses, for example, a love of the military and parades.

Alexandra Fedorovna, as she was known after her conversion, was said to be a great beauty in her youth, although hers was a thin, delicate attractiveness and she was often ailing. She learned Russian with the poet Vasily Zhukovsky and made every effort to assimilate in her new homeland (although she never much took to Orthodoxy), adopting many of the charitable institutions of her mother-in-law Maria Fedorovna after the latter's death, and founding many of her own. The chief element of her image, however, was that of the mother of the expanding Romanov dynasty, devoted to her children, as attested in numerous sentimental group portraits. Given the childlessness of his two elder brothers and the survival of only one daughter from the marriage of his younger brother Michael, the fate of the dynasty rested in Nicholas and Alexandra's hands.

Nicholas was said to be 'faithful' to Alexandra ('Mouffy'), but this did not prevent him from conducting several long relationships with other women. Even before his marriage his alliance with Elena Andreevna Tsvileneva produced several children (known by the name Nikolaev) and there were children from other liaisons too. His long-standing mistress during his marriage was Varvara Arkadievna Nelidova (?–1897), the niece of his father's mistress. Such behaviour was accepted in court circles as long as 'propriety' was preserved, or, to borrow from Wortman, the 'beautiful idyll of the family' was not openly defiled. Baroness M. P. Fredericks wrote: 'What an example Nicholas Pavlovich set for us all in his deep respect for his wife and how sincerely he loved and protected her to the last minute of his life! As is well known, he has love affairs on the side – but what man doesn't?'[23] Certainly Alexandra continued to love him and he seems to have found comfort in her company to the end of his life.

There were seven children from the marriage. The future Alexander II, born in 1818, was followed by Maria (1819–76), Olga (1822–92), Aleksandra (1825–44), Konstantin (1827–92, later admiral, liberal, opponent of serfdom, internal critic of autocracy), Nikolai (1831–91, army commander-in-chief), and Mikhail (1832–1909, inspector general of artillery). The sons produced sons of their own, leading to a rapid expansion of the extended house of Romanov in the second half of the nineteenth century and an increased grand ducal presence in high office in the armed services. Tsarevich Alexander was the first male Romanov to be born to the new generation, a pledge for the future of the dynasty, and the first Tsesarevich whose image was openly propagated and celebrated for public consumption. Even his education was a much more public affair than that of his predecessors. Alexander's tutor, the poet Zhukovsky, declared that Nicholas showed concern for both his 'tenderly-beloved son and the happiness of the people, who are beloved of the tsar',[24] stressing the parallelism between the emperor's closeness to and love of his heir and of his people in his concern for the education of both.

This was typical of Nicholas's efforts to bolster autocracy by increasing respect for the imperial family in what Wortman called the 'dynastic scenario', in which Nicholas presented himself as the embodiment of modest virtue within a family setting.[25] Nicholas's coronation (22 August 1826) publicized the ruling dynasty, 'glorifying' the family as the rest of the elite stepped into the background. All the living Romanovs were the recipients of loyal eulogies, especially the eight-year-old heir, but also the dowager empress, the tsar's brothers Constantine and Mikhail Pavlovich (now regent), and even his brother-in-law Prince Karl of Württemberg and others more distantly related by marriage.[26] Nicholas embraced Constantine and handed him his sword before taking communion as an expression of dynastic reconciliation and solidarity. A centre of attention was Empress Alexandra, who sat on the golden throne of Tsar Michael next to her husband on Tsar Alexis's gem-studded throne.[27] All present were, according to press and personal accounts, overcome by sentiments of emotion (*umilenie*) and rapture (*vostorg*), which conveyed themselves to the eye-witnesses of all classes; family unity guaranteed 'the happiness and prosperity of the fatherland'.[28] A new element in the ceremony was Nicholas's triple bow to the assembled representatives of the people on the Red Staircase outside the cathedral, which later was designated an ancient Russian custom. Popular response became a substitute for institutionalized approval of monarchy, and henceforth reports of 'the great voice of the nation' reacting to encountering the emperor and his family in person – from shouts of 'Hurrah!' to renditions of the

national anthem – became essential evidence of the continuing popularity of
tsarism.

Most often the public encountered the tsar in military settings, which were
supposed to demonstrate not the abject submission of his subjects to regimen-
tation (as visitors like Custine saw it) but loyalty and co-ordination between
the will of the supreme commander and his troops. As visitors remarked, even
court dances had a military element to them, carefully orchestrated steps
and stiff formality. Lavish occasions included the Easter parades, Nicholas's
nameday on 6 December and the review of the Preobrazhensky guards, Russia's
senior regiment, on 14 December. Troops turned out in force at the unveiling
of the Alexander column in 1834 and the Borodino monument in 1839. The
empress's birthday was celebrated at Peterhof on 1 July with more feminine
festivities, culminating in a grand ball with illuminations and fireworks,
although even here among the entertainments laid on were a march past of
her own Cavalier Guards, led by her husband and eldest son. The public was
admitted under close supervision, as they were to the taking of tea at the
Cottage, a mansion-sized residence in the English Gothic style in the grounds
of Peterhof, in a 'theatrical display of domesticity' where a carefully selected
public, including peasants, could witness the acting out of family happiness, a
'cult of family life'.[29] It was one of several backdrops for the medieval pageants
that the imperial couple favoured, the grandest of which was held near Tsarskoe
Selo in 1842 in the form of a carousel, with all the members of the imperial
family in costume, the younger grand dukes dressed as pages. Prints of the event
sold well.[30]

It would be wrong to give the impression that Nicholas was devoted purely
to outward show or sought refuge in mediaeval idylls. He regarded putting
on a good show as just one aspect of his duty as emperor, which turned out
to be a great deal easier than improving Russia. Reform was a duty too, but
Nicholas's approach was a gradualist one. As he wrote in 1826: 'Not by daring
and rash dreams, which are always destructive, but gradually, and from above,
laws will be issued, defects remedied, and abuses corrected. In this manner all
modest hopes for improvement, all hopes for strengthening the rule of law, for
the expansion of true enlightenment and the development of industry, will be
gradually fulfilled. The legitimate path, open for all, will always be taken by Us
with satisfaction. For We do not have, and cannot have, any other desire than to
see Our motherland attain the very heights of happiness and glory preordained
for her by Providence.'[31]

These principles were embodied in His Majesty's Own Chancellery, the
cornerstone of what came to be known as the 'Nicholas System'. The existing
First Section was supplemented by the Second, charged with codifying the laws,

The Alexander Column, Palace Square, St Petersburg (Lindsey Hughes).

and the notorious Third Section, originally intended to supervise foreigners in Russia, which, under Count Alexander Benckendorff, encompassed the corps of gendarmes, with a brief to investigate 'all phenomena'. The Fourth administered charitable and educational institutions, the Fifth peasant affairs.

For the instruction of the public Nicholas's principles were expressed in the so-called 'doctrine' of Official Nationality, based on the key concepts Orthodoxy, Autocracy and National Pride (*narodnost'*).[32] The formulation is associated with the Minister of Education, Sergei Uvarov in 1833, but the concepts were devised and elaborated further through discussions and articles in the conservative press. As Uvarov wrote to Nicholas in 1843:

The Russian devoted to his fatherland will agree as little to the loss of a single dogma of our Orthodoxy as to the theft of a single pearl from the Monomakh crown. Autocracy constitutes the main condition of the political existence of Russia. The Russian giant stands on it as the cornerstone of his greatness. A countless majority of the subjects of Your Majesty feel this truth; they feel it in full measure although they are placed on different rungs of civil life and although they vary in education and in their relations to the government. The saving conviction that Russia lives and is protected by the spirit of a strong, humane and enlightened autocracy must permeate popular education and must develop with it. Together with these two national principles there is a third, no less important, no less powerful: national pride (*narodnost*) ... national pride does not mean going back or standing still, it does not require immobility of ideas. The state apparatus, like the human body, changes in outward appearance as it grows; features change with the years but the physiognomy must not change. It would be wrong to oppose this periodic course of things; it is enough for us to preserve inviolable the sacred shrine of our national conceptions if we take them as the basic idea of government, especially in relation to national education.[33]

Official Nationality was a defence against the threat to tradition from outside (the West) and from within (the Decembrists and their possible successors). This new version of the old 'symphony' of church and state reaffirmed Orthodoxy, as opposed to the rather vague Christian, mystical principles of Alexander I, which Nicholas suspected had a pernicious influence on some of the Decembrists. It assumed that Russia was superior to the West, having preserved true values, and had its own unique path of development which would be pursued by directives from on high.

Some of Nicholas's most successful activities completed the work of his immediate predecessors. Perhaps his greatest achievement was the codification of the laws, carried out under the direction of Mikhail Speransky between 1826 and 1833. The 45 volumes of the *Complete Collection of Russian Laws* provided a historical record that remains invaluable to historians, while the *Digest* of current laws allowed people to ascertain what the law actually was, not least in respect of legal relations between serfs and masters. Nicholas shared Alexander I's view of the need to abolish serfdom, but not now. In a speech to the State Council, 30 March 1842, he declared: 'There is no doubt that serfdom as it exists here at the moment is an evil, palpable and evident to everyone, but to touch it *now* would be even more destructive.' The situation could not last 'forever', but the time was still 'very far off' and any action now would be a 'criminal infringement on social tranquillity and on the good of the state'.[34] Nicholas blamed the danger of 'premature' troubles on those who were making their peasants more aware, for example, by giving them higher education, and also by landowners who abused their powers. All that could be done was to prepare the path for those who came after, to some sort of 'transitional' state, by reiterating Alexander I's law on free agriculturists (1803) and standing firm on the principle that the nobility retained their inalienable right to the land, which did not belong to the peasants. For the time being Nicholas hoped that a change of opinion would be brought about by a combination of paternalism with appeals and measures to encourage, not force, landowners to improve the lot of their peasants. Key words in this and other texts were 'slowly', 'gradually', 'voluntary' (for landlords). Even the secrecy in which these views were given was significant. The text of the 1842 speech was copied down by a member of the council, with the help of two officials. The delegates were sworn to secrecy.

Addressing the nobility of St Petersburg in March 1848 Nicholas again assured them that the land belonged to the landowners, as a 'holy matter', but conceded that there were 'very few good and solicitous landowners' and that they must work harder to take care of the people entrusted in them and hand over 'immoral and cruel' owners to the law. He also warned them not to talk about politics or generally to put ideas into the heads of serfs.[35] Ten secret committees on serfdom were formed between 1826 and 1847. In 1842 the 'Obligated' peasant law was passed, providing for 'personal' freedom for a serf, who would pay dues to his landlord in return for use of land, but this required the landowner's permission and few peasants were able to take advantage of it. In the end, only state peasants were reformed, based on a thorough investigation carried out in 1836–40, and an emphasis upon administrative reform under the new Ministry of State Domains, an important step which did not extend to the landowners' serfs.

Nicholas's 'System' enjoyed considerable successes. There was relative economic prosperity under the regime of E. F. Kankrin, Minister of Finance between 1823 and 1844, who in 1839–43 withdrew devalued roubles. Industry expanded, particularly in metallurgy, cotton and sugar refining, factory workers increased threefold. The railway network was initiated, the Moscow–St Petersburg line opening in 1851, despite Kankrin's warning that railways encouraged 'the restless spirit of our age'. By 1855 the empire had just 650 miles of track, compared with Britain's 7,000, but the network expanded in successive reigns, attracting foreign investment and encouraging the growth of associated industries. Success continued abroad: there were victories in war against Persia (1826–7) and Turkey (1828–9), further expansion in Transcaucasia and the Caspian. There were no major riots within Russia proper, although Poland continued to cause trouble. Crowned king of Poland in Warsaw in May 1829, Nicholas had to contend with the anomaly of the constitution that Alexander I had granted to Poland. Protests against the dispatch of Polish troops to France in response to the July revolution erupted in full-blown rebellion and the declaration of an independent Polish republic in 1830. The dispatch of Russian troops soon suppressed the revolt. The incorporation of Poland into the Empire, ruled by Russian officials and with some restrictions on the use of the Polish language, were seen as a success from Nicholas's point of view.

There was a flowering of literature, which belied the 'police state' label slapped on Nicholas's Russia by many subsequent historians; the 1830s–40s saw the publication of major works by Pushkin, Lermontov, Gogol, Tiutchev, Koltsov, Odoevsky, while Turgenev, Tolstoy and Dostoevsky published their first stories and novels. However, writers had to observe certain limits. Dostoevsky's association with the radical Petrashevtsy group resulted in the life-changing experience in 1849 of being condemned to death and reprieved from the gallows at the last minute, while Pushkin, who got into trouble in Alexander I's reign for incautious expression of views, had to endure the more benign paternalistic guardianship of Nicholas as his personal censor. But real talent still had considerable room for manoeuvre and the court was generous in its patronage. The Academy of Arts, for example, sponsored studentships abroad and commissions for state projects.[36]

In the fine arts, masterpieces of Classicism and history painting by such artists as Karl Briullov, whose *Last Day of Pompeii* (1833) was the first Russian painting to cause a stir abroad, and Alexander Ivanov, whose master work *The Appearance of Christ to the People* (1837–57) was painted in Italy, co-existed with realist trends in the Russian urban scenes of Pavel Fedotov and peasant studies of Aleksei Venetsianov. In thought and philosophy these decades witnessed the debates of the Slavophiles and Westernists, who adopted different approaches to Russia's nature, its mission in the world and to its future development, with an emphasis respectively upon native institutions and virtues rooted in Orthodox principles or on completing Peter I's work by 'catching up' with the West in a mainly secular spirit. Learned societies and journal literature flourished and, without being specifically political in content, spawned a lively debate in the form of literary criticism and history, as well as works of fiction which often appeared first in serialized form. 'Journalism' in the widest sense became the sphere of the emerging class of *raznochintsy* or men who fell between the 'classical' class designations – sons of priests and doctors, government officials and so on. Leaders of the Russian 'intelligentsia', a term which gained currency in the 1830s, with the meaning of radical educated critics of the regime outside official circles, included Alexander Herzen (illegitimate son of a nobleman) and Vissarion Belinsky. They conducted a passionate debate about Russia's past and future, fuelled by readings of German Romantic and materialist philosophy. Tsarism was at the centre of discussion, the Slavophiles wedded to the ideal of an Orthodox tsar in the pre-Petrine mode who would freely consult but not be bound by popular opinion, the Westernists in favour of some form of constitutionalism in the context of modern political institutions. Neither tendency approved of the current Romanovs, among whose fiercest critics was Herzen, who denounced Catherine II among others.

The architecture of Nicholas's St Petersburg embodied the ideals of military discipline in 'parade-like' ensembles, none better than Rossi's designs for symmetrical Theatre Street, leading south from the Alexander Theatre (1828–32) and the Senate and Synod (1829–34). 'The square and the chalk-line accord so well with the point of view of absolute sovereigns that right angles become one of the attributes of despotic architecture', wrote Custine.[37] A focal point was the monument to Alexander I, the Alexander column, unveiled on Palace Square on 30 August 1834, Alexander's nameday. The creation and erection of the column, a single piece of granite, the highest in the world, itself was a heroic feat of engineering, while its design (by Auguste Montferrand) incorporated the motif of Alexander as an angel crushing a serpent with bas relief scenes of his greatest triumphs. Set in front of Rastrelli's Winter Palace and Rossi's General Staff headquarters, with the Bronze Horseman then visible in the distance, the monument was 'a votive object in the emerging cult of dynasty'[38] and one of the capital's major thrusting landmarks. The military parade for the unveiling was one of the grandest of Nicholas's reign.

Classicism was giving way to an eclectic style, epitomized by the grandiose St Isaac's Cathedral by Montferrand, completed only in 1858. Church architecture became a particular focus of national expression through the revival of pre-Petrine motifs. Nicholas's favourite architect in this respect was Constantine Thon (Ton) (1794–1881), who devised a neo-Russian style, starting with a plan for St Catherine's Church in St Petersburg, one of the first projects to break with the Westernized Classicism of the capital. Known as 'Byzantine' style, the favoured model became the five-domed Kremlin cathedrals, including their classical proportions. Thon's most grandiose work was the revived project for Alexander I's Cathedral of Christ the Redeemer, which was transferred from Sparrow Hills to the heart of Moscow. On 10 September 1839 an official foundation ceremony was held, preceded by a liturgy in the Kremlin Dormition Cathedral and a procession of the cross with some of the cathedral's most precious icons – the Vladimir and Iberian Mother of God.[39] Metropolitan Filaret delivered a speech praising Nicholas for completing his 'Blessed' brother's scheme, which concluded: 'And so, Russians (*Rosiane*), in contemporary events we read the ancient book of the Prophets. The Holy times appear before us in the acts of our tsars. What consolation for the faith! What inducement for the Fatherland. Praise to the tsar. May the Redeemer of the world who saved Russia look favourably upon you for creating this House in his name and may he guide your throne forever.'[40] The vast cathedral (which was not, in fact, completed until 1883) could be viewed from another of Thon's massive projects, the Great Kremlin Palace, begun in 1838 and incorporating grand halls for ceremonies of orders: St Andrew, St George, St Vladimir and so on. The facade bore early Russian motifs such as carved window surrounds, reflecting the architecture of the surviving seventeenth-century palaces of Tsars Michael and Alexis.[41]

Stylized Russian motifs appeared in fashion, for example women's court dress for the most formal occasions. As specified in a decree of 1834, it comprised elaborate versions of the high kokoshnik head-dress and adaptations of the loose sarafan gown, which contemporaries referred to as 'patriotic attire', with their references to both seventeenth-century noble and contemporary peasant festive dress.[42] However, European fashion remained the rule for day wear and men, like the emperor himself, kept to military uniform. Music embraced patriotic themes, such as the new national anthem by Aleksei L'vov based on Zhukovsky's *Prayer of the Russian People*, first performed in 1833 for Nicholas's nameday.[43] A key work of national revival was *Ivan Susanin* (1836, renamed *A Life for the Tsar* on the emperor's orders) by Mikhail Glinka (1814–57) on the theme of the heroic peasant who sacrificed his life to save Tsar Michael. The central theme is the peasant's devotion both to Michael and to the principle of tsarism – Russia must have a tsar – and the final scene is of Michael's entry into Moscow (although Michael himself was not portrayed on stage), reflecting Nicholas's own reception in Moscow and the old capital's association with patriotic national feeling. Glinka's other major work, *Ruslan and Liudmila* (1842), took folklore as its theme.

Nicholas's strong sense of family history focused on Peter I, whom he regarded as a role model. Like Peter, Nicholas was frequently referred to as the 'epic warrior' tsar (*tsar-bogatyr)* and portrayed as such in popular prints, even though at 6ft 2–3in he ceded a few inches to Peter's 6ft 7in. 'We are continuing the work of Peter the Great', Nicholas confided to the Marquis de Custine. He had in mind the codification of the laws and reform of government, but he also adhered to Petrine ideals in more symbolic ways. For example, the core of his entourage was Peter's own regiment, the Preobrazhensky guards, who had been the first to come to his aid on 14 December 1825. He even formed 'play regiments' for his younger sons, who were expected to act as role models for their contemporaries. He adopted a 'Petrine' ethic, working from early morning to late at night, interspersed with brisk walks. More widely, Nicholas travelled tirelessly and extensively, always on the move it seemed. He shared Peter's interest in the outward appearance of public buildings, from the humblest trading arcades and public gardens. He was similarly abstemious in his eating habits: 'He was not a great lover of fancy French cuisine but preferred plain Russian cooking, especially cabbage soup and buckwheat porridge.'[44]

The Petrine era was a particular focus of Nicholas's efforts to preserve family history, both for private and public consumption. In 1848 he ordered all objects from the Cabinet of Peter I in the Kunstkamera to be transferred to the Hermitage in the Winter Palace to what became known as the Gallery of Peter I.

Other collections followed, including Peter's wardrobe from Marly at Peterhof (Nicholas liked to wear Peter's capacious dressing gowns), and single items such as Rastrelli's bronze bust of Peter.[45] Visitors were admitted from the end of 1849 under the strict supervision of staff 'to ensure that no visitors touched any of the exhibits'. From 1850 a ticket system was introduced which had to be accessed in the museum chancellery.[46]

An officially approved guide to St Petersburg for children published in 1838 exhorted: 'Get down on your knees, children, before the tomb of Peter I; with hot tears let us bedew this monument and recall the deeds of the one who is hidden beneath this stone.'[47] Reminding them of Platon's 1770 sermon, in which the archbishop had exhorted Peter to 'rise up', the author writes: 'We too ask him to rise up and view the achievements of his successors who try to imitate him', thus calling attention to Nicholas I's admiration for Peter.[48] In 1846 Ivan Pushkarev wrote in similar vein:

'Standing above the tomb of the ruler of millions of subjects, who encompassed in his designs all the world, the father of the fatherland, you are struck by a strange sensation, which you experience fully but cannot express in words'.[49] The personal gratification accessible to individuals through close contact with Romanov memorials and artefacts was to remain a strong element in approved patriotic behaviour for the rest of the dynasty's existence.

Nicholas's concern for national heritage was not confined to the Petrine era. He gave funds for the renovation of the Kremlin cathedrals, the Dormition cathedral in Vladimir and Romanov apartments in Kostroma, where he had a coat of arms installed after a visit in 1834.[50] He sponsored a monument to Ivan Susanin in Kostroma (partly funded by public donations, 1838–51), which featured a bust of Tsar Michael in the Monomach crown.[51] He also erected a statue to Paul I at Gatchina in 1851, the first to be dedicated to the emperor, who was described in the most positive terms, praised for his love of order, respect for 'international morality' and willingness to defend the people of Europe.[52] This, incidentally, was the first ceremony at which Nicholas's grandsons Nikolai Aleksandrovich and Aleksandr Aleksandrovich (the future Alexander III) took a prominent role as members of the guard, underlining the proliferation of Paul I's line and the security of the dynasty's future.

Despite the optimism inherent in the tsar's concern for dynastic heritage, by the 1840s there were signs that all was not well. In 1842 N. Kutuzov submitted a memorandum of a tour of Russian provinces that he undertook at harvest time 1841, when he noted the 'stamp of gloom and grief imprinted on all faces, in all feelings and actions' and this at a time which was usually festive and joyful.[53] He suggested that the emperor was being prevented from seeing the truth by a 'wall' of advisers who shielded him from the people's appeals. As the saying went, it was 'easier to reach the throne of the King of Heaven than that of the earthly tsar'.[54]

Around this time Nicholas himself entered a period of depression, caused by illness and the poor health of his wife; in 1844 his daughter Alexandra died in childbirth and in 1849 his brother Michael Pavlovich passed away. Internal crises, however, such as a cholera outbreak in early 1848 that reached St Petersburg and famine in the provinces directed the popular gaze to domestic issues and reduced support for foreign adventures. 1848 was the crisis year when the System began to crack as Nicholas's attempts to keep the lid on all dissent in Russia extended to suppressing liberation movements abroad and bolstering 'legitimate' regimes, which earned him the soubriquet of the 'gendarme of Europe'. The collapse of the congress system – the fall of Louis Philippe in France, the granting of a constitution by Frederick William IV in Berlin, revolts against the Habsburgs in Vienna, Prague, Budapest, Venice and Milan, rebellions elsewhere in Italy and Germany, even against the sultan in Moldavia and Wallachia – all alarmed Nicholas and galvanized him for action. As he declared in a manifesto of 17 March 1848:

> By the cherished example of our Orthodox predecessors, having summoned the help of the Almighty God, we are ready to meet our enemics, wherever they may be, and without sparing ourselves, we shall in indissoluble union with our holy Rus defend the honour of the name of Russia and the inviolability of our borders.
>
> We are assured that every Russian, every loyal subject, will respond joyfully to the call of his sovereign, to the ancient invocation: 'For faith, tsar and fatherland' and now shall assure us the road to victory, and then, in feelings of reverential gratitude, as now in feelings of holy hope in him, we shall all exclaim together: 'God is with us. And the heathens will be subdued as God is with us.'[55]

In 1848–9 Russian armies intervened successfully to suppress revolt in Moldavia and Wallachia and to restore Habsburg rule in Hungary. Virtually all other revolutionary gains across Europe were reversed, much to Nicholas's encouragement and satisfaction, if not because of his direct aid. His efforts were increasingly focused on stamping out possible dissent at home. From 1849 police surveillance and censorship went to ridiculous lengths, for example the phrase 'Roman emperors were killed' being changed to 'perished'. 'Free-thinking' was further restricted in universities, with the banning of philosophy (in Moscow University) and the imposition of compulsory instruction in theology and Church history. Professorial appointments were made by ministries. All lectures had to be submitted in advance to the Public Library; science had to be based on 'religious truths'. Generally, the number of students was reduced. Raising the price of a foreign passport from 50 to 250 roubles aimed to restrict foreign travel. The trial in 1849 of the Petrashevtsy, a radical discussion group organized by the nobleman Mikhail Petrashevsky and infiltrated by the Third Section, resulted in fifteen conspirators, among them Fedor Dostoevsky, being condemned to death by hanging and reprieved on the gallows at the last minute.

Nicholas felt justified in his measures. His visit to Moscow in 1849 for the opening of the Great Kremlin Palace on Easter Day underlined the belief that in 1848 Europe had drawn even further away from true moral principles and that the Russian people in particular retained a sort of 'sixth sense' that allowed them to appreciate the tsar's authority, thus assuring tranquillity.[56] Links with the past were underlined by the imperial family celebrating mass in Tsar Alexis's Church of the Saviour in the old palace, where, as a contemporary observer remarked, 'the European Emperor is again the Russian Tsar'.[57] The occasion was rounded off with a grand masquerade when nobles wore national costume and various characters from Russian history were represented. However, Slavophiles who hoped for a more radical return to national principles, such as some sort of power sharing in a revival of the old Assemblies of the Land or even the abolition of serfdom, were disappointed.

In the early 1850s the focus of foreign policy shifted to Constantinople when Nicholas became embroiled in a dispute with the French over the guardianship of the Ottoman-administered Holy Places in Jerusalem. In 1853 the despatch of Russian troops to Moldavia and Wallachia provoked war with Turkey. The following year France and Britain entered on Turkey's side to wage war in the Crimea, in what was basically a war over the balance of power and extended beyond the Black Sea to the Baltic and the Caucasus. Nicholas wrote to his brother-in-law: 'Now nothing is left to me but to fight, to win, or to perish with honour, as a martyr of our holy faith, and when I say this, I say it in the name of all Russia'.[58]

The strain of a major war proved too much for the Nicholas System which, it turned out, had failed to deliver the goods both in the economic substructure and in terms of patriotic response. The British and French proved superior at sea. Russian military supplies were slow in arriving. Particularly ironic was that the armed land forces themselves were not properly maintained or run. More emphasis on parades and uniforms than on modern weapons had a negative effect, as did the reliance on loyalty and long service rather than talent and qualifications in appointments to high command. The government at home was moribund: by 1855 the average age of ministers was 65. Nicholas himself died before the Peace of Paris (March 1856) ratified the loss of Russian influence in the Black Sea, which was demilitarized, deprived Russia of Bessarabia and influence in Moldavia and Wallachia, and generally reduced Russia's status as a leading power in Europe. The focus of expansion would henceforth be the Caucasus and Central Asia.

Nicholas's System relied too heavily upon one man. The attempt to see and participate in everything was doomed to failure, especially when the monarch was surrounded by hand-picked favourites. Reliance on loyalty bred stagnation and lies. One critic has suggested that Nicholas was shielded from the truth, only ever exposed to the 'best', the outward glitter – men in uniforms, the fittest, tallest guards in the front row of parades – because people were afraid that any faults would be blamed on them. The System caused alienation and waste of potential talent among the elite, creating the 'superfluous man' of Russian literature, intelligent beings with no stake in the existing system, and in real life subject to varying degrees of radicalism. The all-seeing eyes actually saw rather little. Nicholas 'did not know Russia because he viewed it through the prism of his own doctrine. One will hardly find in the whole of Europe throughout the nineteenth century a statesman so childishly inexperienced both in matters of government and in evaluating phenomena and people as Nicholas. During thirty years on the throne his knowledge of life did not progress one step.'[59] This may seem a rather harsh judgment on one who devoted his whole life to Russia, but it contains an element of truth. Nicholas saw the Russia that he wanted to see, but in the end was forced to confront unpalatable truths,

Nicholas died on 18 February 1855 at the age of 59. The sudden death of a man known for his strong constitution and ascetic lifestyle gave rise to rumours of suicide or malpractice by the court physicians that eventually turned into legends. For later historians, too, the absence of the usual autopsy reports in the archives fuelled speculation. Further rumours were sparked by the fact that the tsar's body was so decomposed that the coffin had to be closed, in defiance of the Orthodox practice of leaving the corpse exposed until the funeral service.[60] His heir Alexander II gave no credence to such rumours. Rather, the medical record underlined his father's devotion to duty and to Russia, sentiments which he himself would uphold. The official description of the course of the emperor's illness, written by Dmitry Bludov,[61] emphasized his refusal, despite feeling ill with 'grippe' (Peter I's 'good death' provided a model), to neglect his duties. He insisted on seeing off guards units leaving for the front during freezing weather and bore with equanimity the devastating news of a Russian defeat at Eupatoria despite suffering from chills, fever and eventually 'paralysis' of the lung. Bludov's account perpetuated the 'scenario' of family happiness and solidarity to the end, as Nicholas embraced his family and they expressed their love for each other. Nicholas's last words to his heir were apologies that he had failed to leave him with a peaceful, happy and flourishing Russia as Providence had deemed otherwise.

By Nicholas's death, Russia was indeed 'failing to flourish', if Western Europe was taken as the yardstick of progress. The leadership role in world affairs that Nicholas inherited, stemming from the Congress of Vienna where Russia was perceived as a leading voice, gave way to a Russia sidelined and seen as the enemy (and a defeated one at that), despite the ambivalent outcome of the Crimean War. It was the end of the 'triumphalist myth'.[62] Increasingly, at a time when former absolute monarchies in the West were delegating power, the Russian monarch was burdened with the obligation of exercising absolute power, not acting as a figurehead in a purely ceremonial role, still less offloading any of his powers. This was true of all the nineteenth-century emperors and became even more pronounced under Nicholas I, who insisted on taking a personal hand in all aspects of government and was deeply reluctant to delegate. This was the model of ideal monarchy passed on to Alexander II, the first emperor to be groomed publicly and unreservedly for his future role, and in turn to his son and grandson. At the same time, the pressure from the elite for a share in decision-making increased, to a level which represented more than a desire simply to 'be close' to the tsar. Reluctant to ignore the falsehood beneath the ceremonial veneer, educated officials now wanted to participate in government.

8

Reform and Reaction: 1855–1894

ALEXANDER II AND ALEXANDER III

[Alexander II] at heart was really more autocratic than his father,
but, having been brought up with immense care and by people
imbued with Liberalism as it was understood at the time in Russia, he
exhibited a curious mixture of despotic and revolutionary ideas …
Alexander III was essentially Russian. Sometimes he called himself
in jest the 'first *moujik*' of his empire … He had … the simplicity
of the *moujik*, and his humble faith in God and the Saints.[1]

Nicholas I once visited his thirteen-year-old son, the future Alexander II, during a lesson with his history tutor, when the topic was the Decembrists. 'How would you have punished them, Sasha?' he asked. 'I would have pardoned them', the boy replied after a moment's thought.[2] Five years earlier, on the afternoon of 14 December 1825, his father brought the future emperor out to greet the Sapper battalion, which had protected the imperial family from the insurgents. Officers duly kissed the heir's hands and feet. The vulnerability of the dynasty and its individual members was thus brought home to Alexander at a tender age. Thirty years on he would kneel at his father's deathbed awaiting his instructions for a good reign. He may have seen alternatives to his father's way of doing things, as in the case of the punishments meted out to the Decembrists, but on fundamental issues he was his father's son through and through, and from childhood he knew what his own fate and duties would be, with little room for deviation. Among his tutors, chosen by his grandmother, Maria Fedorovna, was the poet Vasily Zhukovsky, who believed that the future sovereign must be raised to be a 'human being' and win the love of his subjects. Alexander was the first Russian heir brought up to believe that the people's approval constituted an important moral basis of autocratic rule.[3] A recommended role model was his saintly patron Prince Alexander Nevsky, who would be his 'invisible companion', fierce in battle but also capable of humility and submission to God's will. Another tutor was the German Karl Karlovich Merder, who swore by Ernst-Moritz Arndt's tract *Plan for the Education and Upbringing of a Prince* (1813), among the recommendations of which were that princes' parents must be major influences, representing the female and male spheres, respectively, of faith and love, and strength and order.[4] Nicholas drilled Alexander in the necessity of duty and obedience; if he wept when rebuked, his mother was there to comfort him. Apparently Alexander often felt inadequate. 'I wish I hadn't been born a Grand Duke', he told Merder in 1829.[5] He never felt that he could live up to his father, or combine the strength and humility demanded by his tutors.

Outside the classroom Alexander did better. Like his grandfather, uncles and father before him, he adored the parade ground and he quickly acquired skill and confidence in drilling troops and wearing a uniform to perfection in multiple military ranks, including Ataman of the Cossack Host, Chief of the Don Regiment and Chief of Hussars. Paintings and engravings most frequently showed him in military garb – see, for example, George Dawe's *Alexander II as Most August Ataman*, a full-length study against a dramatic sky. In later life he was luxuriantly be-whiskered and side-burned, but shared his father's dislike of the full beard.

Various rituals punctuated the heir's progress in the public eye. 22 April 1834, Easter Day, was his coming of age, which included his promotion to be flügel-adjutant in his father's suite. One of the impressive new ceremonies devised for the occasion was the taking of the oath of majority, composed by Speransky, in which the key promise was to preserve autocracy. Everyone, not least Alexander himself, was overcome with tears of emotion, culminating in an embrace between him and his parents, which the press recorded in sentimental tones.

Another landmark in Alexander's preparation to rule was an extensive tour of 29 Russian provinces undertaken in the company of Zhukovsky in 1837, which took him to places where no other member of the imperial family had set foot. The itinerary included Perm and Tver, Moscow, Volga cities (Nizhny Novgorod, Simbirsk, Saratov), and Kherson province, where the heir viewed military manoeuvres in Nicholas's suite. Another highlight was Alexander's investiture as honorary ataman of the Don Cossacks, an act of recognition of the close link between the dynasty and the Cossacks, who were a regular feature of the imperial entourage. The tour exercise was intended to strengthen the bonds between the future tsar and people, educating the heir about his subjects and country and also presenting the dynasty to the people in the most positive light. It was an enormous success. The tall, handsome tsarevich made a good impression with his courtesy, charm and piety in church, thus achieving the purpose, as Zhukovsky noted, of creating a sort of love affair, 'an all-national betrothal' between himself and the Russians.[6]

Like his father at his coronation in 1827, during his 1837 tour Alexander bowed from the Red Staircase in the Kremlin and was rewarded by shouts of 'Hurrah'.[7] Such reactions would accompany the Romanovs for the rest of the dynasty's existence; the 'roar of popular approval' at such public appearances was to be a vital gauge of relations between autocrat and people. Popular acclaim represented the sincere reactions of many of those present, heightened

G. Bothinian. Portrait of Alexander II. Image courtesy of Sotheby's.

by the emotion and lavish theatricality of state occasions, but it was a distinctly unscientific means of measuring wider satisfaction, dangerously drowning out more subdued mutterings of disenchantment or blank stares of indifference.

Marriage was part of the popularization exercise and the search for a suitable bride combined conveniently with a major European tour in 1839 (where, among other places, the heir visited Peter the Great's cottage at Zaandam in Holland). But finding the right wife for Alexander proved difficult, not least because, something of a womanizer, he indulged in several premarital affairs. Dozens of eligible girls were pushed in his direction, but his choice fell upon fifteen-year-old Princess Marie of Hesse-Darmstadt (1824–1880), in Orthodoxy Maria Aleksandrovna, with whom he fell in love during a visit to the theatre. She had not been on the list approved by Alexander's parents, not least because of the relative obscurity of her origins. She was also fragile and vulnerable, qualities that appealed to Alexander, but concerned her future mother-in-law who was only too aware of the burdens that an empress must bear in public life. Despite his parents' discouragement Alexander married Maria in April 1841. The press obligingly predicted 'domestic happiness' as a guarantee of Russia's welfare.[8] The new empress came to be respected rather than loved, known for her strict observance of etiquette.[9]

Despite the Grand Duchess's delicate health, the marriage produced eight children: Alexandra (1842–9), Nikolai (1843–65), Alexander (1845–94), Vladimir (1847–1909), Aleksei (1850–1908), Maria (1853–1920), Sergei (1857–1905) and Pavel (1860–1919).[10] Family life brought its sorrows, including the death of their first daughter from scarlet fever at the age of seven (Alexander wore a medallion with her portrait and regularly prayed at her tomb on the anniversary of her death) and, more seriously for the dynasty, the promising heir to the throne Nikolai, their favourite, in 1865. After the latter's birth Alexander was promoted to adjutant-general in his father's suite. More promotions followed, including full general in 1846. Training in government was subordinate, although upon his marriage he was appointed to the State Council and later the Committee of Ministers, as well as sitting on various secret committees, dealing for example with peasant reform and railways. Attendance may have been mostly ceremonial, but Alexander gained a fairly wide view of the empire's affairs. Thus his path was mapped out for him, deeply rooted in dynastic continuity, something he acknowledged in his accession manifesto of 19 February 1855 in which he referred to implementing 'the wishes and intentions of our august predecessors, Peter, Catherine, Alexander the Blessed and our Unforgettable Parent'.[11] His coronation in 1856 struck an optimistic note after the disappointments of the Crimean War, with no expense spared on everything from lavish parades to illustrated albums. Official reports stressed the love of the Russian people for their new monarch and its religious basis and the tsar's wish for co-operation with all elements of educated society in his plans for reform.

Modern historians have long discarded the view that Alexander was a liberal whose goal to transform Russia into a modern democracy was ultimately thwarted by harsh realities. They see him rather as a conservative, determined to preserve what was best from the old system, with a devotion to autocracy scarcely less than his father's. In particular, he was deeply convinced of his own sacred duty and of Russia's special identity. Like his father, at various times he expressed doubts about the loyalty of most sections of society, from the nobles to the peasants.[12] Even his reforms reflected the wishes of his father, who had memorably admitted that serfdom was 'an evil, palpable and obvious to all'. At the same time, he craved the approval of Western monarchs, amongst whose ranks he numbered himself. Modern statehood and serfdom were incompatible.

All this was reflected in Alexander's role as 'Tsar-Liberator'. As he announced to an assembly of Moscow nobles in March 1856, it was better to abolish serfdom from above than to await the time when it began to abolish itself from below. The decision was the culmination of decades of good intentions 'from above' spurred on by events at home and abroad, notably the defeat in the Crimea, which revealed Russia's inability to harness and deploy human and material resources within its own borders. Ideological and moral arguments also fuelled the debate, from the writings of intellectuals to works by novelists such as Ivan Turgenev, whose *Hunter's Sketches* (1847) aroused sympathy for abused serfs. The main aim was not to free up labour and promote 'capitalism' – Alexander and his contemporaries did not think in such terms – but rather to improve the condition of the peasants and reduce the risk of rural revolt.

The emancipation process itself was tightly controlled from the centre but allowed an element of public enthusiasm to oil the wheels, for example the declaration of the nobles of Lithuania and Nizhny Novgorod of their intention of liberating their serfs. It was carried out in the full glare of publicity or *glasnost*, allowed by a relaxation in censorship and by the very public presence and participation of the emperor himself, who toured the country in 1858. Other members of the imperial family also promoted the cause, notably Grand Duchess Elena Pavlovna and Grand Duke Konstantin Nikolaevich. A series of committees pushed the reform through. It was promulgated on 19 February 1861, the fifth anniversary of Alexander's accession to the throne.[13]

The key issue was the granting of personal liberty to twenty million former serfs, who could no longer be bought and sold, made to work, married off or punished by their former lords. Provisions for land distribution were complicated; serfs remained 'temporarily obligated' to their lords, only those who opted for a 'beggar's allotment' acquiring land for free. Anything more substantial had to be bought through redemption payments and the type and location of land had to be negotiated. A further curb on immediate freedom was the preservation of the commune. Communes distributed land, remained responsible for paying collective taxes and administering justice; hence they arguably failed to inculcate independence and a spirit of enterprise among the peasantry. Yet in terms of preserving order, despite sporadic outbursts of protest by those who felt cheated and anticipated a real, 'golden' freedom in the near future (Anton Petrov's uprising at Bezdna in 1861), the emancipation settlement was a relative success.

'Emancipation undermined the whole legal and institutional structure which had existed in Russia since the seventeenth century.'[14] Other reforms followed to cope with the removal of the central institution of serfdom, as well as to further 'modernization' in general, ultimately with the aim 'to increase the opportunities of the people to serve and obey [the tsar].'[15] The Zemstvo Act of 1864 established local councils in Russia's 34 European provinces, with wide functions that included the provision of education and medical services. Importantly, they were based on a system of indirect elections and provided a training ground in local democracy, even though the authorities strongly opposed a national body and conceded only limited rights of taxation. These moderate institutions were to prove a testing ground for autocracy's willingness to compromise further in delegating initiatives. In 1870 councils based on similar principles were established in towns. In many ways the most radical reform was that of the legal system (1864), which for the first time introduced trial by jury and an independent judiciary. Equality before the law replaced the old estate-based system. The culmination of the process was Dmitry Miliutin's military reforms, the need for which had helped motivate the emancipation. Now that landlords were no longer responsible for selecting their serfs for army recruitment a new, more universal system was instituted in 1874, with a six-year active service requirement for all males. The army was reformed, both in training and administration.

In culture the blossoming of literature, art and music continued, much of it informed by national themes. The 1860s–70s saw the publication of major works by Dostoevsky (*Crime and Punishment*, 1866, *Brothers Karamazov*, 1879), Goncharov, Ostrovsky, Saltykov-Shchedrin, Tolstoy (*War and Peace*, 1868; *Anna Karenina*, 1875–7), and Turgenev (*Fathers and Sons*, 1862). Tchaikovsky's works were first performed in the 1860s (Symphony no. 1, 1868), Mussorgsky's opera *Boris Godunov* premiered in 1874 as Russian music developed under the leadership of national composers known as the 'Mighty Handful' (Balakirev, Borodin, Kui, Mussorgsky and Rimsky-Korsakov). In the visual arts a new generation of realist artists led by Vasily Perov, Ilia Repin and Ivan Kramskoy rejected the idealized, 'foreign' visions of academic art, celebrating instead the 'humble' Russian landscape and Russian history and presenting gritty scenes from rural and urban life and a new portrait gallery of progressive heroes. A landmark work was Repin's *Bargehaulers* (1873), a study of the stoicism of a group of 'human pack animals'. In 1871 the Society of Travelling Art Exhibits held its first shows outside the capitals. In architecture the popularity spread of the Neo-Russian style, based on reconstructions of pre-Petrine church and civic architectural styles (see, for example, the Historical Museum on Red Square, 1879), while pastiches of peasant carpentry and wood carving embellished country houses for the elite. At Abramtsevo to the north of Moscow the industrialist Savva Mamontov and his family and artist friends sponsored peasant crafts, ceramics, icon collecting and amateur dramatics on Russian themes. The imperial family actively welcomed Neo-Russian themes in the arts, as long as they were not politicized. The emperor's brother Grand Duke Vladimir even bought Repin's *Bargehaulers*, no doubt seeing stalwart strongmen rather than suffering 'pack animals'.

Dynastic sites were a particular focus for patronage. Despite the adulation that he received from some quarters, Alexander never saw himself in isolation but as first among equals: as leader of the house of Romanov, which, in his view, assured Russia's happiness. His interest in his ancestors and his determination to link his own efforts with theirs was evident from the start of his reign. He had been born in Moscow, a happy coincidence that allowed him to refer to it as 'my native land' and to combine allegiance to the old and new capitals.[16] His attempts to consolidate the dynasty and emphasize its pre-Petrine historical roots alongside its contemporary activities included renovation of the old family mausoleum in the Novospassky monastery in Moscow (where in 1837 he had been impressed by a fresco of a family tree modelled on the rod of Jesse).[17] In 1837 he had visited the Ipatiev monastery in Kostroma, leaving a message: 'With special attention and pleasure we inspected the cells in which together with his mother the young Mikhail Fedorovich Romanov dwelt. In memory of my visit I leave this sheet with my signature.'[18] He completed the restoration of Michael's apartments in the monastery, opening them to the public in 1863.[19] Michael's Kremlin Terem palace was also renovated, by Fedor Solnstev.[20]

In 1856 Alexander purchased the so-called 'House of the Boyars Romanov' on Varvarka from an adjacent monastery, restored it and created a museum there. There was a ceremony of consecration on 31 August 1858 in the presence of the imperial family; a plaque commemorated the 'sovereign originator of the ruling house'. The restoration was an imaginative one, recreating interiors in the early seventeenth-century style and filling them with objects from the Kremlin, among them personal belongings of Filaret, Martha and Michael.[21]

In 1859 an equestrian monument to Nicholas I (Auguste Montferrand, Peter Klodt *et al.*) was unveiled in St Petersburg, a conscious echo of Falconet's monument to Peter I. Plaques celebrating Nicholas's accomplishments included a depiction of Alexander's presentation to the Sappers in 1825.[22] The consecration was attended by the family *en masse*. After the ceremony Alexander wrote to his mother that he continued to serve his father 'in my heart as if he were still alive'.[23]

In 1834 Nicholas I had accompanied his son on a walk around the Peter-Paul fortress, stopping at the cathedral to kiss the tombs of Paul, Alexander I, their wives and Constantine Pavlovich,[24] thus initiating him into the cult of ancestors that he continued to revere. On a visit to the cathedral in 1865 Alexander discovered that many imperial sarcophagi were damaged. He thereupon commissioned white Italian marble casings for fifteen of the tombs from the architect A. A. Puaro. The old tombs were encased in the new ones, which were fitted with new metal plaques.[25]

A major family anniversary was the bicentenary of Peter the Great in 1872.[26] For Alexander, inviting comparisons with his Tsar-Reformer predecessor was a calculated risk which seems to have paid off. The celebrations, culminating in the capital on 30 May, Peter's birthday, centred on processions linking Petrine places and memorabilia – his first cabin, his first boat, the Bronze Horseman statue, and Peter's tomb. The authorities reserved key roles for the elite, but also sought to involve and enthuse the ordinary public, who were offered 'popular readings' on Peter, edifying pictures to illustrate his feats and plenty of refreshments. Events and publications emphasized the progressiveness of Peter's descendants and their fostering of Petrine virtues for the good of the whole nation. In Moscow the celebrations focused on the opening of the Polytechnical Exhibition, which commemorated Peter's promotion of industry and technology and his encouragement of education. The 'grandfather' of the fleet was brought to Moscow for public display, accompanied by Grand Duke Constantine, as an emblem of the potential of small beginnings to grow into major enterprises.[27] Towns with connections with Petrine activity – such as Petrozavodsk and Voronezh – unveiled statues.[28]

Alexander did not neglect the memory of his great grandmother Catherine II. One of the prime aims of the Russian Historical Society, established in 1866, was to publish documents from her reign and 'rescue' Catherine from her radical critics.[29] November 1873 saw the unveiling of M. O. Mikeshin's St Petersburg monument to Catherine, with Alexander's approval and support.[30] Numerous publications allowed a new public to acquaint itself with Catherine, although her *Memoirs* were not published in Russia until 1907 and the first major studies of her reign by Brückner and Bilbasov appeared under Alexander III. Such 'dynastic' promotions paved the way for further celebration of Romanov historical roots in the reigns of Alexander III and Nicholas II.

However, while honouring the memory of his ancestors, Alexander sowed dissension in his immediate family circle. The premature death of Tsarevich Nicholas and the first attempts on her husband's life in the 1860s seriously affected the already fragile health of Empress Maria. Some days she could barely rise from her bed. The couple met during the day and attended public occasions when the empress was able, but the marriage had become a formality. From the mid-1860s Alexander enjoyed the company of Princess Ekaterina Dolgorukaia, whom he first met in 1859, when she was only thirteen, and for a second time at the Smolny Institute in 1864, when he courted her fairly openly with the connivance of her female relatives. At first she resisted, but she too fell in love and by 1866 was his mistress. Alexander is said to have promised to marry her as soon as he was free, since she was his wife in God's eyes.[31] Members of the imperial family, notably the future Alexander III, protested in vain. Somehow a split in the family was avoided and appearances were kept up, despite the scandal that blew up in society over 'a certain lady', whom her enemies uncharitably described as badly educated and even stupid. Alexander emphasized how much Dolgorukaia had given up for his sake. Their fate was sealed by the birth of their first child in 1872.

In July 1880, just over a month after Empress Maria's death and no doubt impelled by the constant threat to his life, Alexander would marry Dolgorukaia at Tsarskoe Selo in the presence of just five witnesses, none from the imperial family. (After her first formal presentation, the tsar's aunt apparently swore 'I shall never acknowledge that impudent gold digger!'[32]) She took the title Princess Romanovskaia-Yurevskaia, which harked back to an ancestor of Tsar Michael's and the founder of Moscow, Prince Yury Dolgoruky. An act of 5 December 1880 conferred this title on the couple's children Georgy (1872–1913), Olga (1873–1925) and Catherine (1878–1959). (Another son, Boris, was born and died in 1876.) They took the patronymic Aleksandovich/ -ovna, arousing fears among the Romanov clan that the second family would claim dynastic rights, with the emperor's support.[33] Despite the clear order of succession established by Paul's law of 1797, the autocrat still had the power to do as he wished and it was known that Alexander regarded his son Georgy as a 'true Russian'. In autumn 1880 he made generous financial provision for his second family and asked his heir Alexander to take care of them in the event of his death. Unlike his father, Alexander II refused to keep his infidelities 'unofficial'. As a recent biographer argues, his insistence upon his own private life, regardless of convention, puzzled high society Russians; by destroying something of the mystical aura that surrounded tsars he made a decisive step towards separating the man from the monarch.[34]

By the time he married Ekaterina, Alexander's life was in grave danger. Far from stemming the flood of revolt, the Great Reforms gave reason and scope for dissident and radical groups, including terrorists, to operate against the system, the political foundations of which remained unchanged. The universities in particular became hotbeds of dissension. Alexander may have allowed, even spearheaded, wide-ranging reforms, but his autocratic power remained untouched: there was no constitution, there were no central representative bodies. Pre-reform *glasnost* permitted a level of public discussion on key issues, but this was soon retracted. A central problem for critics was the crippling 49-year debt borne by the peasants, which they denounced as unjust, since peasants were asked to redeem land that they saw as theirs by right as the tillers of the soil. Peasants fared unevenly, depending on the location of their villages. Wasteful, traditional farming methods were barely touched. Nobles, too, many of whom had already mortgaged their serfs, found themselves in difficulties. Hence the crown risked alienating the two classes of society that it regarded as its bedrock support.

Foreign policy and managing non-Russian nationalities in the empire encountered mixed success. The problem of reclaiming great power status with the West after 1856 was hampered by the rise of Germany and the Russo-Turkish war of 1877–8, into which Russia was drawn in defence of co-religionists in the Balkans, with the enthusiastic support of Panslavists. Russian military successes and the establishment of independence for Montenegro, Serbia and Romania and autonomy for Bulgaria in the Treaty of San Stefano prompted the alarmed Western powers to force concessions from Russia in the Treaty of Berlin (1878), achieving the withdrawal of Russian troops from Bulgaria and Romania. This war was important for the Romanovs in that it inspired a family effort, with the tsar's brothers and sons in command posts, including the future Alexander III, who received the Cross of St George for action on the Danube.

The empire continued to expand in the Caucasus, Central Asia and the Far East, with the subjugation of the Circassians, the consolidation of the governor-ship of Turkestan in the 1860s, the annexation of the khanates of Kokand, Bukhara and Khiva and territorial acquisitions from China in the Amur and Ussuri regions. The port of Vladivostok was founded in 1861. In 1875 Russia reached a settlement with Japan over Sakhalin and the Kurile islands. In 1863 revolt broke out again in Poland, where, following a mutiny of Polish soldiers in the Russian army, an independent 'dictatorship' was declared. The revolt was brutally suppressed and over the next few years most of Poland's privileges were withdrawn, including use of the Polish language in public. More compliant Finland fared better, with Finnish sanctioned as the official language and a separate army created.

There were many grounds for those who campaigned on behalf of the peasants and society in general, including the nationalities, to attack the authorities with the aim of overthrowing tsarism. This gave rise to an amorphous movement of intellectuals known as populism, whose tactics ranged from peaceful propaganda among the peasantry to violent assaults on authority. In April 1866 an expelled student, Dmitry Karakozov, attempted to shoot Alexander, who interrogated his would-be assassin on the spot. Karakozov replied that he had acted to avenge the 'deception' of the emancipation. The tsar ordered an annual procession of the cross to mark his salvation.[35] In Paris in May the following year A. Berezovsky, a Pole, tried to kill the tsar, who was returning from a military parade with two of his sons and Napoleon III. The revolutionary movement gathered momentum, initially in the relatively non-aggressive and utopian 'going to the people' of 1874, when thousands of young educated people flocked to the villages. Most aimed to assist and 'learn from' the peasants, but some tried to raise rebellion. It was this latter element, disappointed by peasant apathy, that eventually devised a radical programme under the name of 'Land and Freedom', which in 1879 spawned the offshoot terrorist organization, 'People's Will', with the express aim of assassinating Alexander, whom it accused of deceiving the people and society, impoverishing the nation, suppressing Poland, extinguishing freedom and maltreating arrested opponents.[36]

The last few years of Alexander II's reign were clouded by violence, all pointing to a bloody reckoning, as terrorists killed government officials all over Russia. In 1878 the populist Vera Zasulich shot and wounded the governor of St Petersburg, General Fedor Trepov, but was acquitted at her jury trial. In March 1879 A. K. Soloviev shot at the emperor in St Petersburg but the bullet only pierced his greatcoat. Six governors-generals were given dictatorial powers and made numerous arrests, but the movement was not halted. In November two attempts to blow up the royal train failed. The 'People's Will' leader Ivan Zheliabov, posing as a smith, managed to lay a mine on the railway track near Aleksandrovskoe, but it failed to go off. Near Moscow another attempt masterminded by Sophia Perovskaia succeeded only in blowing up a wagon of a subsidiary train carrying provisions for the royal table. Both Zheliabov and Perovskaia would escape to plot again.

At lunch time on 5 February 1880 there was an explosion beneath the imperial dining room in the basement of the Winter Palace set off by a terrorist, S. N. Khalturin, who managed to infiltrate the palace staff. (Security was surprisingly lax.) But lunch had been delayed and Alexander was in an antechamber. The future Alexander III recorded in his diary how he witnessed upwards of 50 sentries of the Finnish Guard in the rubble, of whom ten were killed and 47 wounded: 'A pitiful sight – for the rest of my life I shall not forget the horror … Lord, we thank You for Your new mercy and miracle, but give us the means to comprehend how to act. What are we to do?'[37] Alexander also mentions the appointment of Mikhail Loris-Melikov as head of the Supreme Administrative

Commission with extraordinary measures to restore order: 'May God grant him success, fortify and instruct him.'[38] In 1880 more than 31,000 people were under police supervision. In 1879–82 30 revolutionaries were executed.[39]

There was a brief respite. 19 February 1880 was the 25th anniversary of Alexander's accession and the nineteenth anniversary of the emancipation. The tsar was not deterred from appearing in public on the balcony of the Winter Palace with his whole family. Tsarevich Alexander described a grand parade of military bands with units from all the regiments: the music began to deafening cries of 'Hurrah!' from all the officers, soldiers and mass of the people. The national anthem was repeated several times with gun salutes. Receptions for officers and the State Council followed, then a parade of the cross to the main church of the palace for a service ('Never did I see such a huge turn-out of people at such a procession'), a reception for the diplomatic corps and a family luncheon in the Malachite hall. That evening they heard Glinka's *A Life for the Tsar*, which was received with 'huge enthusiasm'; the public mood was 'most enthusiastic (*samoe vostorzhennoe*)', the anthem being repeated six times. 'All in all this day made the most joyful and pleasant impression upon us, and God blessed this solemn and Glorious festival!'[40] The next day, however, there was an attempt on the life of Loris-Melikov, which left him wounded. 'Thank goodness that this man whom poor Russia now needs so much survived!' wrote Alexander.[41]

A mood of gloom and doom prevailed in family circles. On 29 February the tsarevich wrote: 'It's terrible to think what we have lived through these past five years. First the restless years before the Turkish war, then the war itself in 1877–78 and finally the most terrible and abominable years that Russia has ever experienced: 1879 and the beginning of 1880. There could scarcely be anything worse than this time! May God bless us now and give us comfort and may the end of this year give us peace and quiet! Amen.'[42]

After he was appointed Minister of the Interior in August 1880, Loris-Melikov's aim was to restore order and he proposed making further reforms to achieve this. As he wrote to Alexander II, 'the great reforms of Your Majesty's reign seem at the present time incomplete and partly uncoordinated ... The necessary and effective way of continuing the struggle against sedition consists precisely in calling upon society to participate in the elaboration of the measures needed at the present time.'[43] The proposals that followed were ultra-cautious, avoiding 'dangerous experiments', keeping the sovereign power in full control to harness the experience of local leaders and encourage enthusiasm. Alexander told Yurevskaia: 'I have signed the Manifesto. On Monday morning [2 March] it will appear in the papers and, I hope, make a good impression. At least the Russian people will see that I have given them all I possibly could. And all of this is thanks to you.'[44] But the hand of the assassin intervened. On Sunday 1 March 1881 Alexander attended a military parade and visited his cousin Grand Duchess

Ekaterina Mikhailovna. On the way back, at the Catherine Canal, an explosion damaged the emperor's carriage. Alexander emerged unhurt. He insisted on seeing the assassin Rysakov, who had been apprehended, and then on inspecting the site of the explosion, despite the pleas of his guards to drive off. At that point another bomb exploded. Once the smoke cleared, it was obvious that the tsar was severely wounded, his lower body shattered. He was rushed back to the palace, where Yurevskaia took charge, administering oxygen, while recognizing that the situation was hopeless. 'The emperor', she later wrote, 'retained a truly heroic firmness of spirit; not one complaint passed his lips.'[45] He died at 3.30 pm. The assassin Grinevitsky was also mortally wounded.

On 3 April 1881 Zheliabov, Perovskaia, Rysakov, N. Kibalchich and T. Mikhailov were all hanged in what would be the last public execution in Russia. Soon Princess Yurevskaia and her children departed for Nice, where they henceforth created no trouble. Alexander, had he lived, was apparently intending to renounce the throne to join them there, although there were other rumours that he intended to crown Yurevskaia as his consort. Whatever the case, his death averted a dynastic crisis.

'With hope and trust Russia greets its new tsar. He will be true to the memory of his father and he will continue and complete his beneficial enterprises; may the rule of law reign in Russia and may the foundations of correct, rational civil society develop, the first stone of which was laid by Emperor Alexander II.'[46] Thus wrote the liberal newspaper *The Voice* (*Golos*) on 2 March 1881. The circumstances of Alexander III's accession in 1881 were even more shocking than those of his grandfather's in 1825. The unavoidable fact of his father's shattered body brought home even to the most unimaginative observer the wound to the body politic and to Russia itself, arousing horror in ruling circles and hopes among extremists that the Romanov regime was literally and figuratively on its last legs. From abroad Peter Kropotkin's paper *La Révolte* wrote that the assassination had 'inflicted a mortal blow on autocracy'. The prestige of 'God's anointed' was extinguished by a simple can of nitro-glycerine.[47]

The successor did not succumb to despair, however. He may have wavered briefly over how to treat the assassins – with mercy, as the public and intelligentsia demanded, or without compromise, as his former tutor, the Chief Procurator of the Holy Synod Konstantin Pobedonostsev (1827–1907) advocated. The latter's victory in this matter was symbolic of his victory as a power behind the throne.[48] He discerned certain qualities in Alexander, including his 'simple soul', 'Russian heart' and devotion to Orthodoxy that made him the ideal national ruler. He encouraged him to read Russian history, to visit churches, to appreciate Moscow and meet with conservative figures. He also inculcated anti-foreign sentiments, especially anti-German, which extended to officials of German origin.[49] His influence over Alexander was especially strong as the tsar regarded virtually all other members of his circle as dishonest charlatans, few of whom, apart from Pobedonostsev, believed in autocracy any more. (His only two close confidants would be Count Ilarion Vorontsov-Dashkov, minister of his Household, and General Cherevin, head of the Okhrana.)

There would be no compromise, no toying with re-educating the terrorists by kindness. In particular, even the most timid plans for further reform must be nipped in the bud.

Pobedonostsev did not have to use much persuasion as his protégé's conservative values were well entrenched. In January 1880 Alexander had noted with satisfaction the rejection of Peter Valuev's project for a representational State Council (from the nobility, zemstvo and towns) on the grounds that 'it would have satisfied no one, would have confused our domestic affairs even more and all the same might have been one of the first steps towards a Constitution!'[50] On the day of the assassination the new emperor pledged to 'respect his father's will' and issue Loris-Melikov's Manifesto, but that night he halted publication. He and Pobedonostsev argued against a 'chattering shop'; only a close bond between tsar and people based on trust could provide the proper basis for government. As Alexander scribbled on the original of the Manifesto, 'Thank God that this criminal and hasty step toward a constitution was not taken, and that this whole fantastic project was rejected by quite an insignificant minority in the Council of Ministers.'[51] On 29 April 1881 Alexander issued his own Manifesto, written by Pobedonostsev, in which he affirmed the unshakeable foundations of autocracy, sustained by the prayers of the people. It contained a tacit reference to the early Romanovs and the overcoming of 'Troubles' under firm authority.[52] At a military parade on the same day he promised to rule 'autocratically and monocratically' in the manner of his grandfather and father.[53] Alexander rejected even modest proposals, submitted in 1882, for an Assembly of the Land along the lines of the bodies that advised the early Romanovs, on Pobedonostsev's advice that any sort of popular meeting could lead to revolution.[54]

Political conservatism went hand in hand with a belief in Russian supremacy. In 1884 Alexander recalled the consecration of the cathedral of Christ the Redeemer in Moscow after his coronation in May 1883, an event which in itself symbolized the completion of the efforts of his ancestors: 'This great event ... showed to the whole of astonished and morally corrupt Europe that Russia is the same holy, Orthodox Russia as she was under the Tsars of Moscow and as, God willing, she will remain forever.'[55] Conservative nationalists, disillusioned with Alexander II's 'vacillations', welcomed the accession of his son; Westernized intellectuals found themselves excluded. Moscow of the ancient grand princes and the early Romanovs became the favoured source of national inspiration, the heart of the Russian land. Imperial and conservative opinion associated St Petersburg with foreigners.

In summer 1881 Alexander travelled to Moscow and in a gesture inaugurated by Nicholas I bowed three times to the people from the Red Staircase in the Kremlin. Later he visited Kostroma, to do reverence to the beginnings of the imperial line. A mythologized seventeenth century, the time of Michael and Alexis, before Westernization, before reform, became the true source of national life, displayed in everything from church architecture to the design of restaurant menus. At the coronation in 1883 a procession of peasants included representatives of the descendants of Ivan Susanin. At a gala the Bolshoi performed Glinka's *A Life for the Tsar*, which culminates in a hymn of celebration to Michael as he approaches the Kremlin.[56] Russification became the order of the day, in religion, language and culture, further justified by the allegedly revolutionary character of many non-Russian nationalities, especially Jews and Poles. Regulations were issued limiting Jewish residence outside the Pale of Settlement, curtailing the rights of the nobles in the Baltic states and assimilating elites in the Caucasus. The Orthodox Church revived, with many new monasteries being built and new priests consecrated. On numerous religious anniversaries the ruling house demonstrated its dedication to the Church and its role as the support of the state throughout history. These included the 900th anniversary in 1888 of the baptism of Rus.

Alexander curtailed the activities of revolutionary groups early in his reign by imposing strict controls on the intelligentsia and the press and by issuing in August 1881 a series of extraordinary police measures – so-called 'Temporary Regulations' – which remained in force until the fall of the dynasty. The 1884 University Charter curtailed all remaining autonomy and freedoms. Courses for women were closed. (In the days following the assassination students attempted to avoid harassment by discarding their spectacles and cutting their hair.) Counter reforms were instituted under the direction of the Minister of the Interior Dmitry Tolstoy, which strove to limit the power of the zemstvos, urban institutions and local courts. In the countryside a new post of land captain (1889), appointed from the local nobility, was created to police the provinces with comprehensive powers. Justices of the peace were abolished. In 1886 celebrations of the 25th anniversary of the emancipation were banned. At the same time, the government made concessions to the peasants, who were still thought to be devoted to the crown. These included the scaling down of redemption payments and the abolition of the poll tax (1887).

This uncompromising stance at home was initially accompanied by extreme caution in foreign policy, with the aim of avoiding the sort of adventurism that had dragged Russia into conflict with the Turks in the 1870s. Alexander's own experience at the front left a vivid memory of the horrors of war. In 1881 the Three Emperors League (Russia, Austria, Germany) was renewed. Four years later, Alexander veered away from war with Britain over Afghanistan and with Austria over Bulgaria. Avoidance of war earned him the title of 'Tsar Peacemaker'. At the beginning of 1894, however, to the tsar's evident discomfort, Russia signed an alliance with republican France, and entered the more unstable international world of the 1890s with a radical new partner.

Uncompromising authoritarianism was in keeping with Alexander's character and appearance. He was tall and powerfully built, with uncouth manners, his bulky bearded appearance very much in keeping with the vogue in the 1880s–1900s for images of the epic warriors or *bogaytri* of Russian folk saga, who could polish off 100 enemies with one sweep of their sword. He might equally be described as a Cossack Tsar. Invested as ataman of the Don Cossacks in 1869, he greatly admired the Cossacks' loyalty to the crown and Orthodoxy and their way of life. In his own uniform, and in new uniforms introduced into the regiments, he favoured a Russian-style caftan tunic and Russian boots. Nothing in the visual arts captured these associations so well as the posthumous equestrian statue by Paulo Trubetskoy, commissioned in 1899 by competition to coincide with the completion of the Trans-Siberian railway, and unveiled in May 1909 in front of the Moscow Station in St Petersburg. Alexander, dressed in a simple tunic and Astrakhan hat, is seated on a massive horse, which seems to brace itself to hold his weight. The motionless, heavy impression, enhanced by the roughness of the surfaces, was variously interpreted. Some observers saw solid, unflinching

Trubetskoy's statue of Alexander III, St Petersburg. *c.*1916.

Russian virtues, the defensive rather than attacking principle that underpinned Alexander III's reign. The sculptor himself said that he wished to express the power of Russia in his work.[57] Others saw a condemnation of the emperor, seated ponderously on a tightly bridled Russia, or even a joke or caricature, poking fun at the nation. The Soviet commissar A. Lunacharsky thought the statue evoked 'all the shame and all the baseness of autocracy'. The lack of a tail on the horse prompted much comment.[58]

Alexander was born on 26 February 1845, which meant that a crucial ten years of his upbringing were supervised by his grandfather, Nicholas I, whose influence was significant in Alexander's military training.[59] This showed in his love of military parades (although he disliked 'flashy militarism'[60]), an orderly life with regular meals, simple food and so on. He was by all accounts a weak student intellectually, but unusually diligent. Like Peter I, the huge Alexander liked small, cramped rooms and was particularly at ease in the Anichkov palace in St Petersburg, traditionally the heir's residence in the nineteenth century.[61] His favourite palace was Gatchina, the barracks-like residence of his great-grandfather Paul I, where after the events of 1881 the imperial family were able to enjoy increased security. (His mother, to whom Alexander was not close, remarked on his 'unfortunate' resemblance to Paul.)[62]

In his youth he was to some extent shielded from public attention as second in line to the throne, indulging in love affairs, notably with Princess Maria Meshcherskaia, for whom in 1864 he even threatened to relinquish his dynastic rights. Alexander II had raised his eldest son Nicholas as his presumptive heir, declaring him on his majority in 1859. However, during a period of recuperation in the south of France in 1865, tuberculosis of the spine was diagnosed. His parents took a fast train to Nice and were able to spend some time with him before he died on 11 April, apparently of meningitis. Many tributes bore witness to the lost promise of this 'pledge of Russia's future happiness and greatness'.[63] According to one eyewitness, Alexander, declared heir on 15 April, was devastated: 'It was painful to look at poor Alexander Aleksandrovich; he commanded more sympathy than anyone else present'.[64]

Nicholas's death thrust Alexander into the limelight and brought duty to the fore. The following year, despite his continuing attachment to Meshcherskaia and his threat to defy his parents, he married the daughter of King Christian IX of Denmark, Marie Sophia Fredericke Dagmar (1847–1928), Maria Fedorovna in Orthodoxy and Minni to her husband. She had been the late Nicholas's fiancée, summoned to his sickbed in 1865, and was evidently too well connected with Europe's royal houses to be let go: her brother George was king of Greece, her elder sister Alexandra married the future Edward VII of England.

Empress Maria would live through three reigns and a revolution, ending her life back in Denmark. As grand duchess and empress she served as patron of the Administration of Institutions of Empress Maria, which included schools, orphanages, foundling homes and almshouses, the Russian Red Cross Society, the Society for Rescue at Sea, the Maria Charitable Society at the Moscow Marinsky Hospital for the poor and the Maria girls' schools. She was also commander-in-chief of the Cavalier Guards and Cuirassiers. Her activities were not merely token: she tended the war wounded during 1877–8, setting an example for female relatives, including her future daughter-in-law Alexandra.[65] She was more sociable than her husband, compensating to some extent for his discomfort in high society, with whom she was popular for her easy manner and charm. During her reign as empress the court operated with all its former glitter and lavishness. She was also an instant success when the couple toured Russia in 1869–70, visiting churches and warmly greeting peasants.

Alexander remained faithful to his Minni. There would apparently be no repeat of his father's dalliances. As he wrote to her in 1878, may God in his mercy grant the continuation of that 'old, sweet, dear happiness' that they had known for eleven years.[66] Every Easter from 1884 he presented her with an exquisite egg made by the jeweller Carl Fabergé, many of them illustrating the theme of resurrection and rebirth. The first was a simple chicken in a golden shell; later eggs were much more elaborate.[67] Nicholas II continued the custom with annual gifts to his own wife.

The couple had six children, the future Nicholas II (Nicky, 1868–1918), Alexander (1869–1870), George (Georgie, 1871–99), Ksenia (1875–1960), Michael (1878–1918, heir to throne 1899–1904, abrogated succession in March 1917) and Olga (1882–1960). In his diary, Alexander recorded how he wept with joy like a child at Nicholas's birth,[68] while in 1891 he recalled his despair at the death of his infant son, Alexander, 'our angel' who he believed was watching them from heaven.[69] The younger children were their father's favourites. Diary entries for 1880 give a glimpse into his schedule as grand duke, how he went tobogganing with Nicky, skating or simply strolling in the garden.[70] Olga recalled nature rambles, camp fires and sawing wood. Family life was central to Alexander, extending to a liking for his Danish in-laws with whom he shared a love of horseplay and practical jokes.

At the same time, in the 'Enactment on the Imperial Family' (1886) he limited the title grand duke to the sovereign's sons and grandsons. Subsequent descendants took the title Prince (Duke) of the Imperial Blood. The new law also restricted the allowances paid through the Appanages Department. The reform was prompted by the proliferation of the imperial family through the lines of Alexander's uncles, Nicholas I's three younger sons Constantine, Nicholas and Michael, to curb the 'extravagance' of the extended clan by, for example, evicting grand dukes from 'grace and favour' apartments in the palace. The 'disenfranchisement' of future grandchildren led to resentment, as did Alexander's high-mindedness about irregular relationships.[71] He took a dim view of immoral behaviour, issuing sanctions against Konstantin and Nikolai Nikolaevich, both of whom set up households with ballerinas, and exiling his cousin Mikhail Mikhailovich for marrying a foreign countess. On the other hand, those who conformed and set duty above personal life could enjoy high positions, especially in the military, although not exclusively so. His ambitious brother Vladimir (1847–1909), a potential rival, served as president of the Academy of Arts as well as commanding the St Petersburg garrison. Their younger brother Aleksei (1850–1908) was enrolled in the navy from birth, commanding the Danube fleet in 1877–8, for which he won the Order of St George. As chief commander from 1881, however, he was a poor organizer and wasted state funds, more interested in good living and womanizing. He was forced into retirement after the disastrous Tsushimo naval battle in 1905.[72] Brother Sergei (1857–1905) was appointed governor-general of Moscow in 1891, a particularly significant elevation which allowed the ultra-Orthodox and arch-conservative Sergei to turn Moscow into his own personal domain. One of Sergei's conditions for accepting the appointment was that Jews should be expelled from Moscow.[73] Thus the Romanov 'family firm' maintained a prominent position both in society and administration

Alexander III's reign was free of war and terrorist outrages, but it was by no means devoid of family drama. In summer 1888 the imperial family undertook a ceremonial tour of Ukraine, Poland and the Caucasus. On the return journey on the Kursk-Kharkov-Azov railway from Sebastopol on 17 October while breakfast was being served their train crashed near Borki, killing 21 people and wounding many more. Members of the imperial family escaped, officially unscathed. In the empress's words, their salvation was due to 'God's generous kindness and mercy'. She was struck by the concern of the wounded for the tsar's safety.[74] At the risk of damaging his own health, Alexander himself held up the collapsing carriage roof in a feat of strength suggesting that he was a *bogatyr*, a Russian hero of old. The experience made a deep impression on the basically pessimistic tsar, who was reminded of the imminence of death.[75]

The Saviour icon from Peter I's cabin in St Petersburg which accompanied them also emerged intact, with its glass case undamaged. One writer likened the escape to the 'miracle' which saved Peter from Swedish bullets at Poltava in 1709.[76] In 1889 a grateful Alexander III financed the building of two extension wings to the north and south of the outer building of Peter's cabin to accommodate the growing numbers of pilgrims who visited its chapel. Around the Saviour icon were icons donated by pilgrims, including images of St Alexander Nevsky (the emperor's patron saint, whose cult had been revived by Peter) and other saints of the imperial family, presented in gratitude for their rescue.[77] The Neo-Russian Church of the Saviour of the Glorious Transfiguration was built near the site of the crash.

Alexander strove to find a balance between repressive measures and popularity, the latter based on his reputation as a truly Russian tsar, in everything from his beard (he was the first ruler to grow one since the seventeenth century) to his physical strength. In the words of a court historian, 'the majestic simplicity of his bearing … gave him the look of a Russian bogatyr, just as internally he was a bogatyr in spirit'.[78] In the arts official sponsorship continued to favour the Neo-(Pseudo-) Russian or Russian revival style, which mimicked early Russian church architecture and folk motifs in domestic building and decor. A prime example was the Church of the Resurrection 'on the Blood' (1883–1907, architect Alfred Parland), built on the site of Alexander II's assassination as a tribute to a tsar now viewed as a martyr in the manner of the 'passion sufferers' of ancient Rus. Reminiscent of the exterior of St Basil's Cathedral in Moscow with its polychrome cupolas and of the seventeenth-century 'decorated' style in its fancy brick and mosaic work, it satisfied Alexander III's demand for a church 'in the style of the time of the Muscovite tsars of the seventeenth century'.[79] It represented the 'conquest' of Classical St Petersburg by the Russian style, a bold statement of the imperial concept of true Russian architecture.

Grand cathedrals in the same idiom were erected in many major towns of the empire's non-Russian provinces to emphasize the supremacy of 'mother' Russian culture. These included the Cathedral of the Resurrection in Tashkent (1888) and the Alexander Nevsky cathedrals in Tallinn and Warsaw (1894–1912), all presented as symbols of Orthodox rule and Romanov benevolence. A variation on the theme was embodied in the monument to Alexander II (N. Sultanov, A. Opekushin, 1893–1898), which represented dynastic history as much as the emperor's controversial personal achievements. Opekushin's statue depicted Alexander in military uniform and an imperial mantle making a gesture of blessing or perhaps liberation to his people, whose 'love' for their ruler was inscribed on the pedestal. In a gallery beneath the statue were 33 mosaic portraits of Russian rulers from St Vladimir to Nicholas I. Early Russian style was evident in the 36-metre high tent (*shater*) canopy, reminiscent of church architecture and shrines.[80] In the Peter-Paul Cathedral Alexander commissioned a mausoleum for non-ruling Romanovs, who had outgrown the space in the main body of the church.[81]

Icons, religious banners and Orthodox ceremonial permeated all aspects of court and army life. For his coronation Alexander summoned artists from Palekh, thus showing 'loving devotion' towards peasant icon painters.[82] Palekh masters also restored the seventeenth-century frescoes of the Kremlin Palace of Facets, part of the programme to counteract terrorism and dissidence by placing faith in popular creativity. The subjects included legends about the Romanovs' links with Augustus Caesar.[83] Alexander encouraged Russian painters, amassing an impressive collection of works, among them Repin's *Zaporozhian Cossacks*

Writing a Letter to the Turkish Sultan, which he purchased in 1891.[84] In 1898 the Alexander III Museum would open in St Petersburg, the first state-sponsored gallery of Russian art. Lithographs for his coronation album were made from paintings by such leading artists as Ivan Kramskoy, Konstantin Savitsky and Vasily Polenov, and the Russian-style menu for the coronation banquet by Viktor Vasnetsov. The court willingly embraced Russian motifs. In 1883 Grand Duke Vladimir Aleksandrovich gave a ball in the old Russian style, he and his wife clad in boyar costume, the empress attending as a seventeenth-century tsaritsa and the guests as various characters from mediaeval Rus.

Ironically, the shift of the Romanov-sponsored national myth to the seventeenth century coincided with an upsurge of industrialization, spearheaded by the expansion of the railways and financed by high tariffs and rural taxation. Under ministers of finance Ivan Vyshnegradsky and Sergei Witte, the industrial programme was based on foreign investment and expertise. Alexander's conservative government contrived to present even these developments within the national ideological template, on the grounds, for example, that Russian workers differed from their 'rootless' Western counterparts in their rural ancestry and dedication to tsar (who stood above all private interests), motherland and church. Russian industry was state-subsidized and protected by the monarch; its purpose was strongly national, aimed at maintaining Russia's great power status. The Trans-Siberian Railway, for example, initiated in 1891, was emblematic of Russia's mission in the East. Signs of backwardness were ever present, however. A famine and cholera outbreak in 1891, in which almost 500,000 people perished, raised doubts about the efficiency of the government, which had to rely on local zemstvo and voluntary organizations for relief operations.

Alexander's constitution turned out to be less than *bogatyr*-like. In January 1894 he fell ill with nephritis (Bright's disease), a kidney complaint. He rallied, but his condition worsened in the summer. There were plans for recuperation in Corfu, but Alexander died in the imperial residence at Livadia in Crimea on 20 October at the age of only 49. An account of his death by Father John of Kronstadt emphasized its classically 'good' features, the joy of communion, prayer and holy oil, taking leave of his whole family gathered at the bedside.[85] His death provoked a surge of obituaries and condolences not only in Russia but also abroad, where his role in preserving peace was especially lauded. The compliments of Russia's new French allies were particularly effusive. A lying-in-state in Livadia, his sword from the Russo-Turkish war resting on the coffin, was followed by a train journey from Sevastopol to Moscow, with grieving crowds lining the route. In Moscow he lay in state in the Archangel Cathedral, a stone's throw from the seventeenth-century Romanov ancestors that he so admired, before being brought to St Petersburg for burial in the Peter-Paul Cathedral.

The popular press was lavish in its tributes: 'The late tsar was a complete Russian man. From the good-natured face, polite smile, the blue eyes with their soft glimmer, the bright red beard, broad and thick, the powerfully built body, the measured movements, terse speech, the simplicity of manner, directness, the thirst for truth, from all this to steadfastness in work, loyalty in friendship, and including the whole-hearted love for his family – this was a Russian man'.[86]

Censorship did not allow dissenting voices, for which we must turn to later writers: 'The "Russian style" of Alexander III was just as fleeting and empty as the whole reign of that would-be "people's" tsar. Lacking in his veins, probably, one drop of Russian blood, married to a Danish woman, raised in the religious concepts that were instilled in him by the Chief Procurator of the Synod, he wanted, however, to be 'national and orthodox', as often Russified Germans dream of becoming. Even if they don't really know Russian, such people eat black bread and radishes, drink kvas and vodka. Alexander was one of them, but could not write grammatical Russian'.[87]

These criticisms are in many ways unjust in their insistence upon 'blood' as the main determinant of national feeling. Alexander was undoubtedly sincere in his attachment to all things Russian, including his Orthodox faith, whilst following the largely Westernized lifestyle laid out by Peter I. Yet the competing notion that the Romanovs were actually 'Germans' would dog the dynasty for the rest of its existence. Nicholas II inherited an ambivalent legacy.

9

The Last Romanov

NICHOLAS II. (i) 1894–1913

Nicholas II has not a single vice, but he has the worst fault an
autocratic sovereign could possibly have – a want of personality. He
is always following the lead of others. (Maurice Paléologue, 1917.)[1]

The whole collective life of the Russian nation is so to speak summed up
in tsarism. Outside tsarism there is nothing. (Maurice Paléologue, 1917)[2]

It was Nicholas II's misfortune, wrote his leading modern biographer, 'that fate
made him responsible for guiding his country through one of the most difficult
periods in its history'.[3] The extent to which bad luck was compounded by weakness
and stubbornness remains a subject for debate. 'The image of Nicholas II that
dominates historical memory', to quote another source, 'is of a weak, witless ruler,
ill equipped to cope with the challenges of bringing Russia into the modern age.'[4]
Bad omens dogged his early life and reign, from the coincidence of his birthday
on 6 May with the feast of the all-suffering prophet Job to an accident after his
coronation in 1896 when hundreds of his subjects perished. Psychologists have
noted that Empress Maria kept her children close to her for as long as possible,
especially Nicholas, who struck contemporaries as immature when he ascended
the throne at the age of 26 in 1894. He was reluctant to become tsar, sobbing
when he heard news of his father's unexpected death, and declaring himself
'wholly unfit to reign'.[5] He was 'unmanly', even feminine, inheriting his mother's
diminutive stature rather than his father's bear-like bulk. As the wife of the
American minister to St Petersburg memorably remarked, 'Russians will find it
difficult to connect the idea of majesty with one who is so small.'[6] 'His mind is as
small as his person', another critic sharply commented.[7] One might equally cite
the security that Nicholas and his siblings enjoyed, being treated with love and
indulgence by both their parents, with Mama the decisive voice, Papa more of a
soft touch. It was a protective environment, made more so by lessons in the palace
that precluded much contact with 'real life' or the chance to form independent
relationships and judgements. In this Nicholas's upbringing resembled that of
fellow princes all over Europe. He in turn would create his own close family unit,
which played a decisive role in his decision-making.

Nicholas was educated by a governess until the age of ten, when General

Grigory Danilovich took over, a military man who supervised specialist tutors. Nicholas studied four languages: English, French, German and Russian. History was his favourite subject, though the Socialist Revolutionary commander of the guard at Tobolsk in 1917 later recollected that the deposed tsar's 'general knowledge of the history of the Russian people was very weak' and 'all of his discourse on these matters was reduced to a history of wars'.[8] He also studied political economy, international law, military science, chemistry and civil and state law, the last with his father's tutor the Chief Procurator of the Holy Synod Konstantin Pobedonostsev, who preached a pessimistic view of human nature. In particular, Pobedonostsev taught that Russia was too 'primitive', too diverse to embrace democracy and individualism and must maintain a strong monarchy, rooted in faith and tradition rather than rationalist institutional concepts.

Nicholas was, according to some witnesses, a good student with a quick mind, but there was never any sense that he must 'qualify', in the manner of Peter I's principles, to become ruler. To rule was his historical destiny. That hereditary autocracy was enthusiastically upheld by the Russian people seemed plain to Nicholas as he witnessed popular acclaim at such occasions as a family visit to Moscow in 1881 and his father's coronation in 1883. As a manifesto issued by Alexander III on Nicholas's coming of age on 6 May 1884 made clear, 'We believe that there will be heard the universal fervent prayer: may the Lord strengthen the young soul of our first-born and heir in the sacred great behests of service conferred on him by the will of God … and may the grace of God protect him, inspiring and fortifying him in every good intention and just deed.'[9]

In 1887 Nicholas was commissioned into the Preobrazhensky Guards, Peter the Great's own regiment. He enthusiastically embraced military life in the rather artificial setting of cautious camaraderie that an heir to the throne was bound to experience with his peers. It was a life of 'carefree amusement',[10] since there was no war during his father's reign. (At about this time he started an affair with the ballerina Matilda Kshesinskaia.) He adored uniforms and would have many to choose from: in the same year he was inducted as ataman of the Don Cossacks, one of some fifteen honorary military commands. He was also introduced to state service, which he found less congenial, appointed to the Committee of Ministers, the State Council and, in 1893, the Siberian Railway Committee.

Like other heirs before him, young Nicholas was expected to see Russia and the wider world. From October 1890 to August 1891 he travelled to India, Ceylon, the East Indies, Thailand, China and Japan, ending with Siberia. This experience awakened his interest in Russia's Far Eastern policies and a vision of Russia's civilizing role. His companion, Esper Ukhtomsky, taught him that Russians and Asians had a spiritual affinity, that Russia's destiny lay in the East and that 'mergers' of peoples were natural. He felt drawn to Buddhist temples, got on well with local potentates. Yet he remained convinced of Russia's moral superiority.

Russian warships and garrisons in the east aroused feelings of pride, as did Cossacks along his route back home. One of his first acts as tsar to promote his Eastern dream would be the occupation of Port Arthur in Manchuria in 1898.

Nicholas's formative experiences made two overriding principles plain – that he must accept fate in the form of God's will and that his destiny as tsarevich was to rule Russia as autocratic tsar. Fate thus decreed on 20 October 1894, much sooner than he had anticipated. Count Vladimir Lambsdorff, later foreign minister, reported in January 1895 that 'His Majesty still lacks the external appearance and manner of an emperor'.[11] At the same time Nicholas apparently harboured no doubts about the prerogatives of the unlimited power that he inherited from Alexander III. In January 1895, at a reception for various estates bearing congratulations on his wedding, he responded to what he dubbed certain bodies' 'senseless dreams' of a national representative body with the pronouncement that he would 'preserve the principles of autocracy as firmly and undeviatingly as did my unforgettable late father'.[12]

There was a strong dynastic element in Nicholas's dedication to autocracy, which he once remarked he did not maintain 'for my own pleasure'.[13] He shared his predecessors' view that peasant Russia was not ready for democratic rights; indeed, to grant them would be to go against the prevailing popular, religious-based belief in tsarism and play into the hands of radical elements. Nicholas was 'directed by the wish to preserve the crown in the form which he had inherited it from his late father in order to hand it on in the same form after his death to his son'.[14] In short, autocracy must be retained, not least as a duty to past and future generations of Romanovs, a conviction rooted in moral discipline and religious faith which was ultimately to undo the dynasty.[15] Among dynastic values, he favoured military duty first, which was reflected not just in his own upbringing and activities but also in those of his family, including women, who held honorary commands of regiments. A much reproduced print of 1896 shows a splendid array of grand dukes on horseback at a parade, including three sons of Alexander II and four grandsons of Nicholas I, presided over by Nicholas in the uniform of the Chevalier-gardes. Such displays of family solidarity were a familiar sight on the parade grounds of St Petersburg. Nicholas also derived genuine pleasure from imposing military orderliness on his own daily schedule. In this he most resembled Peter I and Nicholas I. This was combined with a need to engage in physical labour and exercise, a dynastic trait going back to Peter I and strongly encouraged by his late father.

Religious faith was central to Nicholas's character. A 'fatalistic spirituality' allowed him to accept setbacks and trials rather than tackling them, in the belief that they were God's will. 'If you find me so little troubled', he once said, 'it is because I have the firm and absolute faith that the destiny of Russia, my own fate, and that of my family are in the hands of Almighty God, who has placed

Lithograph of Nicholas II and the Grand Dukes.
St Petersburg, 1896.

me where I am. Whatever may happen, I shall bow to His will.'[16] The principle
on which there could be no compromise was autocracy, a conviction shared
absolutely by his wife. On 14 November 1894, less than a month after his father's
death and two weeks after the funeral, Nicholas married Alix Victoria Helena
Louise Beatrice (1872–1918), known in Orthodoxy as Alexandra Fedorovna.
Many noted the ill omen of a wedding so close on a funeral. Alexandra's parents
were Prince Louis of Hesse and Princess Alice (1843–78), the second daughter of
Queen Victoria. Ties with the extended British royal family were close. In 1865
the dowager empress's sister Alexandra had married the future king Edward VII.
In 1874 Alexander II's only daughter Maria married Alfred, Duke of Edinburgh,
another of Victoria's sons. Alexandra's elder sister Elizabeth had married
Alexander III's brother Grand Duke Sergei in 1884. Alix was only six when her
own mother and an elder sister died of diphtheria. Thereafter she spent much
time in the company of Queen Victoria, whose devotion to duty and family life
and strict morals she cherished, valuing an English regime of plain food, exercise
and orderliness. Initially Alix refused to convert to Orthodoxy, but relented when
she and Nicholas met at her brother's wedding in April 1894. Her conversion took
place just a day after Alexander III's death. She developed 'an intensely emotional
and mystical faith' in Orthodoxy, with a devotion for icons, crucifixes, relics and

Portrait of Empress Alexandra. Contemporary postcard.

holy men and women,[17] while her philanthropic work, focusing on medical care, owed much to her Protestant upbringing and to her mother's example.

Theirs was a lifelong, intense love affair between two very similar personalities, both with a strong dislike of court life and of officialdom, both with romantic views of the love of the Russian people for their 'little father tsar', both deeply religious. Family life was their cornerstone, marriage the highest expression of Christian love.[18] In 1895 their first daughter Olga was born, followed by Tatiana in June 1897, Maria in June 1899 and Anastasia in June 1901. Until his death in June 1899 Nicholas's younger brother Georgy was heir to the throne, succeeded by their brother Michael, 'until such time as the Lord will deign to bless us with a son and heir'.[19] That long-awaited son, named after Nicholas's most admired ancestor, Tsar Alexis Mikhailovich, arrived on 30 July 1904, a cause for rejoicing in a gloomy time when Russia was embroiled in war with Japan abroad and terrorist acts at home. Sadly, Alexis's life would be constantly threatened by the haemophilia that he inherited from his mother. He had to be shielded from the glare of publicity by keeping his illness secret and from life's hazards by bodyguards, who carried him when necessary. His parents ensured above all that he had God's protection. His bedroom in the family's favourite refuge, Alexander Palace, was dominated by a large five-panelled iconostasis, along with many smaller icons and crosses attached to the walls.[20]

The couple's coronation took place on 14 May 1896, the most lavish so far staged.[21] It was captured on film, as well as in more traditional media by leading artists such as Ilia Repin, Viktor Vasnetsov and Mikhail Nesterov. Romanov family history was evident in numerous details, from the inevitable performance of Glinka's *A Life for the Tsar*, with a portrait of Tsar Michael in the programme, to a banquet menu inspired by a seventeenth-century manuscript. The imperial entourage arrived in Moscow on Nicholas's birthday, 6 May, entering the Kremlin through the Saviour Gate on 9 May, the tsar on a white Arab mare, his mother and wife in separate carriages, to a warm welcome from the people on streets decked with flags and garlands. That night Alexandra switched on the electric illuminations. Vladimir Nemirovich-Danchenko, a correspondent, wrote: 'We held our breath, literally afraid we might disturb this astonishing *fata morgana* by gasping; all we could do was stand and stare, enchanted by the beauty for which no description was adequate, alternating our whispers with suppressed shouts.'[22]

On 14 May a long procession entered Dormition Cathedral, Nicholas in the uniform of the Preobrazhensky Guards, from which at one point (a bad omen) the chain of the order of St Andrew slipped. 'A great, solemn, but, in a spiritual sense, heavy day for Alix, mamma and me', he wrote.[23] In the midst of it all was 'a frail, small, almost insignificant youth, whose Imperial crown seemed to crush him to the ground'.[24] Yet public response to his bows from the Red Staircase and later from a balcony in the Kremlin was loud and enthusiastic. The event confirmed in Nicholas and Alexandra's mind the sacred bond between tsar and people.

On 18 May the royal party was scheduled to visit Khodynka Field in north Moscow for a popular fair at which refreshments and enamel coronation mugs would be distributed. Many still had memories of the successful event at the same location after Alexander III's coronation in 1883. However, the authorities' confidence that the crowd of some 500,000 people would be submissive and grateful proved ill-founded. Early in the morning rumours that there were too few gifts to go round caused a panicked surge that lasted some ten minutes. Trenches used by engineers had not been properly filled in and the ground was unstable. An estimated 1,389 perished, trampled underfoot.

The disaster was a case of inadequate crowd control rather than imperial indifference or malice, but there had to be a face-saving exercise, given the number of foreign dignitaries and correspondents in Moscow. There was discussion about whether to call off the rest of the festivities, but Grand Duke Sergei, Governor General of Moscow, and his brothers Vladimir and Aleksei, who wielded considerable influence over Nicholas, were reluctant for an 'accident' to disrupt the timetable or for any show of 'sentimentality'. At 2 pm that day the tsar duly went to Khodynka where entertainments, including fairground booths and street musicians, went on as planned. The Grand Duchess Olga Aleksandrovna saw cartloads of bodies being brought from the scene which at first she thought were waving. That evening Nicholas and Alexandra earned more criticism by attending a ball at the French embassy, averting a possible snub to Russia's allies who had invested much time and money in the occasion. Both the Russian and the foreign press exploited the obvious contrast between the glittering social occasion and rotting corpses piled on carts. Not everyone viewed the catastrophe quite so negatively, however. Even foreign observers continued to share Nicholas's confidence in the mystical union between tsar and people. The British ambassador Sir Nicholas Connaught reported to Queen Victoria that it was 'difficult to find in history any stronger instance of unbounded fealty than was shown by the thousands of Russian subjects who in the midst of the dead and dying lost all consciousness but that of loyal devotion to their young sovereigns'.[25]

The shocking events following the coronation may be one reason why Nicholas and Alexandra, always uncomfortable with state occasions, retreated to the Alexander Palace at Tsarskoe Selo, where they settled more or less permanently after 1904. The elegant classical palace was designed by Giacomo Quarenghi in 1792 for the future Alexander I; set in a beautiful park with views of lakes, its simplicity contrasted with Rastrelli's nearby baroque Catherine Palace.[26] Here Alexandra was at ease in her Mauve boudoir, first fitted out in 1896, designed for comfort and the accommodation of clutter. She kept the same furnishings until the overthrow of the dynasty.[27] Other rooms in the palace were decorated in Art Nouveau style, including Nicholas's study. Over the years more and more icons found their way into the rooms. Other 'retreats' included the small Upper or New Palace in Alexandria Park, Peterhof, where Nicholas had a comfortable study with splendid views of the gulf of Finland, the new palace at Livadia in the Crimea and the luxurious royal yacht *Standart*, where Nicholas knew all the staff personally. ('This freedom, this rest and particularly life on the water make me as happy as a small child', he wrote to his mother in September 1905 from the Baltic.)[28]

Nicholas II's biographers have noted that he was generally more at ease with peasants, soldiers and servants than with high society, especially its more educated elements.[29] His only close male friend within the imperial circle was Grand Duke Alexander Mikhailovich ('Sandro'), his cousin and brother-in-law, husband of his sister Ksenia. Alexandra too trusted only a very close circle of friends, among them the maids of honour Anna Vyrubova, affectionately known as the 'cow', and Lilly Dehn. Boris Gerua, a page, recalled how 'a sense of unease' was the first impression of meeting the empress: 'She was obviously nervous of conversation and at moments when she needed to show some social graces or a charming smile, her face would become suffused with little red spots and she would look intensely serious.'[30] Prince Sergei Volkonsky, head of the Imperial Theatres, confirms that she was 'painfully shy' and 'could only squeeze a word out with difficulty' and 'never emitted a congenial spark'.[31] Self-discipline and reserve were interpreted as arrogance and frigidity, high moral principles (she deplored the gossip and love affairs of the court) as prudishness. High society even ridiculed her charitable enterprises such as fund-raising bazaars and sewing circles. With the birth of Alexis and the emergence of his illness, the desire for privacy intensified. Her own health suffered, her frequent illnesses and 'funny turns' interpreted by ill-wishers as 'hysteria'. The St Petersburg aristocracy and gossip were merciless. The outcome for the imperial couple was comparative isolation with family, domestic servants and a few friends.

Grand occasions still took place. 'Thanks to the brilliance of the uniforms, superb toilettes, elaborate liveries, magnificent furnishings and fittings, in short the whole panoply of pomp and power', wrote the French ambassador Maurice Paléologue of a reception at Peterhof in July 1914, 'this spectacle was such as no court in the world can rival. I will long remember the dazzling display of jewels on the women's shoulders. It was simply a fantastic shower of diamonds, pearls, rubies, sapphires, emeralds, topaz, beryls – a blaze of fire and flame.'[32] For routine occasions, however, the imperial couple abrogated tedious hosting duties to the 'small courts' of the grand dukes and duchesses, led by such characters as the Lutheran Grand Duchess Maria Pavlovna (née Princess Marie of Mecklenburg-Schwerin, 1854–1920), wife of Grand Duke Vladimir Aleksandrovich, Nicholas II's uncle.[33] Her view of Nicholas was robust: 'Instead of taking some sort of action when things go wrong, he persuades himself that God has willed it so, and then proceeds to surrender to God's will.'[34]

Such alienation undermined Romanov group harmony, as individuals strove for personal happiness and abandoned the solidarity expected of the dynasty. One of several scandals that drove the family apart was the marriage in 1905 of Maria's son Kirill Vladimirovich to the divorced Grand Duchess Viktoria Fedorovna ('Ducky'), who had been married to Empress Alexandra's brother Ernst-Ludwig. Kirill was banished at Alexandra's instigation. Other grand ducal 'renegades' included Nicholas's uncle Pavel Aleksandrovich, who married his mistress in Paris, and the emperor's brother Michael, who married a commoner divorcée in 1912. (Both were eventually pardoned.)

The British ambassador Sir Arthur Nicolson thought that the grand dukes did not 'add much to the popularity and respect' in which the imperial family was held.[35] On occasion they ganged up against the emperor, as when Sergei Aleksandrovich was threatened with punishment for the Khodynka disaster of 1896; on others they attracted public opprobrium. Uncle Vladimir, as commander of the guards and the St Petersburg military district, was implicated in Bloody Sunday (see below), and his brother Aleksei Aleksandrovich in the Tsushimo naval disaster; he was jeered at on the street and resigned from the post of general admiral, which had become more or less a Romanov sinecure.[36] In a speech in 1908 Alexander Guchkov, president of the duma, would denounce four grandsons of Nicholas I, Sergei Mikhailovch (artillery), Peter Nikolaevich (engineers), Konstantin Konstantinovich (military education) and Nikolai Nikolaevich (Council of Imperial Defence) for incompetence.[37] Possibly the grand dukes were no more inefficient than many of their contemporaries, but opinion was becoming less deferential and more intolerant of nepotism. Changes in public attitude struck another nail in the dynasty's coffin.

Military failure had even graver consequences. In January 1904 the Japanese attacked Port Arthur and Russia embarked upon what was memorably and wrongly predicted to be a 'short, victorious war', the outcome of the diversion of Russian interests to the Far East, with Nicholas's enthusiastic support. Seraphim of Sarov, canonized at the instigation of the tsar in 1903, was made the patron of the campaign. The Japanese opposed Russian expansionism through Manchuria and laid claim to the Russian occupied island of Sakhalin. Rooted in Russian underestimation of the 'barbarian' Japanese (as Nicholas viewed them), the war ended in humiliation for the Russian warships that sailed half way round the world only to be sunk by superior Japanese forces, and for ground forces that were poorly led and equipped. In December 1904 the fall of Port Arthur, leased to Russia since 1898, represented a low point in national morale.

Defeat in the Far East fanned troubles at home, which had been brewing since the late 1890s in most sections of society. Among the most disaffected were students (who rioted in 1899 and 1901), the tsar's non-Russian subjects, notably Finns, whose previous high degree of autonomy had been curtailed by integration into the empire for security reasons, and Jews, who in 1903 suffered a pogrom in Kishinev. There was anxiety about peasant riots, most extensive in Kharkov and Poltava provinces in 1902–3, resulting from the impoverishment of the peasantry as a result of industrial policy, heavy taxation and land shortages. Illegal radical and revolutionary parties formed, the Marxist Social Democrats in 1898 (splitting into Bolsheviks, 'the majority', and Mensheviks, 'the minority', in 1903) and the peasant-oriented Socialist Revolutionaries in 1901, the latter launching a programme of assassination of top officials. The Liberation movement (1901; from 1903 the Union of Liberation) represented liberal democrats and the zemstvos, which operated legally under constrained circumstances. After the Minister for Internal Affairs Viacheslav Plehve (1846–1904), notorious for his police methods, was assassinated in July 1904, Empress Maria persuaded Nicholas to appoint the liberal-minded Prince Dmitry Sviatopolk-Mirsky (1857–1914) in his place, awakening expectations in liberal society that the tsar then refused to satisfy.[38] Zemstvo leaders responded with their first congress in November 1904, followed by a series of political 'banquets' that demanded a popular legislative body. When pushed Nicholas issued a number of concessions, but refused to budge on the principle of elected representatives making policy, which he believed to be alien to the spirit of Russian government.

A particular focus of concern were industrial workers, who suffered the deprivations of early capitalism, such as low wages, long working hours and limited rights and, in some key industries, the added pressure of war production. In 1900–1901 the Ministry of Internal Affairs set up its own trade unions under the leadership of the chief of the Moscow security division Sergei Zubatov (1864–1917), in an attempt to inculcate patriotic virtues and divert the workers' movement away from the radicals, thus creating an urban equivalent to the supposedly loyal peasantry.[39] In some ways this paid off, encouraging worker activity that included a loyal demonstration on 19 February 1902 by the monument of Alexander II in the Kremlin and prayers for the health of the tsar. However, the authorities remained suspicious of even such patriotic gatherings and clamped down. From 1903 vestiges of this movement in St Petersburg were rallied by the priest Fr Georgy Gapon, who espoused socialist ideas and used the movement to lobby for civil and political liberties, including a constituent assembly. On what came to be known as 'Bloody Sunday', 9 January 1905, he led a demonstration of an estimated 100,000 workers bearing loyal banners and icons to the Winter Palace to present a petition to the tsar with a broad package of requests. The authorities used the army to control the crowd with inevitable loss of life. The precise casualty figures will never be known, estimates varying widely between the incomplete list of 130 fatalities published at the time by the municipal authorities, and the inflated suggestion repeated in many Soviet accounts that 1,000 died with 5,000 wounded.[40]

Nicholas, who was not even in residence in the palace, wrote: 'A dreadful day! Serious disturbances took place in St Petersburg as a result of the workers' wish to get to the Winter Palace. The troops were forced to fire at a number of points in the city; there were many dead and wounded. O Lord, how painful and distressing!'[41] A potent myth of Bloody Sunday, in which the Little Father

Tsar was depicted with blood-stained hands, immediately sprang up, although Nicholas bore no personal responsibility for the tragedy. The massacre sparked off strikes all over the empire, including a general strike in Warsaw. Less than a month later, on 4 February 1905, the tsar's uncle Sergei was blown to pieces by an assassin in the Kremlin. Onlookers were moved by the sight of his wife Grand Duchess Elizabeth, who was on her way to a Red Cross meeting, attempting to gather together the remains. Both the official manifesto and a right-wing article published slightly later noted the assassin's non-Russian accent and stressed that the main 'nest' of conspirators was based abroad. The authorities found it hard to associate 'true Russians' with such atrocities.[42]

For the rest of 1905 Nicholas found himself under increasing pressure to concede on political rights; lobby groups such as the newly founded Union of Unions, mutinous sailors on the battleship *Potemkin* on the Black Sea, rebellious troops on the Trans-Siberian Railway joined the throng. Rural disturbances spread all over Russia, sometimes to sites where earlier Nicholas had been greeted by patriotic crowds. Still Nicholas would go no further than envisaging a body based on the ancient Assembly of the Land, where 'that unity between Tsar and all Rus, the meeting between me and the people of the land … forms the basis of a system resting on original Russian principles'.[43] In February advisers worked on devising an electoral system weighted towards the supposedly loyal peasantry, excluding most of the urban population. In August Nicholas signed the so-called Bulygin constitution, which created a duma without legislative powers.

It was too little, too late. In mid-October Moscow was gripped by a general strike, which saw the formation of workers' councils or soviets. On 17 October Nicholas issued a manifesto that assured civil liberty based on inviolability of person, freedom of conscience, speech, assembly and association. A state duma, without whose consent no law could be implemented, would be elected on a wide franchise. It established a post of prime minister (Chairman of the Council of Ministers) with significant powers, to be held by Sergei Witte, who had persuaded Nicholas that he must choose between military force or civil liberties. In a letter to his mother on 19 October 1905, Nicholas castigated the railway authorities and the universities for indulging 'the arrogant crowd' during riots. 'My dear Mama, you cannot imagine what torment I was in before doing this.' His only hope was that it was the will of God and would rescue Russia from chaos.[44] Nicholas held 'outsiders' to blame, identifying all the ringleaders among the engineers on the railways as Jews and Poles: 'All the strike and ultimately the revolution itself was organized by them, with the aid of the workers that they had recruited'.[45]

The concession did not end the troubles. Nicholas received as much criticism from the right as from the left, representatives of emergent political organizations such as the reactionary Union of Russian People (Black Hundreds) and the All-Russian National Union complaining that there was 'autocracy, but no autocrat' and that Nicholas was 'a total nobody'.[46] A reduction of censorship allowed national and other groups all over Russia to press further demands. Strikes continued and in Moscow in December turned into armed insurrection. Nicholas was particularly alarmed by peasant revolts, with insufficient troops to quell them, and aggrieved by mutinies in the army. He must hurry to re-establish contact before peasants lost faith, a British eyewitness wrote: 'The halo of semi-divinity with which the peasants were wont to surround [the tsar] was disappearing and now he stood revealed as a shattered idol incapable of performing the miracles which were expected of him.'[47] The London *Spectator*'s correspondent believed that 'only providence [could now] save the House of Romanov from deposition'. This was a 'life and death struggle'.[48] Empress Maria was horrified that certain elements wished to dispossess the imperial family of its appanages, which were their personal and private property. 'It's a scandal', she wrote to Nicholas, 'these strikes! it's the complete ruin of the country and the whole world! No patriotism, no authority, it's a horror. Only God can retrieve us from this chaos and save us.' She hoped that a better time would come with the duma.[49]

The crown and the dynasty survived, heartened by examples of loyalty. Nicholas reported receiving messages of encouragement to maintain autocracy from all over the country.[50] Moderate elements rallied, as the opposition failed to present a united front. Nicholas himself remained calm and refused to be intimidated by a 'handful of anarchists'. He was easily cheered up by a good military parade and a lusty 'hurrah'.[51] The army remained loyal and the regime gained a grip under the ruthless leadership of Peter Durnovo, Minister of Internal Affairs. Punitive expeditions were dispatched all over Russia. Witte secured a foreign loan that prevented financial collapse.

The Romanovs bought salvation at the price of military suppression and the constitution which they had resisted so strongly for more than a century. The new Fundamental Laws of 23 April 1906 removed the term 'unlimited' from the definition of the emperor's powers, but on Nicholas's insistence 'autocratic' remained. Even the 'family business' of the succession was subject to the new structures; Paul I's 1797 Act and Alexander III's 1886 Amendment were included and could only be changed by the existing emperor in agreement with the State Council (the upper house) and the duma.[52] Even so Nicholas, in his own mind and on paper, remained an autocratic monarch, with powers to deploy emergency measures (under article 87), to appoint half the members of the State Council (the newly-constituted upper house), and responsibility for foreign policy and the armed forces. He still agonized over whether he had 'the right before my ancestors to change the limits of that power which I received from them'.[53]

He was assisted in facing the challenge of his new role by the able official Peter Stolypin (1862–1911), who became Minister of the Interior in April 1906 and Chairman of the Council of Ministers in July. Immediately Stolypin launched a reform of peasant land ownership to counter the recent violent eruption of protest. The aim was to abolish the peasant commune and create a class of sturdy peasant entrepreneurs with their own plots, stakeholders in the system through private property. Reform was backed by a relocation scheme to eastern 'virgin lands' and propagation of new farming methods. By 1914 some 24 per cent of peasants had taken advantage of the provisions.

The first duma was elected on a curial system, with scaled representation for landowners, urban dwellers, peasants and workers. This resulted in some 40 per cent of seats going to the liberal Kadets (Constitutional Democrats) and 20 per cent to the peasant Trudovik party. Of the 524 seats, 231 were occupied by peasants, 180 by nobles. On national lines, representatives constituted about 55 per cent Russians, with scaled representation from the rest of the nationalities. Ominously, the state opening in April 1906 took place on Romanov home territory in the Winter Palace, a setting which somehow reduced the duma members to the level of humble petitioners and presented the assembly as the gift of the tsar, rather than the achievement of popular action. Alexandra wore Catherine the Great's pearl tiara. (She regarded the 'dreadful' political parties as 'insignificant'.)[54] The royal party was surrounded by items of imperial regalia. Many deputies, by contrast, wore workers' and peasants' blouses.

Nicholas viewed the duma at best as a modern version of pre-Petrine institutions, with a fundamentally advisory role. It was his creation and it had to earn his confidence, not vice versa. A successful outcome would guarantee the health of autocracy and 'a strong, well-ordered, and enlightened state' to bequeath to his son.[55] For its part, the duma pushed the tsar further than he was prepared to go, particularly on the question of expropriation of noble estates. Examples of clashes include Nicholas's refusal in May 1906 to receive the duma president, S. A. Muromtsev, in person to deliver an 'Answer to the Throne' with various demands such as universal and equal suffrage. In July 1906 the tsar dissolved the first duma. Stolypin became prime minister and the following month suffered the devastation of one of his homes by a Socialist Revolutionary bomb that injured two of his children. A second, even more radical duma followed in February 1907 and returned to the agrarian question. It was dissolved on Stolypin's advice on 3 June when new electoral laws were published as emergency legislation under article 87 to guarantee a more moderate body. Thereafter, the third duma (1907–1911) served a full term. The fourth would be curtailed by revolution. Despite a shift towards landowner representation and drastic reduction in workers' and non-Russian votes, in an attempt to create a body 'Russian in spirit', the duma continued to be at odds with the government over many issues. For example, in 1909 the tsar vetoed the Naval General Staff Bill to stem the duma's encroachment on the armed forces. He also saw the defeat of the Western zemstvo bill in the State Council, one of many examples where the upper chamber rejected the lower chamber's legislation. Stolypin's assassination (September 1911) allowed a shift of power in state administration back to the tsar and the Ministry of Internal Affairs.

The 'constitutional experiment' allowed new forms of public political discourse to develop among educated Russians.[56] There was no turning back the clock. Still, many continued to believe that a constitution could not work in Russia where both society and culture were poorly developed, with a lack of respect for private property and only a rudimentary capitalist economy. The liberal 'centre' had no real support. Only an authoritarian regime could keep the empire together. The most conservative found Nicholas himself inadequate because he 'wavered' too much. He failed to appreciate 'the half-savage instincts of the crude mob' (Durnovo), retaining a sentimentalized, populist view of good peasants. Nicholas was tsar-saint and tsar-*batiushka* ('little father': see Chapter 1), two myths that bolstered his opposition to modern demands for power-sharing, new institutions and so on. He could not even envisage the duma in traditional terms, as a way of removing the 'barrier' or 'wall' between tsar and people by bypassing bureaucracy and, more importantly, the camarilla of 'wicked advisers' who were thought to influence him. Rather, Nicholas came to view the duma itself as a barrier between the tsar and his people, to whom he must appeal directly. Rumours came from the provinces that some peasants received letters from the tsar in which he complained that he had been imprisoned in his palace by ill-wishers and begged the peasants to rise up to free themselves (and him) from the tyrants and oppressors, the nobles and the landlords.[57]

In autocratic mode, Nicholas played ministers off against each other or bypassed them entirely. Many were disarmed by his charming manner (Nicholas hated direct confrontation), only to find that their views had been disregarded. At the same time Nicholas alone could not master all the knowledge and skills required to run a modernizing, multi-ethnic empire, least of all relying on the vague notion of the sound opinion of the patriotic Russian people. He had no private office, nor even a private secretary, which was dangerous when so much business was referred up to him. Alexandra especially strongly embraced 'conservative populism', feeling isolated from court society and alienated by 'outsiders' – Jews, students, intellectuals and radicals in general. Nicholas, with her support, strove to create (or recreate) a 'pure autocracy'[58] in which the bond between tsar and people was not mediated by institutions, still less by competing individuals such as government ministers or party leaders. An official visit to Moscow at Easter 1900, which included a midnight procession to the Cathedral of Christ the Redeemer, meetings with peasants in Kursk in 1902 and the canonization in 1903 of St Seraphim, were several of many occasions when the imperial couple were struck by the inspiring aura of a multitude of pilgrims.[59] The Easter experience prompted Nicholas to write: 'In the unity in prayer with My people, I draw new strength for serving Russia, for her well-being and glory.'[60] The canonization was one of several examples, in order to create new popular shrines, of the elevation of Russian holy men or elders (*startsy*) famed for miracles and prophesy. Seraphin had been venerated by earlier empresses. The ceremonies united the imperial family with 'the people' and the Church. Significantly, miraculous cures of those who bathed in the saint's 'holy spring' were quickly reported; the empress even attributed the birth of her son to the holy waters.

The simple faith of the Russian people and their love for their monarch were notoriously embodied in the self-styled man of God and libertine Grigory Rasputin (1871–1916), first encountered by Nicholas in 1905 and especially influential after 1911. His seeming ability to calm the tsarevich's bleeding when doctors failed was decisive in establishing his influence. Grigory was one in a series of dubious characters who took advantage of the empress's mystical leanings. She felt 'at peace' after speaking with him. Her faith in instinct, heart rather than mind, inclined her to prefer the advice of an uneducated 'man of the people' to that of politicians too clever by half. She was, in the view of one contemporary, in 'a state of religious mania' or 'ecstasy'.[61] There is little evidence that Rasputin had political ideas or policies, at least before World War I, or that there was any sexual impropriety in his relationship with the imperial couple, but his personal scandals and drunken orgies (associated with the banned self-flagellant *khlysty* sect) rubbed off on them, as did his indiscreet boasting about their friendship. He pulled strings for his cronies and gained influence in the Holy Synod. In the words of a close observer, president of the duma Mikhail Rodzianko, 'the mere fact of the close proximity to the Emperor's Throne of a debauched, illiterate and immoral peasant … was in itself sufficient to undermine and uproot all the respect and reverence due to the Crown'.[62] Rodzianko no doubt exaggerated when he claimed in an audience with Nicholas in February 1912 that 'the entire nation, all circles of the community' viewed the *startsy*'s influence with profound apprehension,[63] but the scandal undoubtedly benefited the opposition. A remarkable feature of Rodzianko's account is that it made no reference to Rasputin's control of Alexis's haemophilia, and therefore missed the main reason why the royal couple were so much in his thrall.

Nicholas was by no means blind to public opinion and in the 1900s he grasped opportunities for promoting national pride; past glories proved useful for diverting attention from present crises and humiliations. An intriguing aspect of his view of Romanov family history, and his own dynastic role, is his attitude towards Peter the Great and the Petrine legacy. It was no secret that the slightly-built, mild-mannered Nicholas was uncomfortable with Peter as a role model, preferring the Moscow-rooted image of the 'pious' seventeenth-century Romanovs, but he could hardly ignore a series of bicentenaries, including all Peter's major military victories. From 1896 (the founding of the Russian Fleet) to 1914 (the Battle of Hangö) Nicholas found himself visiting heritage sites and opening monuments and bridges. Such events forced him to leave the relative isolation of family life at Alexander Palace and to mingle with both the court and a wider public of official representatives, with which Nicholas was never comfortable, Alexandra still less. At the same time, such occasions brought them into contact with the 'common' people, whose warm cheers reinforced the royal couple's faith in the loyalty of peasants to tsarism.

There were also dynastic benefits to be reaped. Tsarevich Alexis was usually photographed wearing a sailor suit and was given his own 'play' regiment on the Petrine model, which spawned a movement in schools and churches, where boys did military drill and gymnastics, sang patriotic songs and indulged in other activities, in imitation of the British Boy Scouts. In 1910 the magazine *Play Troops* was launched. All this was a cruel irony given that Alexis's condition prevented him from being more than a token soldier or sailor, the 'hope, the bulwark of all Russia', in the words of the play regiments' official song.[64] Fears for the survival of his only male child must have been a constant heartache, given Nicholas's fervent commitment to the continuation of the Romanov dynasty as a pledge of Russia's future.

The first major Petrine jubilee was the St Petersburg bicentenary in 1903, when theatricalized spectacles recreated the assemblies, balls and masquerades of Peter's time, with gatherings around the Bronze Horseman, *tableaux vivants* on Trinity Square and replica ships on the Neva. Voluntary organizations staged public events on the Field of Mars and other open spaces, where people could enjoy fairground amusements. Souvenirs on sale imitated items produced for Queen's Victoria's jubilees.[65] The whole empire was expected to mark the capital's birthday. In the Tsar Alexander Gymnasium in Reval (now Tallinn in Estonia), for example, the head of History, A. V. Belgorodsky, delivered a lecture to his pupils about 'that true hero, that true epic warrior of the Russian land', praising Peter's self sacrifice and faith in God but stressing that the building of St Petersburg had been accomplished by the whole nation.[66] The royal couple showed little enthusiasm, however. Alexandra's comment in 1905 that 'Petersburg is a rotten town, not an atom Russian'[67] gives a broad hint of their attitude. The costume balls of February 1903 underlined their alienation from St Petersburg culture. Famously, they wore seventeenth-century dress, including in Nicholas's case some of Tsar Alexis's clothes and in Alexandra's an anachronistic imperial crown. Courtiers wore adaptations of 'boyar' fashions.[68] This was actually the first and last occasion on which the imperial couple appeared in seventeenth-century costume in public, but the much reproduced images became associated with deep attitudes towards Russia's historical destiny.

Of all the Petrine anniversaries, the bicentenary of the battle of Poltava, 27 June 1909, received the most official backing, coinciding as it did with the apparent restoration of Romanov authority following the constitutional restrictions imposed in 1907. Nicholas II could relate more easily to Peter's military victories than he could to his Westernizing reforms, and had a special rapport with the Preobrazhensky Guards. Commemorative booklets described the emperor's visit to Poltava in lyrical tones. Even the sun knew its duty, it seems, 'bathing the participants in its gentle rays, as the people greeted their Little Father'. On 26 June Nicholas reviewed the troops, mingling with officers of the Preobrazhenskys, among them three descendants of men who fought with Peter, and visited the communal graves of the Russian dead. On the 27th there was a service in the Church of St Samson and a procession of the cross onto the site of the battle, accompanied by the ringing of church bells, the firing of guns and the beating of drums. In the afternoon there was a further ceremony at the eagle-topped Glory monument.

This was as much Nicholas's day as Peter's. Official descriptions focused on the enthusiastic reaction of the people to their little father, their responses ranging from tears of joy to rapturously powerful hurrahs. In a speech the emperor emphasized the need for all true Russians to support and love their tsar and serve their country and expressed his faith in the people.[69] His 'good-humoured' conversations with peasants at Poltava reaffirmed his belief that the Russian people were devoted patriots and would remain a counterweight to 'alien' elements, including political representatives.

In 1912 attention turned to Alexander I. In August Nicholas and Alexis travelled to Borodino to a ceremony that featured the miraculous icon of our Lady of Smolensk, which was paraded before troops whose regiments had served at Borodino, as in 1812. Peasants figured prominently in the ceremonies, representing their forebears, as well as the tsar-loving peasantry of all Russia.[70] The message of the ceremonies was that the people could overcome all foes with the power of their love of tsar and fatherland. In Moscow nobles delivered the same message, affirming their loyalty and their faith in the union of tsar and people. On the feast of Alexander Nevsky, 30 August, there was a prayer service for Alexander I on Red Square, which affirmed the restoration of peace in Moscow and the predominance of loyal elements. Significantly, duma deputies were not invited to the celebrations.[71] In May 1912 loyal members of the duma had requested to be presented to the tsar, which he found 'unnecessary', relenting only when pressure was applied by the Minister of the Court and Chairman of the Council of Ministers. The ensuing reception was cool, the tsar complaining about certain unwelcome topics of debate with no reference to loyal support. Likewise the duma was affronted when no places were reserved for them during the main Borodino celebrations.[72]

Poltava, Borodino and the Romanov Tercentenary (see below) kept official Russia in a more or less permanent state of self-congratulation. This sense of tsar and people united in acts of collective memory conveyed in some cases genuine popular enthusiasm for the ceremonies in question, bolstering Nicholas's faith in his own popularity and in the power of a direct link with his people to overcome all obstacles. In the words of a booklet published in 1909: 'The Japanese war and its grave consequences – that was our sin. At Poltava we repented and now we can boldly say that a strong, rich and populous Russia *will be unconquerable* for ever as long as it remains a believing, pious *Holy* Rus.'[73] Between 1914 and 1917, in the face of real rather than commemorated war, such sentiments would prove dangerous.

10

From Celebration to Annihilation

NICHOLAS II. (ii) 1913–1918

> Thanks to the Lord God who conferred his grace upon us
> and Russia by allowing us so appropriately and brightly
> to celebrate the 300th anniversary of the accession of
> the Romanovs (Nicholas II, 24 February 1913).[1]

> Oh, God, save Russia! That is the cry of one's soul, morning,
> noon, and night (Empress Alexandra, December 1917).[2]

In 1913 an anniversary occurred in which Nicholas could take unequivocal pride: the last great state occasion of imperial Russia.[3] On 21 February he published a manifesto 'to all our loyal subjects', opening with a narrative of the election of Michael Romanov: 'By the common efforts of the Crown bearers, our predecessors on the Russian throne, and all loyal sons of Russia the Russian state was created and strengthened. Despite many trials the Russian people remained firm in their Orthodox faith; with self sacrificing loyalty to their Sovereigns they overcame misfortunes. The Russian empire became one of the foremost powers in the world ... Observing the three centuries that have passed, we see in all of them the highest feats of valour of the best sons of Russia who spared neither effort nor possessions nor life itself for [Russia's] sake'.

The manifesto commended the 'saints and pastors of the church', the nobility (especially for its good example on the Emancipation), Russia's soldiers, state officials, specialists in science, literature, art, agriculture, trade and industry, and millions of ploughmen (*pakhari*). There was no reference to industrial workers, other nationalities or institutions such as the duma. Loyal subjects should offer prayers to the Almighty 'for the repose of our ancestors on the throne and all those to whom the Fatherland owes its might and greatness'. The manifesto ended with an appeal to God to preserve Russia and 'give us the strength firmly to hold aloft as of old the glorious banner of the Fatherland'.[4]

An official booklet set out the programme for 21 February, emphasizing the tercentenary's all-Russian scope. All the main churches of the empire would celebrate the liturgy, followed by prayers of thanksgiving, wishes of long life for the imperial family and a reading of the manifesto. Before the liturgy, processions of the cross would advance from village churches to cathedrals; afterwards troops would march from all garrisons. In Moscow the main venue would be the Dormition Cathedral, in St Petersburg the Kazan Cathedral. The emperor and his immediate family were to arrive there after the liturgy for the reading of the manifesto and prayers, after which guns would fire from the fortress and church bells peal. Popular entertainments were held at Tsarskoe Selo, Peterhof, Gatchina and Pavlovsk. On the days that followed various events were planned, underlining the celebration's inclusive nature. For example, on 23 February at 11.30 the empress would receive court ladies in Russian dress in the Winter Palace, while at 12.30 the emperor entertained district elders and other representatives of the village population for lunch.[5]

A relentlessly upbeat account of the day itself was left by Fr Smirnov from Tobolsk diocese (founded in Michael's reign), who took to St Petersburg a copy of a miraculous icon of the Mother of God, before which Nicholas had prayed during his travels in 1891. Setting off for the Kazan cathedral, Smirnov's cabby commented that a sunny morning after some gloomy weather matched the joyful mood of every Russian: 'We have waited three years for this festival!'[6] After the liturgy shouts of 'Hurrah' in the distance signalled the arrival of the imperial family, then '*He* entered, desired, awaited with impatience, adored by all.' A tall Cossack carried Alexis, Russia's 'treasure'. The experience was overwhelming. 'My heart swelled with even more limitless love and devotion to our Sovereign and to our dear Motherland, with the desire to serve it zealously to my life's end.'[7]

Later Fr Smirnov attended a reception in the Winter Palace, where the emperor, his children and his mother presided, but not the evidently exhausted Alix. Nicholas asked about Smirnov's icon, kissed it and told him to 'give everyone [in Tobolsk] my heartfelt thanks'. Smirnov was 'touched to the depths of his soul'.[8] The times spent in Kazan Cathedral and the Winter Palace were the brightest and most joyful of his life, consolidating his love for tsar, imperial family and motherland. He castigated the 'negative' intelligentsia, who ridiculed people's beliefs and ideals. He had feared that basic principles were being abandoned and that Russia was heading for another Time of Troubles, but 21 February dispelled all this 'gloom': Russia was 'safe'! 'You had to be in that crowd of ordinary people, you had to listen to their "Hurrahs" to understand how fervent, how genuine is the love of the Russian for his Monarch.'[9]

Smirnov was not alone in his faith in the power of ceremony and direct contact with the imperial family to 'save' Russia. Other observers, however, felt that Nicholas behaved indifferently during the St Petersburg ceremonies, withholding a grand gesture of political amnesty or charity, while 'undemonstrative masses of people … a typical St Petersburg crowd' looked on.[10] According to another source, 'the nation remained indifferent. Its feelings were not in unison with the spirit of the celebrations; it did not share with the Imperial House the joy that House seemed to feel upon so auspicious an occasion'.[11] The same source noted the 'inexpressibly sad' sight of the tsarevich's pinched features, showing 'into what weak and frail hands was entrusted the future of that proud Romanoff Dynasty'. Never in the whole history of Russia did a Sovereign more need the protection of the Almighty than Nicholas II did in the nineteenth year 'of his sad and unfortunate reign'.[12] The imperial couple were criticized for not staging a court ball, Alexandra for leaving after the first act of a performance of *A Life for the Tsar* at the Mariinsky theatre on 22 February.[13] An eyewitness observed her 'trembling convulsively', with an unbecomingly flushed face.[14] She was hardly more relaxed at a ball given by the capital's aristocracy on 23 February, not smiling at all. Later she fainted.[15]

Liberals protested that members of the extreme-right organizations, the Union of the Russian People and Union of the Archangel Michael, played a prominent part in processions and were afforded the privilege of observing the imperial family progressing from their apartments to a state banquet, an honour not enjoyed, for example, by members of the duma. There were high-scale security operations in the capital to avert demonstrations.

Perhaps Nicholas did not expect too much of Westernized St Petersburg, although he did interpret some doves flying up into the dome of Kazan Cathedral as a good omen.[16] His faith in his own popularity was more influenced by the pilgrimage that the family made later that year to Romanov sites. Setting out in mid-May, they visited the ancient Russian cities of Vladimir, Suzdal, Nizhny Novgorod, Yaroslavl, Rostov and (19–20 May) Kostroma. The huge royal cavalcade provided an effective propaganda machine for the towns it passed through, with carefully orchestrated prayers, receptions and entertainments. On the Volga leg of the journey some 50 persons of the imperial blood joined a flotilla (the flagship appropriately named *Tsar Michael Fedorovich*) for a family excursion to the 'cradle' of Romanov history at Kostroma.[17] All along the route the tsar received enthusiastic cheers and spontaneous singing, although there was frequent disappointment when the royal party failed to stop.

Appropriately, Kostroma represented a mix of the old Russia and the new, its 21 textile mills indicative of 300 years of progress under the Romanovs. It also had an active and militant noble assembly, whose marshal greeted the tsar with a provocative speech. Patriotic accounts preferred to dwell on peasant devotion, carried to a pitch of 'holy rapture' as some onlookers leapt into the river to follow the tsar's boat.[18] The presence of the tsarevich excited particular enthusiasm and sympathy, especially when he was seen being carried by his sailor attendant. An official account explained that an ailment of the legs prevented Alexis from walking, but he was on the road to recovery, as evidenced by his 'cheerful expression'. At night the crowds watched the royal boat in silence in order not to disturb the sleeping boy.[19] Alexis's sickly presence was potentially a poignant reminder of the dynasty's fragility, the spectre at the feast, but the rhetoric of 1913 looked to glorious continuity; the Romanov line was to last 'for all time and forever'.[20]

A highlight of the visit was Nicholas's blessing at the Ipatiev monastery with the Fedorov icon of the Mother of God:

> A touching moment. With tears of emotion everyone watched this scene that gripped the soul with its mixture of simplicity and grandeur. The descendant of the modest youth, the powerful ruler of a glorious multimillion empire, humbly bowed his head before that same image of the Immaculate Patron and Protector of the house of Romanov before whom youthful Tsar and Great Prince Mikhail Fedorovich, the first crown bearer of the house of Romanov, raised his prayers for help at a difficult moment. With this same icon of the Fedorov Mother of God the Great Nun, sister Martha Ioannovna, blessed her son on his accession as tsar on 14 March 1613.[21]

Other links with Michael included the presence of descendants of the delegation that came to the monastery in 1613, of peasants who escorted him, and items donated by him to the monastery. The festivities culminated the following day with receptions in the town, the consecration of a monument to the Romanovs and a visit to an exhibition where a section of a 300-year-old oak tree was on show. Descendants of Ivan Susanin attended a dinner for peasants.

In Moscow on 25 May Nicholas was able further to re-enact and relive the events of 300 years before when Michael had been greeted in the Kremlin, walking through the same historical space where Michael and his descendants had been crowned. On the same day the imperial party visited the nearby House of the Boyars Romanov.[22]

It is striking that Nicholas did not visit Moscow between 1903 and 1912, perhaps an indication that he preferred his own vision of the idealized, invented city, frozen in the time of the early Romanovs, to modern reality. In any case, Moscow could be brought to St Petersburg.

Among the commemorative building projects that epitomized the imperial family's retreat from the capital's Westernized world was the Cathedral of the Fedorov Mother of God (architect V. Pokrovsky, 1908–1912) and the adjoining 'mediaeval' village, near the Alexander Palace. The cathedral mixed elements of the fifteenth-century Kremlin Annunciation Cathedral with the couple's favourite seventeenth-century style. The upper church contained a copy of the icon of the Fedorov Mother of God.[23] (It was here that Nicholas claimed to hear an 'inner voice' urging him to take command of the army in 1915.[24]) The couple apparently intended the crypt church, dedicated to St Seraphim of Sarov, as their burial place, which would have broken the sequence of imperial tombs in the Peter-Paul Cathedral.[25] During services in the cathedral Alexandra often worshipped in a recess of the main body of the church, imitating the tsaritsas of old, and Tsarevich Alexis wore Russian dress, underlining their retreat from surrounding reality. The neighbouring village was a Kremlin pastiche, intended for soldiers of the tsar's convoy and His Majesty's Rifles, who wore costumes from Tsar Michael's time.

In 1912 the foundations of a tercentenary church (architect S. S. Krichinsky) were laid in central St Petersburg. The main altar was dedicated in the presence of the emperor, empress and their daughters on 15 January 1914. It was based on 'strict seventeenth-century taste' with a *shater* or tower design with five domes, but with echoes of the Kremlin Dormition Cathedral. The iconography of the church unequivocally celebrated the Romanov dynasty. The main bell was named Nikolai-Mikhail and decorated with the portraits of the two tsars; others were named after Alexandra and the children and inscribed with Romanov coats of arms and double eagles.[26] The lower church was dedicated to Alexander Nevsky and the upper chapels to the Icons of the Fedorov Mother of God and Tsar Michael's patron Mikhail Malein. One of the icons was a tree of the royal genealogy, with Filaret and Michael at its roots.[27] Nicholas was confident that the 'miraculous' church would attract worshippers (it could accommodate 4,000), strengthening them in their faith, and would be 'propitious for the good of our holy Orthodox Church.'[28] It was another piece of Muscovite style superimposed on the heart of Classical St Petersburg.

A secular 1913 project was to create an 'All-Russian National and Imperial Rumiantsev Museum in memory of the 300th anniversary of the House of Romanov', expanding the existing museum in Moscow, near to the site of which Tsar Michael had built a church to St Mikhail Malein.[29] The new extension would contain a memorial chapel with copies of favourite imperial icons, such as the Fedorovskaia, and pictures of churches and monasteries with dynastic connections.[30] However, a proposal to the Tercentenary Committee to establish 'Romanov houses' throughout the land with exhibits to promote patriotic sentiments was not implemented.[31]

In the years preceding the tercentenary Nicholas erected many statues to his predecessors, including two to Peter the Great, in front of the Admiralty, celebrating Nicholas's approval of Peter's 'simple man' identity, which he sought to emulate, and a much more pompous image of Alexander III (1900–1912, by Alexander Opekushin) in Moscow in front of the Cathedral of Christ the Redeemer. The tsar sits impassively on his throne in full regalia like a stone idol, supported by double eagles.[32] An elaborate project for a monument to 300 years of the Romanovs in Kostroma was approved in 1912 and the foundation laid in May 1913,[33] but the war halted work. Statues of sixteen Romanov rulers would have stood around a tent-tower edifice topped by a double eagle, with the novel inclusion of bas reliefs of Nicholas and Tsarevich Alexis (living rulers were not usually depicted on monuments) and contrasting maps of Russia in 1613 and 1913 to show progress under the Romanovs. An allegorical figure of mother Russia blessed the dying Ivan Susanin.[34]

Throughout the empire in 1913 institutions and individuals organized patriotic events. 'On this day', a speaker at the First Male Gymnasium in Simbirsk
declaimed, 'all Russia ... is fulfilling the behest of Pushkin's Pimen and
remembering its great Tsars for their labours, their glory and their good deeds'.
Alexis, the 'incarnation of the holy Russian soul', Peter 'the untiring worker',
'clever, kind Elizabeth', Catherine the 'crowned philosopher', Alexander I 'the
white angel', Nicholas I 'the magnanimous knight of honour and duty', merciful
Alexander II, 'the Tsar Liberator', and the 'truly Russian' Alexander III, 'as well as
our adored monarch now reigning with wisdom, piety, humility, greatness and
firmness'.[35] The monarchs were always in advance of the people, like bright stars
lighting the way, and the monarchical principle was the foundation on which
society and state were constructed. In other words, the Russian principle of
governance did not, as in the West, emanate from society up to state institutions
but the opposite, from above. The peasants had to be protected. According to
this Slavophile point of view, the people did not seek power and the tsar had no
'constituency' in the sense of having to cater to any particular group or party.
The long speech ended with condemnation of those 'internal enemies' who were
trying to destroy Russia with their allies the Jews, Finns, Poles and other 'aliens'.[36]
Such sentiments would have struck a chord with the tsar, who in September 1913
allowed the ritual murder trial of the Jew Mendel Beilis to go ahead, causing a
scandal in educated society.[37]

All over Russia institutions and individuals leapt into print to record their
anniversary offerings. Schools in Smolensk sent a telegram to the tsar, to
commemorate the day when Michael became tsar and express their feelings of
'wholehearted, most loyal devotion and their fervent desire to commit all their
strength to true and selfless service to the Throne and the Fatherland'.[38] At
Prilutskii Girls' Gymnasium on 22 February pupils sat before a portrait of Tsar
Michael draped in national colours, flags and garlands and heard speeches by
the president of the Pedagogical Council on 300 years of Russian history. Pupils'
presentations included Koltsov's poem 'Hurrah!', Zhukovsky's 'Russian Glory',
and a folk song on the election of Michael, while the school choir, like choirs
all over Russia, sang 'Rejoice!' from Glinka's *A Life for the Tsar*. Ivan Susanin's
legendary feat of self-sacrifice was a constant motif throughout the tercentenary
festivities. As Nicholas declared in Kostroma: 'the love and devotion that he
showed for our ancestor will never be extinguished as long as the Russian land
shall live'.[39]

One village with its own little piece of tercentenary history was Nyrob in Perm
province, where in 1601 Michael Romanov's uncle, Mikhail Nikitich, was exiled
in chains by Boris Godunov and reputedly starved and murdered in August
1602 by his guards.[40] When an icon of St Nicholas miraculously appeared at the
site, Mikhail was declared a holy martyr, 'murdered by the wicked enemies of

the house of Romanov'. In February 1913 a new cross and icon for his memorial chapel were sent from Perm. Mikhail Nikitich was a saint by 'popular consent' (*narodnyi golos*) and 'according to the people's belief', as the perhaps sceptical author of an account, one of the Perm delegates, made clear.[41] On 21 February a procession went from the main church to the chapel, where the tsar's manifesto was read out and packs of tea and sugar were distributed to the poor. In the afternoon there were more general celebrations of the jubilee with a rendition of the national anthem, as 'hurrahs' rang out across the village. In the evening a torch procession accompanied a choir singing from *A Life for the Tsar*. A portrait of Nicholas II was brought out of the government office and patriotic speeches delivered about the unity of the Russian people as epitomized by the heroes of the Time of Troubles who saved Holy Russia from ruin.

'In Nyrob as in a drop of water', one speaker declared, 'was reflected the mood which today gripped all the population of the boundless Russian empire. Just as three hundred years ago, when the Muscovite state was faced with the question whether it would survive or not as an independent political entity, today also in the hearts of all citizens of the Russian land awareness has dawned that they are all Russian people and that on each of them rests a great obligation, in case of need, to defend the honour of their Motherland ... in the knowledge that the defence and, so to speak, the Guardian Angel of the Russian state was, is and shall be the Tsar anointed by God.'[42]

Ordinary folk sprang into print. For example, V. Kulchitsky, a cornet of the 12th Dragoons of the Starodub regiment, sponsored a 48-page illustrated pamphlet with cover portraits of Nicholas and Alexis Mikhailovich in seventeenth-century dress and a poem that began and ended: 'Our sun, our Tsar!' A historical essay stressed the victory of the *legitimate* line (through its link with Anastasia) over foreigners and traitors and cited Ivan Susanin's heroism.[43] Another author exhorted Russians to return to the Ten Commandments, family life, sobriety and non-smoking, taking as a direct example 'the Great Sovereign Tsar himself, the first Russian worker and untiring labourer'.[44] Non-Russians were inspired to join in, too, for example, the Jew Krivorog begins his tercentenary offering with a tale from the Talmud about a wanderer in a desert seeking shade and water who suddenly espies a tree loaded with fruit and a silvery spring. He drinks, eats and rests. Before 1613 it looked as though Russia was doomed, but the 'marvellous tree' of the dynasty of Michael Fedorovich appeared. 'Dear Brothers! Are not we, all the inhabitants of boundless Russia, heirs of that wanderer, long roaming in the deserts of time and finding peace under the beneficent protection of the glorious sceptre of the most August line of Romanov? They must pray to their maker that the miraculous tree survive many years.'[45]

Jubilee consumerism was buoyant, from the exquisite and rare to the shoddily mundane. Nicholas's Fabergé Easter gift to his wife that year was a tercentenary egg of gold and white enamel, the outer shell embossed with eighteen miniature portraits of the Romanovs. Inside was a globe of blue steel showing the boundaries of the Russian empire in 1613 and 1913.[46] The Tercentenary icon, for sale in various materials, featured the patron saints of the historical Romanovs. (Ancient icons could be seen at a major exhibition in Moscow.) The duma's tercentenary gift was an icon and a tapestry depicting Tsar Michael welcoming his father back to Moscow.

Russia was awash with Romanov images, of which Nicholas's was central. There were postcards and *cartes de visites* on the market suitable for all pockets. A pamphlet without any text, with a frontispiece of Muscovite and Imperial cross, orb and sceptre on a cushion and a series of notional portraits of Romanovs with their dates, was typical of the sort of material given away as supplements to regular publications.[47] Some 1.5 million tercentenary roubles showing head and shoulder portraits of Nicholas with Michael were circulated and a medal of the same design. (There were complaints about the poor quality and 'ghostliness' of Michael on some later strikings.)[48] In 1913 the reigning tsar's head also appeared on postage stamps for the first time (on the 7 and 10 kopeck values). Ancestors, including Michael (70 kopeck), Alexis (25 kopeck) and Peter I (1 and 4 kopeck), featured on other issues and the Romanov house in Moscow adorned the 3 rouble stamp.[49] Conservatives objected to cancelling the images with postmarks. In general, however, the flood of imperial images was unimpeded, although the censors did caution against handkerchiefs imprinted with the tsar's visage.

The ban on depicting Russian rulers on the stage was lifted, allowing Tsar Michael to appear at the end of Glinka's *A Life for the Tsar* for the first time.[50] Alexander Drankov's film *Three Centuries of the Ruling House of the Romanovs, 1613–1913: Historical Pictures* showed *tableaux vivants* of key moments of history; nineteenth-century tsars were discreetly represented by busts, while Nicholas II appeared as himself in documentary clips, which had proliferated since the coronation.[51] Another 1913 propaganda exercise was the publication of A. G. Elchaninov's *The Reign of the Sovereign Emperor Nikolai Aleksandrovich*, a popular, near-hagiographical biography that struck an uneasy balance between the tsar's frugal, hard-working habits and closeness to the people and his love of distinctly elitist pastimes such as tennis, motoring and yachting.[52]

The warm glow of the tercentenary undoubtedly influenced the mood in which Nicholas went to war in 1914. Although some commentators emphasized the prominence of the 'state idea' (*gosudarstvennost*) and popular mandate in the resolution of 1613, in 1913 the presentation from on high was unequivocally focused on the house of Romanov and its acceptance of God-given rule, without any limitations or contractual basis. The 'crown-bearers' worked and sacrificed themselves on behalf of the people without being limited by them. At the same

Silver tercentenary rouble showing Tsar Michael and Nicholas II and 15 kopeck stamps showing Nicholas I. 1913.

time, numerous representations and re-enactments drew analogies between Nicholas and Alexandra and their seventeenth-century 'forebears'. It was claimed that a princess of the house of Hesse had been considered as a bride for Tsar Michael, and in one publication Alexandra was depicted next to the Fedorov Mother of God, emphasizing her own intercessional role.[53] 1913 imagery reflected an essentially pre-modern view of Russia, before the advent of workers and most of the empire's non-Russian nationalities. Russia's enemies were defeated by faith, patriotism and loyal peasants, as embodied in the mythologized image of Ivan Susanin. Alexandra for one drew the conclusion that forebodings of revolution were wrong, a bogeyman conjured up by government ministers as opposed to the true feelings of the people.

The retrospective atmosphere of 1913 might suggest head-in-the-sand escapism in the face of imminent collapse. Yet the celebratory mood had some justification in reality, even if the latter was largely ignored in official imagery. Nicholas, like his father and grandfather, presided over modernization, the outcome of Russia's defeat in the Crimean War which underlined the need to compete with industrialized, first-rate Western powers. This process was spearheaded by the powerful Ministry of Finance under Sergei Witte (minister 1892–1903) and V. N. Kokovtsov (1906–14), in continuation of Alexander III's programme of industrialization and accomplished with the aid of foreign investment, personnel and technology. In 1897 Witte imposed the gold standard with Nicholas's backing against much protest. Rapid population growth suggests that general trends were positive. Seventy-three million in 1861 grew to 125 million in 1897 and 170 million in 1917. There was progress in education, with three-fifths of peasant children in school by 1914. Peasants now owned as much as one-third of formerly communal land and a programme of selling noble land with cheap credit was in operation. There was evidence that some peasants were becoming more entrepreneurial. There were good harvests and crop yields were now commensurate with the West, with, as always, regional variations. Indeed, the year 1913 marked the high-point of the imperial Russian economy.

Nicholas II's reign, so often dismissed with the imagery of 'doom' 'decay' and 'decline', saw vibrant cultural and intellectual developments when, for the first time, Russia was at the forefront of international creativity rather than always 'catching up' and 'assimilating' the achievements of others. What had already occurred in literature now emerged in music with the compositions of Skriabin and Stravinsky, in the theatre with Stanislavsky and Meyerhold. Diaghilev's Ballets Russes took Paris by storm in 1909. The visual arts saw a rapid succession of Symbolists, Neo-Primitivists, Rayists, Futurists and Suprematists (in 1914 Malevich's revolutionary abstract 'Black Square' was exhibited for the first time), as artists abandoned realism and celebrated urban culture and the modern world of machines and technology. Some were inspired by the pioneering achievements of scientists such as Mendeleev, Pavlov, Sergei Lebedev and Alexander Popov. In literature, writers such as Kruchenykh and Khlebnikov transcended the boundaries of comprehension with their 'trans-rational' language, in 1913 combining their verses with Futuristic sets and costumes by Malevich and radical music by Matiushin in the avant-garde opera *Victory over the Sun*.

Of course, there was ample room for clashes with the retrospective mood of court culture, to the extent that Malevich spoke of the revolution in the arts preceding the political and social revolutions. Nicholas and Alexandra showed no sympathy for cutting-edge trends. (Nijinsky was sacked from the Imperial Theatre in 1911 after a member of the royal family complained that he was indecently dressed during a ballet performance.) More seriously, industrial protest revived after 1911. In April 1912 troops shot some 200 striking miners at the Lena gold field, sparking off sympathy strikes. There were student protests against police encroachment in universities. As more and more peasants found work in non-agrarian sectors, wider experience and new opportunities for education produced a different kind of peasantry, perhaps not so amenable to the allure of the little father tsar.

The challenge was to preserve a traditional monarchy, enjoying support from loyal elements such as the clergy, the upper nobility and the peasants, amid rapid urbanization, industrialization, education and cultural radicalism in an empire where less than half the population were Russians and where nationalist aspirations constantly disrupted the peripheries. Throughout Russia a radicalized section of the educated classes embraced socialist ideas, among which the abolition of monarchy was a prime demand, even for the less extreme. How would the trinity of Orthodoxy, autocracy and national pride stand up to these pressures? The answer, as we know, is that they did not. But the battle was not as uneven as the 'inevitable' 1917 revolutions might suggest; and Nicholas was not entirely deluded in feeling some optimism in the wake of the heady celebrations of 1913, rooted in dynastic pride. His optimism was not dented even by a series of strikes throughout the empire in 1914, culminating in a general strike in St Petersburg when barricades were erected and clashes with troops occurred. Such events made him even more determined to limit the powers of the duma. In any case, the strikers backed down and the troops remained loyal.

One thing deemed essential for the stability of the empire was avoiding a major war at a time when the arms race was escalating. This was achieved after 1905 by maintaining the alliance with France, entering into a Triple Entente with France and Britain in 1907 and keeping on good terms with the biggest threat, Germany. In the Balkans Europe was confronted with the further decline of Turkey and the expansion of Serbia, which Russia generally supported as a fellow Orthodox nation. In a crisis in 1908–9, however, Austria's annexation of Bosnia-Herzegovina, on which Serbia had designs, won Russian support in return for Austria's sanction of Russia's passage through the Straits. This was seen as a betrayal of Slav interests and ended, with German connivance, in Russia's humiliation. By June 1914 when a Bosnian Serb nationalist assassinated Archduke Franz Ferdinand of Austria at Sarajevo, a network of alliances was in place that inexorably drew Russia, France and Britain into war against Germany and Austria. Nicholas at first doubted that Europe would go to war 'to protect the interests of a Balkan state'[54] or that his cousin Kaiser Willy would betray him, but he refused to be pushed around. On 15 July Austria declared war on Serbia. Russian mobilization began the following day, provoking a German declaration of war on 19 July.

Russia's economic, social and political weaknesses made entry into war dangerous, but Nicholas had faith in patriotism, predicting a repetition of the popular response of 1812. In his address to a crowd at the Winter Palace he even repeated Alexander I's pledge of resistance. He was much encouraged by the huge, praying crowds that greeted his appearances in St Petersburg (renamed Petrograd in August) and especially in Moscow. One eyewitness reported that even St Petersburg workers claimed to rally to the tsar 'as to our emblem'. The duma's spirit was patriotic.[55] It proved difficult, however, to sustain enthusiasm for complex war aims among the ordinary Russian soldiers. Following early defeats at Tannenberg and the Mansurian Lakes in East Prussia there were mass desertions, although these were offset by victories in Galicia. Civilian casualties were particularly high in Poland, Lithuania and Latvia, where there were forced evacuations. Some 14 million men would be mobilized, with an estimated 8.5 million casualties.[56]

In summer 1915, against the warning of his ministers (and, indeed, of Rasputin) that he might endanger the dynasty, Nicholas assumed personal command of the army, dismissing the current commander-in-chief, his cousin Nikolai Nikolaevich (Nikolasha) and departing for Staff Headquarters at Mogilev in Belarus. Tsarevich Alexis joined him there in October. The message of dynastic heroism was emphasized by the award for bravery to Nicholas later that month of the Cross of St George, which had also been conferred on Alexander I, II and III. In addition to satisfying a sense of 'sacred' duty and a romantic urge to head his troops, to improve morale and to end mismanagement at Staff Headquarters and tension within the government, this move was an attempt to counteract Nikolasha's popularity. The latter complained of the 'fatal influence' of the empress, especially her ability to make the tsar reverse decisions he had made at Staff Headquarters, while the empress hated the grand duke, whom certain circles regarded as Nicholas's potential replacement. It was widely believed that she expected more scope to interfere in domestic affairs with the tsar away at the front.[57] His ministers' attempts to dissuade him made Nicholas stubborn. As he wrote in a speech circulated widely in December 1915, 'The Tsar directs the war not from the distance of hundreds of miles. He appears in the midst of battle. He feels the mood of the armies.'[58]

In fact, the move was far from a disaster militarily. Summer 1916 saw the initially successful Brusilov offensive at the Austrian front. This, however, was counteracted on the home front by falls in living standards, inflation and food shortages in the towns. Nicholas's health declined, he was nervous and exhausted, although he claimed to find solace in life at the front away from the poisonous intrigues of the capital.

After an initial surge of patriotic support from most shades of opinion, Nicholas had to contend with intense pressures, not least the refusal of various bodies, from the court to voluntary organizations, to co-ordinate their efforts with his. September 1915 saw the creation of the Progressive Bloc of duma and State Council members, aiming to wrest responsibility for the war from the emperor and form a 'ministry of confidence' responsible to the legislature. Simultaneously the Zemstvo and Town Union was formed to co-ordinate the war effort in the rear. Nicholas, suspicious as ever of the duma and spontaneous activity in general, responded by proroguing the duma in September 1915 and appointing a series of apparently incompetent and 'geriatric' prime ministers in a process described as 'ministerial leapfrog'. Between autumn 1915 and autumn 1916 there were three ministers for war, four for agriculture and five interior ministers. Boris Shtiurmer, who was both chairman of the Council of Ministers and Minister of the Interior for part of 1916, was approved by Rasputin, and even Nicholas realized that his last Minister of the Interior, Alexander Protopopov, was hopeless, but in one of several instances of direct intervention, Alexandra persuaded Nicholas to keep him on and not to 'cave in' to the duma.

Warnings against Rasputin's malign sway might have had some influence on the tsar, for example Rodzianko's in February 1916 that Rasputin's perceived interference in government could have 'fatal consequences for the fate of the dynasty'. Empress Maria Fedorovna understood the dangers of Rasputin and tried to persuade Nicholas to banish him, but, as she said, Nicholas was 'so pure of heart that he does not believe in evil'.[59] The decisive factor was that Alexandra would not part with Rasputin, while Nicholas regarded their relationship as a private concern.[60] On 1 November 1916 the Kadet leader Pavel Miliukov delivered a speech in the duma on the theme 'stupidity or treason?' in which he accused the government and Protopopov in particular of incompetence verging on pro-German sentiment, stirred by Rasputin.

Certain grand dukes, notably Aleksandr Mikhailovich and Georgy Mikhailovich, urged Nicholas to concede a responsible government, on the grounds that advice came from people devoted to him. By 1914 some 61 Romanovs were included in the dynastic registers, many of whom took a more modern view of monarchy. Others, however, were time servers promoted to high office beyond their capabilities, for example Sergei Mikhailovich, described by Rodzianko as an intriguer and a disaster for the army. Scandals such as the Bratoliubov affair, when Grand Duke Mikhail Aleksandrovich was duped into handing over state funds to a charlatan, further undermined the grand ducal reputation.[61]

The educated public, not to mention their representatives in the duma, were not inclined to distinguish 'good' grand dukes from 'bad'. Deference for the imperial family in general had declined, as had the solidarity of the family itself. At a time when just having a German-sounding name was dangerous, Alexandra was particularly vulnerable to (and innocent of) accusations of 'German' intrigue to end the war, charges that came as much from the right as the left: the right-wing politician V. M. Purishkevich referred to her as 'an evil genius of Russia and the tsar'.[62] In fact, she had been anti-Prussian since her childhood and her upbringing was more English than German. Her selfless work as a certified war nurse in her hospital at Tsarskoe Selo and other charitable activities such as threading icons for the troops made little impact upon her critics. Early in 1917 Grand Duchess Maria Pavlovna warned Rodzianko of the empress's 'nefarious influence' in driving the country to destruction. She 'must be annihilated'. Grand Duke Mikhail echoed this: the empress was 'fiercely and universally hated' and all were 'clamouring for her removal'.[63] Such opinions emboldened Rodzianko to confront the emperor and ask him to 'save his family' by preventing the empress from exercising political influence. This provoked the melancholy response: 'Is it possible that for twenty-two years I tried to act for the best, and that for twenty-two years it was all a mistake?'[64]

Alexandra saw no virtue in catering to 'bad' people, who now included an ever-growing list of both named individuals ('disloyal' ministers and relatives) and categories (Jews, Poles, students). Her conception of autocracy and of Nicholas as autocrat was firmly rooted in Russian history, or at least her version of it. In a much-quoted letter of 14 December 1916, she urged him to close the duma and to show firmness: 'Be Peter the Great, John [Ivan] the Terrible, Emperor Paul – crush them all under you – now don't laugh, noughty [sic] one – but I long to see you so with all those men who try to govern you .'[65] On the eve of collapse she was still nagging him to show the 'master hand' and to let them feel his fist. 'They must learn to fear you – love is not enough'. 'They' was anyone outside the close circle of friends and officials approved by Alexandra, an ever smaller contingent. Nicholas continued to protest: 'I do not need to bellow at the people right & left every moment. A quiet sharp remark or answer is enough very often to put the one or the other in his place.'[66] Nicholas could be stubborn, but he hated unpleasantness in face-to-face encounters and rarely lost his temper. He was more comfortable with the pious and gentle (tishaishii) aspect of traditional Russian rulership than the stern and 'terrible' (groznyi).[67]

During the war the empress relied more than ever on Rasputin, while others redoubled their efforts to remove him. On 15 December 1916 she wrote: 'even the Children notice how things don't come out well if we don't listen to Him & the contrary – good when we listen'.[68] Two days later Rasputin was dead, murdered by Prince Felix Yusupov, Grand Duke Dmitry Pavlovich and Vladimir Purishkevich. The French ambassador reported that people kissed each other on the streets and lit candles to icons.[69] The Romanovs' response was more muted. Empress Maria, no admirer of Rasputin, found the 'improbable' story of the participation of Felix and Dmitry unsettling: 'The ground is being pulled from under us...'[70] Alexandra visited the corpse and kept the 'martyr's' blood-stained blouse as a relic. There is a gap in her surviving letters until 22 February, when she wrote 'I can do nothing but pray & pray & Our dear Friend does so in yonder world for you – there he is yet nearer to us – Tho' one longs to hear his voice of comfort and encouragement.'[71] Her faith in miracles remained undiminished. In 1917 she visited mother Maria Mikhailovna, a 107-year-old woman of God in Novgorod, who sent an apple for the tsar. She prayed at the site of a chapel being built over Rasputin's grave, where she felt 'such peace and calm', and picked up a piece of wood for Nicholas.[72] She refused to accept the evidence of hostility against her. 'I have the great consolation that the whole of Russia – the real, poor, humble, peasant Russia is with me', she assured a relative.[73] One can imagine Alexandra's growing confusion in 1917 over the contrast between her own idealized vision of the 'true' Russian people, as witnessed during 1913, and revolutionary reality: 'The psychology of the masses is a terrible thing', she later conceded. 'Our people are really very uncultured; because of this they follow the wave like a herd of sheep.'[74] Even in Kostroma, 'the refuge and citadel of the Romanovs', Maurice Paléologue reported, people were tired of the war and there was 'resigned discontent'.[75]

Uncertainty around Rasputin's murder fuelled speculations that some grand dukes were preparing to arrest Nicholas and Alexandra with the help of the guards and declare Nikolasha or Tsarevich Alexis emperor, with Michael as regent.[76] At New Year 1917 Nicholas banished Grand Duke Nikolai Mikhailovich, one of his foremost critics. Other family members left of their own accord. Any plans to save the dynasty were pre-empted by the revolution of February 1917, which broke out in St Petersburg following strikes and bread shortages. Protesting women were joined by workers and radical elements calling for an end to the war and the overthrow of autocracy. The refusal of troops to break up disturbances was crucial in escalating the collapse of authority. 'It's a hooligan movement', wrote Alexandra to Nicholas, 'young boys & girls running about & screaming that they have no bread, only to excite – & then the workmen preventing others fr. work – if it were very cold they wld. probably stay in doors.'[77] It would all quieten down if only the duma would behave. She remained convinced that 'all adore you & only want bread'.[78] The duma, dismissed again, was about to form a committee that was referred to as a 'provisional government', rivalled by the newly formed Soviet of Workers' Deputies.

On 26 February Nicholas received and ignored a telegram from Rodzianko, urging the appointment of a responsible ministry. There is little recognition in his letters and telegrams of the seriousness of the situation, although his silence may have been for the sake of the empress, who was nursing children and other members of the household who had fallen ill with measles. On 28 February the royal train on its way back to Petrograd was diverted to Pskov. Here on 1 March generals browbeat Nicholas to concede parliamentary rule. Initially Nicholas insisted that his duty 'before God and Russia' did not allow it, but agreed after receiving further evidence of the spread of revolution. In this he had the support (although he did not then know it) of Grand Dukes Michael Aleksandrovich, Kirill Vladimirovich and Pavel Aleksandrovich, respectively his brother, cousin and uncle, who had drafted a manifesto for him to sign granting a constitutional order.[79] Then General Ruzsky, commander of the northern front, after news from Rodzianko that 'hatred of the dynasty has reached its limit'[80] informed the tsar that he must abdicate. Almost all members of the high command agreed. Nikolasha sent a telegram imploring Nicholas 'to save Russia and your Heir'.[81] Nicholas informed them: 'For the sake of the well-being, peace, and salvation of Russia, which I passionately love, I am prepared to abdicate from the throne in favor of my son. I ask you all to serve him truly and sincerely.'[82]

Initially it was envisaged that Grand Duke Michael would act as regent until Alexis reached his majority. However, Nicholas heeded medical advice that Alexis's haemophilia was incurable. When Alexander Guchkov and Vasily Shulgin, deputies from the State Council and the duma, arrived, they were astonished to find that no further pressure was needed. Their advice that Nicholas abdicate in favour of Alexis had already been superseded. On 2 March 1917 he signed a manifesto: 'We consider it to be for the good to abdicate from the Throne of the Russian State and to surrender supreme power. Not wishing to part with Our beloved Son, We name as Our successor Our Brother, Our Grand Duke Mikhail Aleksandrovich, and bless his assumption to the Throne of the Russian state.'[83] In his diary Nicholas wrote: 'All around are treason, cowardice, and deception.' But that night he slept 'long and soundly' and the next day read a book about Julius Caesar.[84]

Nicholas had conceded on his own terms, a personal act of abdication that seemed to preserve the old autocratic power structure. In Petrograd popular feeling had gone beyond this, with shouts of 'No more Romanovs!' heard on the street. The transfer of the throne to Michael was not seen as any sort of solution (it would 'pour oil onto the fire', said Rodzianko);[85] his safety could not be guaranteed and his accession was opposed by other members of the imperial house. Monarchists deplored Nicholas's action. The foreign minister Sergei Sazonov lamented. 'Fancy destroying a three-hundred-year-old dynasty and the stupendous work of Peter the Great, Catherine II and Alexander I! What a tragedy! What a disaster!'[86] Michael, regarded by some as 'of weak character and lacking in brains',[87] drew his own conclusion. On 3 March he wrote: 'I have taken the firm decision to accede to the supreme power only in the event that such should be the will of our great Russian people, whom it behoves through universal voting through their representatives in the Constituent Assembly to establish the form of government and the new Fundamental Laws of the Russian state. I beg all citizens of the Russian state to submit to the Provisional government, formed on the initiative of the State Duma and enjoying full power until the Constituent Assembly'.[88]

If one regards Nicholas's transfer of power to Michael as legitimate – it could be disputed on a number of grounds, including the legality of his abdicating on behalf of Alexis, who as a minor was not allowed to renounce his right to the throne – the Romanov dynasty thus ended with Michael II. Significantly, the Provisional Government claimed to have received its power 'by inheritance' from the grand duke, although this nicety was quickly forgotten.[89] The Holy Synod abolished prayers in church for the ruling dynasty.

Nicholas mentioned nothing of abdication to Alexandra, who for some days wrote, in the spirit of 1905, only of 'concessions' that could be withdrawn. 'Two currents – the Duma and the revolutionments [sic] – two snakes which I hope will bite off each others heads – that's [sic] wld. be the reckoning of the situation ... yr. glory will come.'[90] Any promise about a responsible ministry or constitution would be null 'once in power again'; 'we shall believe in a future of sunshine yet on earth, remember that.'[91] On 4 March, now in full knowledge of the abdication, she still foresaw 'glorious sunshine ahead'. Nicholas would be restored by 'the people'.[92]

In the chaos that prevailed, the monarchy's return could not be discounted. In 1917 the Moscow Soviet of Workers' Deputies issued free to soldiers a 16-page pamphlet warning against this eventuality.[93] 'Any who might contemplate restoring the Romanovs should ask themselves who they were and what care they took of working people?' A popular anti-dynastic history begins with the election of Michael by the will of the boyars, then Alexis, 'in general [supported by] the noble-landowning class; to whom he was quiet and humble, overindulging them.' Peter I was clever, decisive and energetic, but 'extraordinarily severe and cruel' and cared nothing about working people, building St Petersburg on bones. The author casts aspersions upon the morals of Catherine I, who was drunk the whole time, went with officers and died of a bad disease which she probably caught from Peter. Soldiers with an interest in dynastic legitimacy should take note that the male line died with Peter II, that the German Biron ruled on Anna's behalf and that Elizabeth was illegitimate, as well as being the last of the Romanov blood line, which had to be restored by her German relative Peter III. In a last resort Catherine II took Orthodoxy and Russian names as a means of restoring the extinguished line of the Romanovs through the Gottorp-Romanov line. Peter III hated Russia and Russians, Catherine II was clever but debauched, spoiling the nobles and tormenting the peasants. Paul's origins were 'obscure', indeed, 'it turns out that our royal house, according to our Russian laws, has no right not only to the name of Romanov, but also the name Gottorp.' Even so, Paul secured the family fortune with the Appanages Department, showering his relatives with unheard of wealth, all 'sucked from the Russian people'.[94] In the ongoing litany of wickedness Alexander I was a hypocrite, Nicholas I stupid and oppressed Russia for 30 years, Alexander II did nothing to relieve the lot of the people, Alexander III was a suspicious, gloomy drunkard and Nicholas II stupid, cruel and duplicitous, spilling rivers of blood. The 1913 celebrations had been 'fake and sham' in an effort to bolster the dynasty's 'stolen' name and put some Russian gloss on their German origins. There was nothing wrong with being foreign, but they had no right to pass themselves off as Russians when there was not a drop of Russian blood in their veins.[95]

Other anti-tsarist writers in 1917 revealed the vast sums extorted by the Romanovs from the Russian people. These included Catherine II's gifts to her favourites and Paul's 1797 law which regulated payments on the basis of closeness to the throne by birth. In 1797–1897 some 236 million roubles were paid out, including 64 million for palaces. It was conceded that in 1862 almost half the former appanage lands went to former serfs, but the imperial family kept the best, including the vineyards that supplied imperial tables, not to mention the tsars' own lands, the Cabinet Domains, which included silver and gem mines.[96]

Voices in favour of the Romanovs inside Russia grew fainter as monarchists fled abroad or, with the outbreak of civil war in 1918, joined the White forces, for whom the restoration of the monarchy was not a priority. On 2 March the new Provisional Government was already considering exiling the imperial family or limiting their movements, while the Petrograd Soviet made plans for their detention (the women of the House of Romanov to be arrested 'gradually, depending on the role each played in the activities of the old regime'.) The Soviet deplored the continuing freedom of 'the deposed Nicholas the Bloody; his traitorous wife; his son, Aleksei; his mother, Maria Fyodorovna, as well as all the other members of the House of Romanov'.[97]

On 9 March 1917 Nicholas, now under arrest, was reunited with his family at the Alexander Palace at Tsarskoe Selo. The family were subjected to insults by 'slovenly' and hostile guards, but they kept busy with a strict regime, digging a garden, shovelling snow, felling trees. Nicholas read the papers and did puzzles. At Easter, in the last days of March, they confessed and took communion in the palace. The priest was astonished by the iconostases in each room, indicating their 'devotion to God's will'.[98] On 10 March the British ambassador announced an offer of 'hospitality' for the imperial family in Britain,[99] but further negotiations collapsed as a result of fears in London that it would 'compromise' the king and let in revolution. Despite happy memories of a family holiday with cousin Nicky on the Isle of Wight in 1909 and warm relations over the years, George V reneged on his initial agreement. The Provisional Government was reluctant 'to make martyrs out of its enemies', but increasingly under pressure to treat 'the bitterest enemy of the people' less leniently.[100] Fears of counterrevolution prompted a change of location. On 1 August 1917 the family left for Tobolsk, which was, incidentally, close to Rasputin's native village. Initially they lived under a relatively benign regime, where boredom was the main enemy.

In Russia political forces were polarizing and the triumph of the Bolsheviks in October 1917 sealed the family's fate. In the spirit of the new order, the guards became more insolent. Regional Bolshevik committees vied for possession of the prisoners, while centrally there were fears of monarchist attempts to free the tsar, plans for whose trial were in the offing. In April/May 1918 the family was transferred on orders from Moscow to the house of the former merchant Ipatiev in the Bolshevik stronghold at Ekaterinburg in the Urals. Their captivity resembled a prison regime, with extra security measures and a drastically reduced staff. (Requests for the tutors Sidney Gibbes and Pierre Gilliard to attend Alexis, who was suffering from swelling in the joints, were refused.) Belongings were pilfered and the house was bedaubed with obscene graffiti. A rescue attempt by 'loyal officers' failed to materialize, as did a possible British secret service rescue through Murmansk, only recently come to light. Yet there were compensations: a warm spring and summer with walks and church services. In June 1918 Tatiana,

Anastasia and Maria celebrated respectively their twenty-first, seventeenth and nineteenth birthdays.

Urals Bolsheviks had a reputation for extreme leftism, which included demands for the destruction of imperial 'bloodsuckers'. At the same time, at the beginning of what would prove a full-scale civil war, anti-Bolshevik White forces were closing in on Ekaterinburg. The 304 years of the Romanov dynasty, that had begun in the Ipatiev monastery in Kostroma, ended in Ipatiev's house in Ekaterinburg when, probably on Lenin's personal orders, Nicholas, Alexandra and their five children were brutally murdered by an execution squad, along with the tsar's doctor and four servants, in the small hours of 17 July 1918.[101] Legend has it that the upstairs room where Tsar Michael lived in 1613 was connected to the ground floor where he received the Moscow delegation by 23 steps, the same number that Nicholas descended to the cellar where he was shot, having reigned for 23 years.[102] The Presidium of the Regional Soviet reported that only Nicholas had been shot, a claim that was made in several documents, but the chairman cabled Moscow 'that the entire family suffered the same fate as its head'.[103] The bodies were taken to an area of mine shafts, where an improvised grave was made and some of the corpses were burnt.[104] Grand Duke

A Photograph (taken by the Tutor Pierre Gilliard) of the Imperial Family in the Park of the Alexander Palace, 1917. Image courtesy of Sotheby's.

Michael, whom some still regard as the 'last emperor', had been shot in Perm on 12–13 June 1918. A day after the execution of the imperial family, several Romanovs, including the empress's sister Elizabeth, now a nun, were flung into a mine shaft near the town of Alapaevsk in the Urals, where they died of further injuries inflicted by explosives flung into the mine or starved to death. The remains of the Holy Great Martyr Elizaveta were later retrieved and taken to Jerusalem. She was declared a saint by the Church in exile in 1981 and the Moscow Patriarchate in 1992.

11

Postscript: 1918–2007

THE ROMANOVS RETURN

Our last chapter begins and ends in a mausoleum. An essential stop for visitors on tours of St Petersburg is the Peter-Paul Cathedral in the fortress, where today's guides provide short biographies of the most famous occupants of the imperial sarcophagi in the main body of the church. All tourists are shown Peter I's tomb by the south wall just in front of the iconostasis, draped with the flag of St Andrew and lined with medals from various jubilees, along with those of Catherine II a few paces to the left, and, in the nave of the church, Alexander II and Maria Aleksandrovna, distinguished by their unusual materials of jasper and rhodonite, and Alexander III and (a recent addition) Maria Fedorovna. On more extended tours other monarchs may get a commentary.

A measure of the cathedral's restored symbolism in the new Russia are the revived fortunes of a part of the building that was until recently neglected, its initial purpose glossed over – the mausoleum of the grand dukes, which, in the words of a recent guide, can now be added to 'the famous list of generally known historic and symbolic monuments of St Petersburg'.[1] The project was commissioned by Alexander III, but lay dormant until 1896 and was completed only in 1909 (architects D. I. Grimm, A. O. Tomishko, L. N. Benois). The main altar was dedicated to Alexander Nevsky. After 1917, in line with the officially negative view of the late imperial grand dukes, the building was declared to be 'of no historical or artistic interest' and all the brass grave plaques were removed from the tombs. For a time it was used for storing paper, then in the 1960s was converted for use as an exhibition hall.[2] It has now been restored as part of the rehabilitation of Romanov history. On 29 May 1992 Grand Duke Vladimir Kirillovich (1917–92) was buried there, after a funeral service in St Isaac's conducted by Patriarch Aleksii. In March 1995 the remains of Vladimir's father, Kirill Vladimirovich (1876–1938), were also transferred there.

The biggest crowds congregate in the cathedral's St Catherine's chapel near the west doors, where on 17 July 1998 Nicholas II was buried after a state funeral designed 'to correspond with historical traditions'.[3] The then president Boris Yeltsin attended. The remains of Alexandra and the children, discovered near Ekaterinburg in 1976, were also buried in the tomb, although controversy

Romanov tombs in the Peter-Paul Cathedral, St Petersburg (Lindsey Hughes).

continues about missing bodies and the authenticity of the bones.[4] This has revived stories that began to circulate as early as 1917 about the survival of members of the imperial family. Space precludes an examination of this fascinating offshoot of Romanov studies, which continues to this day to generate a mountain of literature.[5] In the words of a recent reliable study, the evidence strongly suggests that 'stories of survival are fictive'.[6]

Whether the bones now resting in the cathedral are actually those of Nicholas II is less important than the official decision to stage a funeral and fill the yawning gap in the sequence of Romanov tombs, as a public act of restitution. Streams of visitors and worshippers praying at the new tombs clearly do not share scientists' doubts. In August 2000 the Russian Orthodox Church canonized 1,154 saints, 860 of whom were martyrs of the Soviet regime, among them Nicholas II and his family.[7] They were presented in the tradition of the first Russian princely saints, Boris and Gleb (11th century), for non-resistance to evil. They 'genuinely strove to embody in their lives the commandments of the Gospels ... their sufferings showed the light of the Christian faith that conquers evil, just as it shone in the lives and deaths of millions of Orthodox Christians who suffered persecution for Christ in the twentieth century'.[8] Their individual and collective icons can be bought in church kiosks all over Russia.[9]

It was not always so. In Soviet times Peter I's tomb was the only one honoured with fresh flowers and artefacts in line with the generally favourable assessment of

Icon of Nicholas II.

Peter's achievements that emerged under Stalin. There were no requiem masses even for him, however. Guides concentrated on the deconsecrated cathedral's 'progressive' architectural features in the Petrine context of modernization, glossing over its function as the Romanov mausoleum. The survival of any of the tombs was by no means assured, for 1917–18 saw the beginning of a campaign that continued intermittently and selectively throughout the Soviet era to obliterate reminders of the Romanov dynasty. Lenin's 1918 Decree on Monumental Propaganda ordered the removal of monuments set up in honour of the tsars and their servants. Often mob rule pre-empted edicts. In 1918, for example, crowds in Moscow demolished the statue of Alexander II, whose prominent site in the Kremlin under its own stone canopy made it a particularly prized target. (The canopy and gallery survived until 1928.)[10] Opekushin's monument to Alexander III was toppled in the spring of 1918, a moment immortalized in numerous photographs of the severed head among double eagles and in Eisenstein's film *October*. The pedestal stood empty until it was destroyed in 1932, Lenin's promise to erect a monument to 'Liberated Labour' there remaining unfulfilled.[11] All over the country crowned heads toppled. In Kostroma activists demolished the memorial to Mikhail Fedorovich and Ivan Susanin (the only example of its kind) and in 1918 a statue of Lenin appeared on the plinth of the unfinished tercentenary monument.[12] In Ekaterinodar and Ekaterinoslav monuments to Catherine II were removed, but the director of the local museum saved the latter from further damage by burying it. It was later dug up and erected in the museum courtyard, but has since disappeared.[13] In Nakhichevan-on-Don the empress was replaced by Marx.[14]

Always wary of initiatives outside their own control, the Bolshevik leadership did not advocate spontaneous mindless vandalism even of 'vestiges of tsarism'. Indeed, the preservation of the 'best examples' of the art and culture of the past was official policy, in line with Lenin's much quoted adage that art now 'belonged to the people'. The acceptable heritage included even selected monuments to Romanovs. For example, Russia's first public monument, Falconet's equestrian statue of Peter I (1782), owed its survival to its daring design and also no doubt to its associations with Pushkin and the Decembrists. Even Mikeshin's monument to Catherine II in St Petersburg escaped. An unlikely survivor was the equestrian statue to Nicholas I in St Petersburg, preserved for its artistic and technical qualities. Trubetskoy's equestrian statue of Alexander III was made acceptable by defacing it with verses by the revolutionary poet Demian Bedny, transforming it into a 'bogeyman' reminder of the horrors of tsarism.

However, that even Peter I's image was not sacrosanct was demonstrated by the fate of works by Leopold Bernshtam, *Tsar Carpenter* (1910) and *Peter the Great Saving Shipwrecked Fishermen* near the Admiralty, both destroyed in 1919. Other destroyed Petrine images included Ilia Gintsburg's 1911 bust in front of the Church of the Holy Spirit in Greater Okhta, Vsevolod Lishev's 1914 statue for the bicentenary of the Arsenal, and a bronze figure of Peter in working clothes at Strestroretsk. A further round of destruction occurred in the 1930s, when several copies of Mark Antokolsky's 1909 statue of Peter were demolished, including one in front of the Cathedral of St Sampson and another in front of the hospital of the Preobrazhensky regiment.[15]

Romanov associations were erased in other ways. For example, in 1923 the 'House of the Boyars Romanov' became the 'house of a seventeenth-century boyar'. During the Second World War even this exhibit was dismantled, restored only in 1964 to become a general 'Museum of Exhibits from the State Historical Museum'.[16] A particularly grievous act of desecration was the demolition in 1929 of the Kremlin monasteries of the Miracles and the Ascension. The latter was the resting place of the wives and daughters of the Moscow princes and subsequently the early Romanovs, which included most of the daughters of Tsar Michael and the tsars' wives, including Tsarinas Maria Miloslavskaia and Natalia Naryshkina.

(Even after the founding of St Petersburg, the Russian empresses visited the Ascension convent to pay their respects to their female 'ancestors'.) In 1929 all the remains were removed to a vault in the Archangel Cathedral. In a later and different context in 1977 the Ipatiev house was demolished on the orders of Boris Yeltsin, then Party boss in Ekaterinburg, who wished to discourage its use as a place of pilgrimage.[17]

The trend since the collapse of the Soviet Union has been to preserve and/or restore the Romanov landscape. In some cases, as with Trubetskoy's statue of Alexander III, declared in 1937 to be 'of no artistic or historical significance', it was a simple task of transfer from behind the Russian Museum to the more visible courtyard of the Marble Palace.[18] Bernshtam's demolished *Tsar Carpenter* was replaced by a duplicate from Amsterdam. A copy of a bust of Peter I by Rastrelli replaced a statue of Lenin in the foyer of the Moscow Station in St Petersburg, one of many examples of obliteration of the discredited old regime by the even older.[19] In Moscow the name of the House of the Boyars Romanov has been restored. The chapel of the Iberian Mother of God at the entrance to Red Square, where Romanov rulers regularly prayed on their way into the Kremlin, has been rebuilt, as has Tsar Michael's nearby Cathedral of the Kazan Mother of God, razed in the 1930s.

The most spectacular project was the controversial reconstruction of the Cathedral of Christ the Redeemer, blown up in 1931, with its strong associations with Alexander I, whose scheme was aborted, and Nicholas I, Alexander II and Alexander III, who completed it.[20] This has done more than any restored monument to reimpose a tsarist Russia element upon the post-Soviet skyline, where it vies with the Las Vegas style of contemporary Moscow in a clash of identities. Its reappearance has been characterized as an act of 'repentance' and 'cleansing' from the crimes of Soviet Russia, including the murder of the imperial family, as 'a visible sign of the resurrection of Holy Russia'.[21] Its critics dismiss it as a tasteless and expensive reproduction. Similar protests have been voiced against Zurab Tsereteli's massive monument to the tercentenary of the Russian fleet (1997) in Moscow, featuring Peter I aboard a ship.[22] Among the objections are the cost, the poor design and the lack of consultation. Security also had to be increased when Neo-Bolsheviks threatened to blow it up. Similar threats were made to statues of Nicholas II.[23]

The Romanovs have been rescued from anonymity in less obtrusive ways. An early example of a popular trend was an exhibition staged in 1993 in the V. A. Tropinin Museum in Moscow, *Portraits of Leading Sovereigns of the House of Romanov, 1613–1917*. 'It is no accident', the catalogue states, 'that in our transitional time interest has grown in Russia's past, all our "yesterdays", in the great figures, the rulers of the Romanov dynasty, who were elected to the throne of Russia after wars, internecine strife and popular rebellions of the Time of

Troubles'.[24] Examples of lavish exhibitions devoted to individual Romanovs include several on Peter I and Catherine II and, in 2005, Alexander I.[25] Many such exhibitions travel abroad to demonstrate the new regime's revisionist attitudes. In 2004 an exhibition on Nicholas and Alexandra opened at Hermitage Amsterdam, a new gallery sponsored by Hermitage enterprises. The catalogue foreword from the Hermitage's energetic director Mikhail Piotrovsky reflected current attitudes towards the 'ill-starred couple' and sympathy for the impossible demands of reconciling private life, which they were good at, with public life, which they were not. The abscess in society was not the 'rotting' Romanov regime, but the revolution.[26] The reburial of Empress Maria Fedorovna in September 2006 (see below) in the Anichkov Palace, St Petersburg, was marked by exhibitions on her life in Denmark – *Alexander III and Maria Fedorovna* in the Manege – along with others in the Russian National Library and State Archives, and a display of Russian imperial portraits by the Danish painter Laruits Tuxen. A monument to the empress was unveiled at Peterhof. In galleries all over Russia, and in particular in the former residences at Tsarskoe Selo, Gatchina and Peterhof, imperial portraits have been rescued from decades in storage and returned to the walls.

Another sign of the return of the Romanovs to Russian consciousness is a flood of publications. From the 1920s to the 1980s references to the tsars as individuals were mainly limited to formulaic denunciations of tyranny, oppression and hypocrisy, although generally silence prevailed. Only Peter I and the Romanovs' 'ancestor' Ivan IV were honoured with individual monographs. Collective biographies of the dynasty were impermissible. Even that apparently driest of subjects, genealogical research, in Stalin's era was outlawed as 'a phenomenon of aristocratic-monarchical reaction'[27] and even in less authoritarian times was not regarded as a serious discipline for a historian. This changed in the early 1980s when genealogical charts and pocket calendars bearing royal portraits began to appear on street stalls, along with more substantial books with such titles as *House of the Romanovs*, containing potted biographies, portraits and coats of arms.[28] More recently genealogical studies have appeared under the respectable imprint of the Institutes of History of the Academy of Sciences.[29] The letters and diaries of the last Romanovs have appeared in scholarly editions. Biographies of individual Romanovs now pack the shelves of bookshops, translations from once disapproved foreign authors alongside original works in Russian. The select monarchs deemed worthy of individual studies in the Soviet period have been joined by all the Romanov rulers, perhaps most notably Catherine II, whose German origins once set her beyond the pale.[30] Even Catherine I gets her volume in the influential 'Life of Outstanding People' series. The first Russian empress 'was not among the outstanding state figures', the author concedes: 'she reigned but did not rule, nevertheless Ekaterina was an exceptional personality'.[31] Landmarks in this series (founded 1933) include studies of Tsars Michael and

Alexis and Empresses Anna and Elizabeth.[32] Writers have even vied with each other to say something good about the once denigrated Nicholas I, who has emerged in a recent study as 'strict, but fair' and dedicated to duty. Anecdotes about his willingness to sacrifice workers to complete the renovation of the Winter Palace after the fire of 1837 have been replaced with a story about how he chastised an architect for forcing workmen to sleep in damp conditions.[33] Far from being a philistine, indifferent to culture, he can now be shown as a connoisseur of theatre, a good flute player and a polyglot. Revisionist studies include not only the rulers but also once spurned statesmen. Figures plucked from obscurity and given sympathetic treatment include Grigory Potemkin and Peter Stolypin.[34] A sign of the times is the open acknowledgement by certain Russian scholars of help in their research from modern-day Romanovs and Russian princes abroad.[35]

The last Romanovs and their children arouse especial curiosity and sympathy, to the point of sentimentalization. Recent studies of, for example, the paintings and drawings of Alexander III's daughter Grand Duchess Olga (1882–1960) or Grand Duchess Elizabeth's sponsorship of the Moscow choir, would have been inconceivable in Soviet times.[36] Among a selection of Romanov hagiography to be found on sale in kiosks in churches and monasteries in St Petersburg recently were studies of Nicholas II's daughter Olga, the 'perfect Russian type', of the holy martyrs Alexis Romanov and Elizabeth and others.[37] Right-wing revisionist studies of Nicholas II focus on his saintly self-sacrifice and his attempt to play the role of peacemaker, for example in 1905–7.[38] According to such interpretations, 70 years of communist rule was the price Russia paid for disobeying God's will.

Sympathy for individuals extends to an interest in the links of the Romanovs with the other ruling houses of Europe, not least the British Windsors. Particularly popular in Russia and a frequent visitor is Prince Michael of Kent, grandson of King George V, cousin to Nicholas II. Russians apparently are 'enthralled by his uncanny likeness to Nicholas II'.[39] A sycophantic thirst for royalty and its trappings among certain circles in Russia, especially the revived Russian aristocracy, is one of the more undesirable manifestations of Romanovomania, although understandable given how long this particular fruit was forbidden. Collectors vie for their piece of Romanov memorabilia in the auction rooms, including London, with Russians prepared to pay astronomical prices for anything from a humble photograph to plates with imperial crests and Fabergé masterpieces.[40]

At least some of this Romanov revival is inspired by a desire to see the monarchy restored. On 16 July 1993 several hundred monarchists congregated at the site of the Ipatíev house, including Georgy Mikhailovich (born 1981),[41] whom many regard as the heir to the throne. His line goes back to Vladimir Aleksandrovich (1847–1909), the third son of Alexander II, who for a time regarded his line as the legitimate one, when the potentially fatal illness of Tsarevich Alexis became known and Grand Duke Michael Aleksandrovich (younger brother of Nicholas II) apparently ruled out his offspring with a morganatic marriage.[42] Vladimir's son Kirill Vladimirovich proclaimed himself Emperor of all Russia and head of the Romanov family in 1924,[43] although he was not universally acknowledged. The dowager empress Maria Fedorovna refused to recognize him as such, regarding the proclamation as 'premature' in view of the continuing confusion about Nicholas II's fate. Kirill was 'succeeded' by his son Vladimir Kirillovich (1917–1992). Dynastic purists object to the fact that the line then continued through Vladimir's daughter Maria, who married a great grandson of Kaiser Wilhelm, who was 'legitimized' with the title Grand Duke Mikhail Pavlovich. Maria Fedorovna favoured the claim of Grand Duke Peter Nikolaevich (1864–1931), son of Nicholas I's younger son Nikolai Nikolaevich (1831–1891), whose descendant today is Nikolai Romanov (born 1922), a Swiss resident. His offspring, however, are all female.

Apparently there are no direct male descendants of the Gottorp-Romanovs (Paul I onwards) who cannot be ruled out, according to the 1906 Fundamental Laws, by their contracting of 'unequal' marriages. Yet if one relies on precedent rather than law, it can be said that from the seventeenth century onwards the Romanovs have constantly and successfully renewed themselves and re-established their legitimacy through 'dubious' candidates to the throne by stressing popular acclaim, spiritual descent from earlier monarchs and 'saving Russia'. The German Catherine II is perhaps the supreme example.

As the Romanovs' 400th anniversary approaches it seems appropriate to end with some generalizations about the dynasty's shared principles and collective biography, beginning with the truism that family life and the basic requirement of continuing the line were crucial. In this biological respect the early and late Romanovs were the most successful, Michael and Alexis producing just enough male heirs to avoid the need to recruit outside candidates, the emperors from Nicholas I to Alexander III onwards creating a surfeit, which gave rise to other tensions in the ruling house. In between, thanks to Peter I's 1722 Law of Succession, the Romanovs managed to reinvent themselves with non-biological claims to legitimacy. Individual experience of family happiness varied, but the Romanovs always presented themselves as collectively devoted to the interests of their subjects, their family life a microcosm of Russia's prosperity. Even Peter I and Catherine II, notorious for their harsh treatment of their first-born sons, embraced the virtues of family life, he in his devotion to the children of his second marriage, she to her grandchildren. Anna and Elizabeth were 'mothers' to their subjects. In the nineteenth century all except Alexander I, who failed to leave an heir, celebrated the cult of the family. In the case of Paul, Nicholas I and

Alexander II the family scenario accommodated mistresses, even a second family in the latter's case. Once they were married, not a whiff of extramarital scandal sullied the reputations of Alexander III and Nicholas II, unless one counts the lurid false rumours of sexual shenanigans with Rasputin. The Romanov family always strove to be a model even when they fell short of the ideal.

In this respect making the right marriage was vital for all the male Romanovs. In the seventeenth century the tsars' brides were selected from Russian noble families, always with an eye to balancing alliances at court. Peter I's second marriage to a commoner for love was an individual aberration; but he still set a trend by choosing a German Protestant princess for his son Alexis, which became the pattern for all the male heirs after Peter II, with the difference that unlike Alexis's Charlotte, all the later tsars' brides converted to Orthodoxy and took new names. From Peter I's reign most tsarevny, too, denied marriage in the seventeenth century, were destined for Protestant husbands, linking the house of Romanov ever more intricately to the already intertwined royal houses of Europe. This foreign marriage policy would attract condemnation for 'watering down' the Russian blood in Romanov veins, although in fact it served to strengthen Russia in certain aspects of foreign policy, as well as being in line with dynastic practice all over Europe.[44] It was yet another sign of Russia's integration into European politics as a result of Peter I's reforms.

A stable principle held with varying degrees of personal conviction by all those Romanovs mature enough to form an opinion was the maintenance of autocratic rule, undiluted by representative government. The seventeenth century saw the growth of the tsars' absolute power, with the disappearance of the Assemblies of the Land and the code of precedence and the decline in the authority of the Church. These trends were consolidated by Peter I, who abolished the patriarchate, thereby removing the threat of a 'second sovereign', and had his power enhanced with theoretical defences of autocracy. Thereafter the preservation of autocratic rule was treated as a Petrine bequest, the one example of public rejection of its limitation being in the unlikely hands of Anna Ioannovna in 1730. To quote Catherine II, 'there is no other authority except that which centres on [the monarch's] single person that can act with a vigour proportionate to the extent of such a vast dominion' (The Nakaz, chapter 1, article 10). As the empire expanded further, this argument from the centre became stronger rather than weaker. Under Alexander I it seemed for a time that a constitution, granted to Poland and Finland, would be extended to Russia, but 'liberal' Alexander proved as convinced an autocrat as his father Paul. No such concessions were expected of the 'perfect autocrat' Nicholas I, still less after 1848 saw legitimate regimes abroad toppled or wavering. When under Alexander II it looked as if the Great Reforms would be completed with the granting of civil rights and moderate representation, the growth of terrorism, then the assassination of the tsar dashed any such hopes.

The last two tsars each adhered to the principle of preserving autocracy in his own way, Alexander III in keeping with his bear-like appearance, Nicholas II in apparent contradiction to his mild, evasive manner. From the start of his reign he was under more public pressure than any of his predecessors to concede 'responsible government'. Arguably, despite the constitution of 17 October 1905, he never did and remained convinced that it was his duty to God and the dynasty to maintain his powers undiluted. Empress Alexandra continued to believe that autocracy would be restored.

Another thread running throughout the Romanovs' three hundred years was that of devotion to the ideal of Orthodox Russia. At a basic level this determined that all the Romanovs were patriotic Russians and pious Christians regardless of their ethnic and confessional origins or their 'German' accents, to which opponents of late tsarism frequently drew attention. Russia was the seat of true Christianity, all other churches having fallen into heresy or schism. The formulae changed with time, the Rus of Michael and Alexis giving way in official discourse to Peter I's *Rossiiskaia imperiia*, with more emphasis upon service to the secular state than to the pious monarch. Perhaps only Alexander I deviated, with his enthusiasm for ecumenical brotherly love. Political realities required that alliances be made with non-Orthodox powers, but when the opportunity arose Russia intervened on behalf of Orthodox Christians abroad. In the reign of Alexander I feelings of national identity grew in reaction to Napoleon's invasion and pride in Russia's leading role in Europe. Under Nicholas I the principles ensuring Russia's strength and continuity were expressed as 'Orthodoxy, Autocracy and National Feeling', while under Alexander III and Nicholas II they were embodied in a reinvented ideal of seventeenth-century 'Holy Russia'. Strict adherence to Orthodoxy was maintained in the face of the realities of imperial expansion, which challenged the Romanovs with the dilemma of incorporating non-Russian nationalities, in some cases virtual nation states (Poland, Finland), into the All-Russian Empire. Of other imperial dynasties perhaps only the Habsburgs faced a similar dilemma.

Another fact of Romanov history was that they ruled over an overwhelmingly rural population, comprising some ninety percent peasants. This figure scarcely changed from Michael to Nicholas II, even though a drift into towns and the creation of an urban working class were a crucial factor in the reign of the last tsar. Additionally, until 1861 some fifty percent of the peasantry were serfs. Michael consolidated serfdom and Alexis enshrined it in law in 1649. Peter I's wars and reforms were scarcely conceivable without it, neither was the successful foreign policy of his successors. Yet Russia's rulers from Catherine II onwards acknowledged that serfdom was an 'evil' that kept Russia out of step with Western countries. Its continuation sullied their reputations, as elaborated by historians until fairly recently. Even after the Emancipation the question remained of how these basically Westernized rulers related to the mass of their subjects. The solution for Alexander III and Nicholas II was to stress their own affinity with the peasants through a shared faith and values, and, in the case of the latter particularly, to encourage face to face contact. The idea of the mystical union of ruler and peasants was most clearly expressed and re-enacted in the last decades of tsarism, but it was there from the very beginning in notions of 'naive monarchism', as expressed in the belief that ordinary folk must bypass a 'wall' of wicked advisers to reach Little Father Tsar. Rulers could take some comfort in the idea that the peasants were basically loyal to them and would seek retribution against landlords and government agents, not against them. This could backfire, as it did during the Pugachev rebellion, when the belief that Russia and the peasantry in particular could only flourish under a true tsar allowed the pretender 'Peter III' to press his claims. Even here the comforting factor was that the peasants did not reject tsarism itself. The need not only of peasants but also of other sections of the population for a tsar had allowed the election of Michael, whose main qualification was his links with the old dynasty. The story of Ivan Susanin may have been mainly a nineteenth-century invention, but it stressed the point that from the dynasty's earliest days peasants were willing to lay down their lives to serve it. The Romanovs maintained their faith in the *narod* (or found it wise to express it) until their overthrow.

Space does not allow a discussion of such issues as whether the Romanovs were 'good for' Russia, except in the sense that they made it into and maintained it as a major world power for much of their three hundred years. Certainly no Romanov, with the possible exception of Peter I, ever matched Stalin's willingness to sacrifice millions of his subjects for the sake of some future Utopia. It has been argued that the Romanovs were 'right for' Russia and that the Soviet system was tsarism under another name, portraits of party leaders ('Red tsars') replacing icons and sports parades replacing religious processions for a people with a basically peasant mentality in need of firm guidance. Developments since the collapse of the Soviet Union suggest less nostalgia for old-style, 'benevolent' tsarist autocracy with all the trimmings, more an unformulated adherence to certain of its principles adapted to the modern world. Under Vladimir Putin, who allegedly keeps a portrait of Peter I in his office, the trend has been for firm rule from above, including central control of the media and appointment of provincial leaders, coupled with a 'Petrine' policy of opening up to the West.

In September 2006 attention at home and abroad was again focused on the dynasty and its recent history when the last tsar's mother, Maria Fedorovna, was brought from her native Denmark, where she was buried in 1928, for reburial in the Peter-Paul fortress beside her husband, according to her own wishes and with the sponsorship of Vladimir Putin.[45] It was 140 years to the day since she arrived in St Petersburg to marry Alexander III. A memorial service was held in

Roskilde Cathedral in Denmark on 23 September before the coffin, draped in the Russian national flag, was brought by sea to St Petersburg to lie in state for public viewing in the Alexander Nevsky church in Alexandra Park at Peterhof, one of Nicholas II's favourite retreats. On 28 September the coffin was transferred under a yellow imperial standard to St Isaac's Cathedral, where the service was conducted by Patriarch Aleksii, then carried in motorcade to the Peter-Paul Fortress, processing through the triumphal Petrovsky Gates into the cathedral to the accompaniment of Danish and Russian bands for the reburial service, which was preceded by a liturgy for the empress. The coffin was lowered into a vault next to Alexander III. The events concluded with a 31-gun salute from the fortress and a wake in the Ethnographic Museum. The patriarch described the event as 'an act of repentance on the part of society and the state'. Having fallen deeply in love with the Russian people, 'the empress devoted a great deal of effort for the benefit of the Russian fatherland. Her soul ached for Russia.'[46]

The events took place in the full glare of publicity through international press and internet coverage. Sixty-nine Romanovs attended, along with more distant relatives such as Prince Michael of Kent. Current feuds over the succession were reflected; the guest list was apparently vetted by the Romanov Family Association, which bases its calculation on patrilinear descent.[47] According to the official Danish reports, the current head of the Romanov family is Nikolai Romanov. His younger brother Dmitry accompanied the coffin to St Petersburg, as did Paul Kulikovsky, a descendant of the empress's daughter Olga and her husband Nikolai Kulikovsky. 'We are bringing the Russian empress back to the place where she belongs', said Paul. The funeral represented 'closure' for the family. Yet press accounts were ambivalent about interest among the Russian public, recording both honking of car horns and indifference.[48] Only a few genealogical enthusiasts have a detailed knowledge of the Romanov succession, and as the older generation dies out there is little evidence of a consistent campaign to restore the ruling dynasty, although younger Romanovs take an interest in their Russian roots. That the Romanovs and their history should find their own respectable niche in Russia's current search for a new identity is hardly surprising. The first flush of enthusiasm for this once forbidden subject may have died down, but the Romanovs will remain an essential element of the Russian historical narrative.

Notes

Notes to Introduction

1   On Susanin, see below p. 12.
2   From the author's collection, one sheet, approx 55 x. 40 cc., date and place of publication not indicated.
3   See, for example, J. Bergamini, *The Tragic Dynasty. A History of the Romanovs* (London, 1970); A. S. Rappoport, *The Curse of the Romanovs: a Study of the Lives and Reigns of Two Tsars Paul I and Alexander I of Russia: 1754–1825* (London, 1907).
4   V. Cowles, *The Romanovs* (New York, 1971), p. 11.
5   *Journey of Our Time. The Journals of the Marquis de Custine*, P. Kohler (ed. and transl.) (London, 1980), p. 106.
6   The Muscovite state (*Moskovskoe gosudarstvo*) was formed in the fifteenth century under a series of strong grand princes of Moscow, who began to adopt the title 'tsar'. The official divide between the two is the adoption in 1721 by Peter I of the title Emperor (*imperator*). In the first half of the eighteenth century most foreign powers used the term 'Russian Empire', although the use of 'Muscovy' lingered on.
7   See V. N. Chashkov, 'Romanovy - kto oni?', *Otechestvennaia istoriia*, no. 1 (1998), pp. 167–76; A. B. Kamenskii, 'Byli li Romanovy Romanovymi?', *Voprosy istorii*, no. 8 (1990).

Notes to Chapter 1: Romanov Roots

1   *Du Tsar à l'Empereur: Moscow-Saint-Pétersbourg* (Brussels, 2005), p. 76 (exhibition catalogue).
2   See G. K. Shchutskaia, *Palaty boiar Romanovykh* (Moscow, 2000).
3   E. V. Pchelov, *Romanovy: Istoriia dinastii: 300 let pravleniia* (Moscow, 2001), p. 26.
4   On Anastasia, I. Thyrêt, *Between God and Tsar: Religious Symbolism and the Royal Women of Muscovite Russia* (DeKalb, IL, 2001), pp. 53 ff.
5   According to P. Grebenskii and A. Mirvis, *Dom Romanovykh* (2nd ed; St Petersburg, 1992), p. 9, Varvara Ivanovna Khovrina died in 1552 and Fedor (born 1550) was her son. Elsewhere his date of birth is always given as 1553.
6   B. Shirokorad, *Dmitrii Pozharskii protiv Mikhaila Romanova: Zagadka 4 noiabria* (Moscow, 2005), p. 88.
7   See G. E. Orchard (ed.), *Massa's Short History of the Muscovite Wars* (Toronto, 1982), p. 33.

The claim that he was 'adored by everyone' was clearly an exaggeration.

8   V. Kozliakov, *Mikhail Fedorovich: Zhizn' zamechatel'nykh liudei* (Moscow, 2004), p. 21. According to other sources, his wife's name was Shastunova.

9   Chronicles relate that Riurik, a semi-legendary Viking (Varangian) chieftain, came with his clansmen to rule Rus (the old name for Russia) in the ninth century. Subsequently the princes of Moscow, who ruled most of Rus/Russia by the fifteenth century, traced their line back to him, hence the term Riurikovichi or Riurik(ide) dynasty.

10 See S. Bogatyrev, 'Who Made Ivan IV Tsar? The Muscovite Dynasty and Christian Hierarchs in the 1550's', *SEER*, 85 (2007).

11 This story, first recorded in 1600, was probably untrue. See Orchard, *Massa's Short History*, p. 37. On Boris, S. F. Platonov, *Boris Godunov: Tsar of Russia* (Gulf Breeze, FL, 1973).

12 See C. S. Dunning, 'The Preconditions of Modern Russia's First Civil War,' *RH* 25 (1998), pp. 119–31.

13 See C. S. Dunning's argument that he may indeed have been the real *Dmitry: A Short History of Russia's First Civil War: The Time of Troubles and the Founding of the Romanov Dynasty* (University Park, PA, 2004).

14 M. Perrie, 'Christ or Devil? Images of the First False Dimitry in Early Seventeenth-Century Russia', *Slavica Helsingiensia* 14 (1994), pp. 105–15.

15 Perrie, 'Christ or Devil?', p. 110.

16 With thanks to Maureen Perrie. Dmitry Shuisky in Poland in 1611 claimed that Dmitry was planning to send him with an army to Poland to liaise with anti-Sigismund factions.

17 Shirokorad, *Dmitrii Pozharskii*, p. 359.

18 Shirokorad, *Dmitrii Pozharskii*, passim.

19 Shirokorad, *Dmitrii Pozharskii*, p. 363.

20 Orchard, *Massa's Short History*, p. 183 (letter of 1614).

21 Kozliakov, *Mikhail Fedorovich*, p. 28.

22 On the Susanin legend, *Iubileinyi sbornik kostromskogo tserkovno-istoricheskogo obshchestva v pamiat' 300-letiia tsarstvovaniia doma Romanovykh* (Kostroma, 1913), pp. 10–17.

23 From Kozliakov, *Mikhail Fedorovich*, pp. 40–41.

24 Description of entry from *Razriadnye knigi 1598–1638 gg.* (Moscow, 1974).

25 For numbering months and days, Muscovy used the Julian calendar, in common with much of non-Catholic Europe in the early seventeenth century.

26 Shirokorad, *Dmitrii Pozharskii*, p. 375.

27 P. Longworth, *Alexis: Tsar of All the Russias* (London, 1984), p. 230.

28 See J. Keep, 'The Regime of Filaret', *SEER*, 38 (1959–60), pp. 334–360.

29 M. T. Poe, *The Russian Elite in the Seventeenth Century,* 2 vols (Helsinki, 2004), vol. 1, pp. 82 ff.

30 B. P. Polevoi, 'Concerning the Origin of the Maps of Russia of 1613–1614 of Hessel Gerritsz', in L. Hughes (ed.), *New Perspectives on Muscovite History: Selected Papers from the IV World Congress for Soviet and East European Studies, Harrogate 1990* (Basingstoke, 1993), pp. 14–23. An important new study is V. Kivelson, *Cartographies of Tsardom: The Land and its Meaning in Seventeenth-Century Russia* (Ithaca, NY, 2006).

31 See E. K. Wirtschafter, *Structures of Society: Imperial Russia's 'People of Various Ranks'* (DeKalb, IL, 1994), p. xiii.

32   R. Hellie, *Slavery in Russia, 1450–1725* (Chicago, 1982).

33   R. Hellie, *Enserfment and Military Change in Muscovy* (Chicago, 1971); R. Crummey, *Aristocrats and Servitors: The Boyar Elite in Russia, 1613–1689* (Princeton, 1983).

34   See Poe, *The Russian Elite*, vol. 1, pp. 82 ff.

35   Poe, *The Russian Elite*, vol. 2, p. 41.

36   On the multiple estates of F. I. Sheremetev, both inherited and by royal grant, see Crummey, *Aristocrats*, p. 119.

37   See R. Hellie, 'Why did the Muscovite Elite not Rebel?', *RH* 25 (1998), pp. 155–62.

38   See below, and N. Riasanovsky, *A Parting of Ways: Government and the Educated Public in Russia 1801–55* (Oxford, 1976).

39   V. Kivelson, *Autocracy in the Provinces: The Muscovite Gentry and Political Culture in the Seventeenth Century* (Stanford, 1997), p. 38.

40   Figures for 1678 in J. M. Hittle, *The Service City: State and Townsmen in Russia, 1600–1800* (Cambridge, MA, 1979), p. 32.

41   Keep, 'Filaret', p. 352. For fuller discussion, see Chapter 2.

42   D. Moon 'Reassessing Russian Serfdom', *European History Quarterly*, 26 (1996), p. 512.

43   See S. Hoch, *Serfdom and Social Control in Russia: Petrovskoe, A village in Tambov* (Chicago and London, 1986).

44   On weddings and bridal shows, see R. Martin, 'Choreographing the Tsar's Happy Occasion: Tradition, Change and Dynastic Legitimacy in the Weddings of Tsar Mikhail Romanov', *SR* 63 (2004), pp. 794–817.

45   Information from Pchelov, *Romanovy*, pp. 14–18. See family tree on p. xi.

46   See B. N. Floria, 'Nekotorye dannye o nachale svetskogo portreta v Rossii', *Arkhiv russkoi istorii*, vyp. 1 (Moscow, 1992), p. 139.

47   'Vklady tsaria Mikhaila Fedorovicha', in *Iubileinyi sbornik* (1913), pp. 96–103.

48   This historic church was demolished in the early 1930s to widen access to Red Square for parades. In the 1990s a reproduction was constructed from old plans and now functions again as a church, one of many resurrected Romanov 'shrines'. Generally, see W. C. Brumfield, *A History of Russian Architecture* (Cambridge, 1994).

49   See L. Hughes, 'Images of the Elite: A Reconsideration of the Portrait in Seventeenth-Century Russia', *Forschungen zur osteuropäischen Geschichte*, 56 (2000), pp. 167–85.

50   A. Olearius, *The Travels of Olearius in Seventeenth-Century Russia*, (ed.) S. Baron (Stanford, 1967), between pp. 150–1.

51   See, for example, an early eighteenth century anonymous portrait reproduced in *Du Tsar à l'Empereur*, p. 75.

52   See, for example, J. Roberts, *The King's Head: Charles I, King and Martyr* (London, 1999).

53   See L. Hughes, 'The Petrine Year: Anniversaries and Festivals in the Reign of Peter the Great (1682–1725)', in K. Friedrich (ed.), *Festive Culture in Germany and Europe from the 16th to the 20th Century* (Lewiston, NY, 2000), pp. 148–68.

54   I. V. Pozdeeva, 'Pervye Romanovy i tsaristskaia ideia (XVII vek)', *Voprosy istorii*, 1 (1996), pp. 41–52.

55   See B. F. Porshnev, *Muscovy and Sweden in the Thirty Years War* (Cambridge, 1995).

56   P. Bushkovitch (ed.), *England and the North: The Russian Embassy of 1613–1614* (Philadelphia, 1994).

57 *Du Tsar à l'Empereur*, p. 84. There is a companion portrait of Tsar Alexis, both from the Museum of Fine Arts in Copenhagen.

58 Kozliakov, *Mikhail Fedorovich*, p. 308.

59 Pchelov, *Romanovy*, p. 26. Orchard, *Massa's Short History*, p. 183.

60 See P. K. Monod, *The Power of Kings: Monarchy and Religion in Europe, 1589–1715* (New Haven, 1999).

61 See M. T. Poe, 'A People Born to Slavery', *Russia in Early Modern European Ethnography 1476–1748* (Ithaca and London, 2000).

62 Olearius, *The Travels*, p. 173.

Notes to Chapter 2: The Pious Tsars

1 *Sobranie pisem tsaria Alekseia Mikhailovicha* (Moscow, 1856); *Pis'ma russkikh gosudarei i drugikh osob tsarskogo semeistva*, vol. 5 (Moscow, 1896). He was the first Russian ruler to leave a substantial body of letters in his own hand.

2 L. Hughes, 'B. I. Morozov', *MERSH*, vol. 23 (1981), pp. 71–3.

3 R. Crummey, *Aristocrats and Servitors: The Boyar Elite in Russia, 1613–1689* (Princeton, 1983), pp. 118–19.

4 See E. V. Barsov, 'Chin postanovleniia na tsarstvo tsaria i velikogo kniazia Alekseia Mikhailovicha', *Pamiatniki drevnerusskoi pismennosti* (St Petersburg, 1882), vol. 16.

5 I. Andreev, *Aleksei Mikhailovich: Zhizn' zamechatel'nykh liudei* (Moscow, 2003), p. 69.

6 P. Longworth, *Alexis: Tsar of All the Russias* (London, 1984), p. 58.

7 Andreev, *Aleksei*, p. 68.

8 See N. S. Kollmann, 'Pilgrimage, Procession, and Symbolic Space in Sixteenth-Century Russian Politics', in M. Flier and D. Rowland (eds), *Medieval Russian Culture*, 2 vols (Berkeley, 1994), vol. 2, pp. 163–81.

9 A. Olearius, *The Travels of Olearius in Seventeenth-Century Russia*, S. Baron (ed.) (Stanford, 1967), pp. 262–3.

10 See L. Hughes, 'Attitudes Towards Foreigners in Early Modern Russia', in C. Brennan and M. Frame (eds), *Russia and the Wider World in Historical Perspective: Essays for Paul Dukes* (Basingstoke, 2000), pp. 1–23.

11 Crummey, *Aristocrats*, pp. 75–7.

12 I. Thyrêt, *Between God and Tsar: Religious Symbolism and the Royal Women of Muscovite Russia* (DeKalb, IL, 2001), p. 174.

13 Of Michael's daughters, only Anna took the veil (as Anfisa) just before her death. Of Alexis's daughters two were forced to take the veil in 1698: Martha (Margarita) in the Dormition convent at Aleksandrovskaia sloboda and the disgraced Sophia (Susannah) in the Novodevichy. See N. S. Kollmann, 'The Seclusion of Elite Muscovite Women', *RH* 10 (1983), 170–87; L. Hughes, *Sophia Regent of Russia, 1657–1704* (New Haven, 1990), pp. 16–22.

14 See R. Hellie (ed. and trans.), *The Muscovite Law Code (Ulozhenie) of 1649, part I: Text and Translation* (Irvine, CA, 1988); idem, 'Commentary on Chap. 11 of the Ulozhenie', *RH* 17 (1990), pp. 308–39.

15 See S. Plokhy, *The Cossacks and Religion in Early Modern Ukraine* (Oxford, 2001); idem, *Tsars and Cossacks: A Study in Iconography* (Cambridge, MA, 2002).

16 There is an extensive literature on this controversial issue, much of it in Ukrainian. See F. Sysin, 'The Khmelnytsky Uprising and Ukrainian Nation-building', *Journal of Ukrainian Studies* 17, nos 1–2 (1992), pp. 141–7.

17 S. V. Lobachev, 'Patriarch Nikon's Rise to Power', *SEER* 79 (2001), pp. 290–307.

18 G. Michels, 'The First Old Believers in Tradition and Historical Reality', *JGO* 41 (1993), pp. 485–8; idem, *At War with the Church* (Stanford, 2000).

19 See P. Meyendorff, *Russia, Ritual and Reform: Liturgical Reforms of Nikon in the 17th century* (Crestwood, NY, 1991); P. Bushkovitch, *Religion and Society in Russia: The Sixteenth and Seventeenth Centuries* (Oxford, 1992).

20 K. Bostrom (ed.), *Archpriest Avvakum: The Life, Written by Himself* (Ann Arbor, 1979).

21 M. Cherniavsky, 'The Old Believers and the New Religion', *SR* 25 (1966), pp. 1–39.

22 Michels, *At War with the Church*, p. 223.

23 Longworth, *Alexis*, p. 178.

24 Longworth, *Alexis*, p. 104.

25 See Michael S. Flier, 'Breaking the Code: The Image of the Tsar in the Muscovite Palm Sunday Ritual', in Flier and Rowland (eds), *Medieval Russian Culture*, pp. 213–42.

26 P. Bushkovitch, 'The Epiphany Ceremony of the Russian Court in the Sixteenth and Seventeenth Centuries', *RR* 49 (1990), pp. 1–18.

27 R. Crummey, 'Court Spectacles in Seventeenth-Century Russia: Illusion and Reality', in D. C. Waugh (ed.), *Essays in Honor of A. A. Zimin* (Columbus, OH, 1985), p. 138.

28 P. Longworth, 'Tsar Alexis Goes to War', in P. Dukes (ed.), *Russia and Europe* (London, 1991), p. 242.

29 See L. Hughes, 'Western European Graphic Material as a Source for Moscow Baroque Architecture', *SEER* 55 (1977), pp. 433–43.

30 L. Hughes, 'The Moscow Armoury and Innovations in 17th-century Muscovite Art', *CASS* 13 (1979), pp. 204–23; eadem, 'The Seventeenth-Century Russian "Renaissance"', *History Today*, Feb. 1980, pp. 41–5.

31 L. Hughes, 'Simon Ushakov's Icon "The Tree of the Muscovite State" Revisited', *FOG* 58 (2002), pp. 1201–12.

32 See L. Hughes, 'Images of the Elite: A Reconsideration of the Portrait in Seventeenth-century Russia', *FOG* 56 (2000), pp. 167–85.

33 Hughes, 'Western European Graphic Material'.

34 See R. Hellie, *The Economy and Material Culture of Russia 1600–1725* (Chicago, 1999).

35 See the discussion and data in G. Marker, *Publishing, Printing, and the Origins of Intellectual Life in Russia, 1700–1800* (Princeton, 1985), chapter 1.

36 L. Hughes, 'S. Polotskii', *MERSH* 29 (1982), pp. 8–11.

37 S. Karlinsky, *Russian Drama from its Beginnings to the Age of Pushkin* (Berkeley, 1985).

38 See Hughes, *Sophia*, pp. 173–5.

39 Jacob Reutenfels, quoted in C. Jensen, 'Music for the Tsar: A Preliminary Study of the Music of the Muscovite Court Theatre', *The Musical Quarterly*, no. 2, 79 (1995), pp. 368–401.

40 Jensen, 'Music', pp. 375, 377. See also inventories of Vasily Golitsyn's possessions, which included an organ, clavichord and flutes, Hellie, *Economy*, p. 616.

41 Based on P. Avrich, *Russian Rebels 1600–1800* (New York, 1972); M. Khodarkovsky, 'The Stepan Razin Uprising: Was It a Peasant War?', *JGO* 42 (1994), pp. 1–19.

42 See P. Bushkovitch, *Peter the Great: The Struggle for Power, 1671–1725* (Cambridge, 2001), pp. 49–63.

43 M. T. Poe, *The Russian Elite in the Seventeenth Century*, 2 vols (Helsinki, 2004), vol. 1, pp. 222–5, 231.

44 See, for example, Reutenfels's account of her opening a carriage window, in Hughes, *Sophia*, p. 37.

45 Andreev, *Aleksei*, pp. 606–7.

46 For a full discussion based on primary sources, Bushkovitch, *Peter the Great*, pp. 88–95.

47 See Hughes, *Sophia*, p. 51.

48 See L. Hughes, 'Fedor Alekseevich', *MERSH* 11 (1979), pp. 77–9.

49 Hughes, 'Images'.

50 F. Kämpfer, 'Die "parsuna" Ivan IV. in Kopengagen – Originalporträt oder historische Bild?', in Waugh (ed.), *Essays in Honor*, pp. 187–98; *Du Tsar à l'Empereur: Moscow-Saint-Pétersbourg* (Brussels, 2005), p. 63.

51 See J. Cracraft, *The Petrine Revolution in Russian Imagery* (Chicago, 1997), p. 190; E. S. Ovchinnikova, *Portret v russkom iskusstve XVII veka* (Moscow, 1955), pp. 47–8, 51–3; F. Kämpfer, *Das russische Herrscherbild von den Anfängen bis zu Peter dem Grossen* (Recklinghausen, 1978), p. 242.

52 E. Kämpfer, 'Diarium itineris ad aulam Moscoviticam indeque Astracanum suscepti anno MDCLXXIII', in K. Meier-Lemgo (ed.), *Engelbert Kämpfer, der erste deutsche Forschungsreisende 1651–1716* (Stuttgart, 1937), p. 13.

53 L. Hughes, '"Ambitious and Daring above Her Sex": Tsarevna Sophia Alekseevna (1657–1704) in Foreigners' Accounts', *Oxford Slavonic Papers*, 21 (1988), pp. 65–89.

54 See L. Hughes, *Russia and the West, the Life of a 17th-century Westernizer, Prince Vasily Vasil'evich Golitsyn (1643–1714)* (Newtonville, MA, 1984).

55 See L. Hughes, 'Peter the Great's Two Weddings: Changing Images of Women in a Transitional Age', in R. Marsh (ed.), *Women in Russia and Ukraine* (Cambridge, 1996), pp. 31–44.

56 B. A. Kurakin, 'Gistoriia o tsare Petre Alekseeviche', in *Rossiiu podnial na dyby* (Moscow, 1987), vol. 1, p. 369. Kurakin was married to Evdokia's sister.

57 *Pis'ma russkikh gosudarei* (Moscow, 1861), vol. 3, pp. 68–9.

58 Hughes, *Sophia*, p. 239.

59 Crummey, *Aristocrats*, pp. 209–11; Poe, *The Russian Elite*, vol. 1, pp. 305–10. Poe's figures indicate additional new entrants and personnel.

60 Kurakin, 'Gistoriia', p. 375.

61 *PSZ*, III, no. 1358, pp. 46–7 (29 October 1689).

62 Testament of Patriarch Joachim, 17 March 1690, in G. Vernadsky (ed.), *A Source Book for Russian History from Early Times to 1917*, 3 vols (New Haven, 1972), vol. 2, pp. 361–3.

Notes to Chapter 3: Transformation

1   See N. Riasanovsky, *The Image of Peter the Great in Russian History and Thought* (Oxford, 1985); L. Hughes, *Peter the Great: A Biography* (New Haven and London, 2002), pp. 227–50. For detailed information about all subjects in this chapter, see L. Hughes, *Russia in the Age of Peter the Great* (New Haven and London, 1998).

2   *PSZ*, V, no. 3006.

3   'The Story of the Ship's Boat which gave his Majesty the Thought of Building Ships of War', in J. Cracraft (ed.), *For God and Peter the Great: The Works of Thomas Consett, 1723–1729* (Boulder, CO, 1982), p. 210.

4   *PiB*, IX, p. 69 (3 February 1709).

5   *DR*, IV, pp. 527–30.

6   L. Hughes, 'A Note on the Children of Peter the Great', *SGECRN* 21(1993), pp. 10–16.

7   B. A. Kurakin, 'Gistoriia o tsare Petre Alekseeviche', in *Rossiiu podnial na dyby*, vol. 1 (Moscow, 1987), pp. 381–2.

8   Hughes, *Peter the Great: A Biography*, p. 31.

9   See L. Hughes, 'Peter the Great: A Passion for Ships', in M. Cornwall and M. Frame (eds), *Scotland and the Slavs: Cultures in Contact, 1500–2000* (Newtonville, MA, 2001), pp. 3–20.

10 *DR*, IV, pp. 853–6.

11 See R. Warner, 'The Kozuchovo Campaign of 1697', *JGO* 13 (1965), pp. 487–96.

12 A. G. Cross, 'The Bung College or British Monastery in Petrine Russia', *SGECRN* 12 (1984), pp. 4–14.

13 See, for example, L. Hughes, *Playing Games: The Alternative History of Peter the Great* (London, 2000); E. A. Zitser, *The Transfigured Kingdom: Sacred Parody and Charismatic Authority at the Court of Peter the Great* (Ithaca, NY, 2004); E. A. Zitser, 'Post Soviet Peter: New Histories of the Late Muscovite and Early Imperial Russian Court', *Kritika* 6, no. 2 (Spring, 2005), pp. 375–92.

14 I. A. Zheliabuzhsky, 'Zapiski', in A. B. Bogdanov (ed.), *Rossiia pri tsarevne Sof'e i Petre I* (Moscow, 1990), p. 221.

15 Kurakin, 'Gistoriia', p. 389.

16 See P. Bushkovitch, *Peter the Great: The Struggle for Power, 1671–1725* (Cambridge, 2001).

17 See G. Herd, 'Rebellion and Reformation in the Muscovite Military', in J. Kotilane and M. Poe (eds), *Modernizing Muscovy: The Changing Face of 17th-century Russia* (Oxford, 1999), pp. 263–90.

18 *PSZ*, III, no. 1536, pp. 220–3. See L. Hughes, 'The Funerals of the Russian Emperors and Empresses', in M. Schaich (ed.), *Monarchy and Religion: The Transformation of Royal Culture in Eighteenth-Century Europe* (Oxford, 2007), pp. 395–419.

19 N. B. Golikova, *Politicheskie protsessy pri Petra I* (Moscow, 1957), pp. 131–2.

20 S. M. Soloviev, *History of Russia*, vol. 26, *Peter the Great: A Reign Begins, 1689–1703*, trans. and ed. L. Hughes (Gulf Breeze, FL, 1994), p. 137.

21 N. N. Bantysh-Kamensky, *Obzor vneshnikh snoshenii Rossii s derzhavami inostrannymi*, 4 vols (Moscow, 1894–1902), vol. 4, p. 208.

22 Quoted in L. Oliva, *Peter the Great: Great Lives Observed* (Englewood Cliffs, 1970), p. 108.

23 A. G. Cross, *Peter the Great through British Eyes: Perceptions and Representations of the Tsar since 1698* (Cambridge, 2000), pp. 10–11.

24 Cracraft (ed.), *For God and Peter the Great*, p. 210.

25 See J. Bowle (ed.), *Diary of John Evelyn* (New York, 1983), pp. 403–4.

26 See J. Hartley, 'Changing Perspectives: British Views of Russia from the Grand Embassy to the Peace of Nystad', in L. Hughes (ed.), *Peter the Great and the West: New Perspectives* (Basingstoke, 2001), pp. 53–70.

27 L. Loewenson, 'People Peter the Great Met in England: Moses Stringer, Chymist and Physician', *SEER* 37 (1959), p. 462.

28 S. Dixon (ed.), *Britain and Russia in the Age of Peter the Great: Historical Documents* (London, 1998), pp. 13–14; *Bishop Burnet's History of His Own Time* (Oxford, 1833), vol. 4, p. 407.

29 L. N. Maikov, *Rasskazy Nartova o Petre Velikom* (St Petersburg, 1891), p. 82.

30 See L. Hughes, 'Images of Greatness: Portraits of Peter I', in L. Hughes (ed.), *Peter the Great and the West*, pp. 250–70; eadem, 'From Tsar to Emperor: Portraits of Peter the Great', in G. Szvak (ed.), *The Place of Russia in Eurasia* (Budapest, 2001), pp. 221–32.

31 Quoted in J. Hartley, 'England "Enjoys the Spectacle of a Northern Barbarian": The Reception of Peter I and Alexander I', *WOR*, p. 12.

32 O. Beliaev, *Dukh Petra Velikogo* (St Petersburg, 1798), pp. 22–3.

33 Quoted from J.-G. Korb, *Diary of an Austrian Secretary of Legation at the Court of Czar Peter the Great*, trans. and ed. Count MacDonnell, 2 vols (London 1863/ 1968), vol. 1, pp. 155–6; L. Hughes, 'A Beard is an Unnecessary Burden: Peter I's Laws on Shaving and their Roots in Early Russia', in Bartlett and Hughes (eds), pp. 21–44.

34 *PSZ*, III, no. 1735, pp. 680–1, no. 1736, pp. 681–2.

35 J. Perry, *The State of Russia* (London, 1716; repr. 1967), pp. 195–7.

36 B. A. Uspensky, 'Historia sub Specie Semioticae', in H. K. Baran (ed.), *Semiotics and Structuralism: Readings from the Soviet Union* (New York, 1976), p. 71.

37 See L. Hughes, 'From Caftans into Corsets: The Sartorial Transformation of Women during the Reign of Peter the Great', in P. Barta (ed.), *Gender and Sexuality in Russian Civilization* (London, 2001), pp. 17–32.

38 Korb, *Diary*, II, p. 92.

39 See, for example, E. Anisimov, 'The Fate of St Petersburg in the History of Russia: Reflections on the Tercentenary', in Bartlett and Hughes (eds), pp. 208–18.

40 W. Bruce Lincoln, *Sunlight at Midnight: St Petersburg and the Rise of Modern Russia* (New York, 2000); A. George, *St Petersburg: The First Three Centuries* (Phoenix Mill, 2004).

41 See J. Cracraft, *The Petrine Revolution in Russian Imagery* (Chicago, 1997).

42 See M. Di Salvo, 'What Did Francesco Algarotti See in Russia?', in Bartlett and Hughes (eds), pp. 72–80.

43 See for example Johannes Hohmann's plan (1710s) of St Petersburg in which Vasilevsky Island is completely covered with a grid of streets, although in fact only the south-eastern 'lines' were actually constructed.

44 R. Pipes (ed.), *Karamzin's Memoir on Ancient and Modern Russia* (New York, 1966), p. 126.

45   See M. Marrese, 'Feminine Intrigue and Ambition at the 18th-c. Russian Court', unpublished paper, AAASS, November 2005, p. 5.

46   G. Marker, *Publishing, Printing and the Origins of Intellectual Life in Russia 1700–1800* (Princeton, 1985); J. Cracraft, *The Petrine Revolution in Russian Culture* (Cambridge, MA and London, 2004).

47   O. Neverov, '"His Majesty's Cabinet" and Peter I's Kunstkammer', in O. Impey and A. McGregor (eds), *The Origins of Museums: The Cabinet of Curiosities in 16th-17th-Century Europe* (Oxford, 1985), pp. 54–61.

48   C. Whitworth, *An Account of Russia as it was in the Year 1710* (Moscow-Leningrad, 1988), p. 14.

49   See P. Englund, *The Battle of Poltava: The Birth of the Russian Empire* (London, 1992), p.155.

50   See W. C. Fuller, *Strategy and Power in Russia 1600–1914* (New York, 1992).

51   V. Ger'e, *Sbornik pisem i memorialov Leibnitsa, otnosiashchikhsia k Rossii i Petru Velikomu* (St Petersburg, 1873), pp. 177–80.

52   *PSZ*, IV, no. 2328, pp. 634–5; no. 2330, p. 635.

53   *PiB*, XI (ii), p. 112 (1 September 1711).

54   *PiB*, XI (ii), pp. 123, 124–5, 133.

55   F. C. Weber, *The Present State of Russia*, 2 vols (London, 1722–3), vol. 1, p. 105.

56   See Hughes, 'A Note on the Children', pp. 10–16.

57   See L. Hughes, 'Peter the Great's Two Weddings: Changing Images of Women in a Transitional Age', in R. Marsh (ed.), *Women in Russia and Ukraine* (Cambridge, 1996), pp. 31–44.

58   D. Bantysh-Kamenskii, *Istoricheskoe sobranie spiskov kavalerov chetyrekh rossiiskikh imperatorskikh ordenov* (Moscow, 1814); L. Hughes, 'Catherine I of Russia: Consort to Peter the Great', in C. Campbell Orr (ed.), *Queenship in Europe, 1660–1815: The Role of the Consort* (Cambridge, 2004), pp. 131–54.

59   N. Ustrialov, *Istoriia tsarstvovaniia Petra Velikogo*, 6 vols (St Petersburg, 1858–69), vol. 6, appendix, pp. 346–8; Bushkovitch, *Peter the Great.*

60   Ustrialov, *Istoriia*, vol. 6, pp. 348–9 (31 October).

61   See Hughes, *Peter the Great: A Biography*, pp. 116–18.

62   Ustrialov, *Istoriia*, vol. 6, pp. 442–4.

63   Bushkovitch, *Peter the Great*, p. 386.

64   G. Vernadsky, *A Source Book for Russian History from the Earliest Times to 1917*, 3 vols (New Haven, 1972), vol. 2, pp. 342–3.

65   H. Bagger, 'The Role of the Baltic in Russian Foreign Policy 1721–1773', in H. Ragsdale (ed.), *Imperial Russian Foreign Policy* (Cambridge, 1993), pp. 38–9.

66   See C. Peterson, *Peter the Great's Administrative and Judicial Reforms* (Stockholm, 1979).

67   *PSZ*, VI, no. 3534, p. 141 (28 February 1720).

68   *PSZ*, VII, no. 4422, p. 205 (20 January).

69   Peterson, *Peter the Great's Administrative and Judicial Reforms*, p. 115.

70   J. Cracraft, *The Church Reform of Peter the Great* (London, 1971).

71   *PiB*, IX, p. 331.

72   Perry, *The State*, pp. 271, 274.

73   H.-F. de Bassewitz, 'Zapiski grafa Bassevicha, sluzhashchie k poiasneniiu nekotorykh sobytii iz vremeni tsarstvovaniia Petra Velikogo (1713–1725)', *Russkii arkhiv*, 3(1865), pp. 212–213.

74   *PSZ*, VI, no. 3893, pp. 496–7.

75   *PSZ*, VI, no. 3979, pp. 662–4.

76   *PSZ*, VII, no. 4507, pp. 285–6.

77   *PSZ*, VII, no. 4345, pp. 150–1.

78   *PSZ*, VI, no. 3970, pp. 656–7.

79   *Pokhodnye zhurnaly Petra I 1695–1726* (St Petersburg, 1853–1855); 1725, pp. 1–3.

80   See Hughes, 'Funerals', in M. Schaich (ed.).

81   *200-letie Kabineta ego imp. velichestva 1704–1904* (St Petersburg, 1911), appendix II, p. 57.

Notes to Chapter 4: The Age of Empresses and Palace Revolutions

1   A solid overview of this period is still lacking in English. P. Longworth, *The Three Empresses: Catherine I, Anne and Elizabeth of Russia* (London, 1972) is lively, but out of date.

2   E. Anisimov, *Rossiia bez Petra* (St Petersburg, 1994). See 'Empire of the Nobility', excerpt in J. Cracraft (ed.), *Major Problems in the History of Imperial Russia* (Lexington, MA, 1994), pp. 128–47. See also N. Pavlenko, *Strasti u trona: Istoriia dvortsovykh perevorotov* (Moscow, 1996).

3   See B. Meehan-Waters, 'Catherine the Great and the Problem of Female Rule', *RR* 34 (1975), pp. 293–307; J. Alexander, 'Favourites, Favouritism and Female Rule in Russia, 1725–1796', in R. Bartlett and J. Hartley (eds), *Russia in the Age of the Enlightenment* (London, 1990), pp. 105–24; idem, 'Amazon Autocratrixes: Images of Female Rule in the Eighteenth Century', in P. Barta (ed.), *Gender and Sexuality in Russian Civilisation* (London, 2001), pp. 33–53.

4   See C. H. Whittaker, *Russian Monarchy: Eighteenth-Century Russian Rulers and Writers in Political Dialogue* (DeKalb, IL, 2003); R. Wortman, *Scenarios of Power: Myth and Ceremony in Russian Monarchy*, 2 vols (Princeton, 1995–2000), vol. 1.

5   See M. Marrese, 'Feminine Intrigue and Ambition at the 18th-c. Russian Court', unpublished paper, AAASS, November 2005.

6   F. Prokopovich, 'Oration at the Funeral of Peter the Great (1725)', in Marc Raeff (ed.), *Peter the Great Changes Russia* (Lexington, MA, 1972), p. 42; L. Hughes, 'Catherine I of Russia: Consort to Peter the Great', in C. Campbell Orr (ed.), *Queenship in Europe, 1660–1815: The Role of the Consort* (Cambridge, 2004), pp. 131–54.

7   On the cult of St Catherine, see G. Marker, 'Peter the Great's Female Knights of Liberation: The Order of St Catherine', in Bartlett and Hughes (eds), pp. 35–47. Substitute mother imagery was not, of course, exclusively Russian. Queen Anne, who failed to leave any surviving heirs, was 'nursing mother' to her people. See J. Miller, *The Stuarts* (London and New York, 2004), p. 229.

8   *Zapiska o konchine Gos. Imp. Ekateriny Alekseevny i o vstuplenii na prestol Gos. Imp. Petra II Alekseevicha. 1727 g.* (St Petersburg, 1913).

9   See L. Hughes, 'The Funerals of the Russian Emperors and Empresses', in M. Schaich (ed.), *Monarchy and Religion: The Transformation of Royal Culture in Eighteenth-Century Europe* (Oxford, 2007), pp. 395–419.

10 A. A. Titov, *Dopolnenie k istoricheskomu geograficheskomu i topograficheskomu opisaniiu Sanktpeterburga* (St Petersburg, 1903), p. 140.

11 S. Novoselov, *Opisanie kafedral'nogo sobora vo imia sviatykh Pervoverkhovnykh Apostolov Petra i Pavla* (St Petersburg, 1857), pp. 283–4.

12 See N. Pavlenko, *Aleksandr Danilovich Menshikov* (Moscow, 1981); and *Poluderzhavnyi vlastelin* (Moscow, 1991).

13 See Hughes, 'Funerals', p. 407.

14 The patronymic 'Ioannovna' comes from 'Ioann', an older form of Ivan.

15 On Golitsyn and his reading of West European history and philosophy, I. de Madariaga, 'Portrait of an Eighteenth-Century Statesman, D. M. Golitsyn', in eadem, *Politics and Culture in Eighteenth Century Russia: Collected Essays* (London, 1998), pp. 57–77.

16 See M. Raeff (ed.), *Plans for Political Reform in Imperial Russia, 1730–1905* (Englewood Cliffs, NJ, 1966), pp. 44–5.

17 Raeff, *Plans*, p. 43.

18 M. Curtis, *A Forgotten Empress: Anna Ivanovna and her Era 1730–1740* (New York, 1974) has some good anecdotes, but is unreliable. A. Lipski, 'Some Aspects of Russia's Westernization During the Reign of Anna Ioannovna', *American Slavic and East European Review* [= *SR*] 18 (1959), pp. 477–88, has weathered well. *CASS* 12 (1978), no. 1, is a special issue on Anna's reign. For details, Soloviev, vols 34 and 35. For a post-Soviet view (in English), see E. Anisimov, 'Anna Ivanovna', *RSH* 32, no. 4 (1994), pp. 37–72, and his book (in Russian), *Anna Ioannovna, Zhizn' zamechatel'nykh liudei* (Moscow, 2002).

19 Hughes, *Russia in the Age of Peter the Great* (New Haven, 1998), pp. 412–13.

20 Hughes, *Russia in the Age*, p. 413

21 E. Pchelov, *Romanovy: Istoriia dinastii* (Moscow, 2001), p. 80. The son and Mamonov both died in 1730.

22 See E. Weeda, 'Rulers, Russia and the 18th-Century Epic', *SEER* 83 (2005), pp. 175–207.

23 B. Meehan Waters, *Autocracy and Aristocracy: The Russian Service Elite of 1730* (New Brunswick, 1984); Anisimov, 'Anna Ivanovna'.

24 See E. Anisimov, *Russkaia pytka: Politcheskii sysk v Rossii XVIII veka* (St Petersburg, 2004).

25 Marrese, 'Feminine Intrigue', p. 10.

26 Hughes, 'Funerals', p. 409.

27 V. B. Gendrikov, 'Traurnye tseremonii v Petropavlovskom sobore', in *Kraevedcheskie zapiski: Issledovaniia i materialy. Vyp. 2.* (St Petersburg, 1994), p. 311.

28 Whittaker, *Russian Monarchy*, p. 81.

29 M. Korf, *Braunshveigskoe semeistvo* (Moscow, 1993), p. 11.

30 A detailed account in Korf, pp. 188–235.

31 The best survey is E. Anisimov, *Empress Elizabeth: Her Reign and Her Russia* (Gulf Breeze, FL, 1995). See also J. Brennan, *Enlightened Despotism in Russia: The Reign of Elisabeth, 1741–1762* (New York, 1987); and (now outdated) R. Nisbet Bain, *The Daughter of Peter the Great* (St Clair Shores, MI, 1969).

32   Pchelov, *Romanovy*, p. 91.

33   See Wortman, *Scenarios*, vol. 1, p. 87.

34   Wortman, *Scenarios*, vol. 1, p. 106

35   S. Dixon 'Religious Ritual at the Eighteenth-Century Russian Court', in Schaich (ed.), *Monarchy and Religion*, pp. 217–48.

36   V. P. Naumov, 'Elizaveta Petrovna', *RSH* 32, no. 4 (1994), pp. 8–38; K. Pisarenko, *Povsednevnaia zhizn' russkogo dvora v tsarstvovanie Elizavety Petrovny* (Moscow, 2003). Also P. Keenan, 'Creating a Public in St Petersburg, 1703–1761', unpublished PhD thesis, SSEES UCL, 2005.

37   Prince M. Shcherbatov, *On the Corruption of Morals in Russia*, trans. and ed. A. Lentin (Cambridge, 1969), pp. 145–7.

38   J. Keith, *A Fragment of a Memoir of James Keith written by Himself, 1714–1734* (Edinburgh, 1843).

39   See E. Anisimov, *Zhenshchiny na russkom prestole* (St Petersburg, 1997), pp. 104–5.

40   *The Memoirs of Catherine the Great*, trans. and ed. M. Cruse and H. Hoogenboom (New York, 2005), p. 39.

41   Anisimov, *Empress Elizabeth*, p. 186.

42   For an overview, L. Hughes, 'Russian Culture in the Eighteenth Century', in D. Lieven (ed.), *Cambridge History of Russia*, 3 vols (Cambridge, 2006), vol. 2, pp. 67–91.

43   See W. C. Brumfield, *A History of Russian Architecture* (Cambridge, 1994).

44   See S. Werrett, 'An Odd Sort of Display: The St Petersburg Academy of Sciences in Enlightened Russia', unpublished PhD thesis, University of Cambridge, 2000.

45   For a recent study, E. P. Karpeev, *Russkaia kul'tura i Lomonosov* (St Petersburg, 2005).

46   See W. G. Jones, 'Literature in the Eighteenth Century', in N. Cornwell (ed.), *The Routledge Companion to Russian Literature* (London and New York, 2000), pp. 23–35.

47   See E. K. Wirtschafter, *The Play of Ideas in Russian Enlightenment Theater* (DeKalb, IL, 2003).

48   See M. Raeff, *Origins of the Russian Intelligentsia: The 18th century Nobility* (New York, 1966).

49   Statistics in I. de Madariaga, 'The Russian Nobility, 1600–1800', in H. M. Scott (ed.), *The European Nobilities in the 17th and 18th Centuries*, 2 vols (London, 1995), vol. 2, pp. 223–73. Only males were counted in censuses.

50   J. Hartley, 'Changing Perspectives: British Views of Russia from the Grand Embassy to the Peace of Nystad', in L. Hughes (ed.), *Peter the Great and the West: New Perspectives* (Basingstoke, 2001), p. 67.

51   See G. Hosking, *Russia: People and Empire: 1552–1917* (London, 1997); and his *Russia and the Russians* (London, 2001).

52   On the economy and finance, A. Kahan, *The Plow, the Hammer and the Knout* (Chicago, 1985).

53   M. Raeff, 'The Domestic Policies of Peter III and his Overthrow', *American Historical Review* 75 (1970), pp. 1289–1310. C. Leonard, *Reform and Regicide: The Reign of Peter III of Russia* (Bloomington, IN, 1993) takes an overly positive view of Peter. For a Russian revisionist view, A. Mylnikov, 'Petr III', *Voprosy istorii*, 4–5 (1991), pp. 43–58; and idem, (ed.), *Petr III: povestvovanie v dokumentakh i versiiakh* (Moscow, 2002). For details, Soloviev, vol. 42.

54 V. K. Ziborov, 'Romanovy i Riurikovichi', in I. A. Froianov (ed.), *Dom Romanovykh v istorii Rossii* (St Petersburg, 1995), pp. 47–54.

55 See V. N. Chashkov, 'Romanovy - kto oni?', *Otechestvennaia istoriia*, 1 (1998), p. 170.

56 Versions of Catherine's memoir, ending with her accession in 1762, include *The Memoirs of Catherine the Great*, ed. D. Maroger (London, 1955); *Katharina II: in ihren Memoiren*, trans. and ed. E. Boehme (Leipzig, 1920); *Mémoires de l'impératrice Catherine II, écrits par elle-même; et précédés d'une préface par A. Herzen* (London, 1859). Quotations here from Cruse and Hoogenboom, n. 40 above, pp. 37, 53–4, 70, 120. Catherine wrote three versions, in 1756, 1771–3 (revised 1790–1) and 1794, ibid., p. xii. This text is based on the 1794 version and does not contain fragments and letters included in some editions. See also M. Greenleaf, 'Performing Autobiography: The Multiple Memoirs of Catherine the Great (1756–96)', *RR* 63 (2004), pp. 407–26.

57 See below, Chapter 5.

58 See, e.g. Mylnikov, 'Petr III'; Leonard, *Reform*, p. 16.

59 Mylnikov, 'Petr III', p. 46.

60 Mylnikov, 'Petr III', p. 49.

61 P. Dukes, ed., *Russia under Catherine the Great, vol. 1: Select documents on government and society* (Newtonville, MA, 1978), pp. 32–5.

62 For Bolotov's memories of Peter III, see *Zhizn' i prikliucheniia Andreia Bolotova, opisannye samym im dlia svoikh potomkov* (3 vols., Moscow, 1931) vol. 2, part 9.

63 *PSZ* contains 193 items.

64 See Whittaker, *Russian Monarchy*, p. 92.

65 *PSZ*, vol. XV, no. 11,582; Wortman, *Scenarios*, I, pp. 111–12. On Catherine's continued conspicuous support of Orthodoxy, see Dixon, 'Religious Ritual'.

Notes to Chapter 5: Philosopher on the Throne

1 Some genealogies refer to the house of Holstein-Gottorp-Romanov from 1762. See, for example, J. E. Morby, *The Wordsworth Handbook of Kings and Queens* (Ware, 1994), p. 169.

2 *The Memoirs of Catherine the Great*, trans. and ed. M. Cruse and H. Hoogenboom (New York, 2005), pp. 112, 117, 119, 128.

3 *The Memoirs*, p. 182.

4 *The Memoirs*, p. 184.

5 *The Memoirs*, p. xiv.

6 Catherine's illegitimate children had no dynastic claims. Her daughter Anna Petrovna lived from 8 March 1757 to 8 March 1759 and is buried in the Church of the Annunciation in the Alexander Nevsky monastery. Catherine created career opportunities for her son by Grigory Orlov, Aleksei Bobrinsky (born April 1762).

7 *The Memoirs*, p. 135.

8 Pioneering works include *CASS* 4 (1970), no. 3, and 23 (1989), no. 1. (special issues on Catherine II); D. Griffiths, 'Catherine II: The Republican Empress,' *JGO* 21 (1973), pp. 323–4; I. de Madariaga, *Russia in the Age of Catherine the Great* (London, 1981) and

Catherine the Great: A Short History (London, 1990). More recently, S. Dixon, *Catherine the Great* (Harlow, 2001). In Russian, A. Kamenskii, *Pod seniiu Ekateriny: Vtoraia polovina XVIII veka* (St Petersburg, 1992), the first study of Catherine in Russian since 1917, and *Zhizn' i sud'ba imperatritsy Ekateriny Velikoi* (Moscow, 1997).

9   Kamenskii, *Zhizn' i sud'ba*, p. 267.

10 Recent primary sources in English include *The Memoirs* (n. 2, above) and D. Smith (trans. and ed.), *Love and Conquest: Personal Correspondence of Catherine the Great and Prince Grigory Potemkin* (DeKalb, IL, 2004).

11 See Isabel de Madariaga, *Russia in the Age*, pp. 27–34.

12 On this 'scenario of love', see R. Wortman, *Scenarios of Power: Myth and Ceremony in Russian Monarchy*, 2 vols (Princeton, 1995), vol. 1, pp. 111–13.

13 Text in M. Raeff (ed.), *Plans for Political Reform in Imperial Russia 1730–1905* (Englewood Cliffs, NJ, 1966), pp. 53–68.

14 S. Montefiore, *Prince of Princes: The Life of Potemkin* (London, 2000), p. 36.

15 See J. Alexander, 'Favourites, Favouritism and Female Rule in Russia, 1725–1796', in R. Bartlett and J. Hartley (eds), *Russia in the Age of the Enlightenment* (London, 1990), pp. 105–24.

16 Smith, *Love and Conquest*, pp. 38–9.

17 See A. G. Cross, 'Catherine through Contemporary British Eyes', in *Catherine the Great and the British: A Pot-Pourri of Essays* (Nottingham, 2001), pp. 29–44.

18 For annotated contemporary English versions, see W. Reddaway (ed.), *Documents of Catherine the Great* (Cambridge, 1931) and P. Dukes (ed.), *Russia under Catherine the Great*, vol. 2: *Catherine the Great's Instruction (Nakaz) to the Legislative Commission, 1767* (Newtonville, MA, 1977). Also W. E. Butler, 'The *Nakaz* of Catherine the Great', *The American Book Collector*, vol. 16, no. 5 (1966), pp. 19–21.

19 W. G. Jones, 'The Spirit of the *Nakaz*: Catherine II's Literary Debt to Montesquieu', *SEER* 77 (1998), pp. 658–71.

20 Original French in de Madariaga, *Russia in the Age*, p. 339.

21 For an overview, I. de Madariaga, 'Catherine II and the *philosophes*', in eadem, *Politics and Culture in Eighteenth-Century Russia* (London, 1998), pp. 215–34.

22 See Griffiths, 'The Republican Empress'.

23 I. de Madariaga, 'The Foundation of the Russian Educational System by Catherine II', in eadem, *Politics and Culture*, pp. 168–91.

24 R.P. Bartlett, 'Russia in the Eighteenth-Century European Adoption of Inoculation for Smallpox', in *Russia and the World of the Eighteenth Century*, eds R.P. Bartlett, A.G. Cross and K. Rasmussen (Columbus, OH, 1988), pp. 193–213.

25 J. Hartley, 'The Boards of Social Welfare and the Financing of Catherine II's State Schools', *SEER* 67 (1989), pp. 211–27.

26 J. L. Black, *Citizens for the Fatherland: Education, Educators and Pedagogical Ideals in Eighteenth-Century Russia* (Boulder, CO, 1979).

27 S. Dixon, *The Modernisation of Russia 1676–1825* (Cambridge, 1999), p. 45.

28 J. Lukowski, *The Partitions of Poland: 1772, 1793, 1795* (London, 1999).

29 W. Bruce Lincoln, *The Romanovs: Autocrats of All Russia* (London, 1981), pp. 362–3.

30 Daughter of Landgrave Ludwig IX of Darmstadt-Hesse and Henriette-Karolina of

Swainbrucken-Birkenfeld. See E. Pchelov, *Romanovy: Istoriia dinastii* (Moscow, 2001), p. 132.

31   R. E. McGrew, *Paul I of Russia (1754–1801)* (Oxford, 1992), pp. 91–104, esp. pp. 93–4.

32   Lincoln, *The Romanovs*, p. 367. Daughter of Count Friedrich II of Württemberg and Frederika Sophia Dorothea of Brandenburg. Pchelov, *Romanovy*, p. 132.

33   Lincoln, *The Romanovs*, p. 370.

34   Daughter of Karl Ludwig of Baden and Amalie of Hessen Darmstadt, the niece of Paul I's first wife Natalia. Pchelov, *Romanovy*.

35   J. Bergamini, *The Tragic Dynasty: A History of the Romanovs* (London, 1970), p. 259.

36   See further, J. Hartley, *A Social History of the Russian Empire 1650–1825* (London, 1999) and D. Moon, *The Russian Peasantry 1600–1930* (London, 1999).

37   See J. Alexander, *Autocratic Politics in a National Crisis: The Imperial Russian Government and Pugachev's Revolt* (Bloomington, IN, 1969); M. Raeff, 'Pugachev's Revolt', in R. Forster and J. P. Greene (eds), *Preconditions of Revolution in Early Modern Europe* (Baltimore, 1970), pp. 161–202; P. Longworth, 'The Pugachev Revolt', in H. Landsberger (ed.), *Rural Protest: Peasant Movements and Social Change* (London, 1974), pp. 194–256.

38   *Khrestomatiia po istorii Rossii XVIII veka*, p. 48.

39   Hartley, *A Social History*, p. 112.

40   J. Hartley, 'Catherine's Conscience Court – An English Equity Court?', in A. G. Cross (ed.), *Russia and the West in the Eighteenth Century* (Newtonville, MA, 1983), pp. 306–18. Also J. P. LeDonne, 'The Judicial Reform of 1775 in Provincial Russia', *JGO* 21 (1973), pp. 29–45.

41   Hartley, *A Social History*, p. 113.

42   J. P. LeDonne, 'The Provincial and Local Police under Catherine the Great', *CASS* 4 (1970), pp. 513–28.

43   See R. Jones, *The Emancipation of the Russian Nobility, 1762–1785* (Princeton, NJ, 1973); and 'The Charter of the Nobility: A Legislative Landmark?', *CASS* 23 (1989), pp. 1–16.

44   J. Hartley, 'Town Government in Saint Petersburg Guberniya after the Charter to the Towns of 1785', *SEER* 62 (1984), pp. 61–84.

45   W. Richardson, *Anecdotes of the Russian Empire* (London, 1784), p. 193.

46   R. Bartlett, 'The Free Economic Society: The Foundation Years and the Prize Essay Competition of 1766 on Peasant Property', in E. Hübner, J. Kusber, and P. Nitsche (eds), *Rußland zur Zeit Katharinas II: Absolutismus, Aufklärung, Pragmatismus* (Cologne, 1998), pp. 181–224.

47   De Madariaga, *Russia in the Age*, p. 532 (quoted in French). D. Shvidkovsky, *The Empress and the Architect: British Architecture and Gardens at the Court of Catherine the Great* (New Haven, CT, 1996).

48   On Catherine as collector, R. Gray, *Russian Genre Painting in the Nineteenth Century* (Oxford, 2000), pp. 14–19; G. Norman, *The Hermitage: The Biography of a Great Museum* (London, 1997), pp. 21–46; A. McConnell, 'Catherine the Great and the Fine Arts', in E. Mendelsohn (ed.), *Imperial Russia 1700–1917: Essays in Honour of Marc Raeff* (DeKalb, IL, 1990).

49   Thanks to Antony Lentin, 'In Our Time', BBC Radio 4, 23 February 2006.

50   M. Piotrovsky (ed.), *Treasures of Catherine the Great* (London, 2000). On painting, A. Bird, *A History of Russian Painting* (Oxford, 1987).

51 For an overview, see W. G. Jones, 'Literature in the Eighteenth Century', in N. Cornwell (ed.), *The Routledge Companion to Russian Literature* (London and New York, 2000), pp. 23–35.

52 See D. Smith, *Working the Rough Stone: Freemasonry and Society in Eighteenth-Century Russia* (DeKalb, IL, 1999).

53 See J. Alexander, 'Catherine the Great and the Theatre', in Bartlett and Hughes (eds), pp. 116–30.

54 See O. Figes's theories in *Natasha's Dance* (London, 2002).

55 On this issue, and foreign policy in general, see de Madariaga, *Russia in the Age*, parts IV and VIII.

56 A. Lentin (trans. and ed.), *Voltaire and Catherine the Great: Selected Correspondence* (Cambridge, 1974), p. 48.

57 A. Kamenskii, *The Russian Empire in the eighteenth century* (Armonk, NY, 1997), p. 210; Marc Raeff, 'Uniformity, Diversity and the Imperial Administration in the Reign of Catherine II', in idem, *Political Ideas and Institutions in Imperial Russia* (Boulder, CO, 1994), pp. 141–55.

58 See J. Klier, *Russia Gathers Her Jews: The Origins of the 'Jewish Question' in Russia, 1772–1825* (DeKalb, IL, 1986).

59 Prince M. M. Shcherbatov, *On the Corruption of Morals in Russia*, trans. and ed. A. Lentin (Cambridge, 1969), p. 251,

60 H. H. Rowen (ed.), *From Absolutism to Revolution: 1648–1848* (New York, 1963), p. 223.

61 P. Dukes, *Catherine the Great and the Russian Nobility* (Cambridge, 1967) p. 246.

62 De Madariaga, *Russia in the Age*, pp. 543–4; A. McConnell, *A Russian Philosophe: Alexander Radishchev, 1749–1800* (The Hague, 1964).

63 W. G. Jones, *Nikolay Novikov: Enlightener of Russia* (Cambridge, 1984).

64 With thanks to Simon Dixon, Janet Hartley, Antony Lentin in conversation on Radio 4's 'In our Time', 23 February 2006.

65 Smith, *Love and Conquest*, pp. 391–2.

66 Henry Hunter, *History of Catherine II* (London, 1800), p. xix.

67 See S. Dixon, 'The Posthumous Reputation of Catherine the Great in Russia, 1797–1837', *SEER* 77 (1999), pp. 646–79.

68 S. Dixon, 'Catherine the Great and the Romanov Dynasty', in Bartlett and Hughes (eds), pp. 195–208.

69 See K. Rasmussen, 'Catherine II and the Image of Peter I', *SR* 37 (1978), pp. 51–69.

70 Novoselov, *Opisanie kafedral'nogo sobora*, pp. 253–6

71 P. Svinin, *Dostopamiatnosti Sanktpeterburga i ego okrestnostei*, 5 parts (St Petersburg, 1816–28), III, pp. 19–20.

72 A. M. Schenker, *The Bronze Horseman: Falconet's Monument to Peter the Great* (New Haven, 2004).

73 Quoted in Dixon, *Catherine the Great*, p. 146.

Notes to Chapter 6: The Napoleonic Era

1   F. Vagis, *A History of Militarism* (New York, 1937), p. 269, quoted in J. Keep, 'Paul I and the Militarization of Government', in H. Ragsdale (ed.), *Paul I: A Reassessment of his Life and Reign* (Pittsburgh, PA, 1979), p. 92. One of many anecdotes about Paul. Other works on Paul in English include papers from a symposium: *CASS* 7, no. 1 (Spring 1973); R. McGrew, *Paul I of Russia 1754–1801* (Oxford, 1992). In Russian, N. K. Shilder, *Imperator Pavel I* (St Petersburg, 1901) has a wealth of primary material. (This was one of the last books read by Nicholas II in exile in Ekaterinburg: K. F. Shatsillo (ed.), *Dnevniki Imperatora Nikolai II* (Moscow, 1991), 3 June 1918, p. 682.)

2   *PSZ*, XXIV, no. 17.530 (6 Nov 1796). See also C. Whittaker, *Russian Monarchy: Eighteenth-Century Russian Rulers and Writers in Political Dialogue* (DeKalb, IL, 2003), p. 182.

3   *PSZ*, XXIV, no. 17.557, p. 2. See L. Hughes, 'The Funerals of the Russian Emperors and Empresses', in M. Schaich (ed.), *Monarchy and Religion: The Transformation of Royal Culture in Eighteenth-Century Europe* (Oxford, 2007), p. 414.

4   R. Wortman, *Scenarios of Power: Myth & Ceremony in Russian Monarchy*, 2 vols (Princeton, 1995), vol. 1, p. 173.

5   V. B. Gendrikov, S. E. Sen'ko, *Petropavlovskii sobor: Usypal'nitsa imperatorskogo doma Romanovykh* (St Petersburg, 1998), pp. 42–3.

6   *Opisanie porgrebeniia Nikolaia I*, p. 63; Gendrikov and Sen'ko, *Petropavlovskii sobor*, p. 43.

7   Nikolai Mikhailovich, *L'Impératrice Elisabeth*, 3 vols (St Petersburg, 1908–9), vol. 1, pp. 239–40, quoted in A. Palmer, *Alexander I, Tsar of War and Peace* (London, 1974), p. 3.

8   Wortman, *Scenarios*, vol. 1, p. 184.

9   In an exhibition at the Michael Fortress, September 2005.

10 W. Bruce Lincoln. *The Romanovs: Autocrats of All Russia* (London, 1981), p. 375.

11 Wortman, *Scenarios*, vol. 1, p. 175.

12 Wortman, *Scenarios*, vol. 1, p. 181.

13 Wortman, *Scenarios*, vol. 1, p. 178.

14 Palmer, *Alexander I*, chapter 1.

15 *PSZ*, XXIV, no. 17.906, 5 April 1797, p. 525.

16 *Velikii kniaz'*. This ancient title is generally translated into English as Great Prince in reference to tsars and princes of Muscovy, but in the imperial period Grand Duke is the preferred term.

17 *PSZ*, XXIV, no. 17.906, p. 530.

18 *PSZ*, XXIV, no. 17.908, pp. 569–75.

19 *PSZ*, XXIV, no. 17.909, p. 588–99.

20 Wortman, *Scenarios*, vol. 1, p. 185.

21 On Alexander's marriage, see below, p. 138. On Paul's marriages, above, p. 114.

22 *Rodina* 1 (1993), issue on 380th anniversary of the Romanovs.

23 Alexandra, a close confidante of Alexander, died in childbirth in March 1801. O. E. Volovik, *Velikaia kniaginia Aleksandra Pavlovna: Zhizn'. Sem'ia. Sud'ba. Pamiat'* (Budapest, 2006).

24 E. Pchelov, *Romanovy: Istoriia dinastii* (Moscow, 2001), pp. 173–4.

25 Pchelov, *Romanovy*, pp. 179–80.

26   Pchelov, *Romanovy*, pp. 198–200; W.B. Lincoln, 'The Circle of Grand Duchess Yelena Pavlovna, 1847–1861', *SEER* 48 (1970), pp. 373–87.

27   Catherine had even approved mistresses for the adolescent Paul; the result of one such union was apparently a son named Ivan (Simeon) Velikii, who died in the navy in 1794. See J. Bergamini, *The Tragic Dynasty: A History of the Romanovs* (London, 1970), p. 257.

28   Bergamini, *The Tragic Dynasty,* p. 265.

29   Pchelov, *Romanovy*, p. 145. An illegitimate daughter, Marfa Yureva, was born to one of the empress's ladies-in-waiting after Paul's death.

30   R. Blakesely, 'Maria Fedorovna and the Rise of the Woman Artist in Russia', *SGECRN* 31 (2003), pp. 18–23.

31   Wortman, *Scenarios*, vol. 1, p. 183. Keep, 'Paul I and the Militarization of Government', pp. 91–9.

32   See McGrew, *Paul I*, pp. 209–20.

33   Memoirists include Nikolai Sablukov of the Horse Guards, whose officers, he felt, were subject to particular persecution. See *Trekhsotletiie doma Romanovykh 1613–1913. Istoricheskie ocherki s 124 illiustratsiiami* (Moscow, 1913), pp. 249, 250–1.

34   R. McGrew, 'Paul I and the Knights of Malta', in Ragsdale, *Paul I*, p. 46.

35   McGrew, 'Paul I and the Knights of Malta', p. 50.

36   Charles Whitworth, February 1800. Quoted in J. J. Kennedy, Jr, 'The Politics of Assassination', in Ragsdale, *Paul I*, p. 137. His opinion was shared by the Russian ambassador in London, Count S. R. Vorontsov.

37   B. I. Antonov, *Imperatorskie dvortsy v Sankt-Peterburge* (St Petersburg, 2004), pp. 43–4.

38   In the Slavonic text there are 47 letters, said to be a prediction that Paul would die in his 47th year. See N. Sindalovskii, *Peterburg v fol'klore* (St Petersburg, 1999), for this and other legends about Paul and the fortress.

39   See Kennedy 'The Politics of Assassination'.

40   For accounts, see L. Loewenson, 'The Death of Paul I and the Memoirs of Count Bennigsen', *SEER* 29 (1950), pp. 212–32.

41   Quoted in L. Kelly, *St Petersburg: A Traveller's Companion* (London, 1981), p. 111. On the complex history of the memoirs, see Ragsdale, *Paul I*, p. 157–9.

42   Lincoln, *The Romanovs*, p. 381.

43   Quoted in Palmer, *Alexander I*, p. 46.

44   See, for example, *Trekhsotleiie doma Romanovykh*, p. 251.

45   See E. Petrova (ed.) *The Michael Castle* (St Petersburg, 1996).

46   Works on Alexander in English include M. Paléologue, *The Enigmatic Czar* (London, 1938); E. M. Almedingen, *Emperor Alexander I* (London, 1964); A. McConnell, *Alexander I: Paternalistic Reformer* (Northbrook, IL, 1970); Palmer, *Alexander I*; J. Hartley, *Alexander I* (London, 1994). In Russian, N. K. Shilder, *Imperator Aleksandr I, ego zhizn' i tsarstvovanie*, 4 vols (St Petersburg, 1897), rich in primary sources, has not been superseded. More recently (no monographs were published in Soviet times), A. Arkhangelskii, *Aleksandr I* (Moscow, 2000).

47   Quoted from Shilder, *Imperator Aleksandr I*, p. 280–2, in Palmer, *Alexander I*, p. 35.

48   *PSZ*, vol. XXVI, no. 19.779 (12 March 1801).

49   B. Vilinbakhov *et al.* (eds), *Aleksandr I: Sfinks, ne razgadannyi do groba. Katalog vystavki* (St. P., 2005), p. 13. Catherine also cherished the idea of Alexander the Great as Alexander's role model.

50   Vilinbakhov, *Aleksandr I*, p. 20.

51   Daughter of Karl Ludwig of Baden and Amalie of Hessen Darmstadt, the niece of Paul I's first wife.

52   See D. I. Izmail-Zade, 'Aleksandr I i Imperatritsa Elizaveta Alekseevna', in Vilinbakhov, *Aleksandr I*, pp. 98–115; I. E. Liamina, O. E. Edel'man, 'Dnevnik imperatritsy Elizavety Alekseevny', ibid., pp. 116–31.

53   Palmer, *Alexander I*, p. 16, 18.

54   Izmail-Zade, 'Aleksandr I i Imperatritsa Elizaveta', p. 98.

55   Iu. V. Sharovaia, 'Imperatritsa Elizaveta Alekseevna v portretakh', in Vilinbakhov, *Aleksandr I*, p. 134. It hung in the Hermitage Romanov gallery until 1918, when it was removed along with other works of art.

56   Rumour had it that Maria was fathered by Adam Czartoryski and Lisetka by another lover: see next note.

57   Vilinbakhov, *Aleksandr I*, p. 116.

58   Palmer, *Alexander I*, p. 24.

59   A. O'Connell, 'Tsar Alexander I's Hundred Days', *SR* 28 (1969), pp. 373–93.

60   S. Dixon, 'The Posthumous Reputation of Catherine the Great in Russia, 1797–1837', *SEER* 77 (1999), pp. 658–9.

61   See Wortman, *Scenarios*, vol. 1, pp. 195 ff.

62   M. Raeff (ed.) *Plans for Political Reform in Imperial Russia 1730–1905* (Englewood Cliffs, NJ, 1966), pp. 86, 91.

63   M. Raeff, *Michael Speransky: Statesman of Imperial Russia* (Westport, CT, 1957), pp. 263–6.

64   Palmer, *Alexander*, p. 61.

65   'Project of a Most Graciously Granted Charter to the Russian People (1801)', in Raeff (ed.), *Plans for Political Reform*, pp. 76–7.

66   Hartley, *Alexander I*, p. 43.

67   Raeff, *Plans for Political Reform*, p. 94

68   Raeff, *Plans for Political Reform*, pp. 96–7.

69   Vilinbakhov, *Aleksandr I*, p. 2, catalogue nos 62 and 20.

70   See A. Tosi, *Waiting for Pushkin: Russian Fiction in the Reign of Alexander I (1800–25)* (Amsterdam, 2006).

71   See P. W. Schroeder, *The Transformation of European Politics, 1763–1848* (Oxford, 1994), pp. 277, 320–2, quoted at p. 320.

72   Ibid., p. 321.

73   F. N. Glinka, 'Letters of a Russian Officer', quoted in S. Dickinson, 'Representing Moscow in 1812: Sentimentalist Echoes in Accounts of the Napoleonic Occupation', in I. K. Lilly (ed.), *Moscow and Petersburg: The City in Russian Culture* (Nottingham, 2002), p. 11.

74   Alexander Chicherin, quoted in Lilly, *Moscow and Petersburg*, p. 11

75   *Khram Khrista Spasitelia v Moskve: Izdano k predvideniiu 1000-letiia Kreshcheniia Rusi* (New York, 1986), p. 195.

76   A. Shamaro, 'Imeni tvoemu', *Nauka i religiia* 1 (1991), pp. 20–2.

77   Wortman, *Scenarios*, vol. 1, pp. 236–8.

78   G. von Pott, *Glas k Rossiianam na sluchai Velikogo narodnogo torzhestva, prazdnuemogo v tekushchem 1813 godu, v kotorom sovershilis' dva stoletiia so vremena tsarstvovaniia na Vserossiiskom Prestole drevnego Avgusteishago doma Romanovykh* (St Petersburg, 1813), p. 32.

79   Robert Lyall, MD, *The Character of the Russians and a Detailed History of Moscow* (London, 1823), p. 210.

80   D. Obolensky (ed.), *Russian Chronicles* (London, 1990), p. 258.

81   Palmer, *Alexander I*, p. 280.

82   Obolensky (ed.), *Russian Chronicles*, p. 262.

83   *The Pamphleteer* 4, no. 8 (November 1814), p. 312, quoted in J. Hartley, 'England "Enjoys the Spectacle of a Northern Barbarian". The Reception of Peter I and Alexander I', *WOR*, pp. 11–18.

84   Anon., *The Christian Conqueror: Or Moscow Burnt and Paris Saved* (London, 1814), p. 10.

85   M. Jenkins, *Arakcheev, Grand Vizier of the Russian Empire* (London, 1969).

86   The Bible was available only in Church Slavonic, which was only partly comprehensible to the average Russian.

87   Wortman, *Scenarios*, vol. 1, pp. 226–7.

88   In 1817 only his illegitimate daughter Sophia was still alive.

89   Wortman, *Scenarios*, vol. 1, pp. 266–7

90   Palmer, *Alexander I*, pp. 385–6.

91   See G. A. Miroliubova, 'Poslednii put', in Vilinbakhov, *Aleksandr I*, pp. 160–81, 174.

92   A sobriquet that found itself in the title of a splendid exhibition at the Hermitage in 2005. See Vilinbakhov, *Aleksandr I.*

93   Lyall, *The Character of the Russians*, p. 11.

94   Lyall, *The Character of the Russians*, p. 9.

Notes to Chapter 7: Consistent Autocracy

1   Article 1 of the Digest of Laws of the Russian Empire (1832): autocratic = *samoderzhavnyi* unlimited = *neogranichennyi.*

2   G. B. Vilinbakhov *et al.* (eds), *Aleksandr I: Sfinks, ne razgadannyi do groba. Katalog vystavki* (St Petersburg, 2005), p. 113.

3   On the Decembrists, M. Raeff, *The Decembrist Movement* (Englewood Cliffs, NJ, 1966); P. O'Meara, *The Decembrist Pavel Pestel: Russia's First Republican* (Basingstoke, 2002).

4   See N. Riasanovsky, *Nicholas I and Official Nationality in Russia, 1825–1855* (Berkeley, 1959).

5   T. Schiemann, *Geschichte Russlands unter Kaiser Nikolaus I,* (Berlin, 1904).

6   See the revisionist study by W. Bruce Lincoln, *Nicholas I: Emperor and Autocrat of All the Russias* (London, 1978).

7   R.S. Wortman, *Scenarios of Power: Myth and Ceremony in Russian Monarchy*, 2 vols (Princeton, 1995–2000), vol. 1, p. 266.

8   Wortman, *Scenarios*, vol. 1, p. 267.

9   Lincoln, *Nicholas I*, p. 47

10 Wortman, *Scenarios*, vol. 1, p. 277.

11 To Baron Korf, quoted in Lincoln, *Nicholas I*, p. 163.

12 See above, pp. 154–5.

13 Lincoln, *Nicholas I*, p. 60. (Following a visit to Prussia to see his fiancée.)

14 *Journey of Our Time: The Journals of the Marquis de Custine*, trans. and ed. P. Kohler (London, 1980), p. 72.

15 Lincoln, *Nicholas I*, p. 350.

16 L. V. Vyskochkov, 'Imperator Nikolai I glazami sovremennikov', in I. A. Froianov (ed.), *Dom Romanovykh v istorii Rossii* (St Petersburg, 1995), p. 182.

17 Anna Tiutcheva, quoted in Wortman, *Scenarios*, vol. 1, p. 297.

18 *Journey of Our Time*, p. 72.

19 Vyskochkov, 'Imperator', p. 183.

20 Tiutcheva, quoted in Vyskochkov, 'Imperator', p. 185

21 *Journey of Our Time*, p. 58.

22 Wortman, *Scenarios*, vol. 1, p. 254.

23 Quoted in M. Gershenzon (ed.), *Nikolai I i ego epokha* (Moscow, 2001), pp. 14–15.

24 Quoted in Wortman, *Scenarios*, vol. 1, p. 343.

25 Wortman, *Scenarios*, vol. 1, p. 247–8.

26 Wortman, *Scenarios*, vol. 1, pp. 282–3.

27 Wortman, *Scenarios*, vol. 1, p. 287.

28 Pavel Svin'in quoted in Wortman, *Scenarios*, vol. 1, p. 290.

29 Wortman, *Scenarios*, vol. 1, p. 331.

30 Wortman, *Scenarios*, vol. 1, p. 341,

31 Coronation manifesto, 1826, quoted in Lincoln, *Nicholas I*, p. 86.

32 This has been variously translated as 'nationality', 'national feeling', 'national character', with 'Russian' implied.

33 Gershenzon, *Nikolai I*, pp. 153–4. *Desiatiletie Ministerstva narodnogo prosveshcheniia 1833–1843* (St Petersburg, 1864), pp.106–8.

34 Gershenzon, *Nikolai I*, p. 82.

35 Gershenzon, *Nikolai I*, p. 20.

36 See E.L. Perkins, 'Nicholas I and the Academy of Fine Arts', *RH* 18 (1991), pp. 51–63.

37 *Journey of Our Time*, p. 98.

38 Wortman, *Scenarios*, vol. 1, p. 316.

39 A. Orlov, *Torzhestvennoe zalozhenie sviatago khrama vo imia Khrista Spasitelia v Moskve* (M., 1840), pp. 5–6.

40 *Rech' blagochestiveishemu gosudariu Imp. Nikolaiu Pavlovichu pri torzhestvennom zalozhenii khrama vo imia Khrista Spasitelia v Moskve. sent. 10 dnia, 1839 goda, govorennaia Sinodal'nym Chlenom Filaretom, Mitropolitom Moskovskim* (Moscow, 1839), pp. 4–5.

41 E. Kirichenko, *The Russian Style* (London 1991), pp. 74–8.

42 Ibid., pp. 51–2. See Franz Kruger's 1830 portrait of Empress Alexandra Fedorovna, p. 53.

43   M. H. Brown, 'Native Song and National Consciousness in 19th-century Russia', in T. G. Stavrou (ed.), *Art and Culture in Nineteenth-Century Russia* (Bloomington, IN, 1983), pp. 57–84.

44   A. V. Evald, quoted in Gershenzon, *Nikolai I*, p. 185.

45   M. Piotrovsky (ed.), *Osnovateliu Peterburga* (St Petersburg, 2003), pp. 52–4.

46   Piotrovsky, *Osnovateliu*, p. 54. The gallery continued to function until the early 1990s, when most of the exhibits, including Rastrelli's famous wax model of Peter, were transferred to the remnants of Peter's Winter Palace under the Hermitage Theatre.

47   V. Burianov, *Progulka s det'mi po S.-Peterburgu*, 3 parts (St Petersburg, 1838), part I, p. 91.

48   Burianov, *Progulka*, I, p. 93. On Nicholas I's contribution to Petrine museums and memorials, see *Pamiatniki russkoi kul'tury pervoi chetverti XVIII veka v sobranii God. ordena Lenina Ermitazha. Katalog* (Leningrad-Moscow, 1966), p. 16, and L. Hughes, *Peter the Great. A Biography* (New Haven, 2002), chapter 12.

49   I. I. Pushkarev, *Istoricheskii ukazatel' dostoprimechatel'nostei S. Peterburga* (St Petersburg, 1846), pp. 33–4.

50   *Iubileinyi sbornik kostromskogo tserkovno-istoricheskogo obshchestva v pamiat' 300-letiia tsarstvovaniia doma Romanovykh* (Kostroma, 1913), p. 18.

51   K. G. Sokol, *Monumenty imperii* (Moscow, 1999), pp. 35–6.

52   Sokol, *Monumenty*, pp. 100–1; Wortman, *Scenarios*, part I, p. 409.

53   Gershenzon, *Nikolai I*, p. 205.

54   Gershenzon, *Nikolai I*, p. 206.

55   Gershenzon, *Nikolai I*, pp. 80–5. From *SIRIO* 98, pp. 114–17.

56   Wortman, *Scenarios*, vol. 1, p. 397.

57   The historian Pogodin, quoted in Wortman, *Scenarios*, vol. 1, p. 399.

58   J. Bergamini, *The Tragic Dynasty: The History of the Romanovs* (London, 1969), p. 326.

59   Gershenzon, *Nikolai I*, p. 6.

60   I. V. Zimin, 'Physicians and Autocrats: The Perplexing Death of Nicholas I', *RSH* 42 (2003–4), pp. 8–25.

61   D. Bludov, *Poslednie chasy Imperatora Nikolaia Pervogo* (St Petersburg, 1855).

62   Wortman, *Scenarios*, vol. 1, p. 412.

Notes to Chapter 8: Reform and Reaction

1   Count Paul Vassili [Princess Catherine Radziwill], *Behind the Veil at the Russian Court* (London, 1913), p.17, 118.

2   S. Sermanov, *Aleksandr II: Istoriia Tsaria Osvoboditelia, ego otsa i syna* (Moscow, 2003), p. 72. In English, W. E. Mosse, *Alexander II and the Modernization of Russia* (London and New York, 1958).

3   R. Wortman, *Scenarios of Power: Myth and Ceremony in Russian Monarchy*, 2 vols (Princeton, 1995), vol. 1, p. 346.

4   Wortman, *Scenarios*, vol. 1, p. 344.

5   Wortman, *Scenarios*, vol. 1, p. 350.

6   Wortman, *Scenarios*, vol. 1, pp. 362–4.

7   Wortman, *Scenarios*, vol. 1, p. 366.

8   Wortman, *Scenarios*, vol. 1, p. 375.

9   Vassili, *Behind the Veil*, pp. 25–8, for a harsh assessment.

10 E. Pchelov, *Romanovy: Istorii dinasti* (Moscow, 2001), pp. 239–80.

11 *PSZ*, no. XXIX, p. 143.

12 See A. Rieber, 'Alexander II: A Revisionist View', *Journal of Modern History* 43 (1971), pp. 42–58.

13 See T. Emmons (ed.), *Emancipation of the Russian Serfs* (London and New York, 1970); and *The Russian Landed Gentry and the Peasant Emancipation of 1861* (Cambridge, 1968).

14 Rieber, 'Alexander II', p. 48.

15 Rieber, 'Alexander II', p. 55. See also W. Bruce Lincoln, *The Great Reforms* (DeKalb, IL, 1990).

16 Wortman, *Scenarios*, vol. 1, p. 361.

17 Wortman, *Scenarios*, vol. 1, p. 368.

18 *Iubileinyi sbornik kostromskogo tserkovno-istoricheskogo obshchestva v pamiat' 300-letiia tsarstvovaniia doma Romanovykh* (Kostroma, 1913), p. 19.

19 V. Kozliakov, *Mikhail Fedorovich* (Moscow, 2004), p. 38. The restoration had been ordered by Nicholas I after a visit in 1834.

20 E. Kirichenko, *The Russian Style* (London, 1991), pp. 78–82.

21 G. K. Shchutskaia, *Palaty boiar Romanovykh* (Moscow, 2000), p. 10.

22 K. G. Sokol, *Monumenty imperii* (Moscow, 1999), pp. 74–5.

23 Wortman, *Scenarios*, vol. 2, p. 51.

24 Wortman, *Scenarios*, vol. 1, pp. 358–9.

25 E. El'kin, 'Nadgrobiia na tsarskikh mogilakh', *Kraevedcheskie zapiski: Issledovaniia i materialy. vyp. 2. Petropavlovskii sobor i velikokniazheskaia usypal'nitsa* (St Petersburg, 1994), pp. 162–3.

26 See L. Hughes, *Peter the Great: A Biography* (New Haven, 2002), ch. 12. In 1837 Tsarevich Alexander paid homage to Peter by preserving the Church of the Saviour, where Peter prayed, with a stone cladding.

27 M. Sarantola-Weiss, 'Peter the Great's First Boat, "Grandfather of the Russian Navy"', *WOR*, pp. 37–42.

28 See Sokol, *Monumenty*, pp. 36, 40.

29 See S. Dixon, 'Catherine the Great and the Romanov Dynasty', in Bartlett and Hughes (eds), pp. 201–2. For the radical critics, Dixon, 'The Posthumous Reputation of Catherine the Great in Russia, 1797–1837', *SEER* 77 (1999), pp. 646–79.

30 Sokol, *Monumenty*, pp. 60–1. Mikeshin also designed a statue of Catherine for Tsarskoe Selo (1861), ibid., pp. 64–5.

31 L. Liashenko, *Aleksandr II* (Moscow, 2002), p. 135. See also Kniaginia Iurevskaia, *Aleksandr II: Vospominaniia* (Moscow, 2004).

32 Liashenko, *Aleksandr II*, p. 142.

33 *Rodina* 1 (1993), issue on the 380th anniversary of the Romanovs.

34 See Liashenko, *Aleksandr II*.

35 Liashenko, *Aleksandr II*, p. 276.

36 Liashenko, *Aleksandr II*, p. 284.
37 Sermanov, *Aleksandr II*, pp. 400–1.
38 Sermanov, *Aleksandr II*, p. 404.
39 Liashenko, *Aleksandr II*, p. 297.
40 Sermanov, *Aleksandr II*, pp. 405–6.
41 Sermanov, *Aleksandr II*, p. 406.
42 Sermanov, *Aleksandr II*, pp. 409–10.
43 M. Raeff (ed.), *Plans for Political Reform in Imperial Russia 1730–1905* (Englewood Cliffs, NJ, 1966), pp. 134–5.
44 Liashenko, *Aleksandr II*, p. 145.
45 Iurevskaia, *Aleksandr II*, p. 109.
46 Quoted in Liashenko, *Aleksandr II*, p. 309.
47 Quoted in Liashenko, *Aleksandr II*, p. 318.
48 See R. F. Byrnes, *Pobedonostsev: His Life and Thought* (Bloomington, IN and London, 1968).
49 Wortman, *Scenarios*, vol. 2, pp. 180, 183.
50 Sermanov, *Aleksandr II*, p. 395.
51 Raeff, *Plans for Political Reform*, p. 133.
52 *PSZ*, new series, 3, no. 118.
53 Wortman, *Scenarios*, vol. 2, p. 203.
54 Wortman, *Scenarios*, vol. 2, p. 212. For more on Alexander III's politics, see H. W. Whelan, *Alexander III and the State Council: Bureaucracy and Counter-Reform in Late Imperial Russia* (New Brunswick, NJ, 1982).
55 Iu. Kudrina, *Mat' i syn: Imperatritsa Mariia Fedorovna i imperator Nikolai II* (Moscow, 2004), p. 22.
56 Wortman, *Scenarios*, vol. 2, pp. 220, 226.
57 L. Shaposhnikova, *Pamiatnik Aleksandru III: Skul'ptor Paolo Trubetskoi* (St Petersburg, 1996), p. 18.
58 Wortman, *Scenarios*, vol. 2, p. 428.
59 See P. I. Kovalevskii, *Psikhologiia russkoi natsii: Vospitanie molodezhi: Aleksandr III–tsar'-natsionalist* (Moscow, 2005).
60 D. Lieven, *Nicholas II: Emperor of all the Russias* (London, 1994), p. 24.
61 G. Chulkov, *Imperatory: Psikhologicheskie portrety* (Moscow and Leningrad, 1928).
62 Wortman, *Scenarios*, vol. 2, p. 165.
63 *Poslednie dni zhizni i pogrebeniia v boze pochivshogo Gos. Naslednika Tsesarevicha i Velikogo Kniazia Nikolaia Aleksandrovicha* (St. P., 1965), p. 1. This account of Nicholas's 'good death' emphasises his piety, his consciousness of the approach of death and so on. See also *Konchina Naslednika Tsesarevicha Nikolaia Aleksandrovicha* (St. P., 1865).
64 A. P. Gadenko, *Naslednik Tsesarevich Nikolaia Aleksandrovich, 1843–1865* (n. d., [1911]), recounts the building and consecration of a new church dedicated to St Nicholas in the grounds of the Nice villa in 1903.
65 Kudrina, *Mat' i syn*.
66 *Imperator Aleksandr III i Imperatritsa Mariia Fedorovna: Perepiska, 1884–1894* (Moscow, 2001), p. 5.

67   See G. Von Habsburg-Lothringen and A. von Solodkoff, *Fabergé: Court Jeweler to the Tsars* (New York, 1979); A. K. Snowman, *Carl Fabergé: Goldsmith to the Imperial Court of Russia* (New York, 1979).

68   *Imperator Aleksandr III i Imperatritsa Mariia Fedorovna*, p. 18.

69   *Imperator Aleksandr III i Imperatritsa Mariia Fedorovna*, p. 111.

70   Sermanov, *Aleksandr II*, pp. 390, 397, 409 ff.

71   See W. C. Lee, 'Grand Ducal Role and Identity as a Reflection on the Interaction of State and Dynasty in Imperial Russia', unpubl. PhD thesis, SSEES, London, 2000.

72   Pchelov, *Romanovy*, pp. 262–7.

73   Pchelov, *Romanovy*, pp. 268–75; Wortman, *Scenarios*, part II, p. 293.

74   Kudrina, *Mat' i syn*, p. 30.

75   Chulkov, *Imperatory*, pp. 349–50.

76   D. G. Bulgakovskii, *Domik Petra Velikogo i ego sviatynia v S. Peterburge* (St Petersburg, 1891), p. 31. L. Hughes, 'Nothing is Too Small for a Great Man': Peter the Great's Little Houses and the Creation of Some Petrine Myths', *SEER* 81 (2003), pp. 634–58.

77   Bulgakovskii, *Domik*, pp. 10, 23.

78   S. S. Tatishchev, 'Tsesarevich Aleksandr Aleksandrovich', quoted in Wortman, *Scenarios*, vol. 2, p. 192.

79   Wortman, *Scenarios*, vol. 2, p. 245. M. Flier, 'The Church of the Saviour on the Blood: Projection, Rejection, Resurrection', in R. Hughes and I. Paperno (eds), *Christianity and the Eastern Slavs* (Berkeley, 1994), pp. 32–43.

80   Sokol, *Monumenty*, pp. 82–3.

81   See below.

82   A. Jenks, *Russia in a Box: Art and Identity in an Age of Revolution* (DeKalb, IL, 2005), p. 17.

83   Jenks, *Russia in a Box*, pp. 36–8.

84   See J. Norman, 'Alexander III as a Patron of Russian Art', in J. Norman (ed.), *New Perspectives on Russian and Soviet Artistic Culture*, 2 vols (New York, 1994), vol. 2.

85   Wortman, *Scenarios*, vol. 2, pp. 304–5; Vassili, pp. 195–8.

86   *Vsemirnaia illiustratsiia* (1894), quoted in Wortman, *Scenarios*, vol. 2, p. 303.

87   Chulkov, *Imperatory*, p. 364.

Notes to Chapter 9: The Last Romanov

1   M. Paléologue, *An Ambassador's Memoirs, 1914–1917* (London, 1973), p. 708.

2   Paléologue, *Memoirs*, p. 798.

3   D. Lieven, *Nicholas II: Emperor of all the Russias* (London, 1994), p. 21.

4   M. Steinberg and V. Khrustalev, *The Fall of the Romanovs* (New Haven and London, 1995), p. 3.

5   Memoirs of Nicholas's sister Olga, quoted in Lieven, *Nicholas II*, p. 39.

6   R.S. Wortman, *Scenarios of Power: Myth and Ceremony in Russian Monarchy*, 2 vols (Princeton, 1995–2000), vol. 2, p. 323 (1886).

7   Count Paul Vassili, *Behind the Veil at the Russian Court* (London, 1914), p. 212.

8   Steinberg and Khrustalev, *The Fall,* p. 270 (Vasily Pankratov, autumn 1917).

9   *Manifest 6 maia 1884: My Aleksandr III* (Russian National Library).

10 Lieven, *Nicholas II,* p. 37.

11 Lieven, *Nicholas II,* p. 52. See also, p. 102: 'Our young monarch changes his mind with terrifying speed' (1896).

12 Lieven, *Nicholas II,* p. 71.

13 To Sviatopolk-Mirsky, quoted in Lieven, *Nicholas II,* p. 141.

14 General Voeikov, reporting what the tsar told him after his abdication in 1917, in Lieven, *Nicholas II,* p. 216.

15 Steinberg and Khrustalev, *The Fall,* p. 5.

16 Memoirs of A. Izvolsky, quoted in Steinberg and Khrustalev, *The Fall,* p. 14

17 Lieven, *Nicholas II,* p. 47.

18 Wortman, *Scenarios,* vol. 2, p. 334.

19 *V Boze pochivshii Naslednik i Velikii kniaz' Georgii Aleksandrovich, ego zhizn' i pogrebenie* (Moscow, 1899), p. 19.

20 http://www.alexanderpalace.org/palace/alekseysbedroom.html

21 For descriptions, Wortman, *Scenarios,* vol. 2, pp. 344–58.

22 N. Tarasova *et al.* (eds), *Nicholas and Alexandra: The Last Tsar and Tsarina* (Amsterdam, 2005), p. 78.

23 Tarasova, *Nicholas,* p. 75.

24 Princess Radzivill, quoted in Lieven, *Nicholas II,* p. 52.

25 Royal Archives. QV RA VIC/11/H47/11. [Thanks to Claire McKee.]

26 For a description, see G. King, *The Court of the Last Tsar: Pomp, Power, and Pageantry in the Reign of Nicholas II* (Hoboken, NJ, 2006), pp. 191ff.

27 King, *The Court,* pp. 199–202; http://www.alexanderpalace.org/palace/alekseysbedroom.html

28 *Archives Secréts de l'Empereur Nicholas II,* ed. V. Lazarevski (Paris, 1928), p. 10.

29 Lieven, *Nicholas II,* p. 34.

30 Tarasova, *Nicholas,* p. 51.

31 Quoted in Lieven, *Nicholas II,* p. 55. See also Paléologue, *Memoirs,* p. 6: at a banquet 'the veins stood out in her cheeks' and 'she bit her lips every minute'.

32 Paléologue, *Memoirs,* p. 6 (7/20 July 1914).

33 S. Dixon, 'Catherine the Great and the Romanov Dynasty', in Bartlett and Hughes (eds), pp. 195–208.

34 Tarasova, *Nicholas,* p. 49.

35 Nicolson to Grey, PRO FO 881 8864. 2 January 1907 [Thanks to Claire McKee.]

36 W. C. Lee, 'Grand Ducal Role and Identity as a Reflection on the Interaction of State and Dynasty in Imperial Russia', unpubl. PhD thesis, SSEES, London, 2000.

37 Lee, 'Grand Ducal Role', p. 286.

38 On Nicholas's consistent adherence to his autocratic principles and insistence on being 'in charge', see A. Verner, *The Crisis of Russian Autocracy: Nicholas II and the 1905 Revolution* (Princeton, 1990).

39 See J. Schneiderman, *Sergei Zubatov and Revolutionary Marxism: The Struggle for the Working Class in Tsarist Russia* (Ithaca, NY, 1976).

40   See W. Sablinsky, *The Road to Bloody Sunday: Father Gapon and the St Petersburg Massacre of 1905* (Princeton, 1976), pp. 266–8.

41   K. F. Shatsillo (ed.), *Dnevniki Imperatora Nikolai II* (Moscow, 1991), p. 246.

42   See *Vysochaishchii manifest: Muchenicheskaia konchina Velikogo Kniazia Sergeia Aleksandrovicha* (Moscow, 1905); *Muchenicheskaia konchina EIV Velikii Kniaz' Sergeia Aleksandrovicha* (Moscow, 1905).

43   Meeting with zemstvo representatives in June 1905, quoted in Verner, *The Crisis*, pp. 195–6.

44   *Archives Secréts*, pp. 23–4.

45   *Archives Secréts* (12 January 1906), p. 56.

46   S. Podbolotov, 'Monarchists against their Monarch: The Rightists' Criticism of Tsar Nicholas II', *RH* 31 (2004), pp. 1–2, pp. 107–8. (General A. A. Kireev and B. V. Nikolskii respectively.)

47   Major Geddes, PRO FO 881 9304, July 1907. [Thanks to Claire McKee.]

48   *The Spectator*, 18 November, 30 December 1905. [Thanks to Claire McKee.]

49   *Archives Secréts* (2 December 1905), p. 41.

50   *Archives Secréts,* p. 26.

51   *Archives Secréts*, pp. 43, 44.

52   V. N. Chashkov, 'Romanovy – kto oni?', *Otechestvennaia istoriia*, 1 (1998), p. 173.

53   Lieven, *Nicholas II*, p. 152.

54   Conversation with Kokovtsov, 1911: Lieven, *Nicholas II*, pp. 181–2.

55   Wortman, *Scenarios*, vol. 2, p. 404.

56   See G. Hosking, *The Russian Constitutional Experiment: Government and Duma, 1907–1914* (Cambridge, 1973).

57   British ambassador Nicolson to Grey, PRO FO 881/8756, 9 June 1906. [Thanks to Claire McKee.]

58   Wortman, *Scenarios*, vol. 2, p. 366,

59   R. L. Nichols, 'The Friends of God: Nicholas II and Aleksandra at the Canonization of Serafim of Sarov, July 1903', in C. Timberlake (ed.), *Religious and Secular Forces in Late Tsarist Russia* (Seattle, 1992), pp. 216–17. For a more pessimistic view of the canonization, see G.L. Freeze, 'Subversive Piety: Religion and the Political Crisis in Late Imperial Russia', *Journal of Modern History* 68 (1996), esp. pp. 312–29.

60   Letter to Grand Duke Sergei, quoted in Wortman, *Scenarios*, vol. 2, p. 369.

61   M. V. Rodzianko, *The Reign of Rasputin: An Empire's Collapse* (London, 1927), p. 1.

62   Rodzianko, *The Reign,* p. 30.

63   Rodzianko, *The Reign,* p. 41.

64   Wortman, *Scenarios*, vol. 2, p. 420.

65   See L. Hughes, *Peter the Great: A Biography* (New Haven, 2002), p. 238.

66   A.V. Belgorodskii, *Maloe slovo o velikom (po povodu 200-letiia osnovaniia Peterburga)* (Reval, 1903), p. 6.

67   Lieven, *Nicholas II*, p. 137.

68   *Al'bom kostiumirovannogo bala v Zimnem dvortse v fevrale 1903* (St Petersburg, 1904).

69   *Tsar na Poltavskikh prazdnestvakh 26–27 iunia 1909 g.* (St Petersburg, 1909).

70   Wortman, *Scenarios*, vol. 2, pp. 432–5.

71 Wortman, *Scenarios*, vol. 2, pp. 437–8.

72 Rodzianko, *The Reign*, pp. 63–4, 75.

73 *Tsar na Poltavskikh prazdnestvakh*, p. 47

Notes to Chapter 10: From Celebration to Annihilation

1 K. F. Shatsillo (ed.), *Dnevniki Imperatora Nikolai II* (Moscow, 1991), p. 385. Nicholas mentions the 'brightness' of the weather throughout much of the celebrations.

2 To Anna Vyrubova, in M. Steinberg and V. Khrustalev, *The Fall of the Romanovs* (New Haven and London, 1995), p. 213.

3 For overviews, R. Wortman, 'Invisible Threads: The Historical Imagery of the Romanov Tercentenary', *RH* 16, nos 2–4 (1989), pp. 389–408; idem, *Scenarios of Power: Myth and Ceremony in Russian Monarchy*, 2 vols (Princeton, 1995–2000), vol. 2, pp. 439–80; G. King, *The Court of the Last Tsar: Pomp, Power, and Pageantry in the Reign of Nicholas II* (Hoboken, NJ, 2006), pp. 390ff. Soviet historians ignored the topic. For a post-Soviet overview, O. V. Nemiro, 'Iz istorii organizatsii i dekorirovaniia krupneishikh torzhestv doma Romanovykh: 1896 i 1913', in I. A. Froianov (ed.), *Dom Romanovykh v istorii Rossii* (St Petersburg, 1995), pp. 252–60.

4 *Bozhieiu milostiiu My, Nikolai Vtoroi ...* [imperial manifesto] (Odessa, 1913). No pag. Identical sheets were issued in all major towns.

5 *Vysochaishe utverzhdennyi Tseremonial torzhestvennogo prazdnovaniia 300-letiia tsarstvovaniia doma Romanovykh 21go fevralia 1913 goda* (St Petersburg, 1913).

6 Smirnov, *Prazdnovanie 300-letiia Doma Romanovykh* (Tobolsk, 1913), p. 5.

7 Smirnov, *Prazdnovanie*, p. 9.

8 Smirnov, *Prazdnovanie*, p. 12.

9 Smirnov, *Prazdnovanie*, p. 15.

10 Anna Vyrubova, in King, *The Court*, p. 391.

11 Count Paul Vassili, *Behind the Veil at the Russian Court* (London, 1914), p. 403.

12 Vassili, pp. 404–7.

13 Wortman, *Scenarios*, vol. 2, p. 464.

14 M. Buchanan, *The Dissolution of an Empire* (London, 1932), p. 36.

15 King, *The Court*, p. 396.

16 King, *The Court*, p. 391.

17 *Prazdnovanie trekhsotletiia tsarstvovaiia doma Romanovykh v Kostromskoi gubernii, 19–20 maia 1913* (Kostroma, 1914), p. 23.

18 *Prazdnovanie trekhsotletiia*, p. 93.

19 *Prazdnovanie trekhsotletiia*, pp. 74, 127, 207.

20 See Introduction, p. 1.

21 *Prazdnovanie trekhsotletiia*, p. 51.

22 G. K. Shchutskaia, *Palaty boiar Romanovykh* (Moscow, 2000), p. 19.

23 Wortman, *Scenarios*, vol. 2, pp. 410–13.

24 Steinberg and Khrustalev, *The Fall of the Romanovs*, p. 16.

25 http://www.alexanderpalace.org/palace/photo-tours.html (June 2006).

26 *Otchet stroitel'nogo Komiteta po sooruzheniiu v St Petersburge khrama-pamiatnika 300-letiia tsarstvovaniia Doma Romanovykh*, 3 vols (St Petersburg, 1914–16), vol. 1, pp. 5–7. See also Wortman, *Scenarios*, vol. 2, p. 451; E. Kirichenko, *The Russian Style* (London, 1991), pp. 208, 212.

27 *Otchet stroitel'nogo Komiteta,* vol. 3, p. 15.

28 *Otchet stroitel'nogo Komiteta,* vol. 1, p. 15; vol. 3, p. 4.

29 *Proekt muzeia v oznamenovanie 300-letiia tsarstvovaniia doma Romanovykh* (Moscow, 1914), pp. 10–12.

30 *Proekt muzeia*, p. 50.

31 Wortman, *Scenarios*, vol. 2, p. 408.

32 K. G. Sokol, *Monumenty imperii* (Moscow, 1999), pp. 95–6.

33 See *Prazdnovanie trekhsotletiia*, p. 115.

34 Wortman, *Scenarios*, vol. 2, pp. 454–5; Sokol, *Monumenty*, pp. 104–5.

35 I. I. Efimov, *Istoricheskie ustoi verkhovnoi vlasti doma Romanovykh: Rech' proiznesennaia na torzhestvennom akte Simbirskoi 1-oi muzhskoi gimnazii 21 Fev. 1913 goda* (Simbirsk, 1914), pp. 5–6.

36 Efimov, *Istoricheskie ustoi*, pp. 8, 41.

37 See H. Rogger, 'The Beilis Case: Anti-Semitism and Politics in the Reign of Nicholas II', *SR* 25 (1966), pp. 615–29.

38 *Prazdnovanie 300-letiia tsarstvovaniia doma Romanovykh v vysshikh nachal'nykh uchilishchakh g. Smolenska* (Smolensk, 1914), pp. 7–8.

39 *Prazdnovanie trekhsotletiia*, p. 159.

40 N. A. Ordovskii-Taraevskii, *Opisanie prazdnovaniia 300-letiia tsarstvovaniia doma Romanovykh v sele Nyrobe (Cherdynskogo uezda Permskoi gubernii)* (St Petersburg, 1913). For a different version of the story that denies the tale of cruel persecution, see B. Shirokorad, *Dmitrii Pozharskii protiv Mikhaila Romanova: Zagadka 4 noiabria* (Moscow, 2005).

41 Ordovskii-Taraevskii, *Opisanie*, p. 6

42 Ordovskii-Taraevskii, *Opisanie*, pp. 36–7.

43 V. M. Kul'chitskii, *Trekhsotletiie doma Romanovovykh 1613–1913* (St Petersburg, 1913), p. 3.

44 P. Spitsyn, *Russkomu narodu: Iubileinyia temy dlia besed po dushe na 1913-i god. V pamiat' 300-letiia tsarstvovaniia Doma Romanovykh* (Moscow, 1912), p. 14.

45 Krivorog, 1913, p. 7.

46 See G. Von Habsburg-Lothringen and A. von Solodkoff, *Fabergé: Court Jeweler to the Tsars* (New York, 1979), p. 105.

47 *Sviataia Rus' pod skipetrom doma Romanovykh 1613–1913* (supplement to 'Voin i pkhar') (St Petersburg, 1913.)

48 Wortman, *Scenarios*, vol. 2, pp. 482–3.

49 *Stanley Gibbons Stamp Catalogue, Part 10: Russia* (London and Ringwood, 1999), p. 5

50 Wortman, *Scenarios*, vol. 2, p. 484.

51 Wortman, *Scenarios*, vol. 2, pp. 486–7.

52 A. G. Elchaninov, *Tsarstvovanie Gosudaria Imperatora Nikolaia Aleksandrovicha* (St Petersburg and Moscow, 1913), translated into English as *The Tsar and His People* (1914). See Wortman, *Scenarios*, vol. 2, pp. 487–500.

53 Wortman, *Scenarios*, vol. 2, p. 445; idem, 'Invisible Threads', p. 109.

54   D. Lieven, *Nicholas II: Emperor of all the Russias* (London, 1994), p. 199.

55   M. V. Rodzianko, *The Reign of Rasputin: An Empire's Collapse* (London, 1927), p. 109–11.

56   See N. Stone, *The Eastern Front, 1914–1917* (London, 1975).

57   Rodzianko, *The Reign of Rasputin*, pp. 118, 148–9.

58   Adapted from Wortman, *Scenarios*, vol. 2, p. 503.

59   Rodzianko, *The Reign of Rasputin*, p. 38.

60   Rodzianko, *The Reign of Rasputin*, p. 181.

61   Rodzianko, *The Reign of Rasputin*, pp. 164–6.

62   S. Podbolotov, 'Monarchists against their Monarch: The Rightists' Criticism of Tsar Nicholas II', *RH* 31 (2004), p. 117.

63   Rodzianko, *The Reign of Rasputin*, pp. 247, 249.

64   Rodzianko, *The Reign of Rasputin*, p. 254.

65   J. T. Fuhrmann (ed.), *The Complete Wartime Correspondence of Tsar Nicholas II and the Empress Alexandra, April 1914–March 1917* (Westport, CT and London, 1999), p. 675 (*CWC*). The couple corresponded in English, his generally more fluent and accurate than hers.

66   *CWC*, pp. 687, 689 (23 February).

67   Steinberg and Khrustalev, *The Fall of the Romanovs*, pp. 24–5.

68   *CWC*, p. 678.

69   M. Paléologue, *An Ambassador's Memoirs, 1914–1917* (London, 1973), pp. 735, 742–8.

70   *Dnevniki imp. Marii Fedorovny* (Moscow, 2005), pp. 163–4.

71   *CWC*, pp. 686–7.

72   *CWC*, pp. 670, 695. In March 1917 soldiers exhumed the body and burnt it in a forest outside Petrograd.

73   Paléologue, *An Ambassador's Memoirs*, p. 756.

74   Steinberg and Khrustalev, *The Fall of the Romanovs*, p. 152 (May 1917).

75   Paléologue, *An Ambassador's Memoirs*, p. 785.

76   See rumours in Paléologue, *An Ambassador's Memoirs*, p. 740.

77   *CWC*, 25 February, p. 692.

78   *CWC*, 26 February, p. 694.

79   Steinberg and Khrustalev, *The Fall of the Romanovs*, p. 87 (1 March).

80   Steinberg and Khrustalev, *The Fall of the Romanovs*, p. 60.

81   Steinberg and Khrustalev, *The Fall of the Romanovs*, p. 89.

82   Steinberg and Khrustalev, *The Fall of the Romanovs*, p. 61.

83   Steinberg and Khrustalev, *The Fall of the Romanovs*, pp. 100–102; Paléologue, p. 829.

84   Shatsillo (ed.), *Dnevniki Imperatora Nikolai II*, p. 625

85   Steinberg and Khrustalev, *The Fall of the Romanovs*, p. 103.

86   Paléologue, *An Ambassador's Memoirs*, p. 856.

87   Paléologue, *An Ambassador's Memoirs*, p. 833.

88   V. N. Chashkov, 'Romanovy - kto oni?', *Otechestvennaia istoriia*, 1 (1998), p. 174; Paléologue, *An Ambassador's Memoirs*, pp. 831–4.

89   Paléologue, *An Ambassador's Memoirs*, p. 836.

90   *CWC*, p. 699, 700.

91   *CWC*, p. 701 (2 March).

92   *CWC*, p. 703.

93   S. M. Bleklov, *Dom Samozvanovykh: Krasnyi poriadok soldatu* (Moscow, 1917).

94   Bleklov, *Dom Samozvanovykh*, p. 10.

95   Bleklov, *Dom Samozvanovykh*, p. 15.

96   V. Ia. Iretsky, *Romanovy. (Skol'ko oni nam stoili). Ocherk* (Petrograd, 1917), p. 24.

97   Steinberg and Khrustalev, *The Fall of the Romanovs*, pp. 110, 113 (7 March).

98   Afanasy Beliaev of Fedorov Cathedral, Steinberg and Khrustalev, *The Fall of the Romanovs*, pp. 140–6.

99   Paléologue, *An Ambassador's Memoirs*, p. 853.

100 Steinberg and Khrustalev, *The Fall of the Romanovs*, p. 125.

101 On these and subsequent events, Steinberg and Khrustalev, *The Fall of the Romanovs*, pp. 290–5, especially discussion of the still disputed source of the order for the execution and whether Nicholas alone was the intended victim.

102 P. Grebel'skii and A. Mirvis, *Dom Romanovykh* (St. P., 1992), p. 160.

103 Steinberg and Khrustalev, *The Fall of the Romanovs*, p. 337.

104 From the testimony of Yakov Yurovsky, commandant of the Ipatiev house.

Notes to Chapter 11: Postscript

1   Iu. V. Trubinov, *Velikokniazheskaia usypal'nitsa* (St Petersburg, 1997).

2   V. Gendrikov and S. Sen'ko, *Petropavlovskii sobor: Usypal'nitsa imperatorskogo doma Romanovykh* (St Petersburg, 1998), p. 28.

3   V. Gendrikov, *Poslednii put' (16–17 iiulia 1998 goda)* (St Petersburg, 1999).

4   See for example, *Daily Telegraph*, 12 July 2004, p. 9: an American team of scientists at Stanford University challenged the British research carried out by Dr Peter Gill at the Forensic Science Service which in 1993 purported to prove with 99 per cent certainty that the nine skeletons found in 1976 included those of the tsar, tsarina and three daughters. (Based on a preserved finger of Grand Duchess Elisabeth, which apparently failed to match the tsarina's DNA. Russian investigators were accused of manipulating the experiments with the aim of proving that the bones belonged to the imperial family.)

5   Most prevalent was the Anastasia legend. See, for example, P. Kurth, *Anastasia* (London, 1983); J. B. Lovell, *Anastasia: The Lost Princess* (London, 1992); J. Klier and H. Mingay, *The Search for Anastasia* (London, 1995).

6   M. Steinberg and V. Khrustalev, *The Fall of the Romanovs* (New Haven and London, 1995), p. 295. See also R. K. Massie, *The Romanovs: The Final Chapter* (London, 1995).

7   Elena Hellberg-Hirn, *Imperial Imprints: Post-Soviet St Petersburg* (Helsinki, 2003), p. 57.

8   Patriarch Aleksii, quoted in *Tsesarevich* (St Petersburg, 2004), p. 88.

9   See G. Panfilov, *Romanovy: Venetsenosnaia sem'ia* (2000).

10 K. G. Sokol, *Monumenty imperii* (Moscow, 1999), pp. 82–3.

11 Sokol, *Monumenty*, p. 96.

12 Sokol, *Monumenty*, pp. 34, 105.

13 Sokol, *Monumenty*, p. 54.

14   Sokol, *Monumenty,* p. 58.

15   E. Glickman, http://www.spb.su/lifestyl/146/faces.html
     G. B. Il'in, 'Trudnye sud'by pamiatnikov', *Leningradskoe panorama,* 9 (1987), pp. 33–5.

16   G. K. Shchutskaia, *Palaty boiar Romanovykh* (Moscow, 2000), pp. 19–21.

17   Steinberg and Khrustalev, *The Fall of the Romanovs,* p. 299.

18   L. Shaposhnikova, *Pamiatnik Aleksandru III: Skul'ptor Paolo Trubetskoi* (St Petersburg, 1996).

19   See L. Hughes, *Peter the Great: A Biography* (New Haven, 2002), pp. 246–7.

20   See above, p. 154.

21   *Zhurnal Moskovskoi Patriarkhii,* 6 (1997), pp. 19–20.

22   T. de Waal, 'Moscow Fury as Columbus Dethrones Tsar Peter', *The Times* (18 December 1996), p. 10; A. Sidorov, in *Tvorchestvo,* 1– 2 (1997), pp. 56–63.

23   P. Reeves, *Independent on Sunday* (24 January 1996), p. 17.

24   G. Kropivnitskaia, *Portrety vydaiushchikhsia gosudarei doma Romanovykh 1613–1917* (Moscow, 1993) [leaflet, n.p.].

25   See M. Piotrovskii (ed.), *Osnovateliu Peterburga* (St Petersburg, 2003); L. Iovleva (ed.), *Ekaterina Velikaia i Moskva* (Moscow, 1997); N. Guseva (ed.), *Treasures of Catherine the Great* (London, 2000); B. Vilinbakhov *et al.* (eds), *Aleksandr I: Sfinks, ne razgadannyi do groba. Katalog vystavki* (St Petersburg, 2005).

26   N. Tarasova *et al.* (eds), *Nicholas and Alexandra: The Last Tsar and Tsarina* (Amsterdam, 2005), pp. 10–11.

27   E. Pchelov, *Genealogiia Romanovykh: 1613–2001* (Moscow, 2001), p. 5.

28   See, for example, V. Shevchenko, *Rodoslovnaia tablitsa* (Moscow, 1991); V. Antonov and N. Fadeev, 'Rodoslovie Doma Romanovykh', in M. Nazarov, *Kto naslednik rossiiskogo prestola?* (Moscow, 1996; 2nd edn 1998); A. Bokhanov and D. Ismail-Zade, *Rossiiskii Imperatorskii Dom. Dnevniki. Pis'ma. Fotografii* (Moscow, 1992).

29   A. Sakharov (ed.), *Romanovy: Istoricheskie portrety* (Moscow, 1993).

30   A. Kamenskii, *Pod seniiu Ekateriny: Vtoraia polovina XVIII veka* (St Petersburg, 1992). On trends in biographical writing, L. Hughes, 'Biographies of Peter', in *Russia in the Reign of Peter the Great: Old and New Perspectives,* ed. A. G. Cross (Cambridge, SGECRN, 1998), pp. 13–24.

31   N. I. Pavlenko, *Ekaterina I* (Moscow, 2004).

32   V. Kozliakov, *Mikhail Fedorovich* (Moscow, 2004); I. Andreev, *Aleksei Mikhailovich* (Moscow, 2003); E. Anisimov, *Anna Ioannovna* (Moscow, 2002); idem, *Elizaveta Petrovna* (Moscow, 1999).

33   See L. V. Vyskochkov, 'Imperator Nikolai I glazami sovremennikov', in I. A. Froianov (ed.), *Dom Romanovykh v istorii Rossii* (St Petersburg, 1995), pp. 188, 192–3.

34   *Voprosy istorii,* 6 (1990), pp. 54–75. O. I. Eliseeva, *Grigorii Potemkin* (Moscow, 2005).

35   See Pchelov, *Genealogiia,* p. 12. His book is dedicated to the memory of Grand Duchess Vera Konstantinovna, who died in the USA in 2001 aged 95.

36   *Iskusstvo Vel. Kniagini: Akvareli, risunki, zhivopis'. K 120-letiiu so dnia rozhdeniia V. K. Ol'gi Aleksandrovny* (Moscow, 2003); M. Varakin, 'Vel. Kniaginia Elizaveta Fedorovna i Moskovskii sinodal'nyi khor', *Voprosy kul'turologii,* 3 (2003), pp. 112–13.

37   P. Savchenko, *Russkaia devushka (o docheri Nikolaia II Ol'ge)* (Moscow, 2002); idem, *Tsesarevich* (St Petersburg, 2004); L. P. Miller, *Sviataia muchenitsa Rossiiskaia: V. K. Elizaveta*

Fedorovna (Moscow, 2001); idem, *Tsarstvennye mucheniki: Zhizneopsanie* (Riazan, 2000); idem, *Chudesa tsarstvennykh muchenikov* (Moscow, 1997).

38   See P. Multatuli, *Strogo poseshchaet Gospod' nas gnevom svoim ... Imperator Nikolai II i revoliutsiia 1905–1907 gg.* (St Petersburg, 2003).

39   'A Tsar is Born: Hail "Prince Kentski"', *Observer* (27 June 2004).

40   See catalogues from Russian sales at Sotheby's and Christie's.

41   Steinberg and Khrustalev, *The Fall of the Romanovs*, p. 299.

42   See S. Dumin, *Romanovy: Imperatorskii dom v izgnanii. Semeinaia khronika* (Moscow, 1998); E. Pchelov, *Romanovy: Istoriia dinastii* (Moscow, 2001), pp. 260–2.

43   Pchelov, *Romanovy*, pp. 384–5.

44   A. Kamenskii, 'Byli li Romanovy Romanovymi?', *Voprosy istorii*, 8 (1990), pp. 186–7.

45   Information from the following websites, 23–29 September 2006:
http://www.denmark.dk/portal/page?_pageid=374,520644&_dad=portal&_schema=PORTAL; BBC.co.uk
http://en.rian.ru/
http://www.sptimes.ru/ www.alexanderpalace.org/palace/

46   http://www.sptimes.ru/ Issue 1208 (74), 29 September 2006.

47   See www.alexanderpalace.org/palace/

48   See also A. Blomfield, 'Romanovs Retake St Petersburg to Bury Tsarina', *Daily Telegraph*, 29 September 2006, p. 17. Responses in print include G. N. Korneva *et al.*, *Liubimye rezidentsii imperatritsy Marii Fedorovny v Rossii i Danii* (St Petersburg, 2006), on the empress's favourite residences.

Bibliography

This list contains mainly references to recent and some older English-language works on Russia and the Romanovs in the seventeenth to twentieth centuries. In general, references here are to books and important articles; there is more extensive citation of journal literature in the endnotes, likewise of recent research in Russian.

Alexander, J., 'Amazon Autocratixes: Images of Female Rule in the Eighteenth Century', in Peter Barta (ed.), *Gender and Sexuality in Russian Civilisation* (London, 2001).

Alexander, J., *Autocratic Politics in a National Crisis: The Imperial Russian Government and Pugachev's Revolt* (Bloomington, IN, 1969).

——'Favourites, Favouritism and Female rule in Russia, 1725–1796', in R. Bartlett and J. Hartley (eds), *Russia in the Age of the Enlightenment* (London, 1990).

Almedingen, E. M., *Emperor Alexander I* (London, 1964).

Anisimov, E., 'Anna Ivanovna', *RSH* 32, no. 4 (1994).

——*Empress Elizabeth: Her Reign and Her Russia* (Gulf Breeze, FL, 1995).

Archives Secrets de l'Empereur Nicholas II, ed. V. Lazarevski (Paris, 1928).

Avrich, P., *Russian Rebels 1600–1800* (New York, 1972).

Bagger, H., 'The Role of the Baltic in Russian Foreign Policy 1721–1773', in H. Ragsdale (ed.), *Imperial Russian Foreign Policy* (Cambridge, 1993).

Bartlett, R., 'The Free Economic Society: The Foundation Years and the Prize Essay Competition of 1766 on Peasant Property', in E. Hübner, J. Kusber and P. Nitsche (eds), *Rußland zur Zeit Katharinas II: Absolutismus, Aufklärung, Pragmatismus* (Cologne, 1998).

——*A History of Russia* (Basingstoke, 2005).

Bartlett, R. and Hughes, L. (eds), *Russian Society and Culture in the Long Eighteenth Century: Essays in Honour of Anthony G. Cross* (Münster, 2004).

Bergamini, J., *The Tragic Dynasty: A History of the Romanovs* (London, 1970).

Black, J. L., *Citizens for the Fatherland: Education, Educators and Pedagogical Ideals in Eighteenth-Century Russia* (Boulder, CO, 1979).

Brennan, J., *Enlightened Despotism in Russia: The Reign of Elisabeth, 1741–1762* (New York, 1987).

Brown, M. H., 'Native Song and National Consciousness in 19th-century Russia', in T. G. Stavrou (ed.), *Art and Culture in Nineteenth-Century Russia* (Bloomington, IN, 1983).

Brumfield, W. C., *A History of Russian Architecture* (Cambridge, 1994).

Bryner, C., 'The Issue of Capital Punishment in the Reign of Elizabeth Petrovna', *RR* 49 (1990).

Bushkovitch, P. (ed.), *England and the North: The Russian Embassy of 1613–1614* (Philadelphia, 1994).

——*Peter the Great: The Struggle for Power, 1671–1725* (Cambridge, 2001).

——*Religion and Society in Russia: The Sixteenth and Seventeenth Centuries* (Oxford, 1992).

Butler, W. E., 'The *Nakaz* of Catherine the Great', *The American Book Collector* 16, no. 5 (1966).

Byrnes, R. F., *Pobedonostsev: His Life and Thought* (Bloomington, IN and London, 1968).

Cherniavsky, M., 'The Old Believers and the New Religion,' *SR* 25 (1966).

Cowles, V., *The Romanovs* (New York, 1971).

Cracraft, J., *The Church Reform of Peter the Great* (London and Basingstoke, 1971).

——*The Petrine Revolution in Russian Culture* (Cambridge, MA and London, 2004).

——*The Petrine Revolution in Russian Imagery* (Chicago, 1997).

—(ed.), *For God and Peter the Great: The Works of Thomas Consett, 1723–1729* (Boulder, CO, 1982).

Cross, A. G., 'The Bung College or British Monastery in Petrine Russia', *SGECRN* 12 (1984).

——'Catherine through Contemporary British Eyes', in *Catherine the Great and the British: A Pot-Pourri of Essays* (Nottingham, 2001).

——*Peter the Great through British Eyes: Perceptions and Representations of the Tsar since 1698* (Cambridge, 2000).

—(ed.), *A Lady at the Court of Catherine the Great: The Journal of Baroness Elizabeth Dimsdale, 1781* (Cambridge, 1989).

Crummey, R., *Aristocrats and Servitors: The Boyar Elite in Russia, 1613–1689* (Princeton, 1983).

Custine, Astolphe-Louis-Léonor, Marquis de, *Journey of Our Time: The Journals of the Marquis de Custine*, ed. and trans. P. Kohler (London, 1980).

——'Court Spectacles in Seventeenth-Century Russia: Illusion and Reality', in D. C. Waugh (ed.), *Essays in Honor of A. A. Zimin* (Columbus, OH, 1985).

De Madariaga, I., *Catherine the Great: A Short History* (London, 1990).

——*Politics and Culture in Eighteenth-Century Russia: Collected Essays* (London, 1998).

——*Russia in the Age of Catherine the Great* (London, 1981).

——'The Russian Nobility, 1600–1800', in H. M. Scott (ed.), *The European Nobilities in the 17th and 18th Centuries* 2 vols (London, 1995), vol. 2.

Di Salvo, M., 'What Did Francesco Algarotti See in Russia?', in R. Bartlett and L. Hughes (eds), *Russian Society and Culture in the Long Eighteenth Century: Essays in Honour of Anthony G. Cross* (Münster, 2004).

Dixon, S. (ed.), *Britain and Russia in the Age of Peter the Great: Historical Documents* (London, 1998).

——*Catherine the Great* (Harlow, 2001).

——'Catherine the Great and the Romanov Dynasty', in R. Bartlett and L. Hughes (eds), *Russian Society and Culture in the Long Eighteenth Century: Essays in Honour of Anthony G. Cross* (Münster, 2004).

——*The Modernisation of Russia 1676–1825* (Cambridge, 1999).

——'The Posthumous Reputation of Catherine the Great in Russia, 1797–1837', *SEER* 77 (1999), pp. 646–79.

Dukes, P. (ed.), *Russia under Catherine the Great: Catherine the Great's Instruction (Nakaz) to the Legislative Commission, 1767* (Newtonville, MA, 1977), vol. 2.

Dunning, C. S., *A Short History of Russia's First Civil War: The Time of Troubles and the Founding of the Romanov Dynasty* (University Park, PA, 2001).

——'The Preconditions of Modern Russia's First Civil War', *RH* 25 (1998), pp. 119–31.

Du Tsar à l'Empereur: Moscow-Saint-Pétersbourg (Brussels, 2005).

Emmons, T. (ed.), *Emancipation of the Russian Serfs* (London and New York, 1970).

——*The Russian Landed Gentry and the Peasant Emancipation of 1861* (Cambridge, 1968).

Englund, P., *The Battle of Poltava: The Birth of the Russian Empire* (London, 1992).

Figes, O., *Natasha's Dance* (London, 2002).

Flier, M. S., 'Breaking the Code: The Image of the Tsar in the Muscovite Palm Sunday Ritual', in M. Flier and D. Rowland (eds), *Medieval Russian Culture*, vol. 2. (Berkeley, Los Angeles and London, 1994).

——'The Church of the Saviour on the Blood: Projection, Rejection, Resurrection', in R. Hughes and I. Paperno (eds), *Christianity and the Eastern Slavs* (Berkeley, 1994).

Freeze, G.L., 'Subversive Piety: Religion and the Political Crisis in Late Imperial Russia', *Journal of Modern History* 68 (1996).

Fuhrmann, J. T., (ed.), *The Complete Wartime Correspondence of Tsar Nicholas II and the Empress Alexandra, April 1914–March 1917* (Westport, CT and London, 1999).

Fuller, W. C., *Strategy and Power in Russia 1600–1914* (New York, 1992).

George, A., *St Petersburg: The First Three Centuries* (Phoenix Mill, MN, 2004).

Gray, R., *Russian Genre Painting in the Nineteenth Century* (Oxford, 2000).

Greenleaf, M., 'Performing Autobiography: The Multiple Memoirs of Catherine the Great (1756–96)', *RR* 63 (2004).

Griffiths, D., 'Catherine II: The Republican Empress', *JGO* 21 (1973).

Habsburg-Lothringen, G. von, and Solodkoff, A. von, *Fabergé: Court Jeweler to the Tsars* (New York, 1979).

Hartley, J., *Alexander I* (London, 1994).

——'The Boards of Social Welfare and the Financing of Catherine II's State Schools', *SEER* 67 (1989).

——'Catherine's Conscience Court – An English Equity Court?', in A. G. Cross (ed.), *Russia and the West in the Eighteenth Century* (Newtonville, MA, 1983).

——'Changing Perspectives: British Views of Russia from the Grand Embassy to the Peace of Nystad', in L. Hughes (ed.), *Peter the Great and the West: New Perspectives* (Basingstoke, 2001).

——'England "Enjoys the Spectacle of a Northern Barbarian": The Reception of Peter I and Alexander I', in *WOR*.

——*A Social History of the Russian Empire 1650–1825* (London, 1999).

——'Town Government in Saint Petersburg Guberniya after the Charter to the Towns of 1785', *SEER* 62 (1984).

Hellie, R., *The Economy and Material Culture of Russia 1600–1725* (Chicago, 1999).

——*Enserfment and Military Change in Muscovy* (Chicago, 1971).

—(ed. and trans.), *The Muscovite Law Code (Ulozhenie) of 1649, part I: Text and Translation* (Irvine, CA, 1988).

——*Slavery in Russia, 1450–1725* (Chicago, 1982).

——'Why did the Muscovite Elite not Rebel?', *RH* 25 (1998).

Herd, G., 'Rebellion and Reformation in the Muscovite Military', in J. Kotilane and M. Poe (eds), *Modernizing Muscovy: The Changing Face of 17th-century Russia* (Oxford, 1999).

Hittle, J. M., *The Service City: State and Townsmen in Russia, 1600–1800* (Cambridge, MA, 1979).

Hoch, S., *Serfdom and Social Control in Russia: Petrovskoe, a Village in Tambov* (Chicago and London, 1986).

Hosking, G., *Russia and the Russians* (London, 2001).

——*Russia: People and Empire: 1552–1917* (London, 1997).

——*The Russian Constitutional Experiment: Government and Duma, 1907–1914* (Cambridge, 1973).

Hughes, L., 'Attitudes Towards Foreigners in Early Modern Russia', in C. Brennan and M. Frame (eds), *Russia and the Wider World in Historical Perspective: Essays for Paul Dukes* (Basingstoke, 2000).

——'A Beard is an Unnecessary Burden: Peter I's Laws on Shaving and their Roots in Early Russia', in R. Bartlett and L. Hughes (eds), *Russian Society and Culture in the Long Eighteenth Century: Essays in Honour of Anthony G. Cross* (Münster, 2004).

——'Catherine I of Russia: Consort to Peter the Great', in C. Campbell Orr (ed.), *Queenship in Europe, 1660–1815: The Role of the Consort* (Cambridge, 2004).

——'From Caftans into Corsets: The Sartorial Transformation of Women during the Reign of Peter the Great', in P. Barta (ed.), *Gender and Sexuality in Russian Civilization* (London, 2001).

——'From Tsar to Emperor: Portraits of Peter the Great', in *The Place of Russia in Eurasia*, ed. G. Szvak (Budapest, 2001).

——'Images of the Elite: A Reconsideration of the Portrait in Seventeenth-Century Russia', *Forschungen zur osteuropäischen Geschichte* 56 (2000).

——'The Funerals of the Russian Emperors and Empresses', in M. Schaich (ed.), *Monarchy and Religion: The Transformation of Royal Culture in Eighteenth-Century Europe* (Oxford, 2007).

——'The Moscow Armoury and Innovations in 17th-century Muscovite Art', *CASS* 13 (1979).

——'A Note on the Children of Peter the Great', *SGECRN* 21 (1993).

——'"Nothing is Too Small for a Great Man": Peter the Great's Little Houses and the Creation of Some Petrine Myths', *SEER* 81 (2003), pp. 634–58.

——*Peter the Great: A Biography* (New Haven and London, 2002).

—(ed.), *Peter the Great and the West: New Perspectives* (Basingstoke, 2001).

——'Peter the Great: A Passion for Ships', in M. Cornwall and M. Frame (eds), *Scotland and the Slavs: Cultures in Contact, 1500–2000* (Newtonville, MA, 2001).

——'Peter the Great's Two Weddings: Changing Images of Women in a Transitional Age', in R. Marsh (ed.), *Women in Russia and Ukraine* (Cambridge, 1996).

——'The Petrine Year: Anniversaries and Festivals in the Reign of Peter the Great (1682–1725)', in K. Friedrich (ed.), *Festive Culture in Germany and Europe from the 16th to the 20th century* (Lewiston, ME, 2000).

——*Playing Games: The Alternative History of Peter the Great* (London, 2000).

——*Russia and the West: The Life of a Seventeenth-century Westernizer, Prince Vasily Vasil'evich Golitsyn (1643–1714)* (Newtonville, MA, 1984).

——*Russia in the Age of Peter the Great* (New Haven and London, 1998).

——'Russian Culture in the Eighteenth Century', *Cambridge History of Russia* 3 vols (Cambridge, 2006), vol. 2, ed. D. Lieven.

——'The 17th-century Russian "Renaissance"', *History Today* (February 1980).

——'Simon Ushakov's Icon "The Tree of the Muscovite State" Revisited', *FOG* 58 (2002).

——*Sophia Regent of Russia, 1657–1704* (New Haven, 1990).

——'Western European Graphic Material as a Source for Moscow Baroque Architecture', *SEER* 55 (1977).

Jenkins, M., *Arakcheev: Grand Vizier of the Russian Empire* (London, 1969).

Jenks, A., *Russia in a Box: Art and Identity in an Age of Revolution* (DeKalb, IL, 2005).

Jensen, C., 'Music for the Tsar: A Preliminary Study of the Music of the Muscovite Court Theatre', *The Musical Quarterly* 2, no. 79 (1995).

Jones, R. E., 'The Charter of the Nobility: A Legislative Landmark?', *CASS* 23, no. 1 (1989).

——*The Emancipation of the Russian Nobility, 1762–1785* (Princeton, 1973).

Jones, W. G., 'Literature in the Eighteenth Century', in N. Cornwell (ed.), *The Routledge Companion to Russian Literature* (London and New York, 2000).

——*Nikolay Novikov: Enlightener of Russia* (Cambridge, 1984).

——'The Spirit of the *Nakaz*: Catherine II's Literary Debt to Montesquieu', *SEER* 77 (1998).

Kahan, A., *The Plow, the Hammer and the Knout* (Chicago, 1985).

Kamenskii, A., *The Russian Empire in the eighteenth century* (Armonk, NY, 1997).

Kämpfer, F., *Das russische Herrscherbild von den Anfängen bis zu Peter dem Grossen* (Recklinghausen, 1978).

Karamzin's Memoir on Ancient and Modern Russia, ed. R. Pipes (New York, 1966).

Karlinsky, S., *Russian Drama from its Beginnings to the Age of Pushkin* (Berkeley, 1985).

Keep, J., 'The Regime of Filaret', *SEER* 38 (1959–60).

Kelly, L., *St Petersburg: A Traveller's Companion* (London, 1981).

King, G., *The Court of the Last Tsar: Pomp, Power, and Pageantry in the Reign of Nicholas II* (Hoboken, NJ, 2006).

Kirichenko, E., *The Russian Style* (London 1991).

Kivelson, V., *Autocracy in the Provinces: The Muscovite Gentry and Political Culture in the Seventeenth Century* (Stanford, CA, 1997).

——*Cartographies of Tsardom: The Land and its Meaning in Seventeenth-Century Russia* (Ithaca, NY, 2006).

Klier, J., *Russia Gathers Her Jews: The Origins of the 'Jewish Question' in Russia, 1772–1825* (DeKalb, IL, 1986).

—and H. Mingay, *The Search for Anastasia* (London, 1995)

Kollmann, N. S., 'The Seclusion of Elite Muscovite Women', *RH* 10 (1983).

Korb, J.- G., *Diary of an Austrian Secretary of Legation at the Court of Czar Peter the Great,* ed. and trans. Count MacDonnell, 2 vols (London 1863/1968).

Kotilane, J. and Poe, M. (eds), *Modernizing Muscovy: The Changing Face of 17th-century Russia* (Oxford, 1999).

LeDonne, J. P., 'The Judicial Reform of 1775 in Provincial Russia', *JGO* 21 (1973).

——'The Provincial and Local Police under Catherine the Great', *CASS* 4 (1970).

Lee, W.C., 'Grand Ducal Role and Identity as a Reflection on the Interaction of State and Dynasty in Imperial Russia', unpubl. PhD thesis, SSEES, London, 2000.

Lentin, A. (ed. and trans.), *Voltaire and Catherine the Great: Selected Correspondence* (Cambridge, 1974).

Leonard, C., *Reform and Regicide: The Reign of Peter III of Russia* (Bloomington, IN, 1993).

Lieven, D., *Nicholas II: Emperor of all the Russias* (London, 1994).

Lincoln, W. B., *The Great Reforms* (DeKalb, IL, 1990).

——*Nicholas I: Emperor and Autocrat of All the Russias* (London, 1978).

——*The Romanovs: Autocrats of All Russia* (London, 1981).

——*Sunlight at Midnight: St Petersburg and the Rise of Modern Russia* (New York, 2000).

Lipski, A., 'Some Aspects of Russia's Westernization During the Reign of Anna Ioannovna', *American Slavic and East European Review* 18 (1959).

Lobachev, S. V., 'Patriarch Nikon's Rise to Power', *SEER* 79 (2001).

Loewenson, L., The Death of Paul I and the Memoirs of Count Bennigsen', *SEER* 29 (1950).

——'People Peter the Great Met in England: Moses Stringer, Chymist and Physician', *SEER* 37 (1959).

Longworth, P., *Alexis Tsar of All the Russias* (London, 1984).

——'The Pugachev Revolt', in H. Landsberger (ed.), *Rural Protest: Peasant Movements and Social Change* (London, 1974).

——*The Three Empresses: Catherine I, Anne and Elizabeth of Russia* (London, 1972)

——'Tsar Alexis Goes to War', in P. Dukes (ed.), *Russia and Europe* (London, 1991).

Lukowski, J., *The Partitions of Poland: 1772, 1793, 1795* (London, 1999).

Lyall, R., *The Character of the Russians and a Detailed History of Moscow* (London, 1823).

McConnell, A., *Alexander I: Paternalistic Reformer* (Northbrook, IL, 1970).

——'Catherine the Great and the Fine Arts', in E. Mendelsohn (ed.), *Imperial Russia 1700–1917: Essays in Honour of Marc Raeff* (DeKalb, IL, 1990).

McConnell, A., *A Russian Philosophe: Alexander Radishchev, 1749–1800* (The Hague, 1964).

McGrew, R., *Paul I of Russia* (Oxford, 1992).

Marker, G., 'Peter the Great's Female Knights of Liberation: The Order of St Catherine', in Bartlett, R. and Hughes, L. (eds), *Russian Society and Culture in the Long Eighteenth Century: Essays in Honour of Anthony G. Cross* (Münster, 2004).

——*Publishing, Printing, and the Origins of Intellectual Life in Russia, 1700–1800* (Princeton, 1985).

Martin, R., 'Choreographing the Tsar's Happy Occasion: Tradition, Change and Dynastic Legitimacy in the Weddings of Tsar Mikhail Romanov', *SR* 63 (2004).

Meehan Waters, B., *Autocracy and Aristocracy: The Russian Service Elite of 1730* (New Brunswick, NJ, 1984).

——'Catherine the Great and the Problem of Female Rule', *RR* 34 (1975).

The Memoirs of Catherine the Great, ed. and trans. M. Cruse and H. Hoogenboom (New York, 2005).

Meyendorff, P., *Russia, Ritual and Reform: The Liturgical Reforms of Nikon in the 17th century* (The Crestwood, NY, 1991).

Michels, G., *At War with the Church* (Stanford, CA, 2000).

Miller, J., *The Stuarts* (London and New York, 2004).

Monod, P. K., *The Power of Kings: Monarchy and Religion in Europe, 1589–1715* (New Haven, 1999).

Montefiore, S., *Prince of Princes: The Life of Potemkin* (London, 2000).

Moon, D., 'Reassessing Russian Serfdom', *European History Quarterly* 26 (1996).

——*The Russian Peasantry 1600–1930: The World the Peasants Made* (London, 1999).

Mosse, W. E., *Alexander II and the Modernization of Russia* (London and New York, 1958).

Naumov, V. P., 'Elizaveta Petrovna,' *RSH* 32, no. 4 (1994).

Neverov, O., '"His Majesty's Cabinet" and Peter I's Kunstkammer', in O. Impey and A. McGregor (eds), *The Origins of Museums: The Cabinet of Curiosities in 16th–17th-Century Europe* (Oxford, 1985).

Nichols, R. L., 'The Friends of God: Nicholas II and Aleksandra at the Canonization of Serafim of Sarov, July 1903', in C. Timberlake (ed.), *Religious and Secular Forces in Late Tsarist Russia* (Seattle, 1992).

Norman, G., *The Hermitage: The Biography of a Great Museum* (London, 1997).

Norman, J., 'Alexander III as a Patron of Russian Art', in J. Norman (ed.), *New Perspectives on Russian and Soviet Artistic Culture*, 2 vols (New York, 1994), vol. 2.

Obolensky, D. (ed.), *Russian Chronicles* (London, 1990).

Olearius, A., *The Travels of Olearius in Seventeenth-Century Russia,* ed. S. Baron (Stanford, CA, 1967).

Oliva, L., *Peter the Great: Great Lives Observed* (Englewood Cliffs, NJ, 1970).

Paléologue, M., *The Enigmatic Czar* (London, 1938).

Palmer, A., *Alexander I: Tsar of War and Peace* (London, 1974).

Perkins, E., 'Nicholas I and the Academy of Fine Arts', *RH* 18 (1991).

Perrie, M., 'Christ or Devil? Images of the First False Dimitry in early 17th-c. Russia', in R. Reid, J. Andrew and V. Polukhina (eds), *Structure and Tradition in Russian Society* (Helsinki, 1994).

Perry, J., *The State of Russia* (1716; repr. London, 1967).

Peterson, C., *Peter the Great's Administrative and Judicial Reforms* (Stockholm, 1979).

Piotrovsky, M. (ed.), *Nicholas and Alexandra: The Last Tsar and Tsarina* (Amsterdam, 2005).

—(ed.), *Treasures of Catherine the Great* (London, 2000).

Platonov, S. F., *Boris Godunov: Tsar of Russia* (Gulf Breeze, FL, 1973).

Plokhy, S., *The Cossacks and Religion in Early Modern Ukraine* (Oxford, 2001).

——*Tsars and Cossacks: A Study in Iconography* (Harvard, 2002).

Podbolotov, S., 'Monarchists against their Monarch: The Rightists' Criticism of Tsar Nicholas II', *RH* 31 (2004).

Poe, M. T., *'A People Born to Slavery': Russia in Early Modern European Ethnography 1476–1748* (Ithaca, NY and London, 2000).

——*The Russian Elite in the Seventeenth Century,* 2 vols (Helsinki, 2004).

Porshnev, B. F., *Muscovy and Sweden in the Thirty Years War* (Cambridge, 1995).

Raeff, M., *The Decembrist Movement* (Englewood Cliffs, NJ, 1966).

——'The Domestic Policies of Peter III and his Overthrow', *American Historical Review* 75 (1970).

——*Michael Speransky: Statesman of Imperial Russia* (Westport, CT, 1957).

——*Origins of the Russian Intelligentsia: The 18th century Nobility* (New York, 1966).

——(ed.), *Peter the Great Changes Russia* (Lexington, KY, 1972).

——(ed.), *Plans for Political Reform in Imperial Russia, 1730–1905* (Englewood Cliffs, NJ, 1966).

——'Pugachev's Revolt', in R. Forster and J. P. Greene (eds), *Preconditions of Revolution in Early Modern Europe* (Baltimore, 1970).

——'Uniformity, Diversity and the Imperial Administration in the Reign of Catherine II', in idem, *Political Ideas and Institutions in Imperial Russia* (Boulder, CO, 1994).

Ragsdale, H. (ed.), *Paul I: A Reassessment of his Life and Reign* (Pittsburgh, PA, 1979).

Rasmussen, K., 'Catherine II and the Image of Peter I', *SR* 37 (1978).

Reddaway, W., (ed.), *Documents of Catherine the Great* (Cambridge, 1931).

Riasanovsky, N., *The Image of Peter the Great in Russian History and Thought* (Oxford, 1985).

——*Nicholas I and Official Nationality in Russia, 1825–1855* (Berkeley, 1959).

——*A Parting of Ways: Government and the Educated Public in Russia 1801–55* (Oxford, 1976).

Rieber, A., 'Alexander II: A Revisionist View', *Journal of Modern History* 43 (1971).

Roberts, J., *The King's Head: Charles I, King and Martyr* (London, 1999).

Rodzianko, M. V., *The Reign of Rasputin: An Empire's Collapse* (London, 1927).

Rogger, H., 'The Beilis Case: Anti-Semitism and Politics in the Reign of Nicholas II', *SR* 25 (1966).

Rowen, H. H. (ed.), *From Absolutism to Revolution: 1648–1848* (New York, 1968).

Sablinsky, W., *The Road to Bloody Sunday: Father Gapon and the St Petersburg Massacre of 1905* (Princeton, 1976).

Sarantola-Weiss, M., 'Peter the Great's First Boat, "Grandfather of the Russian Navy"', in *WOR*.

Schenker, A. M., *The Bronze Horseman: Falconet's Monument to Peter the Great* (New Haven, 2004).

Schneiderman, J., *Sergei Zubatov and Revolutionary Marxism: The Struggle for the Working Class in Tsarist Russia* (Ithaca, NY, 1976).

Schroeder, P.W., *The Transformation of European Politics, 1763–1848* (Oxford, 1994).

Shcherbatov, Prince M., *On the Corruption of Morals in Russia*, ed. and trans. A. Lentin (Cambridge, 1969).

Shvidkovsky, D., *The Empress and the Architect: British Architecture and Gardens at the Court of Catherine the Great* (New Haven, 1996).

Smith, D. (ed. and trans.), *Love and Conquest: Personal Correspondence of Catherine the Great and Prince Grigory Potemkin* (DeKalb, IL, 2004).

Snowman, A. K., *Carl Fabergé: Goldsmith to the Imperial Court of Russia* (New York, 1979).

Stanley Gibbons Stamp Catalogue, Part 10. Russia (London and Ringwood, 1999).

Steinberg, M. and Khrustalev, V., *The Fall of the Romanovs* (New Haven and London, 1995).

Stone, N., *The Eastern Front, 1914–1917* (London, 1975).

Sysin, F., 'The Khmelnytsky Uprising and Ukrainian Nation-building', *Journal of Ukrainian Studies* 17, nos 1–2 (1992).

Tarasova, N. *et al.* (eds), *Nicholas and Alexandra: The Last Tsar and Tsarina* (Amsterdam, 2005).

Thyrêt, I., *Between God and Tsar: Religious Symbolism and the Royal Women of Muscovite Russia* (DeKalb, IL, 2001).

Tosi, A., *Waiting for Pushkin: Russian Fiction in the Reign of Alexander I (1800–1825)* (Amsterdam, 2006).

Vernadsky, G., *A Source Book for Russian History*, 3 vols (New Haven, 1972).

Verner, A., *The Crisis of Russian Autocracy: Nicholas II and the 1905 Revolution* (Princeton, 1990).

Warner, R., 'The Kozuchovo Campaign of 1697', *JGO* 13 (1965).

Weber, F. C., *The Present State of Russia*, 2 vols (London, 1722–3).

Weeda, E., 'Rulers, Russia and the 18th-c. Epic', *SEER* 83 (2005).

Whelan, H. W., *Alexander III and the State Council: Bureaucracy and Counter-Reform in Late Imperial Russia* (New Brunswick, NJ, 1982).

Whittaker, C. H., *Russian Monarchy: Eighteenth-Century Russian Rulers and Writers in Political Dialogue* (DeKalb, IL, 2003).

Whitworth, C., *An Account of Russia as it was in the Year 1710* (Moscow-Leningrad, 1988).

Wirtschafter, E. K., *The Play of Ideas in Russian Enlightenment Theater* (DeKalb, IL, 2003).

——*Structures of Society: Imperial Russia's 'People of Various Ranks'* (DeKalb, IL, 1994).

Wortman, R., 'Invisible Threads: The Historical Imagery of the Romanov Tercentenary', *Russian History* 16, nos 2–4 (1989).

——*Scenarios of Power: Myth & Ceremony in Russian Monarchy*, 2 vols (Princeton, 1995–2000).

Zimin, I. V., 'Physicians and Autocrats: The Perplexing Death of Nicholas I', *RSH* 42 (2003–4).

Zitser, E. A., *The Transfigured Kingdom: Sacred Parody and Charismatic Authority at the Court of Peter the Great* (Ithaca, NY, 2004).

——'Post Soviet Peter: New Histories of the Late Muscovite and Early Imperial Russian Court', *Kritika: Explorations in Russian and Eurasian History* 6, no. 2 (Spring, 2005).

Index